The History of the Contractual Thoughts in Ancient China

Yunsheng Liu

The History of the Contractual Thoughts in Ancient China

Springer

Yunsheng Liu
Law School, Research Centre of Real Estate
Guangzhou University
Guangzhou, China

ISBN 978-981-15-5767-5 ISBN 978-981-15-5768-2 (eBook)
https://doi.org/10.1007/978-981-15-5768-2

1. Funded by Chinese Fund for the Humanity and Social Science.
2. Translated by Sun Lin, Duan Jing.

This Springer imprint is published by the registered company Springer Nature Singapore Pte Ltd.
The registered company address is: 152 Beach Road, #21-01/04 Gateway East, Singapore 189721, Singapore

Preface

This book is a pioneer for exploring the evolution of the ancient contractual theories in China. Prof. Kaiguo Li, one of the founders of civil law in China, commended that, "this book has filled the vacancy in the field". At the same time, it adopts a new angle to demonstrate the concept of contracts ever since the Western Zhou Dynasty. With empirical researches and historical materials, it also rebuts the hypotheses and assumptions that the civil and criminal laws were an integrated system in ancient China. After its first publication in 2000, the book brought a group of scholars on the issue, and a substantial number of students have been inspired. The author and the press have received a good deal of correspondence for opinion exchanges. Thus, we found it necessary to translate the book so as to introduce it to more interested readers for further discussion and to promote cultural exchanges among different countries. Howsoever, it is not easy to even make the first step, because of too many ancient concepts and ideograms, as well as the characters in bone, bronze, bamboo, silk scripts in different dynasties which posed a big obstacle in front of us. Much work including consulting professors and doing literature review has been done to solve the difficulty and fathom the complexity of understanding those ancient Chinese expressions and the culture behind them. Additionally, as translators, though we have cooperated in several projects previously, still, we both are so fully engaged in our daily work that we usually feel pressed for time to complete such a great book's translation this time. It took us more than three years to read and study the book itself and additional two for translation. Nevertheless, after more than five years' work, it is finally done. We thought we would be excited at the final moment, except we were not, since the translation work has been a routine in these past years, now the ending of the work is just a wave goodbye to an old friend.

The translation of this book demanded not only English and Chinese language understanding, but ancient legal and archaeological knowledge. It will not be done without the assistance and help of the following people: Dr. Tian Lei and Dr. Chen Kun, who helped in verifying the meaning of ancient scripts and in discussing the proper translations of terms; Eli Zhang, Yaoyao Liu and Jane Shu, who helped in the primary study and format proofing during the process; Xinting Cai helped to sort out the dynasties with the names, time and capitals in the appendix so as to make a clearer guide for those who are less familiar with Chinese dynasties.

The utmost gratitude we would like to express is to Prof. Yunsheng Liu, whose work has been a profound material for understanding and studying the ancient Chinese contractual concepts, and whose confidence in us has been a tremendous encouragement in the past five years and will always be an unforgettable memory in our life.

Chongqing, China

Sun Lin
Duan Jing

Contents

Chapter 1
Introduction: Freedom of Contract Under Ethical Justice

When it comes to researches on ancient Chinese contractual culture, ethical justice can be anything but ignored. Any organic society relies on related both inside and outside binding force. In Chinese traditional society, the most important binding bonds were ethics and contracts. Ethics comprises the internal motivation of contracts while contract is the external manifestation of ethics, which not only constituted the nature of Chinese traditional society but also served as the means to achieve its existence and development. In *The New Science of Giambattista Vico*, Giovanni Battista Vico, an Italian ideologist, visualizes the wane and wax between the nature and the means of human development through the conclusion of three phases in the history of human races, namely Age of Gods, Age of Heroes and Age of Civilians.[1] French sociologist Emile Durkheim focuses on the synchronic study of collectivist tradition in the social development and develops the theory of social connection (unity). The so-called social connection refers to the social bond that unifies individuals, which can be divided into mechanical ones and organic ones. Mechanical connection, as the primary form, is based on a strong collective consciousness and the supporting criminal law so as to unify homogeneous individuals into one society. While the organic connection, with social division of labor as a precondition for existence, is based on the interdependence of heterogeneity of social members. However, the function of social division of labor does not lie in the increase of individual utility or happiness as Hebert Spencer and Britain individualists have addressed, but in the forced establishment of moral order.[2]

In light of theories of Vico and Durkheim, this chapter intends to explore the internal connection and mutual impact between ethics and contracts.

[1] See International Aesthetics [1].

[2] Mitchell [2].

Y. Liu, *The History of the Contractual Thoughts in Ancient China*,
https://doi.org/10.1007/978-981-15-5768-2_1

Ethics: The Connection Means of Chinese Traditional Society

Focusing on human, some scholars claim that Chinese traditional society has experienced three stages, respectively being witchcraft (divinity)-connected in Xia (2100–1600 B.C.) and Shang (1600–1100 B.C.) Dynasties; ethics-connected from Western Zhou Dynasty (1100–771 B.C.) or the reign of Emperor Wu of Han Dynasty (156–87 B.C.) to the May Fourth Movement (1919 A.D.); contract-connected since May Fourth Movement, and that the three-stage change is a process in which people have kept breaking through restraints for emancipation.[3] Though it is ignorant of the internal connection between ethics and contract in the diachronic development of traditional China, this three-stage division oriented in social development from the perspective of ethics and law, is more scientific and objective than the dynasty-oriented or social-structure-oriented division recognized by academic circle in recent years.

The ethical characteristics of Chinese traditional society have raised increasingly polarized concern and comments. For instance, Hegel comments that Chinese, lacking individual consciousness, "simply counts on morals and objective filial piety of families' features in their country. What they know and do is limited to their bloodline and natural obligation due to the lack of independent personality". Meanwhile, Chinese administration and law of society are morals-oriented, far from poetic. In Chinese society, patriarchal political system gives rise to a religious consensus that favors simple virtues and good deeds; that is—"a consciousness of liberty, spirit and impartiality".[4] The German philosopher believes that Physics, metaphysics and ethics characterizes respectively in Greek, Indian and Chinese culture,[5] which is shared by Huston Smith in *Accents of the Worlds Philosophies.* H Smith argues that western thinkers reflect on natural phenomena, Chinese philosophy studies interpersonal relationships and India focuses on introspection.[6] Charles A More, a scholar in the University of Hawaii, also the writer of *Philosophy-East and West*, considers ethics fundamental in Chinese Philosophy. Contrary to individualism advocated by the West, he looks upon human society as a whole and holds that people's self-realization is through the achievement of harmony. While the West attaches importance on the cultivation of individuality, the East values more of the individual instead of an individual.[7]Hajime Nakamura, a Japanese professor, summarizes the importance of formality, ethics, identity order and family relations in terms of Chinese behaviors on the basis of western theories.[8] It seems that Chinese scholars, absorbing the ideas of western scholars on a third-person perspective, start to reflect on their own

[3]Chen [3].

[4]Hegel [4].

[5]Hajime [5].

[6]See footnote 5.

[7]ibid.

[8]ibid.

culture. From Neo-Confucianism to new-generation scholars, it is widely deemed that Chinese traditional society is ethic-centered in nature.

The Confucian-ethics-oriented interpersonal relationships, which substantively cover ties of blood, patriarchal system and hierarchy, were family-centered based on blood relationship. Yu Ronggen, an expert in legal culture of Confucianism, once set forth the essence of "Lunli (伦理ethics)". He said, "the term 'Lunli', AKA Lunchang(伦常), namely moral norms of human relations, refers to hierarchical order of human relations based on family and blood relationship in ancient patriarchal society. In a broad sense, it can refer to the rule of the universe and political order of human society".[9] The etiquette and rites system is the demonstration of such ethical order. Emperor Zhang of Han Dynasty had presided over the *White Tiger Temple* conference on studies of Confucian classics, whose minutes, the famous *Baihu General Sense* played the role of code at that time.[10] And the centerpiece of the conference was to elaborate the functions of ethics, rites and music. "Etiquette and rites, as a harmonious result of Yin and Yang (the two models of energy whose interplay constitutes all things in Chinese philosophy), is used to show reverence to gods, hierarchy and morality", "The propriety of the ruler is greeted with the righteousness of the minister, and it is the same with the father and the son. And four seasons thus keep in order, contributing to the growth of all things. ... There exist the distinctions of class, intimacy and seniority. In accordance with the etiquette at imperial court, lord does not give way to loon, thus giving precedence to nobility; In accordance with the etiquette of fellow villagers, the senior does not give way to the junior, thus giving precedence to seniority; In accordance with the etiquette in ancestral temple, kin does not give way to kith, thus giving precedence to intimacy. As all three realized, the Way of King is paved, leading to the development of all things, which will be greeted with national celebration".[11] After extensive reading, we gain knowledge that in Chinese traditional society harmony of family and state and even of all things were logically based on blood ties. In other words, ethics, which gives precedence to seniority over juniority and lord over loon, both whose harmony are based on the clear distinction between each other, is norm inward supported by etiquette, the restraint outward.[12]

Ethics and Etiquette in traditional China both referred to a certain kind of value system for pragmatic uses, such as the concepts of "benevolence, righteousness, propriety, wisdom and faithfulness" and "gentleness, kindness, respect, frugality and forbearance", which gradually developed through the summary by Confucianists of Han and Song Dynasty. And behind these concepts lies the abstract core, namely, "De ("德", refers to morality)". By tracing the development of Chinese philosophical "De", we can have a clear knowledge of how Chinese society evolved into an ethics-centered one. At the beginning of this century Wang Guowei once said, "Shang and Zhou Dynasty have witnessed the greatest change in Chinese politics and culture".

---

[9] Yu [6].

[10] See Hou et al. [7]. Or see [8].

[11] See *Baihu General Sense* (Volume I(b): *Rites and Music*).

[12] Xu [9].

The Pre-Qin De was a kind of ethics that valued what Pre-Qin religion valued, namely unity of man and Heaven. The Shang Dynasty was a typical thearchy, focusing on worship of ancestor and god through witchcraft rites. However, Zhou Dynasty not only differentiated god, gnome, man and ghost but named a rational supreme god "Heaven" and its reincarnation "King". It was deemed that ancestors had the power to communicate with "Heaven" (the Supreme Being), indicative of the early unity of religions. As a result, "Heaven" turned from the protector of clans and tribes to that of state. It depended on no longer blood ties but governance performance, namely in accordance with "De", whether Heaven favored you as man's king. No exercising De and protecting people, no Heaven's favor. Hence, Chinese ethical values evolved from the hierarchy merely based on blood ties into the moral ideal advocating the unity of man and Heaven. Ba Xinsheng once drew a correct conclusion in his article that the development of Pre-Qi De has experienced four stages: totemism in primitive society, ancestor and god worship in Shang Dynasty, governance in accordance with De in Western Zhou Dynasty, and ethics and morals in Spring and Autumn Period.[13] If it had not been for the national policy "Exercising De and Protecting people" of Western Zhou Dynasty, man would not be distinguished in the chaotic world, becoming the dominant driving force to society and history. It is more than a value judgment that "Man is lord of gods" for it gives the historical function of people unprecedented attention, regarding it as the only defining force to fate of state and king. While the West emphasizes on the value and interdependence of an individual, as seen from the sayings repeated such as "Know Thyself" (Socrates), and "Man is born as political animals"(Aristotle), etc., since Western Zhou Dynasty China has focused on the cultivation of the individual who obeys the kinship-oriented ethics and moral obligations taking "De", the personality and humanity inward, and external etiquette system as the means and the target of moralization. The ethics China underlines is holistic and ethnic, namely other-centered in Liang Shuming's explanation.[14] This ethnic-group-centered ethical values, enriched by the Confucian "Tri-unity" (namely the unity of Heaven and man, unity of knowledge and practice, and unity of mood and scene), evolved into social ethics from a family one. And combined with law, it was externalized into an effective restraint mechanism and internalized as ethnic morals, gradually becoming one of the most important binding forces to Chinese families, society and even state.

Complementing and Fighting Against Each Other: Ethics and Contracts

The contract also plays a role as important maintenance of Chinese traditional society. That's why ethics is said to merely be one of the most important binding forces to

[13]Ba [10].

[14]Zhang [11].

Chinese families, society and state. Ethics and contract both have been the engine of Chinese civilization development in the past thousand years.

It does not run counter to historical rationality that we study the relationship between ethics and contracts from its logical base. Generally speaking, the structure of Chinese ethical moral culture is logically based on the cultivation of man's goodness. In other words, with the good aspect of humanity motivated, a man thus subordinates and devotes himself to the development of family and state. And contract, logically with the intention to restrain the evilness, contributes to mutual reciprocity based on the balance of personal interests so that one does not enjoy too much benefit and the other will not suffer too much from the former's gain. In terms of means, ethics lays a basis on blood and family ties and requires compliance and obedience of an individual, for which his inborn goodness and bloodline-incurred natural obligation can account. And contract, limited to rights and obligations, focuses on mutual satisfaction and recognition between individuals or families. One's rights are reversed as the obligation of another which leads to a reciprocal relation between rights and obligations. As seen from the evolution of history, identity has been not only the precondition for existence of ethics but its base and pursuit. Without identity, ethics is an empty shell. As a result, an identity-oriented Chinese traditional society finally takes shape, where one performs his duty according to his identity. On the contrary, contract goes against identity privilege and for ultimate equality. Naturally, it is supposed to be impartial.

It thus seems that ethics and contracts are born incompatible. However, it is not the case in history and reality. Ethics goes hand in hand with contract throughout traditional and modern China, whose mutual complementation, interaction and infiltration give rise to a unique legal cultural style.

As mentioned above, ethics constitutes the essence of contracts while the contract is the physical expression of ethics. Commendably, contractual spirit is embedded in ethics. Although moral human relations are the ultimate pursuit of Chinese traditional society, if diachronically studied we can see that the early Confucianists, such as Confucius, Mencius and Hsün Tzu, attached importance to etiquette in order to keep human relations and king's governance in order. There existed primitive democracy in their views that right and obligation inter-infiltrated and complemented each other. Benevolent father, filial son; righteous husband, obedient wife; wise king, loyal minister; and vice versa. And taking identity-emphasis to an extreme, Confucian ethics in Han and Song Dynasty provided that one who was inferior or junior merely assumed the obligation without enjoying the rights, which not only failed to develop Confucianism but also blocked its sound development. Necessarily, in contract lies the adherence to basic morality and society-recognized ethics in the pursuit of interests. In essence, contracts can be anything but divorced from ethics, whose enrichment and judgment prevent man being subject to interest, efficacy and desire.[15]

It is noteworthy that there are many arguments regarding ethics in Chinese traditional society as the moral core and even direct connotation of contract but few about

[15]Jiang [12].

their relationship and the development rule and regulation function of contracts. As is known to all, ethics does exert an influence on the development of Chinese ancient contract, ranging from contractual spirit and system to customs, which can be concluded as follows: Firstly, ethical rules imposes identity limits; that is, contractual behavior is subject to the identity of the parties to the contract, and civil rights and civil obligations vary from party to party. In terms of property rights, it is expressly stated from Tang to Qing Dynasty that the inferior and the junior were forbidden from exercising the right to sell family property without authorization while the superior and the senior enjoyed broad authority. This will be detailed later. Secondly, ethical rules play a great part in the formation and development of contractual spirit. No matter satisfying their desire or winning benefits, the parties to the contract are subject to the obedience of ethics. Mutual assent, equality and integrity are not only the elements valued but the existence and development motivation of contract. And they all derive from ethics and morality. Thirdly, ethical rules bring about the unique system of integration in Chinese traditional society, which affects the contractual customs in depth. The control in Chinese traditional society was realized in three aspects. One was the "rule of law" of the government. The "law" here merely referred to "ruler's decrees",[16] which is aimed to serve monarchy. The other was the "rule of etiquette" of the squire class in communities. Fei Hsiao-tung has defined "etiquette" as "civilized customs that voluntarily conform to tradition".[17] Etiquette has been the most important means for local elite, including squire and bureaucrat, to hold a stable and peaceful regional ruling and the direct inheritance of primitive Confucian spirit.[18] The third was the "rule of morality" over people, namely the moral restraint mechanism gradually developed in folk life, which was good-deed-oriented and followed theory of retribution.[19] Influenced by ethical culture, "law", "etiquette" and "morality" are bound up with ethics and morals which can date back to Western Zhou Dynasty. They each impose a direct impact on the formation and development of Chinese contractual customs, especially the latter two.

Judging from the development of Chinese ancient contracts, ethics and contracts complement each other and fight against each other as well. Imposing too much ethical restraint promises deprivation of contractual freedom, but no control imposed on contract will endanger society stability and state security. As a result, ethics and contract are mutually developed "in balance" on the basis of mutual promotion, infiltration and restriction, which impedes the development of the spirit of contractual freedom and leaves China short on the abstract and holy spirit of contract. However, it is undeniable that the "balance" not only becomes a unique feature of Chinese culture but lays the foundation of long-term stability of Chinese society.

We are not intended to glorify Chinese culture. But as L. A. White has put in *The Evolution of Culture*, the function and purpose of culture is to guarantee the stability

[16]See [13].

[17]Fei [14].

[18]See *Mencius: Lianghui Wang* (*Part II*) where Mencius once claimed propriety and righteous proposed by Sage.

[19]Ma [15].

of human life and continuation of human race.[20] And that is the part the peculiar relationship between ethics and contract plays in Chinese traditional society.

It seems that we have paid too much attention to ethics so far. But the point is that only in this way can we have a general idea of what Chinese ancient contracts are and how much they cover.

So, the question is, that what ethics and contracts, falling into different categories, rely on to keep their close connection. If not, we cannot have a profound understanding of the spiritual nature and historical evolution of Chinese ancient contracts.

The Medium: Abstract and Concrete Justice Concept

Talcott Parsons believes that society, marked by shared value orientation and a high level of self-sufficiency, is a system in which people interact with each other.[21] But Hugevilt differentiates capitalist society from socialist society. He holds that the same as their purposes are, namely accelerating economic growth and creating social wealth, the latter, whose development strategy is combined with such basic values as social justice and equality and so on, agrees with values favored by the majority including the intellectual elite and the former motivates wealth pursuit with the promise of more allocable material benefits in the future.[22] It can be said that his theory of social development has got to the root. Why China follows nothing but socialism after the breakdown of thousand-year feudal regime? The argument in political textbook is weak or at least surface-scratched. A change of political system depends more than on military force. Communists' theory of "people" and "common prosperity" win the "popular support" from the perspective of values. As the prerequisite for assuming and consolidating power, "whether or not popular support is inclined", which has been underlined by political elites and political culture of different dynasties, is necessarily worth attention. He who wins the popular support will rule the world; He who loses the popular support will be ruled. Or he who follows "Tao" enjoys great support while one, if not, finds little. These are official expostulations examined by the intellectual history of Chinese political culture and Chinese political system. The foregoing "Tao" and "popular support" reflect the very value idea of justice and equality Hugevilt has mentioned. And the abstract but concrete concept of justice is precisely the medium that connects ethics with contract.

It is necessary to first study the justice concept in eastern and western culture, from which we can see the historical factors shaping the close connection and mutual dependence between Chinese ancient contractual rules and ethical rules.

---

[20] Cited in Zhang et al. [16].

[21] Hugevilt [17].

[22] Hugevilt [18].

In *Institutions*, Justinian clearly defines "law" as "science concerning justice and injustice" and "justice" as "the permanent desire to guarantee everyone what he deserves".[23] Comparing Greek legal concepts with Roman ones, M. T. Cicero gets the idea of the essence of law. He is convinced that the Greek word nomos, which derives from *Veuw*, means allocation, namely things are fundamentally intended to give every man his due. And the Latin word *lex* implies conception of selection, called a *legendo.* In Romans' view, law means equality of selection. Meanwhile there exists distinction between jus and lex in Roman law. Jus is an art of goodness and justice. In other words, the essence of law is justice because jus originates from Justitia (justice).[24] Plato regards law as the means to defend justice. From his view, justice means to help friends fight against enemies[25] and thus "a ruler judges with the purpose to prohibit anyone from infringing on other's property and to protect everyone's property from infringement"; only in this way can fairness be guaranteed so that "everyone enjoys what belongs to him and does what he should have to do".[26] Aristotle further classifies justice as distributive one and commutative one. Distributive justice refers to the distribution of right, power, obligation and duty among members of the city-state according to their social status, which is equal in distribution quota. Interests are equally shared among equal people and otherwise unequally shared.[27] At the same time, the distribution principle is compatible with political system. Wealth is shared on average in democracy while on the merits of competence and contribution in aristocracy.[28] Commutative justice is the code of conduct supposed to be followed in transactions. In *Leviathan,* Thomas Hobbes has detailed and developed Plato and Aristotle's theories of justice. He believes commutative justice refers to the performance of contracts in purchase and sale, hire and employment, debita and credit, transaction, barter and other contractual deeds. But distributive justice, that of the arbitrator, involves the distribution of equivalent interest to people under equal conditions.[29] The classical contractualism in nineteenth century laid stress on the absolute validity of contract. Respecting the freedom of individual will, law merely defended the right of the contractor to contract, which can be positively proved by the claim that contract is justice. Schwartz, a scholar familiar with the intellectual history of American laws, holds that justice in contractual law is protective toward legal contracts in nature[30] and that the contractual spirit then gives rise to a clear logical judgment; that is, "Contract is justice" and "Justice is freedom". Accordingly, it is concluded that "Contract is freedom". The rise of neoclassical contractualism suggested the coming of the age of social restraint on

[23]Justian [19].

[24]Cited in the note 14, 21, 20 of On the Spirit of Western Law. 1996. *Journal of Comparative Law,* (1).

[25]Plato [20].

[26]Cited in [21].

[27]Bodenheimer [22].

[28]Aristotle [23].

[29]Hobbes [24].

[30]Schwartz [25].

individual freedom. Although classical contractualism recognized the equality in rights, it however lead to actual inequality[31] due to the ignorance of "unequal relations between contractors".[32] With the increasing spread of the theory of reliance interest, contractual rules started to lean towards humanity, gradually embraced social customs and moral code and upgraded good faith as the general clause of contract, all of which implied that the development of contract law in twentieth century "turns law into potential morality"[33] instead of a "bargain" in which both parties shared interest at the same time.

As seen from above, justice concept in western philosophy of law develops as follows: each gets his due, individual freedom or state (social) restraint, of which the key is to take law as the means to realize justice so as to protect everyone's rights and guarantee his interests. It is inevitable that social restraint be included in contractual rules under such a circumstance. And finally comes into being two types of justice concept. One is that contracting parties are free to contract under bona fides and another is that society or state, when trusted to adjudicate, is supposed to impartially deal with allocating one what he deserves.[34] Briefly, justice is freedom of contract for contracting parties, impartial adjudication for social ruling parties[35] and the equal realization of interests of both parties as a consequence of contracting deed.

The development of justice concept in Chinese traditional society followed the people's will and kept compliance with Tao, namely people's feelings, rationality and law all taken into account. The Confucian concept of justice aims that people all over the world benefit from the grace of the emperor to obtain what they want. In terms of its realization, it bears a stamp of gift as people's contracting deeds, required as it is, do not matter as much as imperial kindness and official concern about people's feelings. In the absence of western awareness of man's natural rights, individuals in Chinese traditional society were subject to "privilege" of family and class, devoid of the awareness of seeking profits individually. Profit-seeking was subject to both the external restraint from family customary law and state law and the internal examination and assessment of traditional ethical culture. That is not only the real reason why merchant class had difficulty in shaping in China but the root of the absence of contractual freedom and independence. Take Huizhou merchants as an example. The hundreds of years, during which Huizhou merchants rose and reached its peak, have seen the establishment of pro-wealth value ideal and the popularity of Confucianism-binding practice among merchants. It was said that he who was too ineloquent to do business would turn to be a Confucianist, thus ranking

[31] *A Source Book in Foreign Civil Law* (p. 83). 1983. Law Press. p. 83.

[32] Atiyah [26].

[33] Bodenheimer [27].

[34] Hobbes [28].

[35] The Wealth of Nations, wirtten by Adam Smith, has dealt with the main points of economic liberalism, putting that the government is the "protector and watcher" of free competition, and that law can only provide convenience for parties to contract though universal norms.

merchants high over Confucianists.[36] However, the traditional Confucianism brought about the very decline of Huizhou merchants. In terms of ethical tradition, Huizhou merchants were obedient regardless of being the richest one; they kept their behaviors in accordance with Confucian ethics. In *Guide to scholarly merchants* written by Cheng Chunyu in Ming Dynasty, it is encouraged that hardworking and thrifty be given priority to by discreetness-oriented businessmen, which can be seen from such statements as "hardworking promises rich future and greed is born of laziness"; "subdue oneself and be selfless"; "be sincere and kind, and be honest and upright". And it is discouraged that "one takes advantage of his power, wealth or talent to bully others". In the book such statements are beyond count.[37] From the perspective of system and custom, the rise of Huizhou merchants was attributed to joint effort of family. Adjustment of capital lied with family, causing the expansion of merchants and consumption of capital as well. In the meantime, merchants were protected in family-centered rural social structure while the accumulation of commercial capital was hindered due to the idea of doing good and righteous deeds and appropriately accumulating or spending money. Some scholar insightfully holds that since there was no commercial law in ancient China, state compulsory law especially Confucian familyism constituted the internal restraint on commercial capital and commercial spirit.[38]

It was double-edged that Confucian ethics imposed impact and restraint on commercial activities. On one hand, it regulated business conduct and introduced morals into business which made up for legal deficiency, gave rise to good commercial spirit. On the other hand, it did limit the mental motivation of merchants, the main contracting party, to pursue wealth accumulation and placed barriers in their way to accumulate capital in the name of family system.

Confucian-ethics-oriented value did not impose negative impact on the rapid development of Chinese ancient contracts. On the contrary, contractual justice such as equality, freedom and fairness tookdeep root in Chinese traditional society. To put it simple, ethics does not block but provides moral compass for the advance of contract. Only aware of this can we explain the true nature and evolution of Chinese ancient contract.

As mentioned above, subjection to Tao has constituted the majority of regulation on contract from ethics. Though it can be perceived by every person, the so-called "Tao" is too vague to be defined clearly. If required, Tao can be explained as people's feelings, rationality and law. It seems that accordance with law does not matter much to Chinese, but "accordance with people's feelings and rationality" is required in everything. It has been a rule for Chinese officials or businessmen and a vague but concrete criterion for social measurement and appraisal. People's feelings, rationality

---

[36]Wang Daokun. *Taihan Collection (Vol. 54): Epitaph for Mr. Wu, a late prominent personage in Xiyang in Ming dynasty.*

[37]Cited in The Business Principles of Huizhou Merchants in Ming Dynasty Observed from *Guide to Scholarly Merchants*. 1994. *Academics in China*, (6).

[38]Gao [29].

and law jointly constitute the unique justice concept, which was the very means to connect ethics with contract, in Chinese traditional society.

The justice concept has been dually influenced by ethics and contract, be they Chinese ancient one or western one. Ethics motivates man's "goodness" from the perspective of morality while contracts restrain the deluge of man's "evilness" in the mutual satisfaction of interests, thus reaching a balance between "goodness" and "evilness", the ideal existence order. It is noteworthy that ethics, freed of the favor from Heaven, gods and witchcraft, has borne a stamp of humanity since Western Zhou Dynasty.[39] It is also since Western Zhou Dynasty that Chinese ancient contract system has come into gradual maturity, playing the role of regulating the entire social life, especially the daily economic life of people and complementing the development of traditional Chinese ethics and vice versa. And the bond is the justice concept mentioned above, whose ultimate pursuit is the Mean (Impartiality) and equilibrium and harmony, certain life wisdom and life attitude. The concept of "Music (Yue in Chinese)" introduced into ethical philosophy by Confucianists and combined with "Rites (Li in Chinese)", the "rites and music culture" took shape which had been intrinsic to Chinese culture. The Chapter *Music* of *The Book of Rites* dwells on the importance of Li and Yue to social restraint. "Ancestors created Li and Yue not for sensual enjoyment but to educate people on the discrimination between goodness and badness and thus put them back on the right way. Men are born to be quiet-favored in nature but become active under instinct for the perception of things. When perceiving things, man shows preference or abhorrence. Failing to control their preference or abhorrence and to perceive and properly treat the outside temptation, they will totally lose their nature. The outside world has been imposing impact on man. Under this circumstance, if they do not control their preference and abhorrence in the perceiving of things man will be assimilated by things. In other words, man's nature has got lost while their desire has run out of control. The intention of disobedience and dishonesty as well as the behavior of debauchery and rebellion is incurred. The powerful thus oppress the weak; the majority bully the minority; the crafty defraud the fool; the bold torment the coward; and the sick, the old, the young and the childless are not taken care of, all of which lead to world disorder. As a result, ancestors created Li and Yue, a restraint made by man". Both Li and Yue were made for balancing and controlling man's desire so as to keep society stable and people civilized. Confucian doctrine is consistent with Aristotle's political theory; that is, state is meant for providing a moral environment. And it is not because of philosophical cognition of human frailties but assumption of disorderly competition resulting from resource shortage that the claims of Han Fei and Shang Yang (two representatives of legalist school) were cruel and severe. Therefore, legalists control people's behavior through rewards and punishments while Confucianists control people's mind through the system of rites and music.[40] Above is an insightful viewpoint from Gao Daoyun. And Xu Fuguan, a representative of Neo-Confucianism, incisively elaborates the relationship of "Li"

---

[39]Zhang [30].

[40]Karen [31].

and "Yue". In Confucianism, "Yue" can be called fine only in the existence of equilibrium and harmony, behind which lies "kindness" because "Yue", if appropriately adequate, can "motivate people's kindness". The unity of benevolence (whose physical expression is Li) and Yue is underlined by Confucianists. Benevolence belongs to moral category and Yue is a kind of art. The primitive Confucianists believe that morality and art, if both as good as it gets, jointly mark the high level of life.[41] And Ban Gu, a historian of Han Dynasty, materializes the function of Yue in respective of the order of human relations. "Yue advocates harmony. Having taken shape through tuning instruments to coordinate the rhythm, a tune is used to keep in harmony the father-son and king-minister relationship and win people's trust and attachment. That is why ancestors create Yue".[42] It is worth noting that Confucius claims "Yue" to be a kind of mental-influencing force which makes people subdue their desire and conform to Li. However, Confucianism in Eastern Han Dynasty regarded Yue as the means to coordinate human relations, which underlined the extrinsic utility of Yue but ignored the intrinsic moral influence, serving as the prelude to the claim of exterminating the desire proposed by Neo-Confucianists of Song Dynasty. It ran counter to the mode-racy of Confucian claim "subdue one's self and return to propriety".

Under primitive Confucian culture of rites and music, ethical morality norms highlighted class harmony rather than class oppression which has been criticized by many scholars. Racial as Hsün Tzu, he lays stress on the balance between "desire" and "rationality" as much as Confucius and Mencius. "If recognized to be rational, desire, much as it is, will do no harm to state governance; few as it is, desire, if recognized irrational, will do no good to ending the unrest".[43] From the development of Chinese ancient contract, we can know that contract is entered into on the basis of "He (mental harmony)". Although named diversely, Chinese ancient contracts all called for that parties voluntarily entered into them and enjoyed equality in benefiting. Agreements were called "he Tong (和同)" in Tang Dynasty and universally called "He Tong (合同)"in Qing Dynasty. It is entered into voluntarily (with free will) and under good faith rather than force (mental harmony), that is, so-called"contracting on the meet of minds", be they "he tong" or "He tong". The unnatural coincidence above resulted from subtle connection and mutual infiltration between ethics and contract under the influence of Confucinism.

Reasons for Absence Of Complete Written Contract Law in Traditional China

L. H. White has made two presumptions, which seems to be somehow lacking of reasonable grounds yet however thought-provoking. One is that "man can be said to live under ethics", with a social instinct for seeking goodness and avoiding evilness.

[41]Xu [32].

[42]Ban [33].

[43]*Hsun Tzu On Names.*

The other is that men are the carrier of culture rather the primary driving force, the creator or the defining factor of culture. Individuals under certain culture turn the interaction of cultural advance into a potential catalyst and are the media in which cultural advance are expressed.[44] Presuming as above, he intends to elaborate that ethics being the internal binding force of social restraint, whether contract—the corresponding object—is also a social means to regulate human behavior; and that since man cannot create culture (this viewpoint temporarily accepted), what is the motivation of contractual existence?

The former has aroused broad discussion and agreement. As White has put, ethics does form a kind of internal control throughout the development and civilization of society and human being. As social instinct, ethics is to produce social emotions such as shame, empathy and justice which are not innate physiological instinct but cultural product and educational achievement. White has quoted Radcliffe Brown as saying that the so-called conscience is an inward reflection of social approval. And one acts out of conscience for such a long time that he mistakes conscience for an inward reflection of god's will or of instinct, which is post hoc. Therefore, White believes that conscience is the means and medium of ethical behaviors instead of the cause.[45] It seemly can be concluded that sense of shame, goodness and evilness, empathy and justice is a kind of human social instinct generating in the cultural development, intended to restrain human physiological instinct so as to maintain the existing order or achieve the ideal order of peaceful coexistence. So what are the characteristics or the mechanism of contractual system, the contrast of ethics? Having been mentioned above, contract is directly intended to guarantee the interests of both parties without detriment to that of others and society and further to establish and maintain a peaceful and mutually beneficial living environment, of which the later achieves the same end as ethics. But in terms of human nature, both goodness supporters and evilness supporters acknowledge that man tend to be selfish due to instinct (goodness supporters believe) or environment (evilness supporters believe), trying to maximize or optimize their own interests. And thus comes into being a conflict of interest seeking for a solution. It is not man themselves but culture White has referred to that voluntarily adjusts the interests between humans. In other words, in order to protect and gain his own benefits one has to admit and protect interests of others, which respectively belong to the right and obligation of contract. It is in the interaction between right and obligation that man enjoy (not create) a mutually recognized contractual relationship that restrains themselves and others. As some scholars has put, contract is interchange of interests in nature, with the core lying in the "effectiveness of benefiting oneself rather than complementation to benefiting others".[46] Hence ethics belongs to social instinct to seek goodness and avoid evilness while contract is a natural instinct to pursue profits. Leaning towards benefiting oneself, contract enables both parties to pursue the largest profits they consider to be on the basis of mutual recognition. The clan, tribe, and even the state superior to

[44]White [34].

[45]White [35].

[46]Jiang [36].

both parties merely are witnesses and protectors of the contract, and play the role of a neutral arbitrator. And thus market relations, of which the majority can be attributed to contractual relationship, embody interest and wealth rather than ethics. Market is not the moral practicer that shows kindness but the profit seeker asking for the lowest degree of goodness. Above is the general clue to the development of western contract and there is a slight difference from that to Chinese ancient contract, which will be further explained later.

As for the later one, we can argue in the respective of the discussion of a specific question; that is, why there hasn't been any written contract law in traditional China? And is this consequent on human being (traditional system) or a selection of culture?

Ancient China did not see the existence of contract. Actually, by Han Dynasty at the latest, forms of Chinese contract had been totally unified into a national standard.[47] And by Qin Dynasty contract had developed into pretty mature, as developed as ancient Roman law in terms of contract system, contractual spirit and contract management, etc. However, traditional China has seen the enactment of *Market Transaction*("市易" in Chinese) *Law*, *Middlemen and Guarantor*("牙保" in Chinese) *Law* and *Trading law* except a complete and systematic set of modern contract rules. The British scholar P. S. Atiyah believes that British contract can date back earlier to the Middle Ages.[48] The course of British law history and civil law history lags behind the development of Chinese contractual culture, but a complete contract code has failed to come out in traditional China. In terms of the root, the viewpoint of Professor Lawrence Friedman makes some sense. He holds that as a kind of "law" that guarantees the free will of parties, contract is resistant to the intervention of state force. Therefore, contract law is "disinclined to codification (of the contract)".[49] After studying the development history of Chinese ancient contract, we can find that is the truth. The traditional contractual spirit and contract system were mainly embedded in folk secular society and took the form of civil customary law, on which the authority exerted more unrevealing recognition than restraint. Two factors, many scholars suppose, can account for the underdevelopment of Chinese contract law; which are the model of economic life (family-livelihood-oriented rather than profit-oriented) and the official policy of restraining commerce in ancient China. It seems that the failure of a written contract law is man-made. Given all that, Professor Friedman has pierced the veiling at least and located the delay of contract law in the development of contract itself. But the key is that he merely scratches the surface due to his ignorance of the great impact on traditional contractual culture imposed by contract and ethics which were complementary to each other and fought against each other. In other words, it was difficult and unnecessary for contract law to come into being due to the powerful integration function of Chinese traditional ethical culture and thus ancient China failed to see the existence of a complete written contact law.

---

[47]Hugh [37].

[48]See [38]. Also see [39]. It is deemed that the contract law was not attached importance to in the early stage and developed slowly from the seventeenth to eighteenth century. The nineteenth century saw its unprecedented development.

[49]ibid, p. 203.

On the surface, the development of Chinese traditional contract has always been in the dual control of self-discipline and heteronomy, but the most fundamental driving force for the control of contract development is ethics. From the perspective of self-discipline, Confucian economic ethics has always been a moral judge of the economic behaviors of both parties to the contract. The ethical motivation of economic behavior, whether intended or not, has always been a lion in the pursuit of profit. Confucian concept of "Rites" is superficially to discriminate hierarchy and restrain human desire but actually to balance and bring to order the distribution of social wealth so that the gap between the rich and the poor, and between lord and loon will not get wider too much. However, it is far from the real objective of Confucianists. What they really want is the average distribution of social wealth and the permanent stability of society (imperial power, be they Confucius, Mencius or Hsün Tzu). But such average, the same as distributive justice proposed by Aristotle, is confined to those who are equal under the system of imperial power and only in this way can society stability be achieved. Above embodies the true essence of Confucian ethics, namely "Lun (伦)". Lun means sequence or family hierarchy in Chinese. "The way of Lun (lunli (伦理) in Chinese)" refers to that people of the same social status (sequence) enjoy equal rights, assume equal obligations and accordingly do their part. "The emperor is the emperor, the minister is the minister, the father is the father, and the son is the son." Such claim is loaded with the thought of democracy rather than privileged status that Confucianists of Han and Song Dynasty have proclaimed. Confucius once expounded his claim in a sensible way. He said, "I have heard that those in power worry about not the shortage but the uneven distribution of wealth and care about society instability rather than poverty because equal distribution promises no poverty and social harmony and social stability respectively rid them of the worry of manpower shortage and state overturn".[50] Hsün Tzu supposes that the thought of propriety and righteousness is proposed to "make everyone do his own part and win benefits commensurate to his status and contribution, which is the way to keep people live in harmony". And he advocates "distribution according to the thought of propriety, that is, a even one without impartiality".[51] It is a matter concerning the fate of state that benefits are distributed in a fair manner. Paying a little attention to the Chinese history, we can find that peasant uprisings have left great marks on feudal society, reminding rulers of balancing the interests between different classes. The army of Huang Jin Uprising advocated "the Way of Great Peace" and that "Man are born equal and inferior to Heaven"[52] who is fair and impartial. Wang Xiaobo and Li Shun, the leaders of a uprising in Northern Song Dynasty, proposed the idea of average wealth. Zhong Xiang and Yang Yao, the leaders of an uprising in Southern Song Dynasty, further proposed the idea of "eliminating hierarchy and balancing wealth" demanding the equality both in status and in wealth.[53] And Li

[50] *The Analects of Confucius Eight Rows and Eight Lines.*

[51] *Hsün Tzu: Honor and Dishonor*; *Hsün Tzu: Da Lue.*

[52] *Canon of heavenly peace* (*Tai Ping Jing*) Vol. 112.

[53] *Compilation on the Alliances between the Song and King of three dynasties* (*San Chao Bei Meng Hui Bian*) Vol 137.

Zicheng put forward the slogan: "Equal field without tax grain" which attracted a lot of followers.[54] The majority of peasant uprising armies were the great unwashed, uneducated, but it seemed that they knew the truth that Heaven is fair and impartial and that man are born equal. There was not the theory of natural rights in China. In such a political and cultural context, it was not easy to equip illiterate peasants with ideas above. It can be explained only in the way that economic ethics concerning fairness and justice is a kind of "social contract" entered into between peasants and rulers or the rich. Once a breach of contract or damage to their interests occurred, peasants would together rise up in arms. If Chen Sheng and Wu Guang are said to challenge the ruler from the perspective of identity authority ("Is there anyone born to be a king, a duke, a general or a minister?"), uprisings after Tang Dynasty (including the current political power of workers and peasants) have turned the focus on equality and fairness in economic rights. Such ethical spirit hand in hand with the equality (consensus of both parties) and fairness (no damages to both parties) of private contract, ethics and contract thus achieve harmony of spirit and mutual infiltration in practice. But in comparison, ethical spirit, especially the concept of equality and justice, is in chief and embraces the justice concept of contractual concept. As a result, ethics and contract are mutually enriched and developed, imposing great impact on history. On the one hand, as mentioned above, it makes both sides of the transaction ethics-abiding, value honesty and righteousness, and keeps their promise. By virtue of the Buddhist theory of retribution, it developed self-disciplined economic ethical order and trading rules with Chinese characteristics, which contributed to the stable and sound development of economic life. On the other hand, Confucian ethical economic rules took root so deep that they were recognized by both the authority and the people, widely practiced in judicial trials, expressly stated in community pacts and clan regulations and repeated in rules of (business) guild, which left no room for and blocked the development of a written contract law in traditional China. It can be said to have been offset by the premature ethical economic model as well as its core concept of justice, be they the historical motivation for the existence of written contract law or the historical role of written contract law. Explained from the perspective of ethical restraint, the absence of Chinese written contract law is consistent with both historical rationality and historical facts.

The core thoughts of ethical economy, exposed and spread, have influenced the development of Chinese economy from all sides and turned Chinese economy into a premature ethical one instead of a commodity economy or a market economy. However, it cannot be ignored that factors which affect the development of Chinese contract are rationally selected by Chinese culture rather than determined by man as many scholars have supposed.

[54]*A Record Causing Blame on Me* (*Zui Wei Lu*) Vol. 31: *Li Zicheng.*

Evaluation Standards and Research Significance

Research on Chinese ancient contract law has raised rare concern in academic circle for years. And not until 1980s when the research achievement of Japanese and American scholars came into view did a few Chinese mainland scholars initiate the research on Chinese ancient contract with difficulty. However, there have existed few scholars on Chinese ancient contract law so far. What's more, research has been confined to a certain scope due to the shortage of historical materials and the upsurge of "Westernization" in academic circle, failing to achieve great exposure and expansion. In order to change, we have to resolve the following questions: Firstly, what is the standard we will accord to judge Chinese ancient contractual culture? Secondly, what is the connotation and value of Chinese ancient contractual law and are they applicable to reality? This section will respectively provide targeted answers.

As we all know, under the influence of ethics Chinese ancient contract was ethics-oriented in terms of its core of value, which contributed to a system of contract law with the autonomy of patriarchal clans, guilds and villages as the mainstay. And it will be further discussed from the perspective of inner spirit and policysystem.

Considered at the ideology level, the spirit of contract law under the influence of Confucian ethics tended to be moral autonomy of parties to the contract. Judging from the current historical materials ranging from *Rites of Zhou* to civil customary law of Qing Dynasty, the spirit of moral autonomy had been attached importance to without exception. Shang Yang, who advocates agriculture war and severe law, also intends people to be "moral autonomy" driven finally by means of plentiful material wealth and harsh punishments, thereby realizing the ruling strategy of "abolishing punishment with punishment". Different as the way is, the thought of "moral autonomy" is consistent with Taoist thought of "morality of ancestors prevailing over punishment" and Confucianist thought of "punishment and morality complementary to each other" in objective; that is, morality is intended to be the ultimate pursuit and employed to govern the country.[55] The end of Ming Dynasty, a period when Chinese ancient commodity economy was highly developed, saw the existence of devotion to social relief. Those were community pacts and morality books (*Merits and Faults*) on the initiative of squires and officials, intended to regulate behaviors of social subjects. According to the statistics of Cynthia Broaw, morality books were spread throughout the country at the end of Ming Dynasty and there were 10 sets of *Merits and Faults* published and sold to every province during the mere fifty years between 1620 and 1670.[56] Sakai Tadao, a Japanese scholar, has defined "*Merits and Faults*" as "a book that classifies Chinese national morality into good (merits) and evil (faults), respectively gives an account and figures out the number of good and evil".[57] American scholar E. S. Rawski and Peiyi Wu respectively call it "Spiritual Account Books and Moral Book-Keeping".[58] Richard Shek thinks that morality books serve

---

[55]Zeng et al. [40].

[56]Brokaw [41].

[57]Sakai [42].

[58]You [43].

as exhortation for parties to the tenancy contract, promoting harmonious coexistence, a role similar to social contract, thus realizing social stability.[59] Undoubtedly, good and evil or merits and faults included in morality books catalyze the moralization of parties to the contract, being a strong support for Confucian ethics.

Considered at the institution level, the system of contract law, to a greater extent, is a kind of legal norm. It regulates the behaviors of contracting parties by virtue of state laws, clan regulations, community pacts and guild rule, etc. so that they will not deviate from moral economy or ethical economy. Chinese orthodox imperial power imposed the policy of restraining commerce, showing no mercy to businessmen. Han Dynasty is typical of such policy. In Han Dynasty, it was deemed that merchants as the lowest class, if rich, were bound to "disturb the hierarchical order" [60]and doing business regardless of agriculture would leave farmlands uncultivated and annexed, giving rise to the wide gap between the rich and the poor, the shortage of social supply and even social instability.[61] What's worse, due to limited identity privilege, merchants had to align themselves with political forces (which Chao Cuo, a politician of Hang Dynasty, called "collusion with authorities") for effective operation, which was bound to strengthen local forces, endangering the central authority. Hence the authority of Han Dynasty implemented the policy of restraining commerce.[62] The policy expressed itself as political insults, increased taxation, unified transport and averaged price, state monopoly and GaoMin decree (confiscating property once tax evasion is exposed), "strangling" commerce from all sides.[63] Since then, the policy of restraining commerce, not strengthened as it is, has been a political, economic and even cultural strategy for emergency in order to secure state and people and entrench imperial power.

This policy was historical regression. Commerce in Western Zhou Dynasty was valued, causing unprecedented rise in political and social status of merchants so that they could even rise to the status of "manager" sharing power.[64] Szuma Chien still adopted a wise attitude towards "merchants (Huozhi "货殖" in ancient Chinese)". *The Biography of Merchants* in *Records of the Grand Historian* has dealt with the importance of commerce. "Merchants as common people without privilege do no harm to politics and the people. They amass their fortune through time which is a wise way". And mercantilism seems to be adopted as a basic state policy throughout the world. Take Britain as an example. During seventeenth century to mid-eighteenth century when the British market system took shape, the British government actively initiated the enactment of laws and regulations to protect private property and contract

[59]See Richard Hon-chun Shek. Religion and Society in late Ming: Sectarianism and Popular Thought in Sixteenth and Seventeeth Centrury China Ph. D. dissertatioin, 1980: 147–148.

[60]*The History of the Former Han Dynasty Naitional Financial Economy.*

[61]See *Emphasizing Agriculture, Mintage, Conference Foucus* and *Censure on Shangyang* in *On Salt and Iron.*

[62]Ma [44].

[63]Fu [45].

[64]Fan [46].

and finally became the most powerful one over the capitalist world.[65] Freud holds that after the Crusades merchants in Europe gradually infiltrated the feudal organization on account of their satisfying but unharmful character so that they were able to structure their own social apparatus.[66] But the contemporaneous Chinese government of Ming and Qing Dynasties restrained commerce by means of ban of marine trade, ban of the combination of farming and cottage craft and levy of high taxation, which contained the inner motivation for profit-seeking of contracting parties.

Patriarchal system and guild rules correspond to the policy of restraining commerce. The policy of restraining commerce is an economic expression of political concern while clan regulations and guild rules limit individual capacity of contracting parties to engage in economic activities. The patriarchal system advocates public property system which bans private property and unauthorized dispose of property, preemption of relatives and neighbors, and the system of equal division of family property among sons, which weakens the motivation for the development of contract law. And guild rules restrict free competition through monopoly which leaves no historical room for contract law. Having comparing Chinese systems of family, clan and guild, Tachibana Shiraki, a Japanese scholar believes that moral consciousness of guild members constitutes the spiritual pillar of guild activities.[67] Based on the knowledge of traditional China and its background, Kishimoto Mio, another Japanese scholar, believes that Chinese traditional society ignores the "modernization" of individual selection and responsibility.[68]

In conclusion, spiritual restraint (self-discipline) inward and institutional restriction (heteronomy) outward not only lessen the utilization of merchant capital but lead to the nonexistence of an independent merchant class and the root of Chinese ancient contract transplanted into folk secular society, forming customary law of contract. Since the developing process has been expounded above, it really matters what kind of standard we will accord to judge the development and historical effect of Chinese ancient contract.

C. Geerze regards law as a kind of local knowledge. In terms of the specific meaning, the word "local" denotes not only the time and space dimension or class distinction but accent. In other words, local knowledge of what has happened is combined with the local imagination of what will happen.[69] It is the highlights of Geerze's viewpoint that culture itself is elaborated on from the perspective of local cultural characteristics. Every kind of cultural phenomena, if exists, is rational in essence. Simply describing them as "primitive", namely backward and stupid, etc. we will go to extreme. Since the May Fourth Movement, the academic circle, advocating "westernization", has been introducing western values and cultural phenomena into China, which is intended to be a positive motivation for solving the maladies. However, the recent century has seen a tendency in the cultural development, namely

[65]Gao [47].

[66]See the theory of Sigmund Freud, cited in [48].

[67]Tachibana [49].

[68]Mio [50].

[69]Greeze [51].

to compare between western and eastern culture and imply that current eastern cultural education equals the past of western culture and the future of eastern culture amounts to the present of western culture. Emile Durkheim and Max Weber are typical ethnocentrism supporters. Different as their perspectives are in the discussion of culture, they reach remarkably similar conclusions which imply that the East, lagging behind the West, has to follow the western way in order for rejuvenation, otherwise it will always be trading water, failing to enter into the age of modernization.[70] This cultural bias is so widespread that "westernization" and "transplantation" enjoy popularity in jurisprudential circle as well. Books on examining the history of traditional culture are published one after another, in which the successful development of the West serves as s foil to the obsolescence of Chinese ancient culture. Those writers are impetuous and barely objective. The American scholar Philip C. C. Huang is clear-minded. He holds that research on Chinese economic history is to produce concepts and theories in line with Chinese realities instead of following the theoretical framework of modern Western economy. More importantly, such premises on which modern capitalism takes shape must be abandoned as that "economic man" are consistently rational, namely pursuing maximized profit, and that reasonable distribution of resources is met merely in free market. Meanwhile, Huang kindly exhorts scholars to understand economic systems more than on the basis of capitalist economy logic, not regarding it as the only correct standard.[71] Considered from the perspective of reality, China is not as developed as the West indeed, especially in material culture. But this does not mean that we should repudiate our own culture in its totality. Advance is appreciated, but regardless of specific conditions, discarding or bending our national culture to cater for the so-called "advanced" culture or to realize thorough transplant is unappreciated. On many occasions in history, it has been proved that utilitarian imitation brings about nothing but a loss of our own culture.

Although there are just a few scholars on the research of Chinese ancient contract at home and abroad, their spirit of learning about history from history is commendable. In other words, they focus on exploring and verifying the institutions of ancient contract, which is "proof of history" rather than "negation of history". Also, this is where the problem lies. An obsessive exploration is conducive to a thorough understanding of history but devoid of realistic function. "All history is contemporary history," the Italian philosopher Benedetto Croce once said, meaning that research on history is thinking in real time, out of current interest and considered and understood according to current interest.[72] Given above, a rational grasp of contract and ethics, the core concept of traditional culture, not only contributes to a faithful representation of history but a positive effect on reality.

The development of Chinese contractual culture has lasted thousands of years, which can be clearly traced back from *Rites of Zhou* to contract rules in civil law of Qing Dynasty. But to grasp the true essence and connotation of Chinese contracts,

[70]Fei [52].

[71]Huang [53].

[72]Liu [54].

we must pay attention to two points: one is that traditional ethics regulates contract; another is that contract law is mostly embedded in secular folk society, taking the form of civil customary law, which is content-rich and self-improved. No doubt seeking the truth ranks top on the list of historical research, but we must notice that the integration of ethics brings about more than the waste of the "golden opportunity" to enact a written contract law. It is a true fact that the intrinsic rationality of ethical rules contributes to Chinese ancient contract bearing a stamp of premature "morality" and solving lots of practical problems. For example, the foregoing morality books of late-Ming Dynasty guided social elites. It was advocated that the moral practice leaned toward social relief, which alleviated social problems born of the development of Capitalism in Ming Dynasty and made historical contribution to the socialization and moralization of contract from the aspect of contractual spirit, system of contract, contractual institutions and contract obligation. As a result, Mr. Tu Weiming, a representative of Neo-Confucianism, believes that there exists elective affinity between Confucian ethics and East Asian modernity. The core value, summed up as benevolence, righteousness, propriety, wisdom and faithfulness, helps structure the social ideal of turning moderate prosperity into Great Harmony that highlights obligation, empathy, comity, justice and morals. In this case, the tendency of socialization in Chinese contract provides a salutary lesson for legislation, which is the practical significance of studying Chinese ancient contract law. At the same time, institutions of traditional contract are entrenched in folk society, which, if not fully considered and learned, will definitely cause conflict to legislation, increasing the cost of legislation and inconvenience to folk life. Take pawning right as an example. According to historical records, pawning right has been in existence over one thousand years, dating back to Tang Dynasty. Pawn agreements of all kinds have remained in large amounts in the folk. Taiwan's civil code has recognized and adopted the pawning right and a host of pawn agreements in terms of legislative style, which is a historical advance. And mainland China's draft of real rights law (1999) has a separate chapter defining "pawning right", which is not a concession, as some scholars have said, to tradition but rational recognition of customary law of private contract.[73]

J. H. Weakland has put in *Methods of Cultural Anthropology*, "Each culture is an integrated whole, in which even apparently unfamiliar or irrelevant factors can be associated with the whole".[74] Arnold Joseph Toynbee also believes that each model of historical culture is an organic whole, where all parts are interdependent.[75] So knowledge of Chinese traditional culture is a must for the research of Chinese ancient contract Law. No doubt the dominant culture or the literature, such as the relationship between ethics and contract, is important, but folk or secular culture cannot be underestimated, all of which are organic parts of traditional culture and necessary historical materials for exploring the spirit and system of ancient contract.

Compared to heated academic topics such as "westernization" and "transplantation", Chinese ancient contract law is "left to moulder". Neither will we oppose

[73]Du [55].

[74]Wang [56].

[75]Adamson Hoebel [57].

or deny the advancement of western culture, nor are we intended to be a faithful conservative who gets too big for his boots. "A faithful representation of history" is not an unscientific or ineffective way, but we should get aware of the historical role of Chinese ancient contract and its impact on reality. A complete transplantation of western culture, whether possible or not, is bound to bring about cultural conflict and variation, causing the loss of their culture. "One man's meat is another man's poison", as Toynbee has said.[76] On the contrary, it seems much more feasible that cultural contact between the East and the West is left to the rational selection of culture itself rather than man according to White's cultural theory. Most "transplantation" supporters share a preconceived bias, that is, Chinese traditional culture remaining deeply entrenched and greatly enriched, China, if not totally transformed, is bound to fall between tradition and modernity. It may be likened to a healthy man who has his healthy organs removed to transplant artificial ones and then considers the possibility of rejection, seeking the temporary relief regardless of the consequences. As a matter of fact, culture denotes a dynamic process, which, as F. Ratzel has put, is realized through transfer and imitation and whose stages, proposed by V. G. Childe involve not only convergence and differentiation but convergence and assimilation. Generally speaking, it is ridiculous and vain to attempt on cultural resistance or cultural transplantation through personal efforts. Instead, it is more likely to achieve acculturation and guarantee mutual promotion without losing characteristics in cultural contact.[77] So as a cultural heritage and actual cultural force, Chinese ancient contract which exists in contrast with western contract law is valued in terms of its existence and development. This is also why we study Chinese ancient contract. American legal historian Roscoe Pound once rationally and objectively discussed the inherent value of Chinese traditional culture. He has pointed that China needs not to abandon her own historical cultural heritage in the pursuit of modernization of legal system. The ethical system that has been tested by thousand-year history should be taken as the cornerstone of Chinese legislation. And there exists traditional moral philosophy that has been widely accepted as ethical custom in China. It is likely to be turned into a recognized "ideal" on which relations are adjusted and behaviors are regulated.[78] This viewpoint seems to be a reference for current Chinese legislation.

References

1. International Aesthetics. 1985. Series I, 264. The Commercial Press of China.
2. Mitchell, G.D. (ed.). 1987. *A New Dictionary of the Social Sciences*, trans. Yang Zhenyi et al., 98–99. Shanghai Translation Publishing House.
3. Chen Jingsong. 1999. Form and function of social relevancy in traditional Chinese society. *Journal of Renmin University of China* (4).

[76]Joseph Toynbee [58].

[77]Zhang [59].

[78]Pound [60]. Cited in [61].

4. Hegel, G.W.F. 1956. *The Philosophy of History The Oriental World*, trans. Wang Shiyi. SDX Joint Publishing.
5. Hajime Nakamura. 1987. *A comparative History of Ideas*, trans. Wu Zhen, 183–184, 143–145, 170. Zhejiang People's Publishing House.
6. Yu Ronggen. 1992. *The General Theory of Confucian Legal Thought*, 132–133. Guangxi People's Publishing House.
7. Hou, Wailu et al. 1957. *History of Chinese Thought*, vol. II. People's Education Press.
8. Ren Jiyu. (ed.). (1985). *History of Chinese Philosophy: Qin and Han Dynasty.* People's Education Press.
9. Xu Diancai. 1997. Theory of STATE in Baihu general sense. *Journal of Chinese Historical Studies* (2).
10. Ba Xinsheng. 1997. On the origin and evolution of Pre-Qin "De". *Journal of Chinese Historical Studies* (3).
11. Zhang Xingjiu. 1999. *On the Differences between Eastern and Western Political and Legal Traditions in the respective of human view*, vol. 1. Studies in Law and Business.
12. Jiang Shan. 1997. The Gerneralized Integrative Contract. In *Civil and Commercial Law Review*, vol. 6, (ed.) Liang Huixing.
13. Fairbank, T.K. 1960. *East Asia: The Great Tradition*, 84. Boston: Houghton Mifflin.
14. Fei Hsiao-tung. 1984. *From the Soil: The Foundations of Chinese Society*, 53. SDX Joint Publishing.
15. Ma Rong. 1999. Crime and Sin: Rule of Law and Moral Order in China. *Journal of Peking University (Humanities and Social Sciences)* (2).
16. Zhang Meng et al. (ed.). 1987. *Human Genesis: The Origin of Cultural Anthropology*, 253. Sichuan People's Publishing House.
17. Hugevilt. 1987. *The Sociology of Developing Societies*, trans. Bai Hua, and Ding Yifan, 155. Sichuan People's Publishing House.
18. Hugevilt. 1987. *The Sociology of Developing Societies*, trans. Bai Hua, and Ding Yifan, 202–203. Sichuan People's Publishing House.
19. Justian. 1996. *Institutions*, trans. Zhang Qitai, 5. The Commercial Press of China.
20. Plato. 1986. *Utopia*, trans. Guo Binhe, and Zhang Zhuming, 15. The Commercial Press of China.
21. Teaching and Research Section on History of Foreign Philosophy of the Philosophy Department of Peking University (ed.). 1981. *Selected Readings of Western Philosophy*, 117. The Commercial Press of China.
22. Bodenheimer, E. 1987. *Jurisprudence: The Philosophy and Method of the Law*, trans. Deng zhenglai, and Ji Jingwu, 254. HuaXia Publishing House.
23. Aristotle. 1965. *Politics*, trans. Wu Shoupeng, 280. The Commercial Press of China.
24. Hobbes, T. 1985. *Leviathan*, trans. Li Sifu, and Li Yanzhao, 114. The Commercial Press of China.
25. Schwartz, B. 1989. *A History of American Law*, 92. The Commercial Press of China.
26. Atiyah, P.S. 1982. *An Introduction to the Law of Contract*, trans. Cheng Zhengkang et al., 10. Law Press.
27. Bodenheimer, E. 1987. *Jurisprudence: The Philosophy and Method of the Law*, trans. Deng zhenglai, and Ji Jingwu, 183. HuaXia Publishing House.
28. Hobbes, T. 1985. *Leviathan*, trans. Li Sifu, and Li Yanzhao, 118. The Commercial Press of China.
29. Gao Shouxian. 1994. The influence of confucian family-centered ethics on business development in the ming and qing dynasties. *The Northern Forum* (2).
30. Zhang Zhongqiu. 1991. *A Comparative Study of Chinese and Western Legal Culture*, 143. Nanjing University Press.
31. Karen Turner. 1994. Rule of Law Ideals in Early China. In *Recent American Academic Writings on Traditional Chinese Law*, ed. Karen Turner, and He Weifang, 229. China University of Political Science and Law Press.
32. Xu Fuguan. 1987. *Spirit of Chinese Arts*, 13–14. Chunfeng Wenyi Press.

33. Ban gu. *Baihu General Sense*, vol. 2. Rites and Music.
34. White, L.H. 1988. *The Science of Culture: A study of Man and Civilization*, trans. Cao Jinqing, 149, 171–172. Zhejiang People's Publishing House.
35. White, L.A. 1988. *The Science of Culture: A study of Man and Civilization*, trans. Cao Jinqing, 149–150. Zhejiang People's Publishing House.
36. Jiang Shan. 1997. The gerneralized integrative contract. In *Civil and Commercial Law Review*, vol. 6, ed. Liang Huixing.
37. Hugh Scogin. 1994. Between heaven and man: Contract and the state in han dynasty China. In *Recent American Academic Writings on Taditional Chinese Law*, eds. Karen Turner, and He Weifang, 174. China University of Political Science and Law Press.
38. Gilmore, G. 1996. *The Death of the Contract*, trans. Cao Shibin, Yao Jianzong, and Wu Wei. In *Civil and Commercial Law Review*, vol. 4, ed. Liang Huixing, 222.
39. Yang Zhen. 1997. *Anglo-American Law of Contract*, 25. Peking University Press.
40. Zeng Zhengyu et al. 1997. From law to de: An analysis on the social ideal of Shangyang. *Journal of Chinese Historical Studies* (1).
41. Brokaw, C. Changes in social ideology in the morality books of the Ming and Qing. *Newsletter for Modern Chinese History* (16): 38–39.
42. Sakai Tadao. 1993. *Merits and Faults Studies*, trans. Yang Sheng. In *Selected Japanese Academic Writings on Chinese History*, vol. 7, ed. Liu Junwen, 497.
43. You Zi'an. 1997. The popularity of *Merits and Faults* in late Ming and early Qing and the Jiangnan society it mirrors. *Journal of Chinese Historical Studies* (4).
44. Ma keyao. 1997. *A Comparative Study of Chinese and Western Feudal Society*, 374. Xuelin Press.
45. Fu Zhufu. 1980. *Chinese Economic History Review*, Book 2, 618–621. SDX Joint Publishing.
46. Fan Wenlan. 1978. *History of China*, vol. 1, 9–97. People's Publishing House.
47. Gao Debu. 1997. The origin and establishment of the three-dimensional structure of western market economy. *Journal of Renmin University of China* (3).
48. Kardiner, A., and E. Preble. (eds.). 1987. *Studied Man*, trans. Sun Kaixiang, 380–381. SDX Joint Publishing.
49. Tachibana, Shiraki. 1936. *Chinese Thought Studies*, 276–277. Japanese Translation and Commentation Company.
50. Kishimoto, Mio. 1998. civil society of China, cited in *Civil Trial and Civil Contract in Ming and Qing Dynasties*, 355. In Wang Yaxin, and Liang Zhiping, eds. Law Press.
51. Greeze, C., 1998. *Local Knowledge: A Comparative Study of Facts and Law*, trans. Deng Zhenglai. In Liang Zhiping ed., 126. SDX Joint Publishing House.
52. Fei, Hsiao-tung. 1997. Reflection on my academic achievements. *Academic* (9).
53. Huang, Zongzhi. 1999. Studies on economic history, social history and cultural history of chinese legal system. *Journal of Chinese Economic History* (2).
54. Liu, Chang. 1987. *The History in Mind: A Review of Contemporary Western Historical Theories*, 144. Sichuan People's Publishing House.
55. Du, Weiming. 1997. Opportunity for confucianism innovation. *Academic* (9).
56. Wang, Zhigang. 1997. *On Pawning*, vol. 1. Law Review.
57. Adamson Hoebel, E. 1993. *The Law of Primitive Man: A Study in Comparative Legal Dynamics*, trans. Zhou Yong, 199. China Social Sciences Press.
58. Arnold, Joseph Toynbee. 1988. *Civilization on Trial*, trans. Shen Hui, 276. Zhengjiang People's Publishing House.
59. Zhang, Meng (ed.). 1987. *Human Genesis: The Origin of Cultural Anthropology*, 272, 285–286. Sichuan People's Publishing House.
60. Roscoe, Pound. 1984. *The Comparative Law and History: The Foundation of Chinese Law*, vol. 61, 749–762. *Harvard Law Review*.
61. Karen, Turner, and He Weifang (eds.). (1994). *Recent American Academic Writings on Traditional Chinese Law*, 47. China University of Political Science and Law Press.

Chapter 2
Archaeological Research on the Origin of Contracts

The history of Chinese ancient contract can be traced back to the Western Zhou Dynasty (B.C. 1045–771), and scholars in related fields have already made plenty of fundamental researches from the perspective of the origin, evolution and the name of contract. In this chapter, the previous researches will be used for references, and based on the sources of contract concept, this chapter attempts to explore the motivation, historical premise, function, and types of contract, so as to sketch out the general lineament.

Names of Contract: "Agreement (契约)" to "Contract (合同)"

The name of "agreement" has some synonyms in a broad sense, such as covenant, indenture, deed, and contract, which all mean that both parties enter into the agreement with a meeting of minds upon certain subject, and with the stipulations of their rights and liabilities. In Chinese language, Qi Yue (契约, which means an agreement or a contract) are two separate characters yet sharing the same meaning, according to *Interpretation Dictionary of Chinese Characters* (≪说文解字≫), which was edited in Han Dynasty and dubbed as a most influential dictionary in Chinese history. "Qi is Yue", so this word (Qi Yue) itself was a combination to demonstrate the idea of agreement. Qi refers to the behavior that both parties entering into the agreement, and Yue emphasizes the rights and liabilities. In *The Book of Rites* (≪礼记≫), a famous collection of treatises on the rules of propriety and ceremonial usages in ancient China, Qi Yue was also explained as "important agreement". *Shiren Ancient Epigraph* (≪矢人盘铭≫) of Western Zhou Dynasty (B.C. 1045–771) has proved that the conception of Qi Yue had once inscribed in that period. Much other ancient Chinese classic literature could also reveal the trace of such word, such as in *Legend of Spring and Autumn Century* (≪左传≫) by Zuo Qiuming, according to which, there was a new policy promulgated in the sixth year of Wengong (631 B.C.) called "Youzhiyao

Y. Liu, *The History of the Contractual Thoughts in Ancient China*,
https://doi.org/10.1007/978-981-15-5768-2_2

(由质要)" which referred to the agreement between parties when disputes arose in civil cases. Also in *The Analects of Confucius* (≪论语≫), and He Yan's *Interpretation of Confucius Anthology* (≪集解 ≫), they all mentioned the concepts of agreement in the form of Chinese characters "要 (Yao)" and "约 (Yue)". Together with those terms, there was a term called "Panshu (判书), a judgment witnessing the processing of entering a contract)". In *Rites of Zhou* which is considered as one of the classic Confucius works, it records a description of the putative organization of the government during the Western Zhou period. And the words "Panshu, a judgment witnessing the processing of entering a contract" was also written in different Chinese characters as "别" or "莂" or "傅辩", which were in accordance with the same meaning explored in Liu Xi's book—*Expounding Names* (≪释名≫). In the year of 1996, some wooden and bamboo manuscripts were unearthed in Zoumalou (走马楼) of Changsha city, Hunan province. Those relics are deemed as the proofs of the process of the establishment of an ancient contract, among which some of wooden and bamboo manuscripts were carved with the Chinese character "莂 (bie)". This founding can also verify the theory proposed by Liu Xi.[1] Wang Xianqian in Qing Dynasty wrote a book named *Expounding Names—supplementary version* (≪释名.疏证补≫), which revealed an anecdote that in the year of 284, "Bie (莂)" was survived in Shanyin of Zhejiang province. All these relics and textual researches can prove that the partial texts in ancient contracts are not isolated evidences.

From foregoing information, at least three levels of meanings in ancient contract can be revealed:

Firstly, judging from the carving of ancient contract, it is obvious that the characters such as "契 (Qi)" "券 (Quan)" "判 (Pan)" "别/莂 (Bie)" "剂 (Ji)" were carved on the golden or wooden manuscripts; that's the reason why their Chinese affixes are "刀", which refers to knife; meanwhile, those characters carved on bamboo, paper, and silk were named as "约 (Yue)" and "要 (Yao)".

Secondly, judging from the behaviors of entering a contract, ancient people were prone to adopt practical and physical measures. They actually had preferential access to use knives to cut, and use silk and other materials to be cut because they were easily to tear into two or more. Consequently, these behaviors to cut things with contract contents on, with the help of knife and tearable material in the process of contract establishment, were conducted to give parties concerned for binding purpose in some ritual forms that were apart of people's daily life.

Thirdly, symbolically speaking, the fact that ancient Chinese chose knife and silk as the Chinese affixes to form hieroglyphic characters demonstrates the initial contract concept. For those characters with knife as Chinese affix, simply shows that, in ancient China, the physical contract was cut into two pieces with a duplication to each party, or with one of the pieces kept by the creditor, the other by governmental division called Meng Fu (盟府) (this mostly was applied in the real estate transaction in Western Zhou Dynasty) for mutual trust. Thus the interpretation of the knife affix will stand for the meaning of mutual assent, and it will also serve the purpose of the good faith in the cutting form with determination of realizing the contents of

[1]Hu and Song [1].

contract. Besides the idea of good faith, it also can expand two more meanings of the knife affix used in contract from the angle of philology, One is multi-binding: the characters "约 (Yue)" "要 (Yao)" both bear the meaning of trussing, and tying, which directly shows the essence of a contract is its binding force. The other is no regretting once entered a contract: take "剂 (Ji)" as an example. In *Interpretation Dictionary of Chinese Characters*: "剂 (Ji) refers to 齐 (Qi), which stands for the meaning of being consistent." And according to Duan Yu's *Notes for Interpretation Dictionary of Chinese Characters*: "those characters with 'knife'as their affix, bear the meaning of being as neat as cut by knife." The connotation thus is: both parties engaged in the contract should be deemed to be decided and they shall not regret.

The mentioned three levels consist of the initial concept of ancient contract which could be concluded into three phrases—"with good faith", "by mutual binding forces", and "no regret after signing". As these have been seldom discussed in previous works, the book will consequently place the findings in this chapter.

It took a long time for the name "agreement (Qi Yue)" evolving into "contract (He Tong 合同)". As a matter of fact, the name of contract (He Tong) has been used for quite a long time. In *The Book of Rites,* the famous collection of treatises on the rules of propriety and ceremonial usages, the name of "合同" (He Tong, contract) had already appeared with the meaning different from that in today's "contract". From historical evidences and materials, the existing contract is deemed to be equal with the one written in late Wei Dynasty (220–265 A.D.). Wang Guowei's *Archeology Study of Drifting Sand* has considerably detailed description and the rubbing documents, which can still be taken as references. Till Tang and Song Dynasty, "agreement" gradually became "contract (He tong 和同)" or "contract agreement (合同契)", and in official documents like *Law Code of Tang Dynasty,* and *Criminal Code of Song Dynasty*, it was all written as "consensus (He tong)", while in cases reviews it could be in the form of "contract agreement (合同契)" or "contract of agreement (合同文契)". For instance, *Law Reports of Southern Song Dynasty (1127–1279 A.D.)* has recorded: "… the law provides, the behaviors of pawning real estate property shall be with contract; this shall be known by all as a common sense."

For the name of "He tong (和同)" and "He tong (合同)", it is worth to value whether they were the same in essence, or whether they were just in different names? This can be answered in an easy way. According to the historical evidences unearthed from Duanghuang and Turpan, nearly all kinds of contracts were using the form of "He tong" instead of "he tong". There were a number of set phrases like "contract under consensus", "equal stipulations by both parties face to face", "equal stipulations", and "both parties involved", which all demonstrated the contract was deemed to be entered by both parties with free will and equal conversation. The word "He tong" bears two meanings: one is that this kind of contract has to be signed by both parties in person, which refers to other people cannot represent the party to enter it in accordance with legal provision, and the other meaning is that the both parties should have consensus in certain subject, thus the default shall not arise in future morally nor legally. Most importantly, the contract shall be entered with free will and under equal conditions without any threat, tempting, or deceiving. By observing contracts in Ming Dynasty and Qing Dynasty, there were many expressions as "such contract is entered of both parties' accord", which can be seen as a historical continuous evidence of "He tong". The Chinese character "He (和)" stands for a meaning of both parties having face-to-face meeting, and with free will, while "Tong (同)" for consensus made by both parties.

As for the word "he tong", form Song Dynasty and Yuan Dynasty to the present, this word has become the common usage in various transactions. Zhai Hao in Qing Dynasty wrote: "… nowadays, when people are engaging in real estate transaction, they always write a big character on the back of the agreement, then tear the agreement into two pieces. This is so called contract (which in Chinese was he tong), so you can see the fact that the term *agreement* which has been used for ages, has gradually been replaced by the term *contract* instead".[2] In the same time, Ping Buqing also provided a comment on contract: "… after signing the contract, the parties fold the contract and write the word of 'he tong' on it, then each of them takes a duplicate for further consideration. This form of contract can be traced back to the contracts of Xuanzong period in Song Dynasty (1100–1200s)".[3] With the two Qing Dynasty scholars' theories together, it is obvious that in "he tong", the Chinese character "he (合)" stands for the meaning of both parties having reached the agreement to enter into contract for transaction under certain conditions, and they adopted the historical forms to cut the contract into two which were left to both sides for future purposes, which actually was designed for dispute resolution. As for the concrete procedure for dispute resolution, according to Zhao Yi in Qing Dynasty, was that the parties put the duplicates together, on which the word "he tong" was wrote on both, then each party took one copy.[4] Once dispute arose, the parties were supposed to reveal the one with the partial word in order to identify whether it was authentic. In early phase, it was only one character "tong" on it, and later on, the both characters of "he tong" were written on the contract.

From aforesaid evidences, it is not a coincidence that "He tong" has evolved into "he tong" solely for the same pronunciation. Actually, the focuses of the two words were not the same: "He" emphasized on the free wills of parties, while "he" paid more attention to the process of entering and examining the contract. In fact, "He" and "he" both could be analyzed with multiple meanings, which brings difficulty to fathom why they eventually fused together in the expression of the term to describe the name of contract. Howsoever, the answer now can be found in semantics sense and legal historical sense world widely. For instance, the word "pactum" in ancient Roman law means "the agreement reached by two or more parties on their interested issue through negotiation", which is "the form presenting consent and agreement between parties". Domitius Ulpianus has conducted a research on the origin of the

[2]Zhai [2].

[3]Ping [3].

[4]Zhao [4].

definition of "pactum", proving that it came from "pactio (agreement)" and "pax (peace)".[5]

The Primary Form and Evolution of Contracts

The development of contract theory of ancient Rome processed gradually, and it experienced four phases.[6] Meanwhile, the parallel period witnessed the contract of China equipped with considerable comprehensive theory, which mirrors its similar evolution process with that of ancient Rome's. However, as a result of lacks of adequate historical records, it is impossible to compare ancient Roman contract law in exact Anno Domini years. This book will take the four development phases of Roman contract law as references to analyze the primary forms and evolution of China's ancient contracts.

During the developing process of Roman contract law, oral contract was the first phase, which could be divided into nexum and stipulazione. Nexum, a symbolic transfer of rights that involved a set of scales, copper weights, and a formulaic oath, which required the parties together with five witnesses, took specific measures and terminology to demonstrate the agreement of transaction by both parties. Stipulazione, as the oldest form of contract, derived from religious and oath-making ceremonies. The offer of both parties constituted convention, without which, the relations of contract or obligatio could not be formed.[7] The status of contract in Common Law system is named By Word of Mouth of simple contract.[8] The condition in China was quite the same. In Zhou Gong King's time (?–900B.C.), the inscriptions on *Wusi Wei tripod*, and on *Nine-year Wei tripod* which were letters on ancient cooking vessels, they all described the process of entering into the contract During such process, when it came to the exchange or transfer of real property, forest property and valuable hand-made property, both parties would first engage in oral offer and acceptance. Take real property exchange as an example. The parties should report the relevant subject to authorities and the King, and should get approval from the King. The following exchange was supposed to be witnessed by an authoritative governor, who often took the form by asking: "do you agree to exchange the land?" and the parties were supposed to answer: "yes, we do." Then both parties would take oath on the mentioned subject. After these steps were done, the agreement was deemed to be effective.[9]

[5]Ulpianus, Ad Edictum, a commentary on the Edict, in Ding Mei translated version of Sandro Schipani, *Obligatio, Obligatio in Agreement*, 1992, pp. 72, 74; origination version D.Z. 14, 1.2, D.50, 12, 3, Pr.

[6]Zheng [5].

[7]Ulpianus, Ad Edictum, *A commentary on the Edict*, in Ding Mei translated version of Sandro Schipani, *Obligatio, Obligatio in Agreement*, 1992, D45.1.75.10, and D2.14.1.3.

[8]Yang [6].

[9]Kong and Hu [7].

Though *The By Word of Mouth* agreement was simple to be implemented, it was difficult to ensure the stability of transaction. *Litter is (*written contract) thus appeared to replace the *By Word of Mouth* agreement. Gaius divided ancient Roman agreements into three categories, which were obligatio credit document, handwriting instrument and written agreement.[10] In order to make a comparison with this, we shall discuss about China's condition in Western Zhou Dynasty, when the agreements were also divided into three categories as Fubie (傅别), Shuqi (书契) and Zhi Ji (质剂) that were recorded on the surfaces of bronze containers (such as Zong Yi, and Dan Tu, those containers were for religious and other significant occasions). The recording was about the entire process of how the parties entered into the agreement, and consequently could be used as evidences in law suits if any disputes arose in the future.

Among the three categories in ancient China, Fubie, according to Rites of Zhou, was "the loan contract admissible in civil litigation". Zheng Xuanzhu further explained by quoted Zheng Zhong's argument that: "Fubie, one of the instruments, suggests there is a binding force in such document, and this instrument will be cut into two, one for each party." In fact, in most occasions Fubie was used in borrow and loan contract, more specifically, in the occasion of the civil behavior concerned borrowing and loan with interest. Shuqi meant the civil behaviors as obtaining, accepting and donating. Zheng Xuan pointed out that "Shuqito the obtaining, accepting and donating behaviors was as an abstract to an article." Meanwhile, Jia Gongyan had observed that Shuqi was used in government loans without interests, and also used to adjust the relations between people's transaction and donating behaviors. In Sun Yirang (a scholar of Qing Dynasty)'s book Textual Criticism of Rites of Zhou, it wrote, "… those offers made by documents will be written on papers or tickets, or brochure, which are all called Shuqi." The third category was Zhi Ji, which was used for the purpose of adjusting the contractual relationships concerning trading, security, and pawn. According to Interpretation Dictionary of Chinese Characters: "Zhi, is a deposit of personal property to a creditor." It suggested that the function of Zhi was covered but not limited to the behaviors of security and pawn. However, Zhi was somehow also related to the behavior of trading. The Rites of Zhou recorded that there was a position called Zhi Ren, whose duty was to "take in charge of city's goods, people, cows and horses, weaponry, and the precious. For those who were involved in trading, it's necessary to sign Zhi Ji. "Big transaction" used Zhi, "small" one used Ji." That's to say, Zhi Ji was divided into bigger and smaller ones. Zheng Zhuyun wrote in his book Zhi Ren (≪质人≫): "Zhi Ji is an instrument that for parties to hold. 'Big transaction' is the transactions concerning people, cows and horses. To call it big is because the long ticket will be applied in such cases. Conversely 'small transaction' is the transaction concerning weaponry, the previous, and the name of 'small' is because short ticket will be applied accordingly." In his other book Xiao Zai (≪小宰≫), Zheng addressed: "longer one is called Zhi, shorter one is called Ji." In Wang Guowei's archeological studies on bamboo manuscripts, he explored that there were different sizes of ancient manuscripts, which were 2.4 Chi (Chinese unit

[10]Huang [8].

of length, equals 0.3 m), 1.2 Chi, 8 Cun (Chinese unit of length, equals 13 decimeters), and 6 Cun, all these manuscripts demonstrating the use of Zhi Ji. Collection of Mr. Wang Jing'an of Hai Ning, Vol. 26, Research on Written Manuscripts. The name of Zhi Ji existed in Han Dynasty, when it entered Tang Dynasty, becoming "Fenzhi Qi (分支契)".

Briefly speaking, "Fubie", "Zhi Ji" and "Shuqi", though targeted on different adjusting objectives, still shared something in common, which was that they were all carved on metal, or written on silk or bamboo manuscripts. *Rites of Zhou* recorded that "the larger contract and Ji are craved on bronze containers, and the ones concerned with smaller amount, are carved or written on the silk or bamboos." According to Zheng Xuan, "larger contract and Ji are the ones with respect to county and city, which are supposed to be supervised under gods, while smaller ones are relevant to people, which are the relationships between parties." From those arguments, it's obvious that the contracts and agreements were divided into at least two categories, larger one and smaller one. The former is between the government and people, and the latter is between people. The scholar Sun Yirang, in his *Textual Criticism of Rites of Zhou*, also stated that "Zong Yi, the bronze containers with letters; Dan Tu, the silk or bamboo manuscripts with letters, are all for the purpose of establishing a credit relationship." Tts extent, the development of China's ancient contract law was even more delicate than that of ancient Rome's.

The real contract is the third phase in Ancient Rome's four evolutionary phases. Real contracts targeted the subject matter as an important condition, and were divided into loan for consuming purpose, using loan, bailment, and pledge. All of the four were considered to be the primitive forms of agreement, yet as a result of its stability, the world has using it for years. The ancient China was no exception. To leave the condition of early Western Zhou Dynasty apart, the debit and credit relationships of parties were recorded in *Rites of Zhou*, and they were in a clear division thus debit or borrowing (借) and credit (贷) could be distinguished from the writing forms. In *A Guide to Academics of Official Personnel* in Yuan Dynasty, it made an effort to tell the difference of debit or borrowing and credit: "to borrow objects to others means debit or borrowing and to ask others for objects means credit".[11] Back in Western Zhou Dynasty, debit or borrowing and credit were distinguished into two types with different norms. The first type was debit or borrowing and credit with interest. In the Section of Quanfu in the Chapter of Diguan* of *Rites of Zhou*, it read "the behaviors of citizens engaging in loans from government shall be supervised by the relevant administrative officers and then be approved. The interest rate shall follow the national standards." The supervision of relevant administrative officers is called "Bian (to differentiate)". Zheng Xuan explained that it referred to the process of determining the value of the goods, and the interest rate of national standards referred to the tax being paid to government. Furthermore, Zheng explored the interest rate standards in that period: "the loan mode means the authority lend money to citizens.

[11] Li [9].

*Translator's annotation: Quanfu: a division of wealth reserves; Diguan: the official position to administrate the financial business.

If the interest is too high, the citizens will benefit little. Therefore, the interest rate should be adjusted to the different conditions. For instance, if the silk is mainly produced in some region, the tax can be paid by silk there; if the kudzu cloth is mainly produced, likewise, the tax can be paid by it." A very resembling example was Fubie as mentioned earlier. The other type was debit or borrowing and credit without interest, which was adjusted by Shu Qi. Also in Chapter of Diguan of *Rites of Zhou*, it recorded a position named "Lv Shi (旅师)", who was in charge of providing loans and administrating the loans to citizens in accordance with the policy of "providing loans in the form of material matters in barren and infertile time, collecting loans in harvest time". The scholar Jia-Gong Yanshu in Tang Dynasty made an effort in differentiate the terms of Fubie from Shu Qi. He said, "the debit or borrowing and credit with interest is for gaining the interest, while providing loans in the form of material matters is to give loans without profits. The authority helps the people, and the people in turn can live a better life, which is beneficial to the authority." As for other security measures, pawn, and bailment, the development of which were quite advanced in ancient China with detailed documentary. In the mid-Western Zhou Dynasty, the royal family declined and economics expanded, accordingly the mortgage concerned of real estate was a common phenomenon at that moment, then the pledge, pawn, and contract emerged and developed.

When it came to the phase of consensual contract in ancient Roman period, it suggested that the set of contract theory in ancient Rome had already developed maturely and comprehensively. The premise of consensual contract was consideration between parties. In this sense, no set formality would be realized nor would the subject matter be paid to. In Gaius's *Institutes,* there are four consensual contracts involved: purchase and sale, leasing, partnership, and entrusting (emptionibus et venditionibus, locationibus conductionibus, societatibus, mandatis). From historical materials of ancient China, the origin of China's consensual contract began in an early time. Take partnership as an example. No later than in the Western Zhou Dynasty, the partnership concerned with property has been formed. According to *The Rites of Zhou,* there was a position called "Sikou (司寇)", who was in charge of managing "the partnership of properties, and the people committing illegal behaviors shall be punished by law." So, it demonstrates that if parties had reached an agreement to form partnership, they were supposed to comply with laws. Some observed that the business partnership in China began in Spring and Autumn and Warring States Period (770 B.C.–221 B.C.). Those unearthed relics reveal the fact that China's complete contract was found no later than Han Dynasty. The wooden manuscripts with the name of "the contract of trans-marketing" recorded the information of investment, personnel, property management, liability of partners, and punishment in detail, which is deemed to be the earliest existing systematic partnership contract.[12] Additionally, the contract of purchasing things on credit was a typical type of consensual contract, which can be found in *The Rites of Zhou.* As in the Chapter of Diguan (the official position to administrate the financial business), the position of Quanfu was in charge of wealth administration, who would also take charge in managing selling

[12]*Cultural Relics*, Vol. 6 of 1974, graphic demonstration 2.

goods to people on credit. Still, the preliminary purchase contract was thought to be one of the consensual contracts. For instance, the Luoyang peony in Song Dynasty enjoyed high reputation back then, the merchants "enter into contract in the autumn, when the next spring comes, peony blooms, the value of peony can be realized".[13] Another example will be the litchi in Fuzhou City, which "was brought by merchants by signing the contract when they were in blossom".[14] These two examples illustrate the fact that preliminary purchase contract was considerably developed before Song Dynasty in China. Other types of contracts such as leasing and entrusting were parallelly developed in ancient China, which will be analyzed later.

To conclude, it's undeniable that the contract evolution in both ancient China and Rome were pacing with the same speed in the past. In Zhou Dynasty, the division of ancient China's contract has also made itself distinguished.[15] From the nature of contracts, the ancient contracts can be categorized into "contract of god", "contract on containers", "sincere contract" "civil contract", "real estate contract", and "contract of rewarding"; the former three were dealing the cases concerning offering sacrifices to gods and ancestors, predicating the fortune, and etiquette; while "contract of rewarding" was the contract of providing rewards, "real estate contract" was the contractual document of land and territory, "civil contract" was for adjusting the residential register and taxes.

Contracts and Obligatio

The premise of contract is recognition of parties' rights, based on the ensuring of each one's profits. Both parties in contract make clear about their rights and duties, and such relationship is debt. Therefore, any contract in ancient Roman contracts would logically follow three aspects: one was "agreement" as an evidence of parties' consent; the second was "debt" as shared by parties with the mutual rights and duties; third was some specific ceremony which posed the debt on the agreement to take the binding force into effect.[16]

The relationship between contract and obligatio can summarize that contract is the source of obligatio while obligatio is the measure to meet the needs of contract. In early Roman laws, assenting contractual behavior and property transaction behavior bore no legal meaning independently, only when these two components combined together, would the legal meaning be exist.[17] An assenting agreement without obligatio legally attached to, would be merely a "naked/hollow brief agreement", which is impossible to be the source for litigation. Thomas Hobbes in his *Leviathan* states that: "the contract without sword is no more than nothing because it's powerless

[13] *On Peonies of Luoyang* (Ancient Chinese lyric).

[14] Cai Xiang, *Charting of Litchi.*

[15] See Footnote 7, pp. 57–58.

[16] Yang [10].

[17] Tong [11].

to protect man's security", and "if the binding force is not taken into consideration, the contract would be soft and vulnerable, which cannot provide any constraint to human's ambition, greed and other passions."[18] Hobbes also observes that "the exchange of rights is the so-called contract", "all contracts are the exchange or transfer of rights". Meanwhile, the binding force of contract is not the origin from its nature but the concerns of parties who obviously don't want to bear the consequences of breaches. Hence, if one party waives or transfers his rights, he will thus be responsible for not preventing the one accepts to enjoy the said rights.[19] Kant to some extent agrees with Hobbes by holding the view that contract is the free minds of parties, so no matter from the point of view of methodology or historical thinking, the measures of constructing the contract poses no influence, since all the liabilities with binding force come voluntarily.[20]

To think in line with legal thoughts, Saint Thomas Aquinas believes that laws are the regulations and norms for people to allow or prohibit certain behaviors. "…because lex (law) is from ligare (restriction). So accordingly the nature of law is to bind."[21] Natural Law is about the obligation, such concept has become the philosophy basis of contract spirit. The theory that obligatio is originated from consent is the theoretical fundamental of Roman law. The wishes expressed in *nutus* can bring obligatio into being, which supports the theory that obligatio is originated from consent.[22] In Domitius Ulpianus' book *Ad Edictum,a commentary on the Edict,* Chap. 11 views that the *contrahere* (entering into a contract) was to build a relationship of obligatio, which was just the bilateral contracts referred by Greeks, and this type of contract was often used in purchase and sale, leasing and partnership occasions; while *convetio* (agreement), referred to all issues agreed between parties in order to reach a consensus or settlement.[23]

Contract produces obligatio, and obligatio in turn releases the rights in contract, which reflect the dialectical relation of contract and obligatio. As said by Kant and Hobbes, the reason why obligatio of contract bears enforcement power, or to put in another word, bearing legal power, is the consent of both parties. So, consensus is the media of contract and obligatio. Gaius believed that neither further expressions nor written forms were required for the mentioned contract during the process dealing with the obligatio in purchase and sale, leasing and partnership issues, as long as parties concerned had reached agreement.[24] It is notable that Gaius holds the view that the production of obligatio was not only about money to be paid, but about the animus of obligation for payment or accepting payment.

Based on the Roman advanced theory, contract law in occidental world thus gained its lively energy for further development. Comparatively, China's ancient contract

[18]George and Liu [12].

[19]Thomas [13], pp. 99,100, 102.

[20]See Footnote 19, pp. 487–488.

[21]Zhang [14].

[22]See Footnote 7, pp. 6, 7, D.44.7.52.4, and D.44.7.2.9-10.

[23]ibid, pp. 8, 9, D.50.16.19, and D.2.14.13.

[24]ibid, p. 12, D.47.2Pr, and D.44.7.3.1.

theory relied much on the Confucius ethical philosophy sharpened since Western Zhou Dynasty, either from philosophy perspective or institutional-building perspective. Howsoever, this point is not enough to embarrass Chinese scholars. Despite it lacked deeply-rooted and systematic contract spirit in China, it has already set an effective "consent" device from contract system and custom laws to resolve some issues as misunderstanding, coercion, and taking advantages of other's precarious position, which will be discussed later in this book.

On the enforcement of the implementing and completing of obligatio, China's ancient contract system employed considerable fair measures to ensure the creditor's rights. Judicial remedies were deemed to be the last option by public who would usually feel reluctant to resort to. Stipulations of contract always specifically stated the obligation and rights in hope of avoiding risks. In the meantime, there were also some methods such as complaint to the government, and ethical restrains to ensure the objective of realizing the obligation. When mentioned about the effectiveness of the stipulations, the rights transfer clauses, guarantee clauses, and breach clauses were the three most significant types among other clauses. The appearance of mediator and guarantor also accordingly ensured the implementing of realizing the obligation.

The rights transfer clauses in ancient China usually would clarify the subject matter and its quantity, scope, region, date of delivery, and so on. More precisely, they would make further explanation about the relevant issues to spare future problems. Here are some examples: the first one recorded in *The Land Purchase Instrument of Sun Cheng* (171B.C.) was the transaction of real estate:

> In the year of 171, at five to seven p.m on 28th of September, Sun Cheng has bought one Ding (ancient Chinese unit, approximate to one hundred square meters) from Zhang Boshi who is a male citizen of Luo Yang City. The price of this transaction is fifteen thousands and is paid in full at the same time. The range of the land is illustrated in the contract, so are the appendages on the land. Meanwhile, there are some witnesses and notaries presenting during the transaction process. After that, the buyer and seller will buy some wine from the market to ask people to celebrate.[25]

In this contract, it's obvious that ancient Chinese people made it clear about the subject matter (the land), the range of it, the price, the appendage, and they were aware of finding people to witness and notarize. The behavior of buying wine to celebrate was a publicized proclamation of land purchase. To be mentioned, the transfer clause and annexed clause were set to avoid future disputes, of which the annexed clause specifically stipulated the appendages on the land, which still seems delicate in current standard. From then on, the clauses stipulating appendages in later time of ancient contracts can be found hence, and that kind of clause gained its own name of "Pi Zao", which were recorded in other historical books as in *The Sale Contract of Land by Zhou Wengui in Song Dynasty*, and *Contract of Horse Using Land in Jin Dynasty*. The second example that will be illustrated is about the "Guo

[25]Luo Zhenyu, *Historical Events in Artemisia* ≪ *蒿里遗珍* ≫ , Original text: 建宁四年(171年)九月戊午朔廿八日乙酉, 左骏厩官大奴孙成从洛阳男子张伯始买所名有广德亭部冢百田一町, 贾钱万五千, 钱即日毕。田东比张长卿, 南比许仲异, 西尽大道, 北比张伯始。根生土著毛物, 皆属孙成。... 田东西南北以大石为界。时旁人樊永、张义、孙龙、异姓、樊元祖皆知券约, 沽酒各半.

Ge Li Ye" system in ancient China. This system actually referred to two parts: one was to transfer the taxes, and the other was that the seller delivered his property to the buyer for managing. Altogether, these two parts are consisted the necessity of title change. In *Law Reports of Southern Song Dynasty*, it says: according to law, the transaction of land shall transfer owner's taxes, and the authority shall change the name to collect the taxes of land.

It's in the very progress that the guarantee system came into historical stage. The guarantee measures in ancient China were mainly about the guarantee for rights and for default of delivery. To categorize the guarantee measures by methods, ancient China could be classified into four types: (1) security by people, who mostly acted as witness, notary, and the mediators; (2) Using physical property to guarantee, which required the debtor provide some physical property, as in pledge and pawn; (3) The debtor offered his labor force to the creditor for guarantee; (4) Security of property, as in attachment of the debtor's property to secure the payment to the creditor. Despite the difference of these measures, they all played important role in securing the rights of creditor, and imposing pressures on debtor both financially and morally.

Another progress in ancient contract will be the application of breach clause. In Western Zhou Dynasty, when arising disputes between parties became unsolvable by themselves, the creditor and debtor would resort to local government or public community for settlement. During such procedure, the remedies would be equivalent to the debt, though there might be some punishment at the same time, the scale were controlled considerably well by the local government or public community. From a historical point of view, not later than Northern and Southern Dynasties (420–589 A.D.), there were clauses stipulating the punishment of breach in contract, as in Luo Zhenyu's book[26]: "… after the signing of contract, no parties shall breach. Those who breach the contract first shall be charged of five Pi (ancient Chinese unit, equals 33 m) of thin silk." In a word, this system was no longer making damages according to its equivalent value, but also bearing sanction functions financially. Since Tang Dynasty, this kind of breach clause has existed widely in contracts, and approved by official authorities, consequently served the purpose of securing the rights of creditor.

The Historical Premise of Contracts

The relationship between contract and obligation can be deemed as the consent of parties, which suggests that only under the condition that debt is annexed to such consensus, can ensure the exchange of liability and rights. This section will discuss the historical premise of contract from a diachronic view.

The high level of commodity development is one of the necessary premises of contract. The process of labor division-exchange-purchase and sale is the internal logic of human economic life, which brought about three consequences as followed:

[26]Luo Zhenyu, *Analysis on Real Estate Instrument*.

I. The massive residual product is thus produced by the division of labor, and such residual product has to be led into the market to trade equivalent things to sustain a family (buying and selling). Therefore, the commodity economic axis begins to operate. That's to say, the division of labor is the premise of buying and selling. According to the idea, Emile Durkheim holds the view that the connection means in human society is based on the division, which links the needs of all walks in a society, and accordingly fails to provide the context of self-sufficient and self-contained.

II. The development of currency serves as equivalent things. In Chap. 33 of Paulus'*Ad Edicta*, emptio (purchase and sale) originates from exchange. Because there was no nummus (currency) in the past, the method of exchange would be fulfilled in practical objects, thus with neither merx (commodity), nor pretium (price).[27] The major difference between contract of purchase and sale and exchange is that, the former produces the relation of debt in the exchange process under the assent of parties engaged.[28] As one of equivalence, currency has promoted the development of commercialization of commodities, essentially ushering the productive factors into commercialization or materialization. Since Tang Dynasty, China has witnessed plenty of currency related managerial organizations emerging, like golden and silver store, old-style private money house, private banks, exchange agencies, and remittance and conversion center, which altogether provided the drive for financial evolution in China.

III. The new class of living on business thus appeared. As a matter of fact, in Spring and Autumn and Warring States Period (770 B.C.–221 B.C.), there were a lot of people who conducted business activities for a living, yet as a result of Reforms of Shang Yang**, the sprout of business class was under smother for quite a long time in Chinese history. Not until the battle of Chu and Han (206–202 B.C.), had the business class rose again, some of whom became very affluent figures in that period. After Song Dynasty, business class has developed into a considerable scale with some family capital involved. In Qing Dynasty, there was a trading house called "DaShengkui (literally referred as big, prosperity, and primary)", which employed 6000–7000 staff at its climax period. It also owned 16,000–20,000 camels, and partial estimate capital (just in Mongolia) reached ten million Liang (a Chinese unit of weight, equals 50 g) silver.[29] Professor Zhuang Guotu of Xiamen University addressed that the oversea network of Chinese business class started around Song and Yuan Dynasty, and in fifteenth century, it has already formed, arriving its peak in seventeenth to eighteenth century. The Min-nan (Southern Fujian Province) business group was especially outstanding. Even till today, according to Forbes, the Min-nan (Southern Fujian Province) business group have occupied 25% ratio among all Forbes list, if Taiwan be taken into account, the ratio to be hitting 75%.[30] The "Yong (甬,

[27]See Footnote 7, p. 61, D.19.4.1.2.

[28]See Footnote 7, p. 59, D.18.1.1Pr.

[29]Sun [15].

[30]Zhuang [16].

referred to Ningbo City)" business group enjoy high reputation in the modern time, as they have taken six seats in top nine banking and financial families in Shanghai. Their long-lasting influence has made a huge difference in modern financial and industrial fields.

The privatization of property and individual-owned title are the crucial factors of contract. Author Linton Corbin once said: "The term 'legal relation' should always be used with reference to two persons, neither more nor less ... but not between person and property."[31] The privatization of property and individual-owned title developed synchronically, and with greater privatization, came more attention on legal rights of individual's property. Contract, a legal text based on exchange of personal property, reflects the relation of owning and occupying, and also pushes forward the privatization and makes it more complex and regular. In the western history, the social ranking position and property have existed symbiotically, and once someone has obtained his position, he would naturally enjoy according property. Spartan citizens called themselves *homoioi* (equal people), which demonstrates they had equal citizenship, and with correspond property.[32] The needs and interests of individual will be valued as the true drive for civil society's appearing and developing. The civil society defined individual to be free and with ability to own his property who should also be a man of laisser-faire with free mind to pursue his own desires, but not a man with political wisdom and morality. Britain political philosopher Michael Oakeshott believes that, the modern civil society was not civil association any more. Instead, it's the enterprise association. Meanwhile, in her book *The Human Condition*, Hannah Arendit pointed out that, till the modern times, the value of human life had turned to personal profits from public life and moral responsibility. Human, at the same time, turned into economic animal from political animal.[33] The revolutionary change of position to contract in the west world has led the capitalism to expand in many aspects: social, economic, and political, consequently, and it successfully became the mainstream culture that many scholars are proud of. While some family enterprise and syndicate occurred in China, which may conceal the influence of individual blaze, but there still were some important influences of individual during the long lasting feudalism. First, the privatization level was rather high. Take land as an example. Fu Zhufu believes that the private land system was built in China since Warring States Period, when the land was seen as a commodity which could be bought and sold by currency. The private land being commodity and sold freely was the natural selection of market pattern. In Tang Dynasty, the central government promulgated a policy of land equalization, which means that the government would

---

[31]Corbin [17].

[32]Huang [18].

**Translator's annotation: began in 356 B.C., Shang Yang made a series of reforms targeting from the title of land, the rewarding of war-time credit, the new political system in his time, to the most influential topic—the restrain of commercial and encouragement of agriculture, in order to maintain the governance of the authority.

[33]Zhang [19].

distribute a certain amount of land according to one's domicile registration.[34] Even in this very policy, scholars still found traces to prove that there were a lot of private lands in Tang Dynasty.[35] Moreover, some discovered that the purchase and sale of land had become a regular thing in Tang Dynasty despite the policy, and finally the government chose to indulge.[36] Secondly, the commodity level was high. Take the main consumption of foodstuff as an example. Wu Hui listed some data: Northern Song Dynasty's commodity foodstuff ratio was 17%, which reduced in Mid-Ming Dynasty (16%), and when it came to Qing Dynasty, the ratio increased to 17.26%, and in late Qing Dynasty, it even to 20.7%. At the same time, the non-agricultural population in China was at 20–30%.[37] These numbers successfully demonstrate the base for labor in commoditization. American scholar Zhang Gang's research shows that, the labor market has been in China since the Warring States Period, and the relation between employer and employee should be thought of a nexus of purchase and sale rather than a feudal relation. In recent years, the scholars in mainland China also proved the massive labor relations in Spring and Autumn Period.[38] As the labor became a commodity, the social division of labor would grow in a more diversified way, which could lay a foundation for the perfection and development of contract. Thirdly, the rights of personal ownership and disposal bore duality character. On one hand, the rights of personal ownership and disposal were constrained by family power and public-owned institution; on the other hand, the subject of which laws protected was the third party with good faith when the transaction regarding personal or non-personal ownership of family property in the forms of sale and pawn was made, only if the transaction was legit. In 1929, He's Family in South Sea specifically stipulated that: "without a clan conference (family administration institution), those who engage in real estate transactions shall be reprimanded to hand in back to their lands and deprived for ten years' profits and rights of electing and being elected."[39] That's to say, when transaction concerning family owned organizations arose, it was not common to pursue the liability of the third party who was with good faith, but to reprimand the ones who sold the family property, this was for the purpose of securing the purchase and sale behavior.

The neutral position authorities stood was the external context for the emerging of contracts. Grotius of Natural law school believes that besides selfish instinct, human traits also had social instinct, which meant people loved to socialize, and were "eager to live an organized and peaceful life. Such wish helped with the maintenance of social orders, consequently formed the sources of nations and laws." The core idea or principle of this theory was: "(people) don't possess other person's property, and are supposed to give back others' property with profits; (people shall) fulfill their promises, (shall) make compensations for our damages, and (shall) be punished in

[34]Zhao [20].
[35]Yang [21].
[36]Zhao [22].
[37]Wu [23].
[38]Zhao [24].
[39]Yang [25].

accordance with their faults."[40] Kant presented a parallel theory that the anti-social trait of human actually built the human society, and he held the view that individual's evil made the base for the integrate good in human society, further pushed the human history forward in their mutual confronts and conflicts. It's obvious that Kant and Grotius shared the same idea that human's selfish instinct and social instinct are the driven power for human society. To be exact, it is because of the pursuing of selfish instinct that human turn to the social instinct to prevent inappropriate selfish instinct to construct an ideal world. And Kant's theory however, inspired Hegel in his dialectal theory of good and evil. Hegel said: "without the desires for glory, power, and wealth, human will live a life of the shepherd in Arcadia, harmoniously, mutual-caringly, in self-gratification, and will bury their potential gifts. Supposing people's tempers were as even as sheep's, they would fail to realize the value higher than their farming animals'."[41]

Meanwhile, the theories of Kant and Grotius can be used in the research on origin of contract. There is a very significant issue lying in here: when the people have to obey some social norms and agreements, if the governors breached of those, then there must be some riots and chaos in order to form a new government, together with new social norms and agreements. That's to say, violent revolution is the balancing weight on the scale to maintain social norms and agreements. As for contract between citizens, what is the balancing weight then? Consciousness and morality are psychological binding force in such case, yet they are too flexible. So additionally, people do need some device or measure to be imposed to the defaulters by the government power or regional customary laws. E. Durkheim once said: "when I am implementing a contract, ... I am performing the liabilities and duties of laws and customs." "liability and duty are not invented by contract involvers, but by education. Education provides the sense of liability and responsibility for involvers in effective contract, makes clear that the breach of a contract would bring about consequences and punishment, even more damages to bear. Hence it can establish a binding force both psychologically and socially."[42] Hobbes also stated that the nature and source of justice were the abidance of effective agreement, which relied on mandatory social power to keep people to obey. Only when the mandatory social power has established, will the effective agreement be implemented, and the owner title be maintained.[43]

When the justice concept of adherence to the contract has been accepted to the social logic, another issue came out: how should the public power intervene in the contract? Or in other words, to what extent and in what way should the public power gain its goal? The free will of parties entering the contract should not be intruded by the national public power, nor should the free rights to enter into a contract be limited by the public power. This concept was the core principle in contract liberalism era. To put the west contract evolution in a nutshell, one cannot deny the fact that the contract's development depended so much on the market economics and

---

[40] *He's Family Regulations of Hexi County, Southern Sea, 1929.*

[41] George [26].

[42] Walsh [27].

[43] Emile [28].

democracy political entity. More importantly, many elites have done a lot thorough analyses from the perspectives of philosophy, economics, politics, and legal, in order to explore the nature of "freedom".[44] Humanity philosophy successfully liberated the status that human was affiliated to gods, making it possible that human could be a social subject with independent character and free will.[45] Adam Smith, the master of liberal economic theory, provided his opinion for supports from the point of view of how economical rules worked: "Every man, as long as he does not violate the laws of justice, is left perfectly free to pursue his own interest in his own way, and to bring both his industry and capital into competition with those of any other man, or order of men."[46] As long as Adam Smith concerned, the tasks for government and power should be in the direction of protecting the mentioned free competition. School of classic natural law actually put more weight on person per se, with person as the core, and advocated to emancipate the minds, to embrace free minds. John Locke stressed that the ultimate goal to implement laws was not to restrain nor abolish the freedom of human, but to protect and broaden freedom; Montesquieu put the individual's freedom as one nation's most urgent priority.[47] Famous English jurist Sir Gorge Jessel also sequenced the contract freedom in front of public order: "adults and rational people are supposed to have adequate free power to enter into contracts, as long as their contracts are made according to their free will, they shall be deemed as sacred ones, and be enforced by courts mandatorily."[48] All these statements listed above illustrate the relation between contract freedom and neutral government standing point. To be more explicit, only when one party fails to fulfill his obligation of the contract, and jeopardizes the other party or the society at large, can the public power be engaged in such practice. The objective value of law is no more than providing a legitimate measure, procedure or enforcement power, and then creates a reasonable protective system.[49] The role of courts, is supposed to be independent arbitrator or adjudicator, mainly performs the duty of supervising the rules of game be obeyed rather than be involved in the game.

Compared with the freedom tendency of west legal system, Chinese ancient official administrative level was higher, especially in the ranges of real estate, slaves, and transaction of properties. Take real estate as an example. The transfer and exchange of land would be done with length formalities in many trivial details. Not only did the debtor obtain the contract, but the national administrative authority would keep a copy for reference in case they'd be examined someday. The privatized level of land skyrocketed since Warring States Period, which could be seen in the frequent purchase and sale behaviors, and those behaviors of private contracts were under the national laissez-faire policy which did not just simply ignore the transactions of lands. On the contrary, the government distinguished the private contracts of land

[44]Thomas [13], pp. 108–109.

[45]Su [29].

[46]Adam [30].

[47]Edgar [31].

[48]See Furson [32].

[49]Bernard [33].

from authority contracts by naming them "white contract (private contract)" and "red contract (official contract)", and resorted to uniformed contract format and tax system to administrate the purchase and sale of lands. Meanwhile, a new career came into the stage, people who did this new career called "Ya ren (牙人, the two characters literally refer to tooth man)". Later the career gained its name as "Ya hang (牙行, the two characters literally mean the tooth career)". This career took the task of administration and tax collection, and they actually played the role of media, who not only went between the parties in the contract, but also communicated with government officials. No matter "white contract (private contract)" or the "red contract (official contract)", there was very modest effect in preventing the prevailing of private transactions, which can be demonstrated by the fact that since Song Dynasty, the "white contract (private contract)" had been developed incredibly fast. One reason for the prevailing of private contract might be that people wanted to escape from taxes. Another reason was that the effectiveness of private contract was no less than the official contract, and it was even more appealing to common people. Plus, as in some litigation circumstances with private contract, the court also deemed it as a powerful evidence in the case, which can be seen as an example for the laissez faire practice back in that time.

The emergence and development of market provided living space for contract. Market, on one hand, played a role as the physical platform for exchanging contracts, on the other hand, served as the measure of the government to manage contract. In western European countries of medieval time, fair broke the economy of monorail system, made the contractual relations marketizational and socialized, laid the foundation for the developing of contract. Still in western European countries of medieval, there was fair officer preforming his duty at fairs with the seal of the Duke, to signet every important contract in the fair. In the case of ancient China, villages and castles have be formed in early Xia Dynasty (twenty-first century-sixteenth century, B.C.), and when it came into Western Zhou Dynasty (1045–771 B.C.), towns and cities have be separated. Afterwards, the integrate city concept in the view of historical shape has be set, which offered possibility to build a national wide and complex market.[50] German economist of historical school Karl Bucher analyzed: "the change of the extension of human economic activity scope and the relation between producing and consuming is from family economy to city economy, then to the country economy."[51] One necessary factor of such evolution would be the high level of development of market. The period from Western Zhou Dynasty to Tang Dynasty is that which scholars conclude as *Classic Economy* time, which bears distinguished feature of the combination of market administration and city-town administration.[52] As a matter of fact, the market in Western Zhou Dynasty was with highly administrational tendency. The market could be only open in set place at set times. The central government arranged special officer to be in charge of the market, namely, Sishi (司市, market

[50]Zhang [34].

[51]*Address on Traditional Market and Market Economy*, China Economy History Research, 1994, Vol. 4.

[52]Wei [35].

officer), whose duty was to manage, administrate, and make regulation regarding market issues. There were three types of markets in that time, big market, morning market and evening market.[53] Besides, the "national roads" connected every courier station in the country, and in every fifty miles,[54] there was a market in order to meet the needs of people to trade things. Till Han Dynasty, the city size has been escalated onto a new level, and the market thus expanded accordingly. Take Chang'an city as an example. There were nine markets designed in the city, among which six located in the western city, three in the eastern city. Each market covered area of six miles, with extensive citizen area of one hundred and sixty miles, and all the nine markets accounted for 18.5% of the total city area.[55] In the *Ode to the West Capital*of Ban Gu***, it says the city of Chang'an "sets nine markets for different kinds of commodities, and they are so congested that people can hardly turn around, nor can a horse walk; it seems that people could break the city wall as a result of congestion; the dust by people's steps mixes together with the fog, which depicts the scene as a Chinese monochrome painting." After mid-Tang Dynasty, with the development of commodity, modern market pattern has gradually set, free handicraft industry, business class came into the historical stage, together with Ya ren, they all playing very important roles in enhancing and pushing forward the commodity exchange and contract development. Till the time of Song Dynasty, the transaction of lands became even freer than before. "Internal" of market was also dominated by a free atmosphere, which led the system declined, a system used since Han and Tang Dynasty placing the authority as its core to set price and test quality. Instead, the free market took over the charge and stimulated quite a lot national markets. In Tang Dynasty, the government gathered the same industry in one place, called Hang (行). This tradition reached its peak in Song Dynasty, and in Ming and Qing Dynasty, the production element markets in China have all developed well, including real estates, financial, financial instrument, and labor market. Thus the market systematically functioned in very positive orders. Take Jiang Nan silk industry as an example. It formed a full system of producing, providing and selling, meanwhile, and the contract relations were gradually complete, such as the relations of deputizing, hiring, loaning, and contracting to finish certain project, which could all find their correspondent regulation and customs, and further be written down into related contracts.[56]

Commercial ethics which are effective and well-observed are the internal motivation and external regulating form for the development of contracts. That's to say, contract spirit and institution have to rely on the binding force of commercial ethics, which can be seen as the pillars for the whole system. The protestant ethic under the Capitalism commodity economics accelerated the capitalism production method development. The concepts of abstinence, benevolence, and devotion to one's duty were the demonstrations of capitalism contract ethics, which filled the loopholes in

---

[53] *Rites of Zhou, Di Guan, Judiciary II, Sishi.*

[54] ibid,*Yi Ren.*

[55] Li [36].

[56] Pan [37].

the contract regulation, system, and laws.[57] Historian Mr. Ye Xian'en gave a theory about China's traditional society, as he puts it, that traditional China is a country led by Confucius doctrine, and it takes the advantages of the vendors, which is a quite reasonable thought. As mentioned in preface, the Confucius ethic and contract made reflection on each other. To be more explicit, the traditional Chinese commercial ethics and contract merged in the following aspects:

I. Good faith. Traditional Chinese moral standards emphasized much on good faith, while in *Uniform Commercial Code* of US today, it states that "good faith means honesty in fact and the observance of reasonable commercial standards of fair dealing." In Japan, there are also plenty of detailed and rational comments on this matter. Yoishimi Sinkei, HoshiNo Eilchi have made some valuable comments, and KanNo KouTakeshi further cut four categories of the functions of good faith: the function to specialize the laws; to balance the equity of laws (to make it possible that law enforcement would secure ethical norms); the function of modifying the laws; and the function of making new laws (to amend the loopholes in existing laws in accordance with time, and to solve new problems rising in contract relations). There were provisions of good faith in ancient Chinese official documents. Moreover, the good faith as a doctrine had been applied very comprehensively in transaction customs. In Spring and Autumn and Warring States Period (770 B.C.–221 B.C.), the vendors in Lu country fed sheep and goats in the morning, fed the cocks and hens in the evening in order to make the animals heavier when they were sold at the market. Some vendors encouraged people to buy their goods by exaggeratedly bragging. It's said that when Master Confucius went to Lu country to take the position as Sikou, he made great effort to prevent such maleficence. Confucius ethical moral code has influenced Chinese commercial and contract a lot, which will be discussed in later chapters.
II. Against extravagance and amassing. Traditional Confucius ethic advocated the attitude against extravagance and amassing, to avoid the result of losing oneself. This attitude, as a national trend, could accumulate national property by not spending lavishly, which was correspondent to the concept in Protestantism, yet the anti-amassing concept actually yielded negative result in accumulating. There was an idea prevailing in Chinese commercial culture, which was, once something was gathered, it should be distributed in a certain way, or the owner would be followed by some curse. The variant for this idea in the traditional philosophy of "using treasure to fix jinx" actually urged people to make the commitment in charity and help the more vulnerable. These two aspects impacted traditional Chinese contract ethics, which showed more demands in filial duties and doing favors to others. Max Webber once said that Chinese local religions' encouragement was an ethical moral for common people.[58] Though this argument seemed a little extreme, it, however, suggested the distinguished feature of traditional Chinese culture. The filial duty and the wish and burden to offer favor to others

---

[57] Ye [38].

***Translator's annotation: 32–92 B.C., a well-known Chinese historian in Han Dynasty.

[58] Max [39].

indeed weigh more in Chinese culture, even when compared with interest and profit. In the year of 1686, there was a person named Zhang Deyu, who built a house in Huizhou City and then left his hometown. Twenty years later, he came back to his old house, and not until the clan entered a Filial Duty Contract with him, could he be admitted into his own house.[59]

To sum up, the task of comparison between China and west contract theories is completed briefly in the five aspects which cover commodity economics, privatization level, and neutral position of authorities, market system and commercial ethics. The ancient China's contract came into being in the grounds of the blend of civil exchange, official administration, Confucius ethic, and the market economics as well.

Functions of Contracts

A. L. Corbin once put: "The term 'legal relation' should always be used with reference to two persons, neither more nor less … but not between person and property."[60] This assertion tells people that all exchange nature is not about the material or thing, but about the owner's rights. Further, the material or thing is just the tool of exchange, but the core still lies in the exchange of rights. To this extent, Hobbes believes that "the exchange of rights is the so-called contract" and "all contracts are about the exchange and transfer of rights".[61] The nature of the origin of contract is to transfer the right to different owner by a "promise", according to which, the one who transfers is supposed to obtain interest or profit. On the surface, it seems that the original contract relations incline more to the exchange between physical subjects, but to explore deeper, it's not that difficult to find the fact that the existence of exchange between physical subjects is due to the implied or expressed "promise", which is the core of a contract. When the exchange between physical subjects began to fade in history, the relations bonded by "promise" finally caught its attention. People stopped solely exchanging subjects but to conduct transaction activities in order to gain what they wanted. This kind of promise not only limited in vows and oath, but evolved to a set of systematic symbols, which was the contract.[62] In both China and west contract law histories, when taking the theory and system of contract into account, it's important to realize that it is this very set of symbols which enable us to discuss further and more sensible about the functions of contract.

Synchronically speaking, there are three functions of contract:

1. To establish a bond between different people and to create credit for people. M. E. Opler observes that, an implied or expressed basic hypothesis or value orientation usually controlled or stimulated human activities. His cultural themes theory

[59]Chen [40].

[60]See Footnote 32.

[61]Thomas [41], pp. 100–102.

[62]Yang [42].

paralleled the theory of philosopher's value theory, anthropologist's *premise theory,* Parsons'basic value attitude theory, and Linton's ideal mood theory, finally completing the evolution from a theory to a norm adjusting human behaviors.[63] The foundation for contract is based on similar theories, A believes B can fulfill his liability, thus A finishes his duty first and vice versa, which is the premise and value for entering a contract, and hence the most significant function aims at the establishment of the bond between A and B, to transfer the rights. In ancient China, the earliest way to establish a bond was to knot as a symbol for mutual consensus, then it developed into the form of written agreement and contract. Likewise, other cultures in this planet have also experienced similar evolution. As in historical record, the tribe of Yao did not have written letters in their culture, but they still figured out an own system for contracting, which was made "with the message of contrast carved on two blocks of woods and each party possessing one wood".[64] In *The Travels of Marco Polo*, it records that in Yunnan province, the parties of contract would carve information on a wooden stick, which would be cut into two for each party. Once the debtor had paid off, he could get back the half from the creditor, to complete the contract.[65] The book in Qing Dynasty called *Zi Bu Yu* tells a story in Hainan province: just like in Yunnan province, the people in Hainan province also cut their contract into two pieces when concerning real estate transaction. Once the land was going to be re-sold, the new buyer would check both pieces to investigate the title of the ownership.[66] Back to the position of Sishi (market officer), one of their duties was to supervise the purchase and sale conducted under the formality of contracting, in hope of reducing disputes and litigation. Actually, it would be ready to go on with the references here to demonstrate the first function also the premise of contract, which is to establish a bond between different people and to create credit for people. Yet there is still something notable that is worth to point out. The contract customs in Roman Law in fact appeared in the same time as Han Dynasty contract. According to Hugh T. Scogin Jr., an American scholar, the Roman contract rite was unilateral. To be more clearly, it was one side's absolute power and the other side was supposed to accept the former's offer; while Han Dynasty contract rite was entered and bond by moral relations, which demanded people to fulfill the liability as a result of morality. In such circumstance, the individual behavior was confined by social moral norms and rites.[67] To fulfill the duty in a contract was not only an economical or legal behavior, but was also the level for someone concerning morality, which could be thought as a social ethic as well as a business ethic. In *Huai Nanzi,* a collection book of philosophy in Han Dynasty, it concludes the importance of morality, and advocates people to realize their promises. This long-haul pursue for morality and ethic in China

[63]Thomas [41], p. 13, see Footnote 2.

[64]Zhou Qufei, *Ling Wai Culture,* Vol. 10, Wooden Contract.

[65]*The Travels of Marco Polo*, Vol. 2, Jinzhou County.

[66]Yuan Mei, *Zi Bu Yu*, Vols. 1–2, Bamboo Slip.

[67]Hugh [43].

has cultivated a deeply-rooted national thoughts in Chinese people, asking them to be Xin (faithful, keeping their promises) and Yi (giving the sincere honor to others), both of which were conveyed in contract.

2. To serve as a voucher and proof for rights and liability. Contracts, are not solely a proof to demand another party to fulfill his duty, more often, it is a proof for both parties of their rights and liability. The contract per se, normally was about real rights. In Zhou Dynasty, one of the necessary approaches to transfer the real property was to enter a contract with mutual consent clauses, and to carve the contract bronze container. Those symbols in fact replaced the real property. However, in the long time for Zhou Dynasty to Republic of China (since 1911), the focus has been on Usufruct rights rather than the ownership, which was further stated by a Japanese scholar, Hiroaki Tarada who specifically pointed out that "In China, it's impossible to find even one existence of factual title or ownership of real property, there is just a system on paper in the form of contract to secure the purchase and sale of real property". It would make more sense to see the subject as a "right of management" than the subject itself, for the transferring and possessing of real property has been always for the purpose of profits by managing. Plus, the system of owning land failed to establish itself as a national system.[68] As a matter of fact, the real property right in ancient China was not quite true with Hiroaki Tarada's observation. Howsoever, judging from economic and contractual historical documents, Tarada is right in saying that China paid more attention on the factual title or ownership of land and houses, which had laid the foundation for any other type of rights. Consequently, there are two questions stimulated by Tarada's observation: one is that, why the contract, as the certification for real property, has captured so much attention in ancient China, while the factual title or ownership of land and houses were somehow ignored? Take Song Dynasty as an example. In Law Reports of Southern Song Dynasty, the quotation concerning legal provisions and customs all indicated great attention on law. In the Reports, there was a case regarding to the financial dispute between Zeng's brothers. The relating documents said: "the law provides the behaviors of pawning real estate property shall be with contract, each party shall have one copy of aforesaid contract, and this shall be known by all as a common sense … now there is a case that one man pawns his clothes and loses his receipt under which he cannot redeem his clothes. You cannot do with clothes, let alone real estate property!" The second case in the Reports was regarding to Mo Ruhong's suit upon property dispute, on which the magistrate wrote as followed: "the lawsuit will be decided on the basis of contract once a dispute arising." The third case is the dispute between Yang and Huang on real property in which the county judge made the ruling by saying that "where a dispute arising on real property, contract is the sole evidence". And the forth case is the judgment of Hu Shibi (or, Hu Shiying): "generally speaking, when a judge is considering a real property case, he will resort to contract to rule his findings of evidence and he

[68]Hiroaki [44].

will take legal provisions into consideration."[69] The other question stimulated by Tarada's observation is that, since ancient China attaching so much attention on contracts, did they showed equal attitude on actual possession? That's to say, did possession bear the force of real rights alternation? According to the current historical materials, as a symbol of real rights alternation, possession did have legal effect and force to some extent. Once the contract had come into force, the seller should hand out his property, and the buyer should take it in. This could be seen as the first step for contract of its effect which was based on the procedure of property transfer. Pursuant to the law in Song Dynasty: "…without a cl1ear stipulation in contract, or the possession time reaches twenty years, or the decease of the debtor, a lawsuit concerning real property shall not be filed."[70] Thus the possessor could enjoy the possession if there was no clear stipulation in real property contract, or under the circumstances that the possession over twenty years' limitation, or the decease of the debtor. In this case, the assumption in law was made according to the possession time of twenty years to ascertain the title and ownership of the real property. As for the possession without any contract, because the lack of proof in current condition, it's very hard to draw any conclusion.

3. To prohibit fraud and reduce disputes. In customs of common public, the contract was put on great emphasis to realize their rights. Among the authorities in ancient China, the emphasis was the same because the contract itself could prohibit fraud and reduce disputes, and moreover, it could maintain good transaction order and social harmony. No doubt the contract served as a tool for the authorities to regulate civil behaviors corresponding to customs and laws. When a dispute arose, the trial should be conducted on the basis of contract and to charge since the dispute day. According to *Rites of Zhou*: "the Fubie can be used in civil litigation for determining the liability", "the Shuqican be used as the proof of selling and buying at trial", "the Zhi Jican be used for the purpose of adjusting the contractual relationships concerning trading, security, and pawn", and "the parties concerning property disputes" should provide the Fuor Yue Jias evidences so that "the decision shall be made according to evidences".[71] There was no specialized bureau in Zhou Dynasty of ancient China to administrate the contracts, so "(there were six positions) to collect all the copies of the contract parallels today's notary system. If any changes happened in contracts, the officers in the previous six positions shall alternate accordingly."[72] Jia Yanshu in Tang Dynasty observed: "those six positions were so busy to fulfill their duties of collecting contracts, then they formed a rule to make a copy to Dali (the highest rank among the six positions) for references." In the research of Kong Qingming, a jurist on jurisprudence and history of law, it records that "the contract in Zhou Dynasty

[69] *Law Reports of Southern Song Dynasty,* Southwest Institution of Political Science and Law published, 1985, pp.79, 81, 102, 116.

[70] ibid, p. 50.

[71] *Rites of Zhou,* Shishi, Zhaoshi.

[72] *Rites of Zhou,* Dali, original text: 凡邦国都鄙及万民之有约剂者藏焉,以贰六官,六官之所登.

was divided into left and right parts, of which the right part was the main one held by the parties concerned for the proof of rights of debt and property, while the left part was the counterpart stored in the government branches for the proof of justice."[73] The *Rites of Zhou* also made a recording: the two parts of a contract were designed to guarantee the rights of parties, who were supposed to pay for the fees in advance, and after three days the trial would be conducted; both of the parties should appear in the court to prevent the injustice, the trial should begin after they paid all fees. Zheng Xuan made a further explanation: the lawsuit concerning property should ensure the rights of both parties to present at court to give their own grounds, and each party's payment could serve as deposits (Shushi). Under such circumstance, the absence in court or in deposit should be deemed as a lack of justifiable reasons. From the above, the way of charging fees can be easily seen that only after the payment was done, the trial would begin. However, the charge of fees was not to raise the burden of the parties, but to regulate the mechanism of lawsuit in order to prevent the lawsuit among citizens, and promote a spirit of realizing the contract provisions. Plus, in the *Rites of Zhou,* the party who was not in his good faith would be punished in Mo sentence****; if the circumstances are serious, the punishment could introduce the death penalty after ascertaining the documents collected by the six positions. It's safe to say that all those devices and punishment concerning contract disputes were based on the contract itself, and this mechanism didn't find its way out of the historical stage from Zhou Dynasty to Republic of China.

Synchronically, the functions of contract focused on the enforcing aspect which demonstrated that when two parties enter into a contract, they are supposed to obey the stipulations they made and not to breach them. Diachronically, the functions of contract are mainly embodied in the way that the authorities regulated the parties to abide by the law and customs in methods of punishment, correction and encouragement so as to maintain a stable transaction order of the national market.

Types and Forms of Contracts

Compared with the well-developed contract theory in the western countries, the ancient Chinese obviously paid more attention on the pragmatic aspect such as construction of contract's system and the forms. To be pointed out, they highlighted the contract's system of national statute law and civil customs, which was designed for balancing the economic and social function of the country in an impartial and just measure. As a matter of fact, the just and impartial spirit lied beneath the emphasis of the system in ancient China, yet regrettably it failed to draw the comprehensive notice among the academics.

[73] Kong and Hu [45].

****Translator's annotation: Mo means ink, this punishment was to tattoo the criminal's face or forehead.

According to the classification in current standards, we can classify the contracts in ancient China into two classes, namely, legal philosophy class and pragmatic class, from which we can analyze the developing path and evolving levels of the contract:

1. **Bilateral and Unilateral Contracts**
   In this type, the focus was on the fact that whether the parties placed the consideration as a premise for their rights and liabilities. If the both parties enjoyed their rights and bore the burden of liabilities, it would be a bilateral contract. Conversely, if one party only enjoyed the rights without liability, it would be called a unilateral contract. The bilateral contract in ancient China was more common than unilateral contract. The bilateral contract in ancient China would demand both parties to sign the contract in order to confirm their liabilities. Plus, the both parties would hold one copy of the contract for future purpose. In southern part of China, Hainan Province, the Li's adhered to a local custom to carve the bamboo when concerning the transaction of real estate, which meant that the contract of transaction would be carved on the bamboo slip, and the buyer and seller would hold a piece of the bamboo. For example, the real property contract in the year of 1808[74] (13th year of Jiaqing Emperor) stimulated the time, names of parties, location, specific considerations in the contract, and in the end of which, it clarified that in order to make a proof, such contract was carved and divided into three pieces, for both parties and the mediator to hold. This kind of contract was a little different from those used in other parts of ancient China, yet with even higher credit.

Besides bilateral contract, there was unilateral contract existing in ancient China, which suggested that only one party would bear the burden of rights, and the contract would be collected by the rights owner once it was signed. Debita and credit contract was the typical form of it. For example, the unearthed Dunhuang contract titled *Borrowing Contract of Wheat and Maize of Zhaixinzi in the year of 886 (Bingwu Year)* stipulated that, Zhaixinzi, the borrower, made a contract to Nanding Jun, to ensure that Zhai would pay back the wheat and maize he borrowed from Nanding Jun in previous year.[75] In such contract, the interests were not written in, and the ending part of the contract was missing. However, according to conventions at that time, the missing part of the contract should be the signatures of witness and guarantor, which could be confirmed by other ending parts of contracts at that time.

2. **Consensual Contracts and Real Contracts**
   Both China and the western world's contractual evolution share a resemblance, which is that they all place the delivery of the subject matter as an important condition because the behavior of delivery and payment can be used as proof of consensus. Conventionally, common people believed in the principle as "cash on delivery", which demonstrated that the both parties put the other side's delivery as the premise of the transaction. This could parallel the real contract, a initial form of contract still used in many summary procedures in transactions. However, there

[74]Zhang [46].

[75]Files of Dunhuang (1st Edition).1961. Zhonghua Book Company, p. 376.

were some inconveniences in real contract, and to clean up those inconvenient obstacles, the consensual contract would come into use. Scholars found that in *Law of Twelve Tables* (451 B.C.–450 B.C.), the theory of consensual contract has already been founded and differed from real contract.[76] In China, consensual contract could find its solid cultural basis and comprehensive conventional room. The principle as "cash on delivery" and the practice of bartering had being used for quite a long time in history. As for the transaction of real estate, the deed was deemed as the proof of a real property, and its function was served as an important part in payment: the seller received the payment and then he would hand out the deed, which became the premise of a real property contract. Zhejiang Province published a governmental document in the year of 1773 (Qianlong 38th year), in which the authority permitted the customs among common people: "the (financial) practice among civilians are based on the deed, in which it will stipulate and record the amount of money, and that will be the same as used in cash. In practice, people all obey the rule that exchange the deeds and the money, then enter into contract … thus, deed means the ownership of a land—no deed, no land."[77] Also, in the pawning system in ancient China, the person himself could be a subject matter in a contract for amount of money, and only the person paid off the debt, he could be free again. In such contracts, the premise remained the procedure of delivery, which meant that, the subject matter—the person, should go to the creditor's house first, then the creditor would pay. *The Kuimao Contract of Wu Qingshun* unearthed in Dunhuang records that "the three brothers of Wu Qingshun were in deep debt, and now Qingshun will be sold to the family of Suoseng in Longxing Temple. In return, Qingshun will be paid some wheat, jute, and maize. Once the payment is accepted, the person will work without any salary, and he will work under any order of the creditor till the day he pays off the debt."[78] This example shows that the practice of pawn of people is the same as other subjects, which all concentrate on the delivery of the subject matter on the occasion of purchase and sale. Plus, it demonstrates the real contract plays an energetic role in people's daily life in the history of ancient China. As a matter of fact, to pawn a person for debt was so common that even during the time of Republic of China (since 1912), it was still used in the nation around Zhejiang and Jiangsu Provinces.

It's very difficult to determine the exact original time of consensual contract in ancient China, but the scholars all agree that the time would be no later than Song Dynasty, when the consensual contract in China was well developed and gained the approval of the authorities. The typical consensual contracts in that time were purchase-in-advance contract, and purchase on credit contract. In Song Dynasty,

[76]Zheng [47].

[77]*The Regulations of Administrating Zhejiang*, vol. 1, quoted in Yang Guozhen's *The Report on the Contracts and Deeds in Ming and Qing Dynasty*, People's Press. 1988.

[78]*The Research Report on Civil Customs*, 2000, edited by the former Judicial Department of Nanjing Government of the Republic of China, proof read by Hu Xusheng, Xia Xinhua, Li Jiaofa, China University of Political Science and Law Press, p. 383.

Pengzhou city in Sichuan Province abounded in teas, which attracted the tea dealers to conduct business there, where the most popular way of purchase was to pay in advance. According to historical research: "the production of tea from farmers raised from hundreds to tens of thousands Jin (unit of weight, equals to a half kilo). The buyers will pay in advance before the tea is made according to its previous output. In the next spring, the buyers will prepare for money and food to hire workers to pick off the teas. Then the buyers will sort the teas in different categories by the quality, so that the tea can be sold. In this way, the tea merchants can depend on themselves in this industry, some of whom will make it as a family business to keep on."[79] This kind of purchase-in-advance gradually became the reservation system, which meant that the merchant would deposit the down payment to the tea farmers to set certain restrain. Another example was Fujian Province, where the Jianyang paper was very famous. The Jianyang paper was usually sold to Jiangsu buyers, who "pays the front money for reservation and forbids the producer to sell to other people."[80]

To define the nature of the contracts above, the key is to figure out "down payment, front money", and "capital". Liu Qiugen calls those kind of "down payment, front money", and "capital" usurious loan, which seem reasonable enough if judging from the results. Howsoever, as considered from the viewpoint of contract per se, the nature of "down payment, front money" is more like an advanced promise before transaction, and it bears the features of advanced payments. The design of this device was aimed to control the destination of some products. In *The History of Song Dynasty*, the official authority was recorded to engage in the purchase-in-advance activities: "all the tea in the market has to be sold to the authorities, and it will be firstly paid then delivered. The payment is called capital." This can prove that in the ancient times, the producer would gain their capital in the form of advanced payment. Nevertheless, the stipulation and delivery of down payment or front money were the proof and guarantee of the contract, and it was inappropriate to deem the down payment as a usurious loan in such sense, even if the down payment had performed the duty of usurious, it still played the role of proving and paying. Thus, to enroll the purchase-in-advance into consensual contract is a feasible thinking of listing. And it is the same with the situation in Rome, where once the parties through bargaining, have reached a consensus upon the price, even without down payment or other payment, it was deemed to be a valid agreement. The *arrhae* was no more than a proof of the agreement.[81] Gaius actually holds alike idea with Justinian in this, believing that it was necessary to pay *arrhae* in the transaction process, yet it could not nullify the validity if the *arrhae* was not completed, it rather suggested that the acceptance had been reached.[82]

3. **Onerous Contracts and Gratuitous Contracts**
   To distinguish onerous contract and gratuitous contract is to exam whether a contract will gain a profit or not. In the evolution of contract history, onerous

[79] *Jing De Collection*, Vol. 1, *Purchase and Transaction of Tea.*

[80] Guo Bocang, *Records of Fujian Province*, Vol. 1.

[81] Justinian [48].

[82] Gauis, *Edicts of Magistrates*, part X, D.18.1.35Pr.

contract has occupied a prominent role during the whole process. The essence of a contract is to establish mutual benefits or exchange mutual rights. And in this sense, a contract without considering benefits has been in a very limited portion. In ancient China, the gratuitous contract usually took the form of unilateral contract, while other contracts such as in purchase and sold, loan, pawn, and lease, all involved with benefits and profits. Taking debita and credit relations as an example, within which, to borrow money would cause no extra interest, while to loan would result in interest. In Tang Dynasty, the laws did not attempt to protect the debts with interest, which demonstrated the fact that the debtors could only resort to their private methods for remedies. In the provision of Tang Dynasty: "to borrow and loan money to other people, despite the presence of any contract, the authority shall treat those contracts as personal behaviors, and shall not accept any case based on those evidences".[83] So, in Tang Dynasty, the debita and credit relations were considered as a private behavior without any legal protection. As long as the interest was within a reasonable level, the authorities would leave the parties to resolve disputes on their own. In the year of 867 (Xiantong Year of Yi Emperor of Tang Dynasty), the government provided that "to charge compound interest is prohibited".[84] In pawn industry, the doctrine was to provide money to those who need it and was able to pawn something equally worthy, which in fact played the role of adjusting financial market, and a method for traditional poor class of getting through financial shortage. Thus, the pawn began its formative stage in Southern & Northern Dynasty (around the year 220–589, A.D.), and today it still thrives as it used to be. In Qing Dynasty, the sixth year of Tiancong (天聪, 1632 A.D.), the emperor Abahai, (AKA Huang Taiji, 皇太极) prohibited the pawn in his regime. Under such circumstance, a high ranking minster, Hu Gongming dedicated to the emperor, saying: "The poor often need to go the pawnshop to resolve cash-flow problems. Now if Your Majesty decide to put restriction on operating pawnshops, the poor will be out of options, and in a possible scenario, they may begin to steal necessary things to live on … In my opinion, we should keep the pawnshops running so long as the shop owner will not conduct anything unethical and set the interest too high … In this way, the poor people can have an option when they are really short of cash, and further to stabilize the society in the most convenient way." There were a lot of social celebrities who held the same opinion as this minister, one of whom was Gao Shijun, who was a literature scholar in authority bureau, and said: the pawn industry "helps the rich and the poor in the same time, enables them exchange the goods and cash". To both the people and the government, it was a "win–win situation", so all the government needed to consider was how to regulate the formalities and decrees to administrate the market.[85] There was a system called "Xiao Ya (literally speaking, the two words themselves mean that 'pawn for a short time')" whose rule was that the pawn would take a period of three months;

[83]*Provisions in Tang Dynasty*, quoted in *The Criminal Theory Collection of Song Dynasty*, Vol. 26.

[84]*Legal Provisions in Tang Dynasty: Government Administration,* Vol. 6.

[85]Luo Zhenyu, *Dedicating form Ministers in Tiancong Year*, p. 7.

the cash paid by the pawnshop would be 90% of the total pawn value, and the monthly interest would be at 30% of the total pawn value. Such system in that time was a very heavy load for the poor.[86] Thus, in the war time of Qing Dynasty, the officials of the central government advocated to "open pawnshop to help the poor in need", and they did arrange state financial resources to open pawnshop to fight against the pawnshops adopting the system of "Xiao Ya (literally speaking, the two words themselves mean that 'pawn for a short time')".[87]

Gratuitous contract was usually applied to the cases of borrowing, gift, and will. As in gift contract, there was a public club constructed in Suzhou city, where businessman Lu Jitong donated one of his houses to the club, and Lu asked his son Lu Huiqing to hand over the title deed to the public club. A few years later, Lu's family went through a major business failure, and the son, Lu Huiqing wanted to get back the house which was sent as a gift to the club. He filed a complaint to the local authority in the hope of getting back. The judge in the government decided that, once the gift had been given, the title of the house had consequently been transferred to the public club. But as the Lu's family was in sore need of money, as good faith and "to memorize the merit of Lu's father", the judge ruled 60 Liangs (weight unit, one Liang equals to1.8 oz) of silver to Lu's family as a "remedy for the house", and ruled that "all the members of Lu's family shall not sue the case based on the same ground".[88] The judgment in this case indicated that once the establishment of gift contract was valid, the cases of will also appeared as gratuitous contract. In Ming Dynasty, a lot of Pi Qi were used for transferring the real estate property to inheritors in Huizhou City.[89]It's necessary to point out that, the popularity of Pi Qi in that time was to prevent the disputes of the ownership and title, which can be seen as a special form in Chinese contracts.

4. **Format Contracts and Informal Contracts**
   In format contract, the word "format" refers to the fact that the formative form or procedure to perform is its condition. The traditional Chinese society has been adopting format contract as major form, while informal contract as supplementary form. Professor Kong Qingming has observed the civil relations in the *Rites of Zhou,* and then concluded that the exchange of real property has already used the form of civil legal procedure by contracts.[90] To be specific, when two parties entered into a contract to exchange of a land, it did not end after the signing. Instead, the parties should put on file to the government, who would conduct an investigation of the land to determine the range, and then carve the detailed information on the Dan Tu (a bronze container). Furtherly, the government would make a record in specific division. Meanwhile, there was another necessary procedure, say, a fine treatment of dinner to the guests to publicize

[86]Wei [49, 50].

[87]ibid, pp. 443–445.

[88]*Collection of Industrial and Commercial History of Suzhou in Ming and Qing Dynasty*, Jiangsu People's Press, 1981, p. 327.

[89]Zhou [51].

[90]Kong and Hu [52].

the transaction. About the treatment of dinner, Professor Kong Qingming sees it as a "tradition of Chinese people, as they can always feel sincerely happy when someone obtained a piece of land".[91] To throw a dinner has been always a tradition in China concerning of contracts, and the core meaning is just like today's notion of "acknowledgment and publicity" in Property Law. It's very easy to find out the expressions of treatment dinner and banquet in the contracts of Han Dynasty, which coincided with the meaning in the *Rites of Zhou.* In Song Dynasty, the formalities of contracts had been simplified a lot, yet to put on a file to the government authority was still one of the necessities to follow. Moreover, in order to obtain the approval and notary of the government authority, it required some set formalities. Taking agricultural land purchase and sold contract as an example. A valid contract should bear the following formats: (1) The object in the purchase and sold contract shall be in accordance with legal provisions, which means that, the name of parties in the contract, the range of agricultural land, the quality of the land, the location, the margins, the origin, the reason for purchase and sold, the security measure to guarantee the transaction, and the breach clause are all need to be covered in the contract. In the provision of Song Dynasty: "if any person is trading land without a contract stimulating the range, four margins, neighbor guarantor, and written agreement, he or she will break the law and the land concerned will be confiscated." In the tenth year of Shaoxing (1140 A.D.), the provisions went even stricter: "where the real property contract is entered into without appropriate format, nor the guarantor with signature, its validity will lose and the involving parties shall be pursued corresponding legal duty."[92] (2) Again, the provision further put some rules that after three days of the establishment of the contract, "the government will summon a conference participating by the parties, guarantors, neighbors, and drafter of contract." (3) When the previous procedures have done, the government authority will then complete the registration format and confer the proof of payment to the party. (4) When all the formalities have been confirmed, the government authority will seal on the contract endowing its legal effective force, and all the procedures now are finished. So, from these four procedures, we today can drive a conclusion that in the Tang and Song Dynasty, the governmental registration system has been developed into a full shape.

From the viewpoint of daily practice, the types and forms of contracts can be divided into contracts of exchanging, trading, purchase and sold, lease, loaning, pawning, contracting, employing, partnership, and identity confirmation (such as to confirm the inheritor in a will, marriage certificate, a man married to a woman and became a member of her clan*****, concubine issues). This division is in the scope of contract system and theory, which is mentioned in several related books. This book will not choose it as the main focus.

As for the forms of contracts, the "Pan Shu (a judgment witnessing the processing of entering a contract)" and "Bie (a contractual instrument, meaning to cut the

[91] Brief Historical Collection in Song Dynasty, Vol. 61, pp. 65–66.

[92] ibid, p. 26.

contract into two, each party would get one with equal effect)" were the earliest forms of contracts in ancient China since Zhou Dynasty (1045–771 B.C.). And from Jin Dynasty, contracts and attached tax certificate have been integrated into one, named "Wen Quan (文券)". When it came to Tang Dynasty, contracts and attached tax certificate separated again, and they were given a name of "Shi Quan (市券)". Then in Song Dynasty, the tax certificate was designed to glue to the contract, and this format has been adhered till Republic of China (1912–1949 A.D.)

In addition, there was a form of contracts called "Xia Shoushu (literally speaking, the words meaning a document with hand prints on)", which was a device that with the contract carved on two woods with the same contents the parties concerned and the guarantors would press their hand/finger prints on each wood. Then it evolved into "Hua Zhiqi (a contract with fingerprints on)" in Tang Dynasty, which we will go further in this chapter.

According to the original and duplicate copies, the contracts can be divided into lateral and unilateral contracts, the former usually bears both the original and duplicate copies, and the latter usually applies in the selling situation for the buyer to prove the transaction,[93] which is detailed in Professor Zhuang Chuanxi's *Research on Qin and Han Dynasty* that can be used as references.

References

1. Hu, Pingsheng, and Shaohua Song. 1997. *Importance of Newly Unearthed Manuscripts in Zoumalou. Guangming Daily* (January).
2. Zhai, Hao. 1958. *Collections of Popularities. Property. Contract*. Edited by (Qing Dynasty). Commercial Press of China.
3. Ping, Buqing. 1982. *Contract* of *Xia Wai Jun Xie* ≪ 霞外捃屑 ≫ , a collection of essays in Qing Dynasty, vol. X. Shanghai Guji Press.
4. Zhao, Yi. 1990. *Gai Yu Cong Kao* ≪ 陔余丛考 ≫ (a history notebook). Hebei People's Press.
5. Zheng, Yunrui, 1997. *The Origin of Western Contract. Journal of Comparative Law* (III).
6. Yang, Zhen. 1997. *On Common Law Contrac*t, 8. Beijing: Beijing University Press.
7. Kong, Qingming, and Liuyuan Hu. 1996. *Civil Law History of China*, 21. Jilin People's Press.
8. Huang, Feng. 1997. Translated version of *Institutes*, 228. Gaius, China University of Political Science and Law Press.
9. Li, Zhimin. 1988. *Ancient Civil Law of China*, 174. Law Press of China.
10. Yang, Zhenshan (ed.). 1995. *Roman Laws, China's Laws and Civil Codification*, 344. Beijing: China University of Political Science and Law.
11. Tong, Ansheng. *Civil Legal Behaviors*, 3–4. China Renmin University Press.
12. George, H. Sabine, and Shan, Liu (Trans.). *A History of Political Theory*, 527. The Commercial Press of China.
13. Thomas, Hobbes. 1988. *Leviathan*, 99, 100, 102. Translated by Li Sifu, Li Yanbi. Commercial Press.

---

[93] Zhuang [53].

*****Translator's notes: a man married to a woman and became a member of her clan, it may sound normal nowadays, yet in ancient China, and most scenarios were opposite: a woman married to a man and became a member of his clan. So when a man became a clan member of his wife, it meant that he would be no longer a member of his own family, in Chinese, the phrase is called "Ru Zhui".

14. Zhang, Naigen. 1996. On the spirits of Western Law. *Journal of Comparative Law* 1.
15. Sun, Xiangyi. 1998. *History of Financial Trading*, 442. China's Financial Press.
16. Zhuang, Guotu. 1999. Network of oversea trading in ancient times. *Journal of Xiamen University* 3.
17. Corbin, A. L. 1919. Legal analysis and terminology. *The Yale Law Journal* 29, 165. In *The Law of Primitive Man*, 51, ed. E. Edamson Hoebel's. Translated by Zhou Yong. China Social Science Press.
18. Huang, Yang. 1997. *The Historical Origins of Civilis*, vol. 5, Du Shu.
19. Zhang, Runlun. 1997. *The Meaning of Pragmatic Philosophy*, vol. 5. Du Shu.
20. Zhao, Yunqi. 1998. The real estate purchase under Tang Dynasty's land equalization. *Social Science Front*, 2.
21. Yang, Jiping. 1998. Discussion of private land in Tang Dynasty. *Researches in Chinese Economic History*, 3.
22. Zhao, Yunqi. The developing changes in Tang Dynasty's land policy. *Chinese Ancient Society Research.*
23. Wu, Hui. 1998. *The evaluation of historical commodity foodstuff ratio. Researches in Chinese Economic History*, 4.
24. Zhao, Gang. 1986. *Historical Analysis on Chinese Economic System*, Part II. Labor Market, Linking Publishing.
25. Yang, Shanqun. 1996. Brief introduction on private economics during spring and autumn period. *Shanghai Social Science Journal*, 1.
26. George, H. Sabine. 1968. *A History of Political Theory*, 480. Translated by Liu Shan. The Commercial Press.
27. Walsh, W.H. 1960. *Philosophy of History, An Introduction Harper Torchbook*, 125.
28. Emile, Durkheim. 1988. The rules of sociological method. In *The Science of Culture: A Study of Man and Civilization*, ed. L. White's, 139. Translated by Cao Jinqing, Zhejiang Renmin Press.
29. Su, Haopeng. 1999. The historical backgrounds and values for the free rise of contract. *Legal Science, 5.*
30. Adam, Smith. 1974. *An Inquiry into the Nature and Causes of the Wealth of Nations*, 252. Commercial Press, Chinese version.
31. Edgar, Bodenheimer. 1987. *Jurisprudence: The Philosophy and Method Of the Law*, 53–54. Translated by Deng Zhenglai, Ji Jingwu, Huaxia Press.
32. Furson, M.P. 1991. *Law of Contract*, 12th ed. Butterworth & Co.
33. Bernard, Schwartz. 1990. *The Law in America.* Translated by Wang Jun, China University of Political Science and Law Press, p.131; Grant, Gilmore, *The Death of Contract.* Translated by Cao Shibing, Civil Law Theses Collection, vol. 3.
34. Zhang, Quanming. 1998. Three stages of Chinese ancient city. *Journal of Central China Normal University*, 1.
35. Wei, Tian'an. 1997. *Guild System History of Song Dynasty*, 1, 11. East Press.
36. Li, Shan. *Collection of Ode to the West Capital*, vol. 1.
37. Pan, Shuzhi. 1997. Market system of Jiang Nan village. *China Economic History Research*, 2.
38. Ye, Jingyi. 1999. Webber: Protestant ethics and capitalism spirit. *Journal of Peking University*, 4.
39. Max, Webber. 1997. *Konfuzianismus und Taoismus.* Translated by Hong Tianfu, 178. Jiangsu People's Press.
40. Chen, Keyu. 1995. On how Huizhou clan administrating. *China History Research*, 3.
41. Thomas, Hobbes. 1985. *Leviathan*, 100–102. Translated by Li Sifu, Li Yanbi. Commercial Press.
42. Yang, Zhen. 1997. *Contract Law in Common Law System*, 88. Peking University Press.
43. Hugh, T. Scogin Jr. 1994. *Between Heaven and the Man: Contract and the State in Han Dynasty China, in Observations of American Scholars on Chinese Legal Traditions*, ed. Gao Daoyun, et al., 192. China University of Political Science and Law.

44. Hiroaki, Tarada. 1994. Rights and unjustice: Civil procedural Laws. In *Civil Trial Contracts*, ed. by Wang Yaxin, Liang Zhiping, 192. Law Press of China.
45. Kong, Qingming, and Liuyuan, Hu. 1996. *Civil Law History of China*, 60. Jilin People's Press.
46. Zhang, Xuehui. 1998. The research on the agricultural lands in the border area in Ming and Qing Dynasty. *The Research of Chinese History*, 4.
47. Zheng, Yunrui. 1997. The Origin of Western contract. *Comparative Law Research*, 3.
48. Justinian. 1996. *Institutes*. Translated by Zhang Qitai, 174. Beijing: Commercial Press of China.
49. Wei, Qingyuan. 1993. The social functions of pawning industry in Qing Dynasty. *Political University History Journal of Taiwan*, 6.
50. Wei, Qingyuan. 1995. New findings of Ming and Qing Dynasties. China Social Science Press, 451.
51. Zhou, Shaoquan. 1992. *The classification of document in Huizhou. Social Science of Huizhou*, 2.
52. Kong, Qingming, and Liuyuan, Hu. 1996. *The History of Civil Law in China*, 20. Jilin People's Press.
53. Zhuang, Chuanxi. 1995. *Research on Qin and Han Dynasty*, 179. Peking University Press.

Chapter 3
Free Will and Lawfulness: Establishment and Related Issues

French socialist Emile Durkheim published the book *Division of Labor* in 1893, in which he stated that the opposing forces made human beings unite in mandatory cooperation for their existence. And the development of specialized labor division in human groups will inevitably lead to the dependent and cooperative relationship among people. In 1912, Durkheim reemphasized the same view on in his book *Elementary Forms of Religious Life*: A society can only exist when the condition of unity and cooperation is not harmed.[1] As is stated in the introduction of this book, Durkheim believes that western society is of an organic connection (unity) model which emphasizes people's individuality and uniqueness. On the one hand, labor division not only makes each individual work independently, but also generates dependent relationship among people; on the other hand, social norms as a kind of "collective body of conscience", which is a system of community reflecting beliefs, sentiments and emotions, regulate the positive connection among people for the necessary common interests of each individual. Durkheim's theory reflected the historical evolution of western contract theory from the sociological perspective. By reviewing comprehensively the ideological history of western contract law, it evolved through an evident process from liberalism to socialization, with "justice" as the mainline during the process. However, the notion "justice" in the freedom of contract emphasizes the security and realization of individual's rights and freedom; while the tendency of contract socialization rising in the end of nineteenth century strived to regulate the "free will" of people in the contract, and let them avoid damaging the interests of the society in realizing freedom, not to weaken or even break the "collective body of conscience" as proposed by Durkheim and lead to the social tragedy of "*Anomie*", for the sustained and stable development of the society and final realization of individual's freedom and rights. It is not hard to conclude that the social connection model of Durkheim has tints of "mutual adaption" theory by Charles Darwin. In 1871, Darwin emphasized in his book *The Descent of Man* that

[1]Quoted from Abram Kardiner and Edward Preble. 1988, in which "They studied man" was translated by Sun Kaixiang, SDX Joint Publishing Company, pp. 164, 165, 178.

Y. Liu, *The History of the Contractual Thoughts in Ancient China*,
https://doi.org/10.1007/978-981-15-5768-2_3

the physiological defects of man were the greatest wealth for human beings, which forced people to maintain a high degree of cooperation and let them go forward from community to society. In the book *Principles of Sociology*, Darwin pointed out that the social systems and customs generated by cooperation were the results of evolution, and they in turn became the motive power for human evolution. The conciliation of the two intrinsic instincts of egoism and altruism brought about the complex system and made individuals obey the group and common interests. At last, Darwin classified two types of society: one is the society dominated by "bellicose spirit", in which the connection of individuals is mandatory cooperation and social position is the foundation of social relations; the second is the "industrialized society", in which people cooperate of their own will and social contract functions as the regulator of social relations.[2] In comparison of the social connection model of Durkheim and social types of Darwin, there is a succeeding relationship between the theories of the two scholars. The reason for the description of the evolution theory and sociological theory above is that, the academic circle has always laid much stress on analyzing and evaluating the origin and evolution of western freedom of contract from the perspectives of legal philosophy, humanities (spirit) and economic liberalism, and ignored the perspective of sociology. One more important reason lies in the fact that ancient Chinese society has deliberate and detailed contract system, but we lack mature and systematic contract theory as in western society. We should not reverse the order of reason and result by believing that there is no humanistic spirits such as profound legal philosophy and economic liberalism as the guide, so there is no systematic contract theory. On the contrary, if we review the ancient Chinese contract system from the sociological perspective, we can sense the delicacy and innate energy in the traditional Chinese contract theory from the institutional perspective. This point is the logistic start of this chapter.

Free Will and Lawfulness: Contractual Justice and Social Justice in Run-In Period

If we try to find out consistent characteristics in contract law between eastern and western traditional societies, we can find out that free will and lawfulness are probably in accordance with the two developing trends: autonomy of will and contract socialization of western society respectively. The difference is that, Chinese ancient contract laid stress on the contract justice "free will" (autonomy of will) and the social justice "conforming to law" (contract socialization), and during run-in and interaction of the two forces, the distinctive contract system and contract theory system were formed.

The autonomy of will theory in western contract served as a historical motive power for the development and maturity of western contract theory. Its emergence and perfection highlighted individual's right consciousness in western contract theory

[2]ibid., pp. 23, 53–54, 60.

and strived to obtain extensive identification from the beginning. The background of the emergence of autonomy of will is manifested in the following aspects, and through investigating this point we can get the significant differences between Chinese ancient contract law and western contract law.

1. Theoretical foundation of legal philosophy. The Stoic school of philosophy was the first to demonstrate human "rationality" and "equality" from the perspective of natural law, and believed it is injustice to discriminate people for the difference in gender, social class, race or nationality. This view directly influenced the political philosophy and jurisprudence.[3] The footstone of western political and legal system lies in the view that man's idea of freedom derives from the idea of equality by nature. Immanuel Kant placed freedom as the core of morality and law, and classified freedom as moral freedom and legal freedom. And legal freedom means primary and intrinsic rights by nature, which is the manifestation of the idea of equality and means that each man is independent and the master of him.[4] Hegelianism believes that the great ideal of human historic movement is to realize freedom, which signifies that what individual possess is not the rights at one's own will, rather, is the rational freedom that can realize freedom with the precondition of respecting others' personality and rights. Therefore, Hegel advocated that as long as individual doesn't violate the interests of the whole society in exercising his right, the nation should endow its citizen with the rights of possessing private assets and concluding contracts freely.[5] English philosopher and socialist Herbert Spencer took freedom as the core of justice, and believed that the intrinsic instincts of egoism and altruism proposed by Darwin both have tints of justice. According to Darwin, the egoistic elements of justice push individual to obtain the utmost interests from his natural instincts and abilities; the altruistic elements of justice let every individual realize the fact: in exercising rights, other people with the same demand would pose restrictions. Based on this view, Spencer combined the two elements of justice into one: "law of equal liberty", with the essential idea that "each has freedom to do what he wills provided that he infringes not the equal freedom of any other." E. Bodenheimer explained it as "justice is that the freedom of each person can only be restricted by the same freedom of any other."[6] For this reason, Spencer believed that the government should not restrict individual freedom, but should improve it, restricting its activity within the range of executing contract and providing protection for the two parties concerned. Leonard Trelawney Hobhouse in the same era of Spencer was more close to the thought of freedom of contract. He believed that there were two definitions for freedom: first, freedom was a kind of doing things that would not harm any other; second, this kind of right was restricted in considering that others had the same right. Law as a means to achieve freedom should restrict any individual to do "all that he wills" to avoid causing the fear of

[3]Bodenheimer [1].

[4]ibid., p. 77.

[5]ibid., pp. 81–83.

[6]ibid., p. 95.

bringing about infringement or oppression to others. Derived from the function of law, Hobhouse believed that state has three functions: to protect the security of life and property; to maintain individual's right of labor and work; to establish public services. What the state strives for is justice rather than charity, namely, creating certain economic conditions to let citizens in physical and mental health to get ample food and clothing for themselves and families through their labor.[7] It is obvious that the Stoic school of philosophy and the notions of "freedom" and "justice" in legal philosophy have formed the philosophical and political basis for the theory of autonomy of will and offered great opportunity for the improvement of the theory.[8]

2. The Laissez-faire economics. To some extent, emergence of the bourgeoisie in the historical arena in seventeenth–eighteenth century was the outcome of social economic development, and this kind of social economy was generated by the thought of liberalism and laid a solid foundation for the economic mode for the current capitalism and finished the valuable primitive accumulation. It can be observed that, the uprising of western bourgeoisie was the outcome of city money (later became capital) overcoming feudal estate, city getting rid of feudal rule for autonomy, autocratic state replacing feudalism, and the notion of libertarianism and rationalism taking the place of class discrepancy.[9] The Laissez-faire economics of Adam Smith upheld libertarianism and rationalism, and in the meantime pushed the state's function of autocracy to democratization. What's more important, the Laissez-faire economics freed people from status society, let them be engaged in economic activities with independent property and personality, and treat each other as equal parties of the contract, thus the sensitive molding of freedom of contract and autonomy of will was accomplished. Later, induced by the history of legal thoughts of Henry Maine and improved by Pandekten of the Continental Europe, the complete theory of freedom of contract was formed and the principle "autonomy of will" became the soul of "private law".[10]
3. Humanism spirit and social contract theory. The essence of freedom of contract is the freedom of man himself, which includes not only liberating man from God's embrace, but also becoming a member of the society with independent will and abilities. These two kinds of freedom were established and matured with the help of humanism spirit and social contract theory in the western society. As is universally known that, in the Medieval Ages, human beings existed as member of one race, nationality, family or community. At that time there was the catholic doctrine "the one who belittles oneself will be respected by the God." The holy flame of humanism was first lit in Italy, which was the first to make man become "spiritual individuals",[11] and Martin Luther had the unprecedented statement,

---

[7]Qigang [2].

[8]Tian [3].

[9]Xu [4].

[10]Jingkun [5].

[11]*The Changes in Italian Renaissance*, the Commercial Press. 1979, p. 125.

"my faith has become free, thus I am free." He demonstrated repeatedly that each one is the subject of his spirit and the master of this faith. This independence of faith was the prelude of personality independence.[12] Hegel was content in evaluating the basic contents of religious reform, "man is destined to become free by depending himself."[13] Martin Luther dragged man to reality from the God; while social contract theory and democratic government system established by the humanistic masters like Locke, Montesquieu and Rousseau liberated man from the feudal autocratic regime and let man release glaring brilliance and amazing energy. The subjectivity perspective of the two views above laid a solid foundation for autonomy of will as the core of freedom of contract.[14]

Taking justice as the core idea, and equality and freedom as the means, western contract liberalism executed historical propelling force in molding the structure of liberal capitalist's economy, politics and culture. Taking western contract liberalism as a reference system, it is hard for us to find a same criterion for equality and freedom in ancient China. In terms of equality, the equality of personality is the precondition of commodity economy as well as the precondition of contract. Hegel stated in discussing the nature of contract, "Contract means the two parties concerned treat each other with direct and independent personality."[15] The value target that the idea of equality seeks for is that the two parties concerned of the contract have equal rights and duties in the content of the contract. As for the procedure of the contract, the two parties concerned are equal in personality, as well as in procedure interests.[16] In terms of freedom, the parties have their inborn right to establish rights and duties on their own will, and this right should not be deprived or infringed by any "public power". Thus the free will of man is not only the origin of rights and duties, but also the original basis for their emergence. Some scholars believe that the development history of western contract theory is the liberation history of man, in which contract liberated man from the status of god's servants and helped them to obtain independent personality; it is a sum-up of their understanding of the world.[17] Compared to the western society, the contract in Chinese ancient society also attaches importance to equality, but with totally different connotation. In the contract law in ancient Chinese society, equality in the official legal documents as well as the folk customs have the following two characteristics: the first one is equality in ethical sequence, namely, the subjects on the same ethical sequence can enjoy the same rights and undertake the same duties. This phenomenon is the shadow of feudal hierarchical order casting upon contract law. Western society holds a common view that property is a personality, however, traditional Chinese society forbade people from storing private property. For example, the Zheng family in Pujiang county of Zhejiang province which rose in

[12]Pingye [6].

[13]Hegel [7].

[14]Details can be found in the same book of footnote 3, Chapter Three, Section One.

[15]Hegel [8].

[16]Kaixiang and Jiagang [9].

[17]Renyu and Kaixiang [10].

the Jianyan period of Southern Song Dynasty and had experienced the three dynasties of Song, Yuan and Ming, had the family rule of all generations living together with common property and prohibiting private ownership. "For the descendent who privately purchases farmland as property and save money, as soon as their deeds are known, the other members will report them to the head of the family, then the head will call up all family members to the ancestral hall, beat the drums to announce their crimes and announce their crimes on the wall. Afterwards, the head will tell the close relatives and friends of the criminals and detain the criminals to the law court."[18] The inequality of old and young was not only in ethical ranks or law; but also in religious status and property disposition. The disposing and managing right of family properties was held by clan heads, family branch heads, and householders and the transaction activities should be approved with their personal signature before they have the legal validity. This phenomenon signifies that the establishment and validity of folk contract relationship should rely on the will of senior relatives of the family. The male managers' important power was evident in official legal documents. The law of Tang Dynasty and Song Dynasty regulated that, if the inferior young stored private properties would be flogged for ten beats for the property worth ten pi of silk, with every ten pi being flogged for another ten beats, the utmost punishment was one hundred beats.[19] The law of Ming Dynasty and Qing Dynasty regulated that, if they inferior young stored private properties would be flogged for thirty beats for each ten strings of 1000 cash, and with every ten strings being flogged for anther thirty beats, the utmost punishment were one hundred beats.[20] The male managers of each family had the same property disposing rights, however, the inferior young didn't have such rights. Once they acted beyond their authority and had private transactions, they would be harshly punished by regulations of the clan and the family, and even be punished by the state law. The law of Song Dynasty stated clearly that, "The descendent should not privately purchase or sell servants, livestock, farmland and houses and other properties when the family heads are present." The ones who violate the regulation and "those agents of the transactions will be seriously punished."[21] In special cases when the family heads were away in an enemy country or separated by warfare, the inferior young should first send application to the county government before disposing assets, and should not do transactions without the permission of the government. In forbidding the inferior young from privately having property transactions, the state law was in high consistency. It demonstrated a fact fundamentally: the inferior young didn't have property ownership nor free property disposition rights. In this sense, the heads of families were equal, and the inferior young were also "equal"

[18]*Categorization of Learnings* (Ancient Chinese book), the Vol. 34; *Zheng Wenrong: Regulations of the Zheng Family*.

[19]*Law Code of Tang Dynasty*, Volume 12, Law of Household and Marriage-About the Inferior Young Disposing Properties Privately; *Criminal Code of Song Dynasty*, Volume 12, Law of Household and Marriage, about the Inferior Young Disposing Properties Privately.

[20]*Law Code of Ming Dynasty*, Volume 4, Household Law and Household System, About the Inferior Young Disposing Properties Privately.

[21]*Criminal Code of Song Dynasty*, Vol. 13, Law of Household and Marriage, About Transaction of Properties.

to each other. It was the longstanding status that blocked the path for freedom of contract in Chinese society. "Freedom of contract and freedom of disposing properties are the motive power for freedom of operation and activation of individual's creativity and also provide living space for them."[22] The authority of clan elders impeded the freedom and rights of the inferior young, whose reliance on the clan discouraged their motives to seek for economic effects. When the inferior young took the position of elders with higher ranks after some years, they would enjoy their rights and in the meantime suppress and even prohibit the freedom and rights of their young descendent. The same thing circulated from generation to generation and becomes a unique phenomenon of the oriental society. The second characteristic of equality in traditional Chinese contract law is the equality of substantial interests, namely, the two parties concerned in the transaction get their corresponding interests with satisfying results after the transaction and no inequality occurs. This point will be discussed in this book later.

We should not say there is no freedom in ancient Chinese contract law. In a strict sense, the parties concerned of the contract would follow the willingness principle, in signing the contract or not, with whom to sign, and the conditions of the terms of the contract. The legal precondition of validity of the contract was also "approval by both parties" and "willingness of both parties". It is noticeable that, because of the status of the parties of the contract, freedom had very limited operation space, and equality in status would inevitably impede freedom.

It might be a little far-fetched to discuss freedom and equality in ancient Chinese contract law. However, if we analyze and judge from each cases and specified institution, we can find the implied value orientation, namely, ancient Chinese contract law had always been seeking for the internal unity of contract justice and social justice, rather than a period of western contract development history when only freedom of contract was sought for.

Free Will: Autonomy of Will and Declaration of Will

Autonomy of will, as derived from legal philosophy, means that the establishment of rights and duties with the range of contract should be decided by the free will of the two parties concerned of the contract. This kind of autonomy is based on the notion of natural law "everyone is born equal". In the contract relationship, the freedom of man, according to Hobbes, is a kind of right as well as duty, established jointly by the two parties of the contract. Furthermore, one should keep his promise because he himself has the duty based on his own behavior.[23] French scholar V. Gounot further elaborated on the freedom theory of Hobbes, and believed that freedom had two levels of meaning: first, the person concerned should not be restricted by the duties that he once hasn't approved; second, the person concerned should be restricted by

[22]Zweigert and Kotz [11].

[23]Sabine [12].

the duties that he offered to undertake. Based on this, Gounot explained the double meanings of autonomy of will: it implies not only that the person concerned has the freedom of establishing rights and duties for his own, but also he has the freedom of not establishing rights and duties.[24]

Law Reports of Southern Song Dynasty has the following comments: "families that want to purchase farmland and houses should follow the principles of lawfulness and free will."[25] The comment was plain with significant meanings. Since the Western Jin Dynasty and Eastern Jin Dynasty, contract had been called "hetong (consensus)" and "hetongqi (instrument of consensus)",[26] and through Northern and Southern Dynasty and Tang Dynasty, it was called "lianghe" and "Hetong".[27] In Song Dynasty, the name of "hetong" became regular, commonly used among the people and accepted by the government. The foremost essence of "hetong" was the "approved" and "free will" behavior by both parties of the contract, which signifies that the legal relationship of rights and duties established by the two parties concerned is the result of their mutual choice and decision. This point is close to the "autonomy of will" of the western society.

Contracts are the carrier and medium of free will of the two parties concerned in the contract, as well as a written testimony of establishing legal right and duty relationship by the two parties. One evident characteristic of ancient Chinese civil law, administrative law and criminal law is endeavoring to protect the transaction between the parties in the contract under free will, and taking "willingness without being compelled" as the precondition for the effectiveness and validity of the transaction. By reviewing the ancient contracts in China throughout the history, they all had the same words of "willingness of both sides", from Tang to Qing Dynasty. There are similar fixed expressions in the contracts in Tang Dynasty: "making finger marks to signify contract of both parties", "both parties are equal", and "it is forbidden to go back on one's words". In investigating the land pawning in border areas of Ming and Qing Dynasties, Zhang Xuehui showed three contracts in the periods of emperors Kangxi (1622–1722 A.D.), Qianglong (1736–1795 A.D.) and Jiaqing (1976–1820 A.D.) respectively, and demonstrated that the expressions in the contracts such as "it is approved with willingness and the two parties were not forced to sign the contract", and "it is commonly accepted without any suppression" were similar in different places. This proves the importance of free will of the two parties.[28]

A completed contract is composed of offer and acceptance, which was specified by many scholars, hence the author will not analyze in details in this section. According to the characteristics of ancient Chinese contract, we will take two systems with characteristics of a tender contract as an example, the "priority property purchasing

[24]See footnote 8, pp. 18, 13.

[25]*Law Reports of Southern Song Dynasty* (*1127–1279 A.D.*), compiled and printed by Teaching and Research Section of Legal History, Southwest University of Political Science & Law in 1985, p. 104.

[26]Zhimin [13].

[27]Qingming et al. [14].

[28]Xuehui [15].

system for relatives and neighborhoods" and "auction system", and analyze in details the elements of a complete contract.

The first one is *Invitation to offer or Invitation to Treat*. Relatives and neighborhoods enjoyed the priority in purchasing property in ancient Chinese society, the priority property purchasing system for relatives and neighborhoods guaranteed the pre-emption rights for the relatives and neighborhoods. In this system, the proprietor would present a written document containing the details of the property for sale, and invited relatives and neighborhoods with pre-emption right to decide whether to purchase or not. The behavior is called "setting up an account".

There are two accounts of invitation made in the years of 1265 and 1366 (both in Yuan Dynasty) as following[29]:

[1] The properties of one garden, one gazebo, one hill, and one house, etc. locating in East County in Jinjiang belongs to Mahe, who had these properties by inheritance. Now the owner intents to sell these properties at the price of 150 silvers, anyone who is interested can set up a price for further negotiation.

For the purpose of making a credit, this invitation is made.

Time of invitation: July, 1265.

Seller: Mahe

Witnesses: Mahe's neighbors

Notary officer: Huang Longzu

Signatures of those who are not interested: Guhulushe, Gubibi, Guamida, Shuhusamading.

[2] The properties of one mountain with fruit trees locating in East County in Jinjiang belongs to Pu Ayou, who had these properties by inheritance. Now the owner has spent his money in reckless way and entrust the official to sell these properties, anyone who is interested can set up a price for further negotiation, those who are not interested shall clear their intention too.

For the purpose of making a credit, this invitation is made.

Time of invitation: August, 1366

Seller: Pu Ayou

Signatures of those who are not interested: Zeng Da, Pan Da.

One of the two account documents refers to priority purchasing or rejecting for relatives and the other refers to priority purchasing or rejecting for neighborhoods over live-sale of real estate. Signature and cross signed by lot-rejecter illustrates the importance of the account documents. It is worth noting that Mahe marked the price clearly on the account while Pu Ayou did not mark the price of the mountain for sell. It seems that price under Mahe's bid can also conclude a transaction, and there is some leeway for bargaining from the literal meaning of his invitation. Pu Ayou's invitation for mountain neighbors to offer price is similar to auction without reserve price. Thus, both of them have the nature of invitation to offer. They will not go to accept stage if relatives reject the invitation, but if their relatives purchased the property, the invitation would have the nature of an offer, and it can be deemed as

[29] See footnote 27, pp. 470–471.

acceptance when the proprietor approves it. Proprietor's dissent about the price can generate a new offer, the buyer's consent is acceptance, and so forth until the deal is closed. Propriety for relatives and neighborhoods over live-sale of real estate has been formed into a fixed model since Tang Dynasty, but unfortunately, we do not have the chance to take a look at the original contract documents. We can understand the overall content by referring to these two documents in Yuan Dynasty.

The second one is offer. Relatives and neighbors' pricing has the nature of offer. It was no later than Song Dynasty that the integrated competitive contract system existed in ancient Chinese contracts. These systems can be classified into two categories[30]: one is "seal and submit" system for renting out or selling state lands; and the other is "auction system" for assigning the state's managerial authority of commerce. The so-called "seal" means that the written document should be hermetic, and "submit" means that the bidder or lessee shall submit the written document about terms and conditions of purchase or tenancy to the seller or lessor. In August of the first year of Emperor Huizong, Song Dynasty (1119 A.D.), the imperial edict commanded that, apart from those already occupied and cultivated by people, lands generated after the water recede in Zhexi County as well as abandoned lands, wasteland, grassland and mud-land shall be measured with Mu*. The acreage, boundary and location of the land shall be defined and registered. Each piece of land is named after one character from Thousand-Character Classic respectively**. Rental and tax for those lands are slightly lower than that of neighboring lands. The "seal and submit" process lasts for one hundred days, during which people can submit hermetic documents for renting. These documents would be unglued at the expiry, and the land would be rented to the person who offered the highest price. Each tenant would receive a document recording all the information of the land, such as the quality, acreage, boundary, location, rental and tax. The lessee should apply for government's approval and make title deed if he would like to pawn or sell the land in future.[31] This imperial edict indicates that the competitive contract processes with nature of bid are as follows: first, the government issues a public notice with the basic information and the least rental and tax of the subject matter of the contract. It has the nature of auction with reserve and can be deemed as "invitation to offer"; second, the lessee offers a competitive price in the form of hermetic document before deadline, and this can be called "bid" or offering stage; third, the government unglues the documents and picks out the one who offered the highest price and then rents the land to him, and this step is called "award of bid", namely, the accept stage.

The third one is acceptance. Let's take auction (as "pumai" in Chinese) as an example. Auction means that buyers offer competitive price respectively, and the person offered the highest price eventually get the subject matter. Here is an example about the proclamation of Si nong si*** of Xining, Song Dynasty: "the management

---

[30]Jinfan and Chengwei [16].

[31]*The Compilation of Song Dynasty, National Economy*, 63:195.

*Translator's annotation: Mu is a unit of area, and one Mu is about the acreage of 667 m^2.

**Translator's annotation: Thousand-Character Classic is an article with one thousand different characters written by an official named Zhou Xinsi according to the demand of Emperor Wu of Liang in Southern Dynasty.

right of wine workshop and similar industries shall be retrieved by the government at the expire." The government calls for bids beginning with private dealing price half year ago in downtown areas. People who want to buy the subject matter shall "seal and submit" to the box locked and controlled by government during two months. The government will unglue the documents at the expiration and sell the subject matter to the person offering the highest price. The subject matter will be sold to the prior bidder if there exists the same price offering. The buyer can contribute rental in three steps, one step a year.[32] This is a legislation draft with respect to calling for bids over state-own industrial and commercial management rights. The process is similar to that of renting out state-own lands, namely, the government calls for bids beginning with the private dealing price and then bidders offer their competitive bidding. Bidders put their documents into the box in two months. At expire, government will "unlock the box, unglue the sealed documents and sell the subject matter to the person offered the highest price."[33] This is the process of "award of bid" or acceptance. Meanwhile, if there are bidders offering the same price, the fair treating method is selling the subject matter to the prior bidder.

There remain two questions to be illustrated: What is the historical cause of "reach agreement rely on go-between", means the reliance of offering stage in ancient Chinese contracts on go-between's introduction? How to determine the effective time of contracts?

Let's begin with the question about "reach agreement relying on go-between". Go-betweens played vital roles in the conclusion, performance and dispute solutions in ancient Chinese contracts. They acted as media to send messages and started the preclusion of the transaction between the parties before they enter into a contract. We can say that "go-betweens" are required according to both laws and practices from prompt dealing or transaction to block trade in ancient times. When exploring its historical cause, a Japanese scholar Kishmoto Mio believes that "go-betweens" system was originated from the particular relational bonds and etiquette standards in daily life, and was established on the mutual trust in individual personality. This system has dense feudal ethics characteristic. Thus, Kishmoto Mio considered the contracting process in ancient China as "a mixture of ethics and morality and utilitarian trading".[34] In fact, go between system still has the characteristic of pure economic behaviors apart from ethics presented by Kishmoto Mio, such as exploring the market conjuncture, balancing interests of both parties, and undertaking the testify obligation over disputes.

The second question is about the effective time of those contracts. There are two ways to define the effective time according to laws in Song Dynasty: first, contracts are entered into upon being stamped by official based on formal contract principle;

---

[32] *Supplementary Notes of Comprehensive Mirror to Aid in Government*, Vol. 220.

[33] ibid., 32, Chapter 217.

[34] Kishimoto Mio, *Civil Society and China.* See Yaxing and Zhiping [17].

***Translator's annotation: Si nong si is an official title in ancient China, and it governs grain reserving affairs, but basically became an idle organization in the late Tang Dynasty in the fourth year (1071 A.D.).

second, they are entered into on the delivery date of subject matter. The former is principle when the latter is exception. According to legal provision in Song Dynasty cited in Qing Ming Ji****: Court shall bring in a verdict or intercession referring to title deed if one of the parties prosecutes upon disputes about acreage of the land after the title deed is made; and the longest term of protection for real estate pawning is twenty years, beginning from the effective date of contracts. However, the delivery date would be considered as effective date if the parties deliver subject matter after the title deed is made.

Default of the Expression of Meaning and Its Remedies

Both ancient Roman law and ancient Chinese Contract Law praise highly of "formalism". They focus on the standards that whether the legal forms and procedures are complied with by conclusion and performance of contracts, instead of paying attention to default in meaning expressing. The law prohibits actions such as fraud and duress that damage the facticity, integrality and freedom of expression of meaning for "morality" or "commonweal" purpose, not because of its illegality or the purpose to protect the private right of autonomy of will in concluding contracts. The principle of true and free expression of meaning was established in *French Civil Code* in western society, Article 1108 of which provides that, "the contract is null and void if the parties acknowledged that it is concluded due to misunderstanding, fraud or duress." Though there was no deep and detailed theory of meaning expressing in Song Dynasty, there were some provisions in legal documents and Customary Law regulating the parties' expression of meaning. Thus disputes arisen from defective expression of meaning could be corrected, the performance of the contract could be accepted, the interests of both parties could be balanced and the illegal doer of fraud, simulation, duress, undue influence and ethics violation could be punished. The following part will demonstrate furtherly.

The first is fraud. It refers to counterfeiting and modifying contracts illegally or enticing descendants to conduct such actions and deceive the relatives who have priority of purchasing. It is prohibited by civil customs and punished severely by the government. Verdicts in Qing Ming Ji cited a lot of cases, many of which are "counterfeit" and "illegal" transactions. Here are some examples. In a case, Huang Guizi and Yang Digong imposed several deals on one piece of land. Yang asserted that there was a grave of his family in that piece of land and claimed priority to redeem based on priority for relatives and neighborhoods. In another case, Huang Zongzhi attempted to occupy the land through a fake title deed. He was then held "to be flogged for one hundred beats, return the real title deed and destroy the fake one". Li Dingfu, together with other five persons, committed "entice descendants to sell properties" and seduced Sun sold fields without his mother's consent. In this case, Li Dingfu and the persons involved were held "gaining property illegally, enticing the descendants and infringing others' property rights", and were penalized in the light of attempted larceny, being banished, imprisoned or flogged.[35] As for fraud, it refers to doing business secretly and disregarding priority for relatives and neighborhoods. Take one case in Yuan Dynasty as an example. In October of the first year in Yuan Dynasty (1308), "A Tie Jun Hu in Guanzhou County named Zhang Zhu sued a Zheng Jun named Zhou Yuan for selling 53 Mu lands to another person Zhou Er disregarding his priority for purchasing.*****. Ministry of Rite****** held it was a deal violating legal provisions and ordered Zhang Zhu redeems the piece of land at the same price."[36] Fraud is not only regulated by legal provisions, but also be looked down on by government and populace. Zhen Dexiu, a citizen in Song Dynasty, has ever heard a case: a businessman named Yan Wenlong consigned his money in the hands of Li Si and Li Qiwu, and they recorded each deposit and withdraw as evidence. However, Li Si and Li Qiwu attempted to embezzle his property. Yan sued to the court, claiming to regain his property. Zhen Dexiu thought it was a case of felony in which the rich people rode roughshod over the vulnerable people and decided that Li Si and Li Qiwu be flogged one hundred beats and return the property they had embezzled.[37] In cases mentioned above, the buyer and seller did not negotiate about the transaction, or just ran counter to their families, relatives or neighbors' will. "Mutual consensuses" reached by both parties based on their negotiation also requires that both parties conclude the contract with good faith, and fraud is prohibited. This point can be concluded from civil contracts and government documents from Han Dynasty to the Republic of China (1912–1949). The parties attach warranty clauses to the contract, explaining the sauce, quantity, quality of the subject matter and conditions about whether it is assumed with priority for relatives and neighborhoods or overlapped transactions. The circumstance of seller's fraud would be discussed in detail later.

The second is simulation. Simulation means forging fake contracts, redeeming or selling property in other person's name. For instance, Jiang Wenhui was held "simulatedly" for redeeming farmlands of a relative passed away without contract beyond the time limitation. Huang Gongshi******* forged a title deed recording the acreage of the farmland and attempted to steal and sell his nephew's real estate secretly with this fake title deed. He was described as "heartless" and "injustice" by the government. The buyer and guarantor involved in this case were flogged.[38] People who use other's identity would also be punished. For example, Dong Sanba was flogged for eighty beats for asserting himself as posthumous child of Han Zhichen. Chen Yaxing was flogged for asserting himself as posthumous child of Sun Hua because his mother has ever been Sun's servant girl. Xiao Zhensun came to Yao Yue's family at five years old when his mother remarried Yao Yue. Zhensun changed

[35]Footnote 25, pp. 102–103, 95–96, 81–82, 34–35.

****Translator's annotation: Qing Ming Ji is a corpus about court verdicts and state documents in Song Dynasty. It is a valuable resource in studying the history of Song Dynasty.

[36]Cite from footnote 27, p. 504.

[37]*The Enlightened Judgements*, Chapter 11.

[38]See footnote 25, pp. 103–104, 97.

his family name after Yao was dead and thus embezzled Yao's property. He was flogged and ordered to return the property to Yao's family, etc.[39]

The third is duress. Duress means compelling the proprietor or the third party to act against his real will. The purpose of prohibiting duress is to guarantee the safety of transaction and to protect interests of both Parties. According to a case recorded in *Zhe Yu Xin Yu*********. Tong Yingfeng's father concluded a contract to sell a house when he was alive. Yingfeng colluded with borough and go-between and compelled the buyer to pay extra silver, but the buyer agreed to pay half of it. The parties could not reach an agreement and sued to the court. The elderly buyer committed suicide with poison under the duress of borough warden and go-between. The court decided that Tong Yingfeng, together with borough warden and go-between be flogged and awarded damages to the Buy's son. Duress was named "gaining unpeacefully" officially in Tang Dynasty. The *Law Code of Tang Dynasty* noted that: "gaining unpeacefully includes intimidation, deception and extortion". According to legal provisions, all the public or private objects gained by stealing, looting, deceiving and extorting are illegally gained objects. Fructus of original objects are defined as booty, which shall be returned to state or proprietor together with the illegally gained objects. As for cows or horses or something of the same kind, shall be returned to proprietor together with fructus. If the original object is destroyed, the proprietor shall be awarded damages. This is to keep the stability of trading activities. Laws in Ming Dynasty provided that "The government and military shall not disturb the populace or take over their objects for use. Where there is a need for requisition, the government shall compensate the proprietor according to the current price. Government shall pay promptly after purchasing goods from merchants. People who bargains would be punished."[40] It demonstrates that state pays attention its behavior when regulating public trading activities with the purpose to do business with free will and fair principle.

The forth is undue influence. It refers to concluding contracts with the proprietor at unfair price when the proprietor is trapped in trouble. The direct purpose of undue influence is to take properties from proprietor. The court accepts and hears this kind of cases with the aim to protect interests of the weak. For instance, Fan Dayou was getting old and infirm and was near his end, when his clansman Fan Yu embezzled his property and instigated other clansmen to divide up his possessions with the excuse of being his representative. Cai Zhongjie described it as "undue influence" in

---

[39]See footnote 27, p. 458.

*****Translator's annotation: Zheng Jun Hu and Tie Jun Hu are authorized strength of troops in Yuan and Ming Dynasty. Two to three families pick out one person to join the army while other families just provide some subvention for them. Families provide soldiers are called Zheng Jun Hu, while families provide subvention are called Tie Jun Hu.

******Translator's annotation: Ministry of Rites is an official department in feudal China.

*******Translator's annotation: Gongshi refers to people who attend the central imperial examinations in ancient China.

********Translator's annotation: this is the only remaining corpus of verdicts of civil and criminal cases in Ming Dynasty.

[40]*Supplementary Notes of Comprehensive Study of the Written Record*, Chapter 25, *shi.*《市》.

the verdict, and noted that it was extremely immoral for clansmen to embezzle Fan Dayou's property shortly after he passed away. The court imposed severe punishment on them as a warning to others. Fan Yu was flogged for one hundred beats and all the people who have ever taken Fan Dayou's property were named to be punished. In another case, Hong Baisi was ill and has already had one foot in the grave but could not afford a funeral. Hong's neighbor Zhang Guangrui has been keeping his eyes on Hong's real estate for a relatively long time. He instigated his son concluded a contract in the name of his son-in-law. Zhang colluded with Hong Baisi's elder brother Hong Baisan, and attempted to kill Hong Baisi' son but failed. The attempt murder was prosecuted by Hong Baisi's step son Zhou Qian'er. Zhou asserted that Zhang Guangrui "scared his father to death". Wu Andao held that Zhang Guangrui, as well as his son and son-in-law was guilty, and ordered Zhang return the property to Hong's family. Zhang was sentenced imprisonment as punishment.[41] Though Wu's verdict was not fair enough, it showed state's attitude towards undue influence in public transactions.

Methods to remedy default of the expression of meaning are as follows in ancient China:

First, punish according to the Criminal Law. The wrong party shall be flogged with whip, flogged with stick, sentenced to prison or sent into exile to prohibit such bad transactions to the ground.

Second, return the original items. *Law Code of Tang Dynasty* noted that all the public or private objects gained by stealing, looting, deception and extorting are illegally gained objects. Fructus of original objects are defined as booty, which shall be returned to state or proprietor together with the illegally gained objects. Zhangsun Wuji defined blackmails into two categories in Law Code of Tang Dynasty, duress and inducement, and commanded the items be returned to the proprietor. The items shall be returned to the original proprietor though the titles of the crimes are different. The returning of illegally gained items shall comply with this provision.[42] The fructus of the original items shall be returned to proprietor as well, even if the occupier had added additional value to them. For instance, in the case of stealing and selling or staling and cultivating state-own or private farmlands, the farmlands as well as crops attached to them shall be returned to the state or original proprietor. If the parties sell and buy farmlands without the official documents, then the land, money and crops attached to the field shall be awarded to the proprietor. Zhangsun Wuji noted in Law Code of Tang Dynasty that crops here include plants and fruits.[43] Such principle was widely obeyed in cases with default of the expression of meaning, cases with infringement and cases about cultivating grave land and so on.

Third, confiscate the money and goods. Confiscating money and goods to national treasury according to the circumstance of the case in which both parties are in fault is a main solution method to regulate market activities. It is unfair though effective. Moreover, solving civil disputes with administrative means is unreasonable compared

[41] See footnote 25, pp. 40, 67.

[42] *Law Code of Tang Dynasty*—Example 4.

[43] ibid.—Marriage Law.

with the provisions in western Contrary Law. The case of Zhang Guangrui was of this characteristic.

Forth, warrant for contracts. Contract in ancient China praised highly of warranty clauses demonstrating that the contract was entered into based on consensus by both parties. The purpose was to avoid disputes. Remedies relied on government level were the last process of relief. We will take the important conditions in the contract required by seller as an example to illustrate the prevention mechanism in ancient contract.

The warranties in ancient Chinese contract could be divided into two categories: guarantee and earnest money. Guarantee can be divided in detail as guarantee by people and guarantee by property. Guarantee by people is the pure warranty which means a Third Party guarantees to the creditor. The Third Party assumes obligation to pay back completely or partially if the debtor did not fulfill his obligations. This kind of warranty can be continually divided into two categories: suretyship and guaranty. The former means creditor can only request the guarantor to pay back when debtor did not fulfill his obligations; while the latter means that creditor can ask the Third Party to perform his duty directly. Warranties in ancient Chinese contract usually belong to the former, namely, the suretyship. Here is a warranty clause recorded in the unearthed relics in Dun Huang[44]:

> Two Shuo and five Dou of wheat is loaned to Dongsa Clan for their lack of grain in June, Yin year. *********Wheat of the same quantity shall be returned by August. The clan's property would be claimed if there is no returning at expire. The guarantor needs to pay back if debtor is not able to perform his obligations. Both parties concluded with good faith. This contract is made in duplicate.

It is clearly stated that the guarantor shall assume the responsibility to pay back the wheat only when debtor could not perform such obligation.

It is worth noting that debtor's family members became guarantors unconditionally from the beginning to the end. Here is another example: Straw Dealing Contract Concluded by Zuo Chongxi in the First Year of Zong Zhang, Yuan Dynasty (668 A.D.)[45]:

> Zuo Chongxi in Chonghua County bought neighty bundles of straw with forty strings of cash from Zhang Pan in Shunyi county on June, 3rd, 668. If Zuo did not get the straw at expire, Zhang shall return sixty strings of cash to Zuo. If Zhang did not return the money, his wife and children as well as the guarantor shall assume the responsibility. This contract is concluded with consensus. Finger marks are made to signify the good faith of both parties.

This is a contract for purchase with earnest money being paid in advance. People who made finger marks include the Seller, Buyer, guarantor and the witness. Debtor's wife and children shall assume joint liability though they were not attached to the contract. There were a large quantity of terms of this kind.

In addition, guarantee by people did not require independent contract in ancient China, instead, it only requested guarantors sign and make finger marks on the contract.

---

[44]*Dunhuang File* (Series I), Zhonghua Book Company, 1961, p. 353.

[45]Unearthed Documents in Turfan (Vol. 6), Culture Relics Press, p. 424.

Guarantee by property means that debtor take his or other's property as the pawn to perform his obligations. Taking loan contracts as an example, the debtor was requested to provide pawn, called "guarantee acquisition". The creditor can also appoint debtor's personal estate or real estate as pawn. This is called "pawn appointment". Here is an example[46]:

> Teacher Bu in Ningchang County borrowed ten pennies from Wei Feng on January, 28th, 665. The interest is one penny per month. Bu shall return the principal and interest to Wei Feng when he commands. If the debtor did not return the money, his wife and children shall assume the liability. This Contract is concluded based on consensus. Finger marks are made to signify good faith of both parties.

It is provided clearly by some contracts that the debtor could not gain the fructus generated from the pawn. Fructus shall be given to creditor as interests of the principal. In loan contract concluded by Zheng Haishi in the first year of Qian Feng, Tang Dynasty (666 A.D.)[47]:

> Zheng Haishi in Chonghua County borrowed money from Zuo Chongxi on April, 26th, 666. Zheng shall return the principal to Zuo when he commanded. Zheng's items and farmlands are independent from other burdens. If the debtor could not pay back the principal, his wife and children shall assume the responsibility. Laws are promulgated for government to obey, while contracts are concluded for civilians to observe. This Contract is concluded based on consensus of both Parties with their finger marks signed.

It has been formed as practice to guarantee with debtor's property as pawn in loan contracts. The government consents this practice provided that the creditor takes over debtor's property after decision of the court and take the property according to the amount of loan. Property taken by creditor exceeding the loan will be deemed as theft. *Law Code of Tang Dynasty* provided that "creditor ought to sue to the court if there is a need to take over debtor's property. If the creditor takes debtor's property such as servants or poultries without suing, he will be charged with theft".[48] Subsequent legislative spirit coincides with this point. For example, laws in Ming Dynasty provided that "people who take over debtor's property without suing shall be flogged for eighty beats. If creditor takes more than the principal, the extra portion shall be returned to the debtor".[49]

There are little mortgage contracts. Here is an example of Loan Contract of Wheat Concluded by Peng Shunzi[50]:

> Peng Shunzi in Pingkang County borrowed two Shuo of wheat and two Shuo of millet from Gao Tongzi on May, 16th. Peng shall return four Shuo of wheat and four Shuo of millet to Gao by Autumn. Peng pledged with a petticoat. If Peng could not pay back the wheat

---

[46]ibid., p. 526.

*********Translator's annotation: Shuo and Dou are both volume units in ancient China. One Shuo equals to 59.4 l and one Dou is one-tenth of Shuo. "Two Shuo and five Dou wheat" weighs about 110 kg converted to modern units.

[47]ibid., p. 417.

[48]*Criminal Code of Song Dynasty*, Chapter 26, quoted from Law Code of Tang Dynasty.

[49]*Law Code of Ming Dynasty*, Law of Household.

[50]*Dunhuang File* (Series VI)—Contract Documents.

and millet, he shall give the petticoat to Gao in the presence of his wife and nephew. This Contract is concluded as testimony.

The "pledge" contract is like The Pledge Contract on the Wheat of Baiceng Ding in the fourth year of Xian Zong in Tang Dynasty (659)[51]:

> On December 21st of the fourth year of Xian Zong of Tang Dynasty (659.A.D.), Bai Sengding, from the countryside Chong Hua, borrowed the wheat of 40 Dou from Wangcai Huan of the countryside Wu Cheng, by the method that Wangcai Huan could work the land of 2 acres owned by Baiceng Ding. The borrower Baiceng Ding gave the wheat of 40 Dou back to the lender Wangcai Huan who could not work the land of Baiceng Ding any more. After two years, if Baiceng Ding could not give the wheat back, the ownership of the land of 2 acres would be gotten by Wangcai Huan forever. The two parties thus made the pledge contract, it will be effective and credible with finger marks made thereon.

The contract ostensibly seems to be a pledge contract in which one uses one thing as the pledge to exchange for another thing, but its distinctive point lies in the fact that it contains the pawn relation. The lenders don't charge for the interest and the people who are responsible for the loan don't collect the rental. While the land is given back, the duty is given back. It has had the typical right and obligation relations of pawn contract. Expect personal guarantee and material guarantee, during ancient times, there were still institutions such as reducing debts by the labor of themselves, slaves and livestock, which meant that they covered the debts with the labor of their own, their slaves and maid-servants and their livestock. Li Zhimin has made substantial and credible discourses on this point, which can be a supplementary reference for interested audience.[52]

With respect to guaranty contract on advance payment, during ancient times of China, it was called "□", commonly known as "front money", whose rules and procedures were similar to today's. In addition, it also has the same property with the certificate for the contract, liquidated damages of the advanced payment and penalties. Due to space limitations, I'm not going to try to cover all that here.

About the guaranty content, please see the next section for more details.

Lawfulness: Guarantee of Social Justice

The Article 1108 of *French Civil Code* rules as follows: the formation of a contract has to meet four conditions, namely, the consent of the party, the contractual capacity of the party, the subject matter and the legal cause. According to Anglo-American law of Contract, an effective contract should have the essential elements as follows: the offer and acceptance; the consideration or the formal escrow; the parties have the intent to establish legal relations; the parties have the contractual capacity; the declaration of intention had authenticity and consistency, the contractual subject

[51] See footnote 27, pp. 307–307.

[52] See footnote 26, pp. 138–140.

matter must be lawful.[53] In the case of Chinese contracts, the lawfulness not only provides guarantee for the freedom realization of rights, but also places limitations on the rights and freedom, if the true value pursuit of the meeting of minds is complete freedom of contract, which means that the law allows the parties to freely pursue the lawful rights. In short, for the contract law of ancient China, the ultimate goal of the lawfulness is not to meet the wants of personal freedom of rights, but to stipulate the personal behavior so as to make it in conformity with the procedures of the whole social benefit. What the lawfulness pursues is the social justice and not contractual justice which are paid much attention on by the meeting of minds any more.

During the history of western contractual development, the concept that the contract meant the freedom, and the contract meant the justice covered almost two centuries until the end of the nineteenth century. The justice or freedom of contract was gradually substituted by the contractual socialization trend. The original holy brilliance of personal freedom, personal rights and personal ownership were washed off in the socialization tide. The legal lock of social justice was also attached to the contractual justice. In comparison, thousands of years' contractual cultural history of China seemed to be always between the contractual justice and the social justice. The country and government always regarded the interests of rulers as the leading factor, on this premise, complemented by the increase of personal interests and the satisfaction of desires. As the traditional China which didn't break the shackles of identity all along, the contractual freedom was always like the rare bird in the cage and it was difficult for it to fly in the sky. It was a kind of pity. But we have to admit that it is just the mutual friction between the contractual justice and social justice that makes the brilliant Chinese nation stably go forward from generation to generation and maintains the social stability and inherent traditional culture by the distinctive contractual culture. From the perspective of utilitarians, China did lag behind during recent almost three hundred years in the world history and the past glories of Five Thousand Years of Civilization had also become a kind of burden. However, judging from the current situation, we can't throw this culture whose sedimentary accretion has remained for thousands of years into the Pacific and then recreate or transplant a kind of completely new culture. On this account, it seems to be wise to evaluate the traditional culture in an objective and calm way. Studying and finding the contact law in ancient China should also be treated like this. If we only blindly compare the western mature contractual theory with the Chinese careless contractual theory, it is undoubtedly to compare our own disadvantages with the other party's advantages. It finally turns out to be a sigh to our own culture and not the reform.

The "lawfulness" of the contract law in ancient China reflects in three aspects of relevant provisions, including the contractual subject matter, the contractual capacity, the contractual forms, which are respectively discussed as follows:

The first one is the subject matter. There are many tradable things in ancient contracts, but for the public benefit, the national security and maintaining the feudal moral human relations, many personal estates and real estate cannot or are be limited to go into markets as contractual subject matters. It can be separated into five types

[53]Zhen [18].

as follows: (1) The weapon. The weapon may be the tool for criminal purposes. It will not only disturb the social security, but also endanger the country rule. Thus, all the past dynasties make strict stipulations on the weapons trade. The strictest one is to stipulate for prohibition of weapons passing "Across Border" which means going into the surrounding minority tribes. The Han Dynasty law specifies: "In Hu City, both officials and civilians with armament or iron are banned to pass across border. Even though it is bought in the capital city, the law applies everywhere."[54] In Tang Dynasty, it was expressly ruled that anyone who took weapon, gold, silver, iron, coin and silk or any else like that were forbidden to pass across the border in the west and the north.[55] In the April of the fifth year of Dazhong Period of Emperor Xuanzong, Tang Dynasty (851 A.D.), it was ruled that at the border, it was forbidden to trade weapons for the consideration that the weapons could do harm to the society.[56] (2) The fete matter, including the graveyard. It was closely related to ethic, thus related rules were made in the folk under the production of the government. At the end of Qing Dynasty, rule of Xian Family's ancestral temple in Lingnan Region wrote: "ancestral temple, the ancestor's grave and heritage is the fundaments of a clan." Under this condition, since antiquity, clan regulations and ancestral temple's rules have strictly forbidden to sell ancestral grave and land to other clans and to be embezzled by others. "Only if such forbiddances concur, our clan would intolerably dislodge the conductor out of the clan and inform the government."[57] In the year of Guangxu Period, Qing Dynasty, Family Sun rule stipulated that "Those who steals and sells ancestor's grave and heritage shall be expelled, so it is the same with the ones who steals and sells the grave stones and trees". (3) The nation's monopoly on gold, silver, copper, iron, salt, tea and vinegar etc., and the common civil entities were not allowed to trade. In the year of Jianzhong of Dezong Period, Tang Dynasty (780 A.D.), it was clearly stipulated that the natural resources belonged to the State, and should be administrated by a national special officers.[58] Han Hui, Deputy Minister of Ministry of Revenue, submitted official document and said: "the brass and copper are the natural resources, it's illegal for a local officer to handle, but shall be administrated by a national special officers".[59] Take the industry of salt as another example: Wang Jing in Renzong of Song Dynasty once stated that since Tang Dynasty, the salt from lake has been taken benefits to nearly half of the state.[60] Before the mid-Tang Dynasty, salt industry was privately operated and salt trader had to pay salt tax to the state. After mid-Tang Dynasty, the government took the policy of monopolizing

---

[54] *Hanshu*, Vol. 50 and 90.

[55] *Tang Huiyao*, Vol. 86.

[56] *Collection of Tang Dynasty Imperial Edicts and Orders*, Vol. 130.

[57] Genealogy of Family Wei in Yanbu Village of Shangyu Vol. 14 Twenty-four Family Precepts, Quoted from Fei Chengkang: Family Law and Clan Doctrines of China, Shanghai Academy of Social Sciences Press, 1998 (the content of the family law and clan doctrines which is not marked belongs to this book).

[58] *Tang Huiyao*, Vol. 87.

[59] *Old History of the Tang Dynasty*, Vol. 129.

[60] *Supplementary Notes of Comprehensive Mirror to Aid in Government*, Vol. 1.

salt, and sky-high monopoly prices brought about illegal operators mounting. "It was really hard to extinct the illegal traders of salt."[61] At the same time, with local protectionism taken into consideration, the government forbade the inflow of foreign similar product into local market from the border, and the outflow of local superior products into other regions. For example, during Wang Jing's occupancy in Sichuan (891 A.D.), "superior silks made in Shuguo but not the inferior is banned to outflow into Central Plains of China, which is called 'rucaowu' (the outflow of rough goods) by the local people."[62] (4) The public property of clan. The inflow of public property of clan into the market shall subject to related procedures, among which male seniors of clan hold a key position. Such as jitian, yitian, xuetian all called "public land" are publicly-owned by clan and are forbidden to sell. "Jitian (a land used to sacrifice ancestors) is to bring benefits to descendants… The one who privately sells jitian will be charged by clan and clan will inform ancestors about the crime. That person thus will be forbidden to step into ancestral temple and his name will be dislodged from the genealogy."[63] "The stone graved the name and area of public land erecting at the gate of ancestral temple reminds descendants to protect public land generation to generation. Anyone who proposes to pledge public land is regarded as the unfilial",[64] "The one who steals and sells public land will be punished in accordance with law, and that piece of land will be judged to be a public land again".[65] (5) The unqualified products are forbidden to trade in the market, which is expressly stipulated during the period of western Zhong Dynasty. Also in *The Rites of Zhou* expressly ruled: "fakes and counterfeits amounting to 49 kinds are forbidden to trade in the market in which citizen's kinds account for 12, businessmen's for 13; merchants' for 12, workers' for 12." The so-called fakes and counterfeits also gain the name of "buwu (illegal goods)" or "tezhe (evil goods)". In addition, expect the unqualified products, in order to make the market environment clear, Zhou Dynasty prohibited the products ("luxurious goods") which only focused on the luxuriousness and glamour and had no practical usefulness to come into the market. Zheng Xuan made comments that the luxurious goods which were exchanged without usefulness should be prohibited to make the market in good order. Finally, this turned out to be the market order that the harmful influence disappeared and there were very few the luxurious goods.[66]

The second is the contractual capacity. In the contract law of ancient China, contracting parties should be bound by the law in two aspects: one is age, the other is the identity. All the past dynasties regarded age (to be mentioned, it was height to use as a capacity in Qin Dynasty) as the standards to decide whether the contracting party had the full capacity. Most of offenses and crimes of persons limited in disposing capacity would not be investigated. For the aspect of identity, what was directly related with the contractual right and the contractual capacity was not only the age, but

[61] *Ce Fu Yuan Gui*, Chapter 88.

[62] *Comprehensive Mirror to Aid in Government*, Vol. 273.

[63] Genealogy of Family Ji in Gaolv of Pucheng City of the Republic of China, Vol. 1.

[64] Jinhua History, Zheng Yong, *Family Etiquette of Zhen Family*.

[65] Dabishan Collection, Chapter 56, Li Weizhen: *Public Land of Clan Wu*.

[66] *Rites of Zhou Diguan Sishi*.

also one's identity in ancient China, which had close relationships with contracting rights and direct influence on the legal effect of contracts. Even though the persons without some necessary identity had concluded the contracts, it was also difficult for them to get the legal identity or the customs recognition. Generally, the identity can be classified as follows:

1. The persons with special identities could not make relevant contracts. For instance, during the period of Emperor Wu of Han Dynasty, it was prohibited that merchants and their family members took in the land, because of which it was void to make the land transfer contract with merchants and their family members. On the contrary, only by persons with special identities making the contracts, could the relevant contract relation become legally effective. For example, in Tang Dynasty, the travelling merchant who was engaged in the foreign business had "Guosuo" (a certificate of trade license which proved that the official who mastered the foreign trade and customs allowed the foreign merchant to trade in the inland) given by the local governor or the monitor (the military inspector), and the ordinary merchants in most cases failed to own this privilege.[67] For another instance, when Manchu entered and hosted the Central Plains of China, Manchu enjoyed the privilege. In the trade of real estate, people without Manchu nationality could not purchase common houses and residential land, three routines respectively in the nineteenth year (1754), the twenty-eighth year (1763) and the thirtieth year (1769) of Qianlong administration prohibited common people from pawning the land of banner people. In the nineteenth year of Jiaqing administration (1814), it was specified that the land or houses which were possessed by the banner people could not be allowed to be pawned by the common people. Both the owner and seller should be punished due to breaking the systems and in addition, the money of payment for the land and houses would be recovered to be given to the government if there were people who tried to privately pawn by borrowing the others' names.[68]
2. The senior are superior and the junior are inferior. This mechanism held a core position in the Patriarchal Clan System of ancient China where the control of clan property right was handed by the senior and the private sale and usage of such property by the junior would bring about not only the punishment under clan rule, but also the investigation of the government. In Song Dynasty, as long as parents were living, the children had no contractual capacity for handling the property.[69] For example, there were an uncle and two nephews in Liang's family who had a piece of land. One day, his nephews privately dealt with a buyer named Gong, and sold the land to Gong. The court verdict deemed that the private deal of Liang's nephews concealed the senior, which was illegal. In considering that Liang and Gong are neighbors, it was knowable for Gong that this deal was illegal, thus it was ruled "confiscate the money to national treasury; return the land back to

[67] Lihu. 1998. *The Management of Shiboshi and Shibo in Tang Dynasty, The History Research* (3).

[68] Quoted from Jinfan [19].

[69] See footnote 25, p. 63.

the owner" in accordance with the law.[70] Throughout the dynasties in Chinese history, it has been rigorously stipulated that the inferior junior shall not privately steal and sell property which has been repeatedly stressed and strictly stipulated in the rules of ancestral temple and genealogy.

3. The servants are superior and the employees are inferior. The contracts of Tang Dynasty and Gaochang unearthed in Turpan show that one party of employment contract is called "zuoren", which referred to the servants. Sekio Silo, a Japanese scholar, believes that "zuoren" specifically refers to the servants of Gaochang.[71] Superficially, one party of the employment contract is "zuoren", while Sekio Silo and Wu Zheng hold the opinion that the contract is actually concluded by the master of the servant and the employer. Stated another way, "zuoren" was not a party in a contract but a nominal one whose status was as low as a slave.[72] It demonstrates that the contractual right obviously varies from identity, a servant or an employer. The lunar first month of the fifth year of Chongde Period, Tangzong, Qing Dynasty (1642), Huang Taiji (Abahai) ordered Ministry of Revenue that "any loaner of/for food supplies shall be the seniors of a family, the servant shall not be involved in food supplies loan."[73] The seniors could conduct debita and credit between each other, while different identity and status between employers and servants accounted for unequal contract subjects, namely, the contractual right and the contractual capability.
4. The male are superior and the female are inferior. In the Patriarchal Clan System of China, it is an obvious characteristic that the male kept a grip on powers in the aspects such as the religion, the property, the management and education. Not only legally but socially speaking, the status on identity of the female was lower than the male. Thus, only when the male of one family died or had no capacity to make contracts, could the female conclude contracts instead. However, they had to follow the moral codes—they had to make the negotiation from behind a curtain, which meant that they could not bargain and negotiate with the sellers or the representatives of the sellers face to face. In *Zaling* quoted from *The Penal Complex of Song·Household and Marriage Law*, the judicial officials in the commentary wrote that "after carefully observing and studying, we found that if the property was pawned or pledged, the family head or the respected head must sign the contract with the seller or the trusted follower of the seller face to face. Or, the deal could be made only if the female who were hard to face the other party must negotiate from behind a curtain".

The third one is the contract forms. In the contracts of the ancient times, the formal contract acted as the main trend. Zhang Chuanxi divided the contract development

[70] See footnote 25, p. 92.

[71] Sekio Silo. 1995. *Analysis of Document of Zuoren Relation Unearthed From No. 154 Tomb in Astana, Eastern Asia History and Culture* (Vol. 1), Research on the Western Regions, translated by Hou Shixin (1).

[72] Zheng [20].

[73] *Veritable Record of Taizong of Qing Dynasty*, Chapter 59, p. 2.

in ancient China into four phases.[74] The first was from the Western Zhou Dynasty to the Spring and Autumn Period. It was a period when the contract with states and the contract with all the people coexisted. The second phase was from the Warring States to the Western and Eastern Jin Dynasties. It was a period when the private contract of the folk was developed. The third phrase was from the Eastern Jin Dynasty to the Five Dynasties. It was the period when the contacts in paper prevailed and the nation carried out intervention. The fourth phrase was from the Northern Song Dynasty to the Republic of China. It was the standard contract period or nation intervention period. The key point of this section was to start with the specific modality of the contract with studying the contract process during the ancient times, especially the period since the contract in paper system (paper contract systems) of official version of the Song Dynasty started, so as to explore the development track and the gain and loss of Chinese contact itself. It will be discussed from four aspects as follows:

1. The establishment of the contract and unifying of the contract in paper system (paper contract systems). To write and make contracts is a signal of establishment of the civil act and the presupposition of its being lawfulness. As far back as the Western Zhou Dynasty, there was a saying that "the contract which was significant should be written on the bronze container, while the contract which was not important could be written on the drawing paper",[75] Li Zhimin made the interpretation that if the contracts were fairly significant, they should had be carved on the sacrificial vessel of the temples. If the contract was not important, it could be written on the bamboo slip by the cinnabar ink.[76] American scholar Hugh. T. Scorgin, Jr. considered that the uniform contract form of Han Dynasty prevailed and some contract terms were also uniform in a high level. The Sinologist from the Netherlands, Hulsewé thought that this consistency "implied a kind of legal origin".[77] Zheng Zhong who lived in the period from Emperor Ping to Emperor Zhang of Han Dynasty (5–83 A.D.), when making notes on *Rites of Zhou·Qiuguan·Shishi* said that at his time, the transaction was differentiated by the contracts which were concluded. The contracts were respectively given to the seller and buyer. If there were disputes, the contracts could act as the reference. According to the above, it can be known that concluding contracts in Han Dynasty had become the customs and habits, and was also emphasized by the official. The material form of the contract in Han Dynasty nowadays is more common in the Northwestern Frontier Fortress Garrison Regions and Silk Roads. There were not only the common types of contracts such as sales, employment, lease, land tenure and loan, but also the contracts about partnership, contracting, trust and testamentary succession. What's more important was that contracts in Han Dynasty especially sales contracts had come into being a set of uniform form and modality, which set up rules and forms for the future generations. Until Tang Dynasty, the systems of concluding contracts had already become rules

[74] Chuanxi [21].

[75] *Rites of Zhou Qiuguan Siyue.*

[76] See footnote 26, p. 129.

[77] Daoyun et al. [22].

and been upgraded from the "Private Contract" to the national law. "The sales on slaves or the horses and cattle should be examined by this bureau to make contracts."[78] "If the slaves or horses, cattle, mules, donkey had been sold, the buyer who didn't make a contract within three days should be beaten with a stick for thirty times, and the seller could be beaten for twenty times", and "if the deal had been concluded and the contract was made through Shisi beyond the stipulated time, and in addition the number of the exceeding day which was one, he or she should be beaten by thirty times, and if the number was ten, he or she should be beaten for forty times, and the most serious crime should be beaten for one hundred times." In the *Annotation and Critique,* Zhangsun Wuji wrote that the sales on the slaves, horses and cattle had been concluded, and the Shisi who didn't give the contract should be beaten by thirty times for the exceeding one day. The punishment should be carried out by the judicial department. The people who shielded this criminal should be regarded as the head criminal.[79] Thus, we know the establishment of the contract of Tang Dynasty was not only a simple civil act but also an administrative act of nation managing markets and trades. The development of contracts in Song Dynasty was in neater formation. Real property transaction such as pawning land or houses must be in form of concluding contracts, which would not be discussed here in detail. The law ruled that the personal estate transaction such as sales on the livestock, the carriage, the boat and the female labor employment must be in form of concluding contracts. In the meantime, the law of Song Dynasty specified the strict systems of fingerprints and seals in order to make contracts management more normalized. In the beginning of foundation of Yuan Dynasty, it strictly ruled that in live-sale, pledge, land tenure, sub-tenancy, sales and mutual loans of belongings in real estate and expensive personal estate must be in form of concluding contracts. In the November of the seventh year of Yuan Dynasty (1270) it was instructed that the ministry of revenue instructed that recently there were a lot of the live-sales of the lands or the houses, the sellers and the buyers who didn't want to hand in the tax privately negotiated and didn't make contracts by means that they pledged the houses with the excuse of borrowing money. Due to the unclear contract, the disputes which were made to the official could not be judged according to the law. For this purpose, except that the parties in previous transaction didn't need to change, from the date January 11th, the intermediaries and the guarantors should make the formal contract by signature according to the law. In Ming Dynasty, such civil acts generally carried out the contract system. In addition, the variety of contracts with variety of fixed forms was common all around the area. For example, the employment contract could be classified into two types: one was the employment contract form which included aspects such as names of employers and employees, the time limitation of employment, the employment reward and the payment method, and the employee liability for the damage because of breaking contracts or infringement. The other one was the live-sale

[78] Institutional History of the Tang dynasty Taifusijing Duzhushiling.

[79] *Law Code of Tang Dynasty Regulations on Sales of Slaves, Cattle, Horses without Contracting.*

and employment contract. Generally, the parties should hand in all the money of live-sale or employment all in one time, and it was ruled that since the employees were pawned and employed, they had to be subject to the orders, and could not break or put off contracts, be absent without leave or kidnap the property of the employer. The contracts during the earlier and the middle period of Qing Dynasty were generally written by the parties themselves of the folk. The management of the government reflected that every contract should be pasted with the contractual footer issued by the official. Although in the later period of Qing Dynasty, the paper for contracting of the official version was used, but for the private contract in the folk, it was also allowed to paste the contractual footer, which had the same legal effect with the paper for contracting in the official version. More stamp taxes were collected by using the tax ticket which acted as the legal basis for the certificate of contract.[80]

The legalization and standardization of establishment of contracts began from Song Dynasty. It specifically reflected in the appearance of the "standard contract" and the enforcement of uniform contract paper. In the March of the eighth year of the Taipingxingguo Period (983 A.D.), the imperial court ruled that the Business and Tax Bureau of the feudal official and states, the pledge contracts were respectively given to the people related to the pledge of the house or the land. This should be set as the example, if the people broke this, they should be punished by the law.[81] "There were two copies of contracts of the live-on for the land and the house, and one was given to the seller, and another was given to the Business and Tax Bureau". After a long period, "the relatives and the neighbor took in the land or the house because the contract owned by the seller had gone. Also, the contract copy of the Business and Tax Bureau had gone." For getting the remedy, in the first year of Emperor Song Zhenzong Qianxing Period (1022 A.D.) people were informed that the live-sale and pawning the house or the land should be in forms of concluding four contracts: one for buyer, one for seller, one for Businesses and Taxes Bureau and one for the county,[82] so that it could effectively prevent the shortcomings including transactions of the folk in taking in and falsely claim as their own. The unifying of paper contract systems had become common all around the area by the end of northern Song Dynasty. In the third year of Chongning reign of Emperor Huizong of Song Dynasty an imperial order was made that the written contract of houses and lands should be printed and sold by the official. Except for the fees of the paper, writing brushes and the ink, the amount of payment depended on the amount of the contracts.[83] Until April of the sixth year of Zheng He (1116 A.D.), it was instructed that the people who pawned the lands and houses should make a negotiation on the price and within three day make a basic and fixed document first, and fill it up. The county should urge them to hand

[80]See footnote 27, p. 636.

[81]*Supplementary Notes of Comprehensive Mirror to Aid in Government*, Vol. 24, Section "in the March of the eighth year of Taipingxingguo Period".

[82]*The Compilation of Song Dynasty, National Economy, 61:62.*

[83]ibid.

in the document and buy the formal contract within three days.[84] In the end of Ming Dynasty and the beginning of Qing Dynasty, receiving the official contract paper and the system of tax and receipt were transferred to local grass-roots management system. For example, the borough chief must supervise the sales behavior on lands of the folk. The borough chief received the contract paper in official version on sales of lands. The people who wanted to buy or sell the land must receive this contract paper from the borough chief, and fill it up. Then, the borough chief supervised the performance including aspects such as making the contract and concluding the deal and reported county government to print the contract and collect the tax.[85] This method facilitated the work of both the official and the common people. It generally became a kind of routine in Qing Dynasty.

2. The contract clauses. According to the contract theory of the western contractual liberalism, the establishment of contract clause was the result of the mutual consent from contracting parties. The contents stipulated in clauses shall be deemed as the private right of the parties and the state shall not intervene. Based on the current material, it seemed to be difficult to draw that the contract clauses of ancient China were the result of free will. During the period of the Western Zhou Dynasty, the contracting forms in the transfer of right to use (the ownership belonged to King Zhou) in real estate (lands) were similar to the "formal contract" of the ancient Rome. The clauses established through parties' concluding contracts must be reported to the official and get the official's consent. The objective or reason included two aspects: the first one was that the land was owned by the King Zhou and the transfer of lands must be agreed and admitted by the King or the representative of the King. Otherwise, the transfer of the land right (right of use in lands) was void. For example, in the third year of Gongwang, in the *Weihe* it was written that Ju Bo bought the beautiful jade ornament, the red tiger-shape jade, the fur of muntjak and so on which costed seventy peng from Qiu Wei, and Ju Bo made a promise of giving the land of thirteen acres to Qiu Wei. Then Qiu Wei reported this to the five ministers including Bo Yifu, Cha Bo, Ding Bo, Qiong Bo, Shan Bo in order to get their admission about the contract with Ju Bo. The key step in this approval behavior was the content of contract clause about how the rights and obligations of the parties were determined. The second aspect was that through the admission and consent of the five ministers, the private transaction (the main was the transfer of ownership in real estate) was legally binding. From this, we knew that the identification of the feudal official was not only an identification and consent on the contract clauses, but also had the further legal notarization effect. It was used by the future generations that the situation that the contract clauses were admitted and agreed by the feudal official turned into the fact that the feudal official directly supervised the contracts. And finally, the uniform contract system turned out

[84] Zhou Shaoquan: Official in Charge of Grain, Borough Chief and the Old of the Late Ming Dynasty and the Early Qing Dynasty Seen in the Contract Document of Huizhou, *The Research on Chinese History*, 1998 (1).

[85] See footnote 27, pp. 153–154.

to be the detailed issues of the specific contract clauses. For example, in Song Dynasty, contracts documents like live-sale must have the following clauses: (1) The name and domicile of the parties. (2) The subject matter for pawning, including the hectare and acre of the lands pawned (number), situation of the land (quality), the location, square. (3) The reason of pawning. (4) The origin of the industry. (5) The price of closing the deal. (6) The original money of tax and undertaking the tax. (7) The warranty specifications. (8) The responsibility for breach of contract. This kind of clauses was the mandatory clauses. When the parties made live-sale contracts, they must fill up the amended document clearly, otherwise it cannot be admitted by the feudal official and given contractual seal. Back to Han Dynasty, according to the current historical material, we know that contracts in that time were different between counties, yet the main clauses stayed alike. Thus, although Han Dynasty didn't have uniform contract paper system, there were express terms for contracts clauses. Based solely on customary law, it was still difficult to lead to so uniform and complete behavior. Prof. Hu Liuyuan studied contractual forms of Han Dynasty and yielded quite a lot achivements. In accordance with his achievement, we can know that the content of sales contract clauses of Han Dynasty was as follows[86]: (1) the time of concluding the contract. This is the signal of the assignment of ownership and right to use and the transfer of sales goal and also the basis of time limitation of contracts. A common point of the contract in Han Dynasty was that the year, month, day of contractual establishment were expressly specified in the beginning of the contract. For example, there were contracts such as *The Sales Contract on Engraved Stone by Yue Yangtong in the Second Year of Dijie (68), The Sales Contract on Mutian Jade by Wu Miying in the November of the Sixth Year of Jianchu*, and so forth.[87] This kind of form was be followed by the future generations until Tang Dynasty. Since Yuan Dynasty, the written order of the time of concluding the contract had been situated after the main body of contract document. This finally became the fixed form and was passed on until now. (2) The name, the identity and domicile of the parties. (3) The subject matter of the transaction. Sales on land contract had noted to list the surroundings of the land to enclose the area. What's more important was that on the relevant subject matter, there had been complete relationship of right and obligation, which were expressly listed in the contract to bind the behavior of the contracting parties. For example, in the sales contract, a slavery sales contract of Han Dynasty wrote the duty and obligation in detail:

> In the first month of lunar year of Shenjue Period (59 B.C.) Han Dynasty, Wang Ziyuan, a man from Zizhong, bought a slave from Yang Hui, a woman from Anzhili of Chengdu at the price of 5,000 wen**********. It was a must for the slave to obey Master Wang without offend. The slave had to do the things as following: sweep the floor once getting up in the

[86]The original contract seen in [Japan] Noboru Niida: *History of Chinese Legislation. The Land Act. The Citation Act*, pp. 416, 417, 420.

[87]*Taiping Imperial Encyclopedia*, Chapter 598. Wang Bao, *Slave Contract*.

**********Translator's note: this slave belonged to Yang's husband who had died. Entering adulthood, the slave often offended against others, thus no one wanted to buy him.

> morning; get the cookers cleaned after breakfast; drench ditch and enclose it with fence; weed the vegetable garden and loose soil; mend the rough road; make a lianjia (an everyday use to thresh grains) with wood and cowhide; make a tool with bamboo; chisel stone into a duijiu (a mortar to pound grains); accumulate straw into a broom; make a shuiyu (a water container for grinding the ink) with wood; hollow the wood into a jiudou (an everyday use to scoop liquor); weave shoes with reed; trap deer, birds, fishes; grow ginger and taro; feed piggy and colts; at the Vernal Equinox, set water gate in land for trapping fish; clean cups and tidy table; peel garlic in the vegetable garden and cut perilla leaf; no drinking in excess; even a burning desire of drinking could only be satisfied by a sip of liquor; grind the mill; sell zongsuo (a kind of rope made of palm); buy bed-mat in Mianting; on the way home from Miangting, buy rouge in Xindu city; resell the rouge in town; sell geese; buy tea in Wudu; dig the lotus root in Lake Yangshi; no sitting around in the market; no vulgar language; make knifes and mao (a kind of weapon in ancient China) to exchange cattle and sheep in Yizhou (city name); be smart and pinch pennies when trading; cut down trees with axe, then make components of wheels; make clog shoes with the remaining wood; use the leftover material as firewood; and use the burned firewood as charcoal; use bamboo cage with stones in to reinforce embankment; repair the house and build new rooms; whittle bamboo into slips for writing; two or three bundles of dried firewood could make the wish of going back in the evening come true; in April, loose soil and then seed; in May, harvest wheat; in October, thresh beans for paying grain tax; no tasting when the fruits are ripe; warning the neighbors of preventing thieves when the dog is barking… when the slave is in old age, he could exchange for having a rest by pounding a dan (unit of volume in ancient China) grain; when in the evening with nothing to do, wash clothes until daybreak… If the family slave contravenes the rules, he will be flogged one hundred beats.

This text listed the issues in details of the housework that the family slaves needed to do. Despite there being some literary exaggeration, from the other side, it also reflects the fact that there were heavy slavery obligations in the sales contract of Han Dynasty. This contract became effective from the moment that Wang Ziyuan (Bao) stayed in the family of Yang Hui. Wang wanted the slave Bian Liao to buy the wine for him, and Bian Liao took a stick to Wang Ziyuan's home, saying that when you bought me, you just requested me to guard the tomb and not to buy the wine for the other men. Thus, even though it was sales contract of person, the right and obligation of slaves should also be expressly written when the contract was concluded. (4) Prices and methods of payment. The price was generally calculated by the currency in use, also added by the price of the clothes. This calculating method was very common in the unearthed Dunhuang Turpan document of Tang Dynasty. It can be seen that it was caused by the remaining customs of Han Dynasty. There were two methods of payment: the person who paid off the price at one time was called "the money having been paid", the money having been paid at that day or no actual price; payment by installments were listed by the time of final paying off the price, such as "the money of being paid off till the spring", and "the money of being paid off till December". (5) The effective terms in clauses. Most of the sales contracts of Han Dynasty had the words of "Rulvling" to show the binding effect between the parties.

In the clauses of contracts, warranty clauses were the most important. Because it was an effective way to guarantee the creditor to achieve the obligatory right and a strong guarantee through the way of customs in the folk or the feudal official to make "public" remedies. In the contracts such as the sales contract and contract of loan, the warranty clause was a kind of duty and obligation which were added on the creditor to promote the creditor to positively and completely perform the contract obligation. The types of warranties were stated as above in detail.

In the personal warranty, the warrantor in Han Dynasty was called "Renzhe (referred to the guarantor)", Xu Shen in the *Origin of Chinese Characters People* said that "Ren" was the guarantor. The future generation made use of "the guarantor" all around. Through specifically analyzing the meanings of "Ren", its initial meaning had more ethical features, which belonged to "righteousness" of Confucianist and Mohist School. Mocius had ever explained the moral connotation of "Ren" that Ren was the person who did something harmful to himself or herself but good for the others.[88] "Ren was the person who did something that he or she didn't want to do in order to solve the urgent difficulties of the others."[89] From this, we can know that the behavior of "Renzhe" (the guarantor) was a kind of righteous deeds, which meant that the "Renzhe" by his or her reputation and asset met the urgent need of the other people. From the perspective of Mocius, "the behavior that the person had spare efforts but didn't help the others" and "the behavior that the person had the additional money but didn't give it to help the others and knew the good way to solve the difficulty but didn't tell that" were "Injustice".[90] All the people helped each other, which was not only a kind of "righteous deeds", but also a way by which the people could get the interests. This is the so-called saying that the people who care about the others must be cared about by the others and the people who are beneficial for the others must be given benefits by the others.[91] The mutual benefit is a kind of means and benefiting ourselves is the objective. The function of "Renzhe" is also a little similar to that. In the economic life of the folk, acting as the guarantor is not only a kind of righteous deeds and virtue, but also a kind of necessary need. Since as a community, the economic life and especially the advance development of transaction behavior can be promoted only if the people contact and protect each other. It will not lead to the fact that the amount of transaction can be decreased because of lacking transaction safety. It is very inconvenient for the society and life.

About the content of the warranty, this chapter will adopt the inside relationship between the parties do demonstrate.

In the contract document, the contracting parties expressly rule that making warranties clauses is the dependable method to achieve the secured bonds. Since Song Dynasty, warranties clauses upgraded from the folk customs to the national laws. In the contractual clauses, the parties must have the warranties clauses, otherwise they would break the laws. For example, in the live-sale of lands, the people pawned the land, and made the contract which wrote the situation of surroundings that the money of the rental should be paid except the tax. The sellers, the neighbor and the guarantors made contracts written by the people who were responsible for writing. In addition, the behavior which broke the live-sale contract of the land should

[88] ibid.

[89] ibid.·*Jingshuoshang.*

[90] ibid.·*Shangtongshang.*

[91] ibid.·*Jianaizhong.*

be punished. The specific content of warranties can be discussed in the following three aspects.

I. The first one is the warranty with flaws, which means that one party makes the warranty for the other party about the flaws of the subject matter which is delivered, and it is expressly written in the contract document. Once the flaws of the subject matter turn up, the deliverer needs to afford the damage due to the delivery with flaws and gives the compensation. This kind of flaws can be classified into two types: the warranty of number and the warranty of quality. Most of them appear in the contract in which they are delivered by the way of measure, such as the physical credit and the sales of real estate. For example, the *Sales Contract on Land in Han Dynasty* stipulated that if the acres of the land are not enough, the money paid for the missing part of the land should be returned. The so-called "according to the amount with the shortage of land, returning the money" means that if the acres of the land aren't same as the amount of the agreement, the money on the shortage part of land should be given back to the buyer. About the warranty for the quality, in Tang Dynasty it was ruled that the sales of the slaves, the horse, the cattle, the mule… After concluding the contracts, if they had the disease, a sales agreement could be revoked within three days after it was concluded. If there was no deceit about the disease, the contract should be performed according to the law. The people who broke the rules should be beaten for forty times. Zhangsun Wuji explained it specifically that if after the contract was concluded, the disease was known, but it wasn't known during the purchase, the contract could be revoked within three days. After three days of the conclusion of the contract, the buyer found no disease, but he or she wanted to revoke the contract by the deceit. At this time, according to the rule, the people who broke the rule should be beaten for forty times. If there was the deceit about the disease, but the people didn't receive the revocation, they should also be beaten for forty times.[92] From the above, we can know that the buyer enjoyed the right of rescission ("revocation of a sales agreement within three days after it was concluded") based on the following three preconditions: (1) When the slaves and livestock were bought or sold, without knowing that they had the disease, the law made a presumption that if the fact that the cattle had the disease was previously known, the transaction could not be successful. (2) The illness of the subject matter existed before the transaction and not after the transaction. If the illness appeared after the transaction, this kind of risk was afforded by the buyer himself or herself. (3) Based on said preconditions, the buyer had to exercise his revocation right within three days, which was a time limitation. Otherwise, the buyer would lose the right of revocation. The right of rescission was the right which the law gave to the buyer. Accordingly, it was also the obligation added to the seller. That is, the seller must guarantee that his or her slave and livestock didn't have the disease before the transaction. If they had the disease, the buyer must be permitted and agreed to sever the sales contract relation. If the reason was that the seller clearly knew that his or her subject matter

[92] *Law Code of Tang Dynasty*, Chapter 26.

had disease but he or she didn't tell it, not only the buyer should be permitted and agreed to rescind the contract but also the seller should afford the punishment of flogging. In the folk contract document, we can find a lot of examples to explain that the buyer of contracting parties requests the seller to make the warranty clause. For example, in the unearthed *Sales Contract on Cattle in Tiger Year* from Dunhuang,[93] it was expressly ruled in the contract that after concluding the contract within (three) days, if the cattle with the disease didn't eat the water and grass, the cattle should be given back to the original owner. More than three days, the parties should follow the contract and could not stop or go back on the promise. For another example, in the relation of land tenancy, the tenant hand in the grain which must be fit in with the standard and quality which were stipulated by the contract document to the lessor. For example, in the *Tenancy Agreement on the Land by Suo Shannu in the Twenty-second Year During the Zhenguan Times of Tang Dynasty (648 A.D.)*,[94] it was stipulated that on the day of getting the wheat, following the traditional customs, the buyer got the wheat by the measure tool Hu. The wheat should be clean and qualified, and if the wheat was not good, the lessor should winnow the wheat himself or herself. The same clause was still contained in the *Tenancy Agreement on the Land by Zhang Junxing in Tang Dynasty.*[95] The contract requested that on the day of getting the wheat, the wheat should be clean and qualified, and if the wheat was not good, the lessor should winnow the wheat himself or herself. The so-called "Winnow the Wheat" is that if the grain which is delivered by the seller is not fit in with the agreement and the customs, the lessor can "Winnow the Wheat" by himself or herself to make sure of the quality of the grain.

II. The second is the warranty of right or also called warranty of title. It more exists in the sales contract. The seller enjoys the complete and absolute ownership towards the subject matter which was sold. And this is the precondition of closing the deal successfully and also the basis to guarantee the safety of the transaction. In the contract of ancient China, this kind of clause is very common in the sales contract. For example, it was written on the *Purchase Contract on Land by Pan Lijia of the Seventh Year of Guang He in Han Dynasty (184 A.D.)* that[96]:

> On the November 6th of the seventh year of Guang He (184 A.D.), a man called Pan Lijia from Pingyin County, bought the land located in Shiliangbu from a man called Duge Zi and his brother from Luoyang. The number of the land was five acres and the price of each acre was three thousand copper coins. The total price was fifteen thousand copper coins, and it was paid that day. The land covers the area of □, which can be marked at east of □, west of □. (Note: □ refers to the letters cannot be recognized in current time)... Once the land was owned by the people who were not included in account, Duge Zi should undertake this responsibility.
>
> Witness: Du Ziling, Li Jisheng

[93] *Dunhuang File, Series V. Contract Document.*

[94] *Unearthed Document in Turpan, Vol. 5, Cultural Relics Press*, p. 18.

[95] *Otani Document* No. 2828, see footnote 27, p. 294.

[96] See footnote 88, pp. 443–444.

Parties celebrated the transaction by having a drink, and the bill of alcohol was paid by both parties.

This kind of contract is very typical in Han Dynasty. One of the warranty clauses specifies that once the land was owned by the people who were not included in account, Du Gezi should undertake this responsibility. It means that if the land which is bought by the Pan Lijia occurs disputes of ownership with the official, the other people, the Hans and the minority, and that is, the above people think that they have the ownership of the land sold by Du Gezi, all the duties should be afford by the brothers and it has nothing to do with the buyer. After Tang Dynasty, this kind of right clause had become the necessary clause in the purchase contract of the buyer. Most of the unearthed various sales documents of Turpan of Dunhuang are like this kind. For example, in the *Sales Contract on Horse of the twenty-fifth year in the beginning of Tang Dynasty (737 A.D.)*, it was ruled that the deal on the horse had been concluded at that day, and if someone who was the original owner of the horse accused that the horse was the booty and requested the party to return the original thing. This responsibility should be taken by the guarantor and the seller. It had nothing to do with the buyer.[97] A contract of cattle-sale in the year of weinian unearthed in Dunhuang, it was stipulated that the deal on the cattle and the wheat had been concluded at that day, and if someone who was the original owner of the cattle accused that the cattle were the booties (寒盗) and requested the party to return the original things. This responsibility should be taken by the seller who would buy other cattle for the buyer.[98] A contract of cattle-sale in the year of yinyang (寅羊) stipulated that the deal on the cattle and the wheat had been concluded at that day and if someone who was the original owner of the cattle accused that the cattle were the booties and requested the party to return the original things. This responsibility should be taken by the seller who would buy other cattle for the buyer.[99] The warranty clauses in the contracts above show that the buyer, in order to avoid future disputes, specifies the warranty clauses and requires the seller and the guarantor to guarantee for the ownership. The so-called "Handao" actually meant "kedao (theft)", which referred to the accused booty. No matter in what kind of case, the related responsibility shall be shouldered by the seller and the guarantor. The sales contract stipulates that the seller has no duty to return the subject matter which has been sold due to the flaws in ownership.

What is noteworthy is that in the contracts of ancient China, even when the seller's subject to be sold was of his own without any flaw in ownership, as long as the sale and the pawn encroach the priority right of relatives and neighborhoods, possible impair would land on buyers' legitimate right. Therefore, no encroachment on relatives and neighborhoods' right shall be affiliated with the warranty clauses of the contract. If the seller and the pawner conceal relatives and neighborhoods, the responsibility shall be undertaken by the owner not the buyer. Commonly, this kind of pawning is confined to that of real property. But unfortunately, the priority right of relatives

[97] See Zhongluo [23].

[98] See footnote 93.

[99] ibid.

and neighborhoods system corrodes the increasing improvement in the legal effect of such warranty clause. And throughout Yuan, Ming and Qing Dynasty, the effect nearly disappears, which will be detailed in the next chapter.

The selling of goods with unknown source and a deal sold to multiple buyers had been prohibited by the law in all dynasties, which closely links to vital interests of the buyer, thus such warranty clauses exist in many ancient contracts. Meanwhile, in term of pawning real property, it is a must that the tax paid to the state shall be done before the real property is pawned to the next buyer. The contract also expressly stipulates the performance of paying tax and requires the seller to guarantee. Take *The Land-Sale Contract in the February of the Eighteenth Year of Qianglong, Qing Dynasty (1753 A.D.)* as an example[100]:

> Whereas the lack of money, now I am willing to sell the land (2.47 ha) … to … for good. The selling price will be 815 silver …, if the land proven to be stolen or other illegal source, or if it is sold to other buyer, or failure to pay the tax, or any kinship disputes arisen because of it, the current buyer and guarantor shall bear no responsible thereof.

The contract was written in both Chinese and Manchu languages, in which the warranty clauses covered four circumstances: (a) land proven to be stolen or other illegal source, (b) sold to other buyer, (c) failure to pay the tax, (d) any kinship disputes arisen because of it. If any or all of those four circumstances occurs, the joint liability shall be undertaken by the seller and the guarantor, but not the buyer.

III. The third is amnesty guaranty. It more existed in the sales contract and loan contract, which specially stood out during the period of Tang Dynasty when the imperial court exercised the policy of amnestying. In *The Contract of House sale by Zhang Yiquan in the fourth year of QianningPeriod (897 A.D.), Tang Dynasty,* it stipulated that once the deal on the land had been concluded, and if seller's siblings or any others claimed to be the original owner, either the seller deals with the dispute or the government practices amnesty for the tax debt, both conditions will requires no obligations on the buyer. And in *The Contract of House Sale by Sheng Duhe*, it wrote that: when the land has been sold, the buyer enjoys permanent title and ownership of the land, if the relatives or family members of the sellers have any disagreement concerning the tax or title, they can find a nearby place instead of the disputed land, or the government practices amnesty for the tax debt.[101] Until Post Tang Dynasty (936 A.D.), such locution was still common in contract. Such in *The Contract of House Sale by Yang Hulvbu in the Third Year of Qingtai, Tang Dynasty*, it also wrote that: if such deal encounters with the policy of amnestying, the dispute shall not be suitable.

3. The parties of contract make cross. Cross and sign showed the consensus reached by the parties. According to the way of administration, characteristics of clan, market convention and law, the parties on contract were broadly divided into the following four categories: the first one refers to the main parties of contract,

[100] See footnote 28.

[101] See footnote 98.

which was also called "qizhu (means the master of a contract)" or "qishou (means the head of a contract)". Generally speaking, qizhu was the direct parties who concluded the contract and made deals. From the Western Zhou Dynasty to the Northern and Southern Dynasties, the signing form of the parties was to briefly fill name, birthplace and social status in the contract, so was the signing form in the personal property contract and real property contract of the Western Zhou and Han Dynasties. With the development of the form of contract itself as well as the legalization of deal and complexity-oriented formalities, not only the name and birthplace of qizhu had to be detailed in the contract, but also in the end of the contract, qizhu himself had to sign name or make cross for the intensification of the contract credibility. Commonly, qizhu was an individual civil subject, but in the sales of real property or under the priority right of relatives and neighborhoods system, if the qizhu was a junior, only when the senior jointly signed the contract, could the contract enter into legal force for the purpose of preventing future disputes. Such as in *The Contract of House Sale by Yang Hulvbu in the Third Year of Qingtai (936 A.D.), Tang Dynasty* unearthed in Dunhuang, there were two sellers, Yang Hulvbu and his mother Azhang they were the co-owner of the house, both made cross on the contract. Yang Hulvbu made cross with his left hand finger, and his mother right hand finger, which manifests the ancient philosophical thought—male left and female right—of the philosophy of Yin Yang permeated into the contract. The identity of qizhu or qishou always was senior men in a family, if such men passed away, their wife could hence be the qishou. A case recorded in *Law Reports of Southern Song Dynasty* was that Wei Jun, who had four brothers and their father had passed away while the mother was alive, was addicted to drinking and gambling, and his pressure for money drives him to pawn the family's land to others without the knowing of his brothers and mother. In Liu Kezhuang (the judge)'s verdict, it recorded that "when a land is going to be sold or pawned, it shall be conducted in accordance with law. Now the mother in this family being the qishou, if one of the son, Wei Jun desires to sell or pawn the land, he shall have the approval of other brother together with the mother at the same time, otherwise it will not be effective." Thus, it was ruled that Wei Jun's pawn was illegal, the judge gave an order to confiscate the money to the State Treasury, return the house to the original joint owners, and Wei Jun got a official record regarding this case.[102]

The second category of parties was the neighbors, uninterested people and contract notaries who mainly served as the role of witnesses to the contract, meanwhile the neighbors could also be the guarantors. In ancient China mutual help and guarantee among neighborhood was attached importance to the well-field system (the land distribution method in Chinese salve society), Lijia system and the Bao-Jia system (the administrative system organized on basis of households respectively originated in Ming and Song Dynasty) all were positive proof. Hence neighbors and relatives

[102]See footnote 25, pp. 92–93.

tended to be the witnesses to the contract and mutually provided guarantee in transactions. In addition to witnessing the conclusion of contract, their signatures guaranteed them the obligation to witness when called by the official. Then mediators and Yabao (which means middlemen and guarantors) took their place. Uninterested people and contract notaries are mainly required in contract formalities of Han Dynasty. For example, as put in Deed (written on jade) for Horse-purchasing by Wu Miying in Jianchu sixth Year, Zhao Man and He Fei were notaries; Yuan Shuwei served the same role in Deed (written on lead) for Land-purchasing by Wang Moqin in Jianning second Year. In Deed (written on lead) for Field-purchasing by Sun Cheng in Jianning fourth Year, Fan yuanzu, who is of another surname, plays the role of notary and Fan Yong, Zhang Yi and Sun Long are uninterested people. Meaningfully, in Deed for Field-purchasing in Yuanhe first Year of Han Dynasty (181 A.D.), it is put that uninterested people Jia and Liu both were contract notaries,[103] from which we can know that uninterested people and contract notaries play the same role in nature in Han Dynasty. Literally, "contract notaries" are those trusted by both parties to preside over the conclusion of contracts, whose work is procedural, while "uninterested people" are the mere witnesses. "Uninterested people Jia and Liu both are contract notaries". In other words, Jia and Liu, the two witnesses, preside over the conclusion of the contract. In this case, it is no wonder that "uninterested people" and "contract notaries" are used alternatively in some contracts of Han Dynasty while at the same time in other ones. When it comes to neighbors and kinsfolk, two means, if their preemption is involved, can be adopted to testify their knowledge of the transaction. One is signing. By signing the trading contract, relatives and neighborhoods were more than justification of the conclusion of the contract. More importantly, it could be inferred from their signatures that they have been fully informed of the sale or pawn and have waived their preemption. This system not only saved cost but also enhanced the stability and security of the transaction. The *Contract of House-sale by Yang Hulvbu* in Later Tang Dynasty mentioned above is also a demonstration and proof by recording that "Deng Poshan and Xue Ansheng, who live in the same courtyard" signed on the contract as well. Another is publishing the transaction and its result through certain ceremony. Take the custom of Miao people as example. Even though the land price has been agreed between the seller and the buyer of another clan, if the seller's kindred, enjoyed preemption they could get that land. Such custom is still being practiced today in the region. As a result of such custom, in order to ensure a smooth transaction without kinsfolk's grab or intervene, the buyer will entertain the kinsfolk, village head and mediator after concluding the contract. Besides, he will give the seller's first cousins each five kilos of grain, so-called "grain for next of kin". Such full performance promises that the contract formally goes into effect and then next of kin shall not grab the field or the house sold and shall bear the obligation to testify. The third category of parties was Renzhe (which means commercial guarantors) and Ya Bao (which means middlemen and guarantors). In terms of transaction guarantor or witness, although it refers to Renzhe or Yabao in folk customs, Yaren (either official or private one) is more used

103 Qicai [24].

in the market under state management. It is provided by law that they should sign the contract and assume certain legal obligation. The fourth category of parties was Qian Shu, namely documents ghost writer. It is not necessary that contracts be made and written by contracting parties. They can be ghostwritten but the scrivener should expressly state his family name and given name in the contract, showing impartiality. The fifth category of parties was Kinsfolk. It is a practice of Chinese ancient contract system that kinsfolk perform the repayment of debt. Some contracts must be signed by kinsfolk to ensure the creditor's rights. Contracts for sale, loan and mortgage, in particular, are entered into with the signatures of kinsfolk required. Meanwhile, if the title to the real estate is "shared", namely held in family co-ownership, it is a must that co-owners sign the contract for sale or pawn in agreement so as to prevent any dispute in the future. The sixth category of parties was Partners who must jointly sign the contract. Otherwise, the contract will not be concluded and win the official recognition.

And with respect to the signature of the contract, there are a few points worth noting. First, signing marks the conclusion of contract. In the contracts of Tang Dynasty unearthed in Dunhuang and Turpan, it is provided that both parties enter into a contract on agreement and mark their knuckle lengths on the contract in case of verification. Formulistic expression as it seems to be, such necessary clause really matters. Second, their signing is the legal basis for assuming contractual obligation. It thus has been expressly provided by laws since Tang Dynasty. For example, statutory interpretation of Song Dynasty expressly provides, "If a property is sold twice, the original owner, Yaren, neighbors and other people who sign the contract all will be examined on unjust enrichment and be accused of dispossession. Those who do not get money will be fined off 30% to pay the victim. And if the original owner fail to return all, Yabao and neighbors who jointly sign the contract are liable to fill the gap. And the ownership of the property belongs to the original buyer".[104] This is a clear regulation on contractual obligation. And on the other hand, it is a must that the parties to the contract sign the contract because only in this way can the transaction be legal. In Shaoxing tenth year (1141 A.D.) of Song Dynasty, it was enforced that contracts, if not in accordance with format and without signature of Yabao and scrivener, it would be illegal and forbidden. An official from Ministry of Revenue made a proposal to She Ling Suo (an agency that codifies the administrative decrees in Song Dynasty) and then this practice became law. "Future contracts … if not signed by Yabao and scrivener in person and sealed by the official, shall be deemed illegal and forbidden."[105] We can thus know that the authority has made strict rules on the signing by contracting parties respectively from the perspective of the format and obligation of the contract. Third, signing should be made by the parties to the contract in person, otherwise it was invalid. As mentioned above, signing the contract was the mutual assistance and guarantee between contractual parties. Unless signed in person, the contract could not become effective. In the above case where Wei Jun sold land without authorization, one of the parties called

[104]Criminal Code of Song Dynasty Law of Marriage.

[105]*The Compilation of Song Dynasty, National Economy, 65:66.*

Zhang Wushi was exempted from liability and released back home due to the lack of his signature on the contract. Take *The Law Reports of Southern Song Dynasty* as example again. The Lee Cousins fought over the family property. The contract presented was signed by Zhou You under the authorization of Mo Rushan. The local authority held that it was not rare that contract was ghostwritten in a transaction. But the signature, which mattered most, could be anything but ghostwritten. Since Mo Rujiang so his property to Mo Rushan who had no title and then asked Zhou You to ghostwrite the contract, it must be Mo Rujiang that had been in bad faith at the beginning.[106] Fourth, there are two signing forms, namely signature and making one's mark. Signature has been dealt with above. And making one's mark can be divided into two types.[107] One is mark of finger, namely marking one's knuckle length, especially of middle finger and forefinger. And man tends to choose left hand and woman chooses right hand according to folk custom. It is no later than the Han Dynasty that the finger-mark system has become a practice. Contract for Fur-sale by Ou Wei in Jianshi second Year (31 A.D.) of Han Dynasty, for instance, has put that Dong Zifang buys the fur of Ou Wei at the price of 1500 qian with the agreement on payment performed when spring comes, witnessed by Du Junjuan, the uninterested people. There are three lines on the outside of "Uninterested people Du Junjuan" written on the bamboo slips reserved. This, in terms of archaeological materials, is the earliest record of finger mark. Tang Dynasty has seen the popularity of finger mark. Various kinds of documents unearthed have been positive proof. For example, in the Contract of Loan by Zhen Haishi in Qianyuan 1st Year (666 A.D.) of Tang Dynasty, the borrower, two guarantors and the witness all mark three lines under their own name except the lender.[108] That's why contract was called "Finger-marked contract" in Tang Dynasty. And making one's mark has evolved into knuckle or finger tracing since Song Dynasty, which can been seen from the works of Huang Tingjian. "The parties to the contract of servants-buying, if illiterate, mark their knuckle length instead. And contracts of field-and-house-sale in Jiangnan area can also be signed in fingermark."[109] Zhang Chuanxi, a master in fingermark study, believes that four variants have been in existence, namely knuckle tracing (marking knuckle length), fingerprint (impressing one's thumb or forefinger on the contract), hand-print (impressing one's hand or hands on the contract) and hand-and-foot print (that is, the debtor impresses his hands and feet respectively at the both ends of calico on which is written the contract). And since Ming Dynasty, the practice of fingerprint has been on the wane, replaced by signature Li Xu, living in Ming Dynasty, once said, "A tenant who wants to divorce his wife practices finger mark regardless of literacy. But it is not the case when it comes to contracts for servants-purchasing or filed-and-house-purchasing".[110] The other is Yazi (personally special signature).

---

[106] See footnote 25, p. 81.

[107] See footnote 26, p. 122.

[108] *Instrument Unearthed in Turoan*, Vol. 6 *Instrument from No. 4 Tomb in Asitana.*

[109] Huang Tingjian: *Reports Collected by Huang Wengong*, Vol. 11.

[110] Li Xu: *Essay of Jie An*, Vol. 4.

The so-called Yazi refers to that the contracting parties sign their names in semi-cursive script. It is also named "Huaya" for joint-up writing is similar to curlicue. Yazi came in vogue in Sui and Tang Dynasty. And later Yazi turned into marking a cross, Chinese character seven and even a circle. This practice has been reserved till the Republic of China.

4. Transfer, Delivery and Seal System of Contract. A contract goes into effect on the premise that transfer and delivery is finished. So is the fulfillment of rights shared between contracting parties. It is generally involved in procedure Lai Li (trace of origin), Pi Zao (disposal of fixture and change of registration), Guo Ge (transfer) and Li Ye (delivery).

Firstly, the so-called Lai Li (tracing of origin) refers to examination on whether the seller or the pawner has the authority to dispose the property and the relevant certificate, upon which government intervention in the conclusion of private contract mainly relies. Generally speaking, "Lai Li Bu Ming", namely "unknown origin", means that the seller or the pawner cannot justify the source of the property sold, which imposes risk on both parties, especially the buyer, for unauthorized disposal of property will affect the transfer of property rights and even cause the deprivation of ownership which leads the buyer to suffer great economic loss. Hence, ownership of legal origin is a prerequisite for the success of the transaction. Besides, "tracing the origin" can find out whether the property sold or pawned is such public property as land or house for charity and land to be returned to the state upon death of owner. And through the examination on the signing, it can also be known whether the seller (pawner) is an inferior or junior who has no authority to dispose the property; that is, "the unauthorized disposal" is made by an inferior or junior without the knowledge of his superior or junior. If so, the transaction will be investigated, causing great economic loss. In terms of the concern of the buyer, it is more often the first case; that is, is the property of legal origin? It is necessary to find out a way to prove the legal origin of the ownership. A practice concerning ancient contract thus comes into being, called the former contract for transfer of property rights. In other words, if the property to be sold or pawned is owned not through succession but through purchase, the seller has to delivery or display the document of title transfer to the buyer in case of uncertainty. The Song Dynasty saw the popularity of this practice. It was attached great importance to in the judicial practice of Song Dynasty. According to the judgment by Liu Houcun included in *Law Reports of Southern Song Dynasty*, "The former contract for transfer of property rights is a must when it comes to property purchasing." We can thus know that in Song Dynasty it recognized the delivery or display of "the former contract for transfer of property rights" as an objective means to guarantee the legality of title, be they the government or the folk custom. There are four ways to justify the origin: First, relevant muniment of title (including the original contract and official receipt of deed tax) is directly delivered to the buyer as a proof of legal origin, which can be backed up by Contract of Mountain-land

Sale by Wu Gong in Jiading 8th Year (1215 A.D.) of Song Dynasty, collected in the library of Peking University.[111]

> Once sold, the property is at the disposal of Zhu Yuanxing in terms of registration at the government, tax payment and replacing farming with fir planting. Impediment or occupation from other people, if occurs, is to blame on me, the seller, nothing to do with the buyer. And two contracts concerning my buying the property from Zhang Minzhong and his brother, which are sealed by the official, will be delivered to the hand of Zhu Yuanxing.

As can be seen from the text, the mountain land sold by Wu Gong was bought from Zhang Minzhong and his brother with the contract sealed by the official. The delivery of the original contract is to justify the origin and to imply that since the collateral duty (namely the delivery of the original contract) has performed, the loss of original contract or issue incurred will merely blame on the buyer. The practice was enforced by law, gradually turning into a routine. In practice it is often the case that the original contract is delivered. But sometimes the delivery of the original contract is expressly written into the new contract. In the *Contract of House Sale by Liu Yuxi in Tongzhi 10th Year (1871A.D.) of Qing Dynasty* also collected in the library of Peking University,[112] for example, it is put that in witness whereof, the parties hereto have caused this deed in case of the need of proof in the future. Included are the original contract from the owner Liu, the former contract with tax paid from Chen and the contract prior to the former one from JIn. All three ones are delivered to the buyer. There are also such records in Yuan Dynasty, the dynasty between Song and Qing. *Contract for the Sale of Lichi Orchard on Mountain by Pu E'you in Zhizheng 27th Year (1367 A.D.)* of Yuan Dynasty[113] says, "This contract is made in case of the need of proof in the future. And with Gong Ju (namely official documents) delivered, the buyer is liable for tax payment and property management". "Gong Ju", in Zhang's opinion, called "Wen Die" in Tang Dynasty, refers to the license to sale the property which is sealed and issued by the official. In addition to the direct delivery of the title certificate, notes can be added on the original title document to clarify the legal origin and transaction history of the property, whose nature and form as well as the form of liability are similar to "endorsement" on instruments nowadays; that is, he who has signed the contract shall justify the source of power to dispose the property, otherwise will be charged with passing for the owner or unauthorized sale.[114] The third way to account for the power source is to conclude a contract of transfer or write a receipt. In other words, a new contract or other documents are made between the seller and the buyer on the fact of property transfer so as to prove the origin of the property. It is provided as follows in a model contact for land-sale of Ming and Qing Dynasty[115]: The transferor wishes to sell the property out of his need. Both parties agree on the full price of XX under immediate payment. No receipts shall be made otherwise. Upon sale, the land price shall not be increased and the land itself shall

---

[111] See footnote 75, pp. 181–182.

[112] ibid.

[113] Yikui [25].

[114] Youyi [26].

[115] Guozhen [27].

not be redeemed no matter it is farmed or lent. This land is sold voluntarily without any dispute. If any, the seller, not the buyer, is liable to justify it.

From the foregoing cause, we can know that the property in such contract is without heir and has been pawned. And since the property is for sale, the buyer will pay the differentials. And it is a practice that the seller issues a receipt stating that the property pawned has been sold with price increased and shall not be redeemed. And it is stated in the original contract that this contract have been delivered to the buyer without the issue of a receipt, which simplifies the formality. And so is the contract of transfer. When it comes to property delivery, with the original price and the price differentials, etc. agreed on, the seller delivers the tax transfer certificate of the property and notes the price. This case can be backed up by the clause in *Contract for sale by Hong Jiwen and Hong Jixin in Daoguang 12th Year* (1832 A.D.).[116]

> The ownership of the building I share is transferred to my cousin Bian under this contract with the signature of the middleman. The price of the building we have agreed on is 7,000 wen… Upon delivery, the building is available under this contract. The tax will be levied on… paid in the form of grain. The price differential incurred and bonus are paid all at a time. Certain basic tax, if not paid, will not blame on the seller. No such Issues shall occur as price increase or redemption initiated by my brothers, uncles or nephews. The contract of transfer need not be made otherwise.

Though no receipt or contract of transfer has been formally made in the above contract, it still stipulated the formal clause, which guaranteed the right of the buyer to justify his ownership of the property bought. And we can also know that such documents can be included in the original contract instead of being made separately. The relevant clause in the original contract and the separate contract of transfer or receipt are equally authentic. The last way to justify the origin is to note in the contract where the old contract is, why it is not delivered and where it can be found for reference in the future. This case applies to the sale of small property. Binding more than the property, the old contract cannot be partially delivered. Such kind of clause matters no as much as the specific performance of delivery in term of effect. But since the old contract cannot be partly delivered, the relevant clause should be included specifying the cause as much as possible, which will more or less reassure the buyer. For example, it is said in *Contract of Field-sale by Wu Ziji in Jiaqing sixth Year* (1796 A.D.)[117] that the old contract cannot be delivered due to its binding over other property. And if needed in the future, it can be checked for reference.

Secondly, the procedure of Pi Zao (disposal of fixture and change of registration) would be applied, Pi Zao means to dispose of the fixture to the property under the clause of the contract and register the change of title. Take the Han Dynasty as an example. State management of real estate transactions at that time was not as rigorous as that of nowadays. Basically, it was both parties that agreed on how to deal with the transfer of real estate property rights and related fixture. *Positive proof is Deed (written on lead) for Land-purchase in Jianning fourth Year of Han Dynasty* (171 A.D.). It stipulates that those growing on the land all belong to Suncheng, the buyer.

[116]Quoted from Bingyao [28].

[117]See footnote 116.

So is *Deed for Land-purchase by Caozhongcheng in Guanghe 1st Year* (178 A.D.), which stipulates that all that grows the field and weighs over one qian are owed by Cao.[118] The transaction on real estate has fallen under the control of the government since Tang and Song Dynasty. Zhanji Bu (register book of field) and Yulin Ce (register book of land) are created to make records on real property for reference. Meanwhile, Song Dynasty has seen the existence of new documents on rights such as Guanshu (employment contract) and Fenshu (property division contract), etc.[119] Change of registration on Zhanji Bu is an enforced formality, which intends to affirm not only the property but property rights and its limits, especially the key point, namely whether the fixture or fructus to the property belongs to the buyer. Hence Zhang Chuanxi believes that Pizao is to dispose of the fixture to the property. It is stipulated in *Contract of Mountain-sale by Zhou Wengui in Baoyou 3rd Year* (1255 A.D.) of Song Dynasty that the mountain land specified herein as well as the fir trees thereon is sold to Zhang Zhongwen. And the fixture or fructus to the property, the fir trees are expressly specified in the contract to avoid any disputes. Another contract, the Contract of Land-purchasing by *Ma Yong in Dading 28th Year of Jin Dynasty* (1188 A.D.), can be more positive proof. It stipulates that the bamboos and trees growing on the land are not for sale. And rain drainage as well as carriages and cattle can pass there through. It is noteworthy that such clause is designed for reservation of rights. The fixture to the property (namely those bamboos and trees) is still in the possession of the original owner and what's more, easement such as drainage and driveway is expressly specified which helps clarify the right and obligation. If in Wutai County, Shanxi Province, where coal mines are abundant, land sale usually involves the statement of "the black and the white in whole". If not so, the coal under the earth is owed by the seller not the buyer.[120]

Thirdly, Guo Ge (transfer), also called "Tui Shou", means the transfer of tax obligation following the ownership; that is, the grain taxed for realty transfer should be paid by the buyer upon the transfer. The conclusion of the contract between both parties does not promise the immediate transfer of ownership. It is a must that both parties agree on the tax obligation and go through legal formalities before the delivery. Since the Eastern Jin Dynasty, state management of contract has been increasingly standardized to guarantee the smooth and secure going of the transaction. But it is no doubt that levy of contract tax has been another important factor. Although primarily intended to restrain the commerce, levy of contract tax infringes the interest of people in nature. "People going in for business instead of agriculture, reward and punishment involved are intended to adjust the transportation and price which is the just excuse for infringement of interest". The system of contract tax thus "has not been a practice until the Southern Dynasties".[121] The Eastern Jin Dynasty has seen the two kinds of "fixed tax rate". One is "San Gu", tax on transaction without contract. The other is "Shu You", namely contract tax. It can be said that the formation of the unified

118 See footnote 88, pp. 437, 419.

119 See footnote 27, pp. 449–451.

120 Judicial Department of Former Nanjing National Government [29].

121 *Suishu Food Chapter*.

contract system in ancient China was not due to the development of the contract itself but the taxation levied by the state. After the establishment of the Eastern Jin Dynasty, transaction of such property as servants, horses and cattle, and transaction of such realty as field and housing, all involve contracts by deed. And contracts sealed by the official are called "red contracts" while the private contracts are called "white contracts". "If the ownership is transferred to the contracting party who pays the tax, the contract is called red contract".[122] And when it comes to land sale, it is often the case that tax is intended to be avoided and thus the contracting party who should pay the tax does not register at the government. If so, the contract is called white contract.[123] The "tax payment" or "tax avoidance" is aimed at the tax imposed by the government. It is expressly stipulated in law of Song Dynasty that the white contracts are illegal and shall not be used whereby the management of contract tax system is strengthened, infringing the interest of people. In Volume V of The Law Reports of Southern Song Dynasty, Wu Shuzhai rules that judgment concerning transaction should be mainly based on the red contract rather than the white contract and that the former contract for transfer of property rights is a must. In March of Shaoxing 5th Year (1135 A.D.) it was provided that the white contract presented in a dispute over property shall not be enforceable.[124] And in October of Shaoxing 13th Year (1143 A.D.) it was further provided that the case shall not be heard where the sale of field or housing is testified by a white contract and that the subject shall be confiscated.[125] But as early as in Xuanhe 7th Year (1125 A.D.) the three departments (the Zhongshu, Menxia and Shangshu) emphasized that the sale or pawn of field and housing involved the registration at the government with the original contract presented, the tax paid and the new contract concluded. The old one shall go into the procedure of Pi Zao and the new one shall be sealed by the official. And the population registry shall be changed therewith to avoid the tax preserved while the property transferred.[126] Red contracts are designed for tax levy. As a result, the transfer has been the requisite for contract sealed and tax paid since Southern Song Dynasty. He who has the contract sealed before the transfer shall be punished under law and the transaction shall not be protected by the law. All the sale of field and housing involves the review of the property tax and tax for exemption of labor service registered. Upon the payment thereof, the contract shall be sealed.[127] "Tax shall not be paid without transfer in advance".[128] "The official has enacted a strict law against" contracts sealed in advance. Those made before the law can be remedied through "volunteer application for examination and registration in specified time." "if not so, the seller can bring a lawsuit for the return of the property without the

[122]Tao Zongyi: *Historical Notes Recorded in Nancun*, Vol. 17 Slave servant.

[123]Li Xinzhuan: *Jottings in Song Dynasty Since the Year of Jianyan* (1127 A.D.), Vol. 5.

[124]Li Xinzhuan: *Major Events Reports in Song Dynasty Since the Year of Jianyan* (1127 A.D.).

[125]*The Compilation of Song Dynasty, National Economy*, 70:141.

[126]ibid., 35:2.

[127]ibid., 35:6.

[128]ibid., 61:66.

money returned".[129] And cases shall not be heard even if the property owner has the contract if the contract without transfer tax paid is brought to court at other time.[130]

Lastly, Li Ye or Jiao Ye (delivery), which is referred to as "Guan Ye (namely taking charge)" by the buyer, means the process where the original owner deliver the ownership of the subject to the buyer. It was provided in Huangyou years of Ren Zong in Song Dynasty that where the field or housing is pawned, the ownership thereof shall be delivered.[131] And Wu Shuzhai has judged in Volume VI of *The Law Reports of Southern Song Dynasty*: "Under law, the ownership of the field or housing pawned must be transferred". Delivery shall be made in parallel to the contract's being sealed and levied, namely the transfer of tax duty before the official. Mr. Wu thinks of this clause as cutting to the point of pawn; that is, sale contract comes into effect on the premise of contract sealed and property delivered. It is recorded in Volume II of Guideline for Prefectures and Counties that delivery shall be based on the contract sealed in a field sale. Without the contract sealed or the property delivered, the money paid cannot justify the ownership. And even a trial shall be "based on the contract with the charger taken into account", from which we can thus know that the contract sealed and the property delivered are the prerequisite for the going into effect of the contract. Meanwhile, the limitation of action is closely connected with the seal of contract and the delivery of the property. Generally speaking, the date when the contract is sealed marks the beginning of limitation of actions. The record in The Law Reports of Southern Song Dynasty has been clear example. "Under law, pawn date is subject to the contract sealed". However, if the delivery of property is not made in sync with the seal of the contract, the date of the specific performance of delivery prevails. In Song Dynasty, contracts sealed by the official were imposed on time limitation and punishment will be imposed if the time limit is met. According to the memorial from the Ministry of Finance in Shaoxing 26th Year (1156 A.D.), the period is limited to 60 days in general. "If the deadline for the field-and-housing-sale contract's being sealed expires, the party shall be convicted and the property shall be confiscated. Such provision is too strict to be enforced, causing frequent complaint. The limitation specified in the law of Shaoxing years is intended to be followed; that is, the tax return should be filed at the government within 60 days and the contract can be drawn with the tax money in the following 60 days".[132]

References

1. Bodenheimer, E. (US). 1999. *Jurisprudence: The Philosophy and Method of the Law*, trans. Deng Zhenglai, 16–17. China University of Political Science and Law Press.
2. Qigang, Wan. 1998. Comment on the liberalism of Hobhouse. *Peking University Law Journal* 5.
3. Tian, Yin. 1995. *Modern Contract Law in France*, 18. Law Press.

[129] ibid., 61:61.

[130] ibid., 61:63.

[131] ibid., 173.

[132] *The Compilation of Song Dynasty, National Economy*, 54:13.

4. Xu, Liu. 1987. *History in People's Mind: Review of Modern Western Theories of History*, 79. Sichuan People's Publishing House.
5. Jingkun, Fu. 1997. *Contract Law in the 20th Century*, 8. Law Press.
6. Pingye, Li. 1987. *The Discovery of Man*, 128–130. Sichuan People's Publishing House.
7. Hegel, G.W.F. 1956. *The Philosophy of History*, trans. Wang Zaoshi, 464. SDX Joint Publishing Company.
8. Hegel, G.W.F. 1961. *Elements of the Philosophy of Right*, trans. Fan Yang, and Zhang Qitai, 62. The Commercial Press.
9. Kaixiang, Liu, and Liu Jiagang. 1997. *The Procedure of Contract*, vol. 5. Tribune of Political Science and Law.
10. Renyu, Li, and Liu Kaixiang. 1993. *Concept of Contract and Order Innovation*, 188. Peking University Press.
11. Zweigert, K., and H. Kotz. 1992. *An Introduction to Comparative Law*, trans. Pan Handian, 628. Guizhou People's Publishing House.
12. Sabine, Gorge H. 1986. *A History of Political Theory*, trans. Liu Shan et al., 487–488. The Commercial Press.
13. Zhimin, Li. 1998. *Civil Law of Ancient China*, 119. The Law Press.
14. Qingming, Kong, Hu Liuyuan et al. 1966. *The History of Civil Law in China*, 231. Jilin People's Press.
15. Xuehui, Zhang. 1998. A preliminary study on agricultural land issues in border areas of Ming and Qing Dynasties. *Journal of Chinese Historical Studies* (4).
16. Jinfan, Zhang, and Guo Chengwei. 1999. *General History of Chinese Laws*, vol. 5, 182. Law Press.
17. Yaxing, Wang, and Liang Zhiping (ed.). 1998. *Civil Trail and Local Agreement in Ming & Qing Dynasties*, 378. Law Press.
18. Zhen, Yang. 1997. *Anglo-American Law of Contracts*, 14. Peking University Press.
19. Jinfan, Zhang. 1998. *Review of Civil Law in Qing Dynasty*. China University of Political Science and Law Press.
20. Zheng, Wu. 1986. Study on the form of land ownership of family Ju in Gaochang. *Journal of Xinjiang Cultural Relics* (1).
21. Chuanxi, Zhang. 1995. *The Research on the Problem of Qin and Han Dynasties. The Improvement Process on the Contractual Form of Ancient China*. Peking University Press.
22. Daoyun, Gao, Gao Hongjun, and He Weifang. 1994. *Recent American Academic Writings on Traditional Chinese Law*, 174, 179–180. Chinese Political Science and Law University Press.
23. Zhongluo, Wang. 1975. A survey of Turpan unearthed documents of Tang Dynasty. *Journal of Cultural Relic* 7.
24. Qicai, Gao. 1995. *Customary Law of China*, 331–332. Hunan Press.
25. Yikui, Shi. 1957. Land contract of Yuan Dynasty. *Research on History* 9.
26. Youyi, Zhang. 1993. Land system in Huzhou region of Qing Dynasty before Opium War. *Journal of Science and Technology of China Press* 63.
27. Guozhen, Yang. 1988. *Research on Land Contract of Qing and Ming Dynasties*, 162–162. Renmin Press.
28. Bingyao, Shen. 1995. Sales of real estate in Suian County of Qing and Ming Dynasties. *Research on Social and Economic History of China* 4.
29. Judicial Department of Former Nanjing National Government (ed.). 2000. *Record of Civil Custom Investigation Report*, vol. I, 165. China University of Political Science and Law Press.

Chapter 4
Private Contracts as Laws and Decrees: Validity and Responsibilities of Contract

English functional anthropologist Bronislaw Malinowski, based on his observation on "savage culture", defines law as binding obligations which endow one party with certain rights and the other duties, and is maintained by a specific mechanism of reciprocity and publicity inherent in the structure of their society.[1] E. Adamson Hobel, the American anthropologist as well as a historian of legal philosophy, published the book *The Law of Primitive Man,* where he elaborates further Malinowski's idea and believes that "civil law", the positive law governing all the phases of tribal life, consists of a body of binding obligations. Those regarded as rights by one party are "acknowledged" as duties by the other. The norms of "civil law" are kept in force by the consistent mechanism of reciprocity and publicity that exists in the structure of their society.[2] We have no intention of seeking a safe and scientific definition of "law" or "civil law" as anthropologists do when they observe the "savage society", but two unique points of Malinowski's idea about law have definitely drawn our attention. One is that he views law itself as a kind of responsibility or liability, and the other is that he regards the social mechanism that fulfill or regulate the responsibilities and liabilities as "inherent", "reciprocal" and "public". This is also the case with the functions of contract. The rights and duties agreed upon by both parties are reciprocal, and fulfilling duties and realizing rights are seen as "justice", otherwise injustice. On basis of this, this chapter explores how ancient China realized the rights of contract, and how authorities and the civil society made adjustments and coordinate when met with obstacles.

[1]Malinowski [1].

[2]Hobel [2].

Y. Liu, *The History of the Contractual Thoughts in Ancient China*,
https://doi.org/10.1007/978-981-15-5768-2_4

The Realization of Justice: Divine Power-Human-Public Power

A look into the history of language development shows that the word "law" in western languages concerns two aspects: one is the "right" proposed by Greek culture, which means the "justice" that law pursues is to give every man his due, being fair distribution of the state. A Chinese scholar Liang Zhiping has provided some insights about this in his book.[3] The other is the two separate word origins in Roman law culture: jus and les. Jus stems from "justitia" (justice), which emphasizes the fairness of deals among Roman common citizens; and according to Saint Thomas Aquinas, lex originates from ligare (meaning "to bind"), thus the essence of law is to bind based on whether or not one fulfills his or her duties and obligations. And the school of natural law established at a later stage believes that the essential feature[4] of law is to undertake one's duties and obligations for others, which is consistent with Malinowski's idea. The "rights" and "obligations" or "duties" mentioned above are in nature two-dimensional: those regarded as rights by one party are acknowledged as duties by the other and vice versa. Therefore it can be seen from the dynamic semantic symbols that the Greeks attach greater importance to "fair distribution" whereas the Romans "equal choices" or "to bind", the essence being the pursuit of "justice" of law.

In terms of "contract", Roman law defines "making a contract" (contrahere) as establishing a relation based on "obligation". Bilateral contracts such as the contract of purchase and sale, the contract of loan and the contract of partnership are cases in point.[5] As a premise, the contract should be a "covenant (convenio)" under the "consent (consensus)" of both parties. Ulpianus holds that both consensual contract and real contract should contain a covenant, otherwise no contractual relations or obligatory relations would be established. And "covenant" refers to everything decided on by both contractual parties so as to reach an agreement or accommodation.[6]Gaius also puts great emphasis on "consent" by both parties in his discussion on obligation of bilateral contracts including the contract of purchase and sale and the contract of mandate.[7] Paulus, on the other hand, defines that the obligation emerges not only from the "covenant" of giving some money but also from the desire (animus) to set obligation (obligtio) to fulfill the responsibilities of giving and taking.[8]

However, both "consent" and "covenant" are just essential element and process in making a contract, the ultimate goal of which is the pursuit of "justice", that is,

[3]Liang [3].

[4]Zhang [4].

[5]Domitius Ulpianus. *A Commentary on the Edict (Ad Edictum)*. 11th edition. D.50.16.19; [Italy] *Corporis Iuris Civilis Fragmenta Select*. 1992. Edited by Sandro Schipani. Trans. by Ding Mei. China University of Political Science and Law Press, p. 8.

[6]Domitius Ulpianus. *A Commentary on the Edict (Ad Edictum)*. 4th edition. D.2. 14. 1. 3, p. 9.

[7]Gaius. *Institutes*. 3rd edition. D. 44. 7 2 Pr, pp. 12–13.

[8]Paulus. *Institutes*. 2nd edition. D. 44 7. 3. 1, p. 12.

to realize the rights of contract. Before the elaboration of that, one point has to be made clear: the realization of contractual rights depends on the validity of contract.

From where I stand, the so-called validity of contract lies in the binding power and enforceability to both parties. Contract itself, as a set of letter symbols, serves as the substantive public testimony of this mutually binding power and enforceability. Being mutually binding involves the compulsory moral and legal obligations based on the contract reached by both parties in order to guarantee the realization and fulfillment of corresponding rights and obligations. From an etymological perspective, the western world stresses "rights" or "obligations", whereas the essence of contract in ancient China emphasizes "和同 (harmonious agreement)" and "合同 (consensual agreement)", the "rights" and "obligations" of which are stipulated in relevant clauses of the contract. That is to say, western contract law prioritizes the value of "justice", meaning the realization of rights. By comparison, Chinese ancient contract law prioritizes that of "和同 (harmonious agreement)" and "合同 (consensual agreement)", which, being relevant to moral judgment to a large extent, attaches great importance to the will and consent of both parties while making the contract. Despite the differences, both of the two systems share the same ultimate goal of realizing rights.

The internal rationale of binding power is that the contractual parties have reached a consent and made their promises to each other, the ultimate goal of which, of course, is to realize rights or fulfill obligations. In continental law system, *Napoleonic Code* is the first to stipulate this binding power in the form of statute law. According to Clause 1 of Article 1134, "Contracts reached by law shall have the binding power as law does"; and Clause 2 "Rescission of the contract is not allowed unless there is a consensus of both parties or other reasons permitted by law". Both of the two items reflect the principle of autonomy of will, that is, one who declares his or her will shall be constrained by it.[9] The item which forbids arbitrary rescission of contract is the protection and guarantee of the principle and its spirit. This kind of legislative spirit is the proper inheritance of traditional natural law. In his discussion on the binding power of obligation, Grotius believes "An obligation has to be shared by parties involved according to their will so as to be truly binding". And the reason why one should keep a promise is that he or she proposes the obligation based on his or her behaviors. German philosopher Kant holds the same opinion that under all circumstances every binding obligation has to be regarded as self-imposed.[10] Thomas Hobbles believes making a contract is an act of will. Therefore, when one gives up or gives away the rights, he or she is obligated not to interfere with the enjoyment of rights by the recipient. Based on this understanding, Hobbes views fulfilling the contract as the third natural law and also the origin of justice, and that means breaching a contract is an act of injustice.[11]

The enforceability, on the other hand, is the principal means of maintaining the validity of contract. When one party breaches the contract without fulfilling the

---

[9]Yin [5].

[10]George [6].

[11]Thomas [7].

obligations, the other party or state public power can force him or her to fulfill the obligations and make compensation by compulsory means, so as to recoup the losses and guarantee the possible interests for the non-breaching party. It is safe to say that the binding power, to a great extent, demonstrates the "moral theory of honor" proposed by Hobbes, that concerns the fear for the consequences of breaching a contract by the breaching party and the pride and glory the non-breaching party feels.[12] Meanwhile enforceability attaches importance to realizing rights of contract by compulsory means. Both of the binding power and enforceability manifest the pursuit of justice and its realization.

The historical development of Chinese traditional contract law indicates that it doesn't have so profound theoretical connotation as western contract law does, and even it is hard to find theoretical explanation of abiding by civil contracts. However, the civil contract put great emphasis on the validity of contract. As early as Han Dynasty, different contracts all had their special items stipulating their validity. The following are examples:

February of the first year of Jian Ning Period (168 A.D.), Contract of Purchasing a Graveyard in Wufengli:

> In the first year of Jian Ning Period, nine people have bought a hill in Wufengli from Shangong (the land seller) to bury their father Ma Weijiang, which is worthy of 600 thousand Zhu*. The money has been delivered immediately on the day, and the contract has been made in duplicate with each party keeping one. This has been done in the February of the first year of Jian Ning. This contract is as valid as laws and decrees of the authorities.

In the fifth year of Xi Ping Period (176 A.D.), Contract of Liu Yuantai Buying a Grave[13]:

> On July 14th of the fifth year of Xi Ping Period, Liu Yuantai bought a piece of land to build the grave from the wife of Liu Wenping who was from the same county with 20 thousand Zhu. The money was delivered immediately on the day. The land stretches to Guandao in the south, Fendu in the west, Fangqin in the east and Liujing in the north. This contract is as valid as laws and decrees of the authorities.

In December of the first year of Guang He Period (178 A.D.), Land Deed of Cao Zhongcheng Purchasing Land to Build the Grave[14]:

> On December 15th of the first year of Guang He Period, Cao Zhongcheng bought 6 Mu (a Chinese unit of area) of farmland to build the grave from Chen Hunu who was from the same county. The land was worthy of nine thousand Zhu and the money was delivered immediately on the day. Everything in the land would thereafter belong to Cao Zhongcheng. This contract, which is made in the presence of Jia and Liu, is as valid as laws and decrees from the Heaven.

The "laws and decrees" from the above examples were common language among people, which could be interpreted from two perspectives: first, it indicated that the

[12]ibid., p. 107.

*Tranlator's annotation: Zhu: *an ancient unit of weight used as a monetary unit in Han Dynasty.*

[13]*Cultural Relics*. 1980 (6).

[14]The information without indicating sources in this section is all cited from *History of Chinese legal system: Land Law by* Niida Noboru.

contracts made enjoyed the trust of ghosts and gods (the Emperor of Heaven), with both human beings and gods being witnesses. Second, the contract made by both parties should be valid, which was equivalent to law. Thus it developed from the witness and trust of ghosts and gods to validity equal to laws of the authorities, which was written in the contract by both parties. In *Contract of Yang Shao Buying Land in the Fifth Year of Tai Kang Period of Tsin Dynasty* (284 A.D.), the validity of contract was explicitly recorded, "The private contracts made by people are as valid as laws and decrees".[15] Until Tang Dynasty, people gradually gave up depending on the trust of ghosts and gods and the validity of contract lied in the mutual constraint of contractual parties. This, to a certain degree, excluded the limit and intervention of laws of the authorities in private contracts. *Contract of Kang Baoqian Buying Land in the Fourteenth Year of Yan Shou Period of Gao Chang Kingdom* (637 A.D.) recorded that "The private contract is to be approved by both parties with their respective signatures as a symbol of trust".[16] The same expression can also be found in *Contract of Shi Buying Land on May 8th in the Fifteenth Year of Yan Shou Period of Gao Chang Kingdom* (638 A.D.).[17] Judging from other archaeological materials, the sentence "The private contract is to be approved by both parties" was already a formulistic expression then, the essence of which was the mutual recognition of the validity of contract to urge the other party to fulfill the obligations. It is also worth noting that expressions as "The authorities abide by the laws", "People comply with private contracts" are also common language in large amounts of contracts unearthed in Dunhuang including *Contract of An Huanqing Selling Land*,[18] *Contract of Zhang Xizi Buying a House*.[19] These also have proved that people attach great importance to the actual realization of the clauses of the contract when making one, thus excluding the intervention of law of the authorities. Since rights and obligations clauses including interest rates, prices in nongovernmental contracts are different from those of the authorities, especially in contracts regarding buying and selling, debit and credit, mortgage and pawn, people would apply those clauses made by themselves instead of the authorities. After Song Dynasty, the control on nongovernmental contracts by the feudal government became more stylized and strict, therefore few clauses concerning validity of contract could be found. The identification of validity of contract was then transferred from the contractual parties to feudal authorities, marking the official intervention of public power in civil contracts, which lasted till the end of Qing Dynasty. However, on the level of folk customary law, the contractual parties were still entitled to identify the validity of contract. Just as the saying goes, "There is the sun in the day, the moon at night; the authorities have their law and Yao people have their private contracts."[20]

[15]Qian Daxin. *Ancient Books from Qing Dynasty.* Volume 15.

[16]*The Unearthed Documents in Tturfan* (Book 4). Astana—Tomb No. 1.

[17]Cited from Kong et al. [8].

[18]*Dunhuang Documents.* The 1st Series. p.293.

[19]*Dunhuang Documents.* The 5th Series. Contract Documents (A).

[20]Gao [9].

In conclusion, both Chinese and western contract culture confirm the validity of the contract and regard it as the premise of realizing justice. The development of Chinese ancient contract law has undergone the evolution of divine power-human-public power, and then formed the parallel structure of public power and customary law.

Mutual Reinforcement and Restraint: The Dualistic Relation Between the Government and People

As has been discussed above, there is a dualistic relation regarding the validity of contract between common people and the authorities, where they coordinate with and recognize each other, meanwhile confront with and reject each other.

The validity of contract is mainly demonstrated in the following three aspects[21]: first is the enforceability of the contract itself; second is that a contract cannot be changed or rescinded by any party alone once it is made; third is that the performance of a contract has to be based on good will. When a contract is made, there has to exist some clauses or other related items explicitly guaranteeing the performance of the contract, that is, the validity of contract. Generally speaking, nongovernmental contracts adopt the following ways to indicate the validity:

Firstly, to make an oath or promise to the gods and spirits. This check and balance mechanism stems from the ancient oath and covenant, which can be traced back to Shang and Zhou Dynasties. The American sinologist Laura A Skosey provides in his paper an insight into the Chinese characters "告" and "诰", where he believes that "告" means "to report to the ancestors and sprits and gods" and "to sacrifice". It was religiously significant and embodied some kind of religious power from the end of Shang Dynasty to the end of Zhou Dynasty.[22] Henri Maspero, on the other hand, holds that the ancient "oath", as a kind of religious ritual in the first place, evolved into a court practice gradually with less and less connection to religious power.[23] As a matter of fact, both Skosey and Maspero are right about it in the way that Skosey emphasizes the psychological binding force of the oath and covenant itself while Maspero is dedicated to the evolution of it. The "covenant" originates from the blood pledge, blood sacrifice and blood covenant in ancient tribal alliances, where the covenant is made to impose moral duties on both parties that make the oath, with the power of religious gods and supernaturals to regulate them. British anthropologist Rober R Marett believes that making a covenant starts from exogamy and dual organization, and blood covenant means the combination of life, which is expressed by some rituals.[24] The true functions of the oath and covenant system can be easily found in ancient Chinese classics. The *Legend of Spring and Autumn Century* by Zuo

---

[21] Yintian [10].

[22] Laura [11].

[23] ibid. Cited from Henri Maspero, p. 100.

[24] Zhang [12].

Qiuming records that "Covenant is the way to reaffirm trust. Therefore it is bound by sincere hearts, served by jade and silk, completed by words, and guaranteed by gods".[25] From the account some features of covenant have emerged: (1) The covenant is made out of sincerity; (2) Both parties making the covenant have to reach a consensus upon the matter being discussed (completed by words); (3) The content of the covenant has to be externalized or re-expressed by some forms (served by jade and silk); (4) The basic motive of making a covenant is to seek protection and notarization from the gods so as to protect the interests of the non-breaching party and punish the breaching party; (5) However, the actual goal of making a covenant is to build mutual trust and bind it with the power of spirits and gods. This process has since then developed into common set expressions like "May it be taken as evidence by both gods and men". In later generations the practice became the foundation to win the trust of the judge and others. It was a prevailing custom that people involved in legal procedures were required to make a covenant in Zhou Dynasty,[26] which was then already evolved into the "court practice" as proposed by Maspero. Epigrapher Chen Mengjia explored the procedures of making a covenant in the 1960s, which was listed as follows[27]: (1) establish the contents of the covenant, write it on the bamboo tablets and duplicate several ones; (2) chisel the ground to make a pit; (3) offer sacrifices to the gods; (4) the presider take some blood from the sacrifices; (5) all the parties to the covenant smear the blood on their lips; (6) pray; (7) read the covenant loudly to the gods; (8) place the covenant with the sacrifices; (9) bury the covenant and the sacrifices in the pit; (10) one transcript or copy is preserved in the authorities in charge of administrating covenants and related documents. After Chen's study, the famous sinologist W. A. C. H. Dobson also summarized the procedures of making a covenant, further illustrating its impact on ancient contracts. His summary of the procedures was listed as follows[28]: (1) both parties reach an agreement on the conditions of the covenant; (2) kill some livestock as sacrifices, drink some blood and smear the blood on the lips; (3) take an oath (including the names of the parties to the covenant, clauses of the covenant and consequences of breaching the covenant); (4) summon gods and spirits to witness; (5) offer the sacrifices to the gods and spirits; (6) bury one covenant with the sacrifices; (7) agree and exchange the transcripts of the covenant; (8) one transcript or copy is preserved in the authorities in charge of administrating covenants and related documents. Chen and Dobson had a lot in common in their discussions, only Dobson's work being more sophisticated. Two points have to be made here, first, one copy of the covenant being buried with the livestock was to win the trust of spirits and gods, while the other copy being kept by local authorities which were in charge of administrating covenants and related documents was to win the trust of people as well as for future examination and confirmation. Second, the procedures of making a covenant had exerted great influence on those of making a

---

[25] *Legend of Spring and Autumn Century by Zuo Qiuming*. Year 12 of Ai Gong, Year 13 of Zhao Gong.

[26] *Rites of Zhou Qiu Guan Si Meng*.

[27] Chen [13].

[28] Dobson [14].

contract for the generations to come. In fact, some covenants in Zhou Dynasty were in nature civil contracts protecting property ownership and property transfer relations. According to the study of some scholars, the covenants of East Zhou Dynasty were classified into six categories[29]: Zong Meng (宗盟, people of the same family name taking an oath of alliance), Wei Zhi (委质, mortgage), Na Shi (纳室, pledging non-violation), Zu Zhou (诅咒, vowing or cursing), Bu Shi (卜筮, divination) and others, among which the oath of "mortgage" was to mortgage oneself to an owner to show sincerity and loyalty. This kind of "mortgage" was usually due to debt, survival problems or the purpose of seeking refuge, and the legal status of the person being mortgaged was inferior to that of Zhuhou (seigniors in feudal China), Gongqing and Dafu (high-ranking officials in feudal China) and superior to that of "Qunmeng" (the great unwashed) such as Chen (subjects), Zao and Li (Yamen runners in feudal China). At that time, this class of people being mortgaged was called "Shumin" (the multitude), who could make a living on their own and whose special legal status and rights were based on and defined by their "mortgage" covenants with those high-ranking officials including Zhuhou, Gongqing and Shifuren. As for "Nashi", it was a kind of covenant where leaders of alliances reached a consensus and pledged non-violation of others' slaves, properties and assets.

After getting a basic idea of the covenant system, we can move on to the functions of the covenant itself, which can be generalized from three aspects. The first is that of publicity, that is, people would make a covenant with the presence of a great number of people as witnesses and under the supervision of gods and spirits. The second is that of testimony. The actual goal of publicity is to guarantee the mutual conformity to the covenant. The institution of covenant and its relevant rituals all serve as the testimony of the existence of the covenant and its unchangeable validity. In *Rites of Zhou*, there is an official title called "Zu Zhu", who is in charge of presiding over eights kinds of deeds including making covenants, conferring honors, etc.[30] Zheng Xuan once said: "All the words of the people involved in those eight kinds of deeds should be heard by the gods and spirits. Making a covenant are usually concerned with important matters, with major ones being decided by Meng (盟 covenant), and minor ones by Zu (诅 vow)." And the documents of the covenant served to enhance the validity and credibility of the government. Meanwhile, there is also the official position or title of "Si Meng", who is responsible for the regulations and administration of making covenants. As it records, "Whenever there is disbelief, conflicts or disharmony among vassal states, the official Si Meng would preside over the covenant, record the contents and rituals of the covenant, and then face north and report it to the gods and spirits by reading it out". "In the same way, make covenants with those who violate the orders and decrees of the monarch, and make covenants with those who breach their pledges."[31] The third function concerns its binding power, which is the essence of the covenant system. The fundamental goal of publicity and testimony is to bind the parties involved to abide by the covenant. People

[29]Li [15].

[30]*Rites of Zhou Chun Guan Zu Zhu.*

[31]*Rites of Zhou Qiu Guan Si Meng.*

also tend to depend on power from the gods and spirits and the other parties involved in the covenant to prevent each other from breaching it. If there is a violation or breach of the covenant, they would make a plea to the heaven for punishment; or the other parties would make concerted efforts to force the breaching party. Thomas Hobbes once described a similar situation, "Making a promise or a vow is the linguistic form added to a promise. The person shows his compliance with what he said through a promise or a vow, otherwise he or she would get the punishment from the gods." "Making a promise with religious rituals will augment the fear of breaking it."[32]

The covenant system has made a huge impact on contract and the most important is that its spirit of honesty and good faith evolved into the basic principle of civil law later. It is easy to find in related literature of Spring and Autumn Period that honesty and trust are things valued greatly in trade. Records of Jin State advocated that "Honesty should be attached importance to when dealing with others."[33] Duyu clearly explained that "Cheating is not allowed and be honest and trustworthy". Another example from history could further elaborate this point: Zheng Huangong (the first emperor of the State of Zheng) made a covenant with the merchants of the state and reached an agreement to abide by: "The emperor Zheng Huangong and the merchants all migrated from the region of Zhou. They mowed the grass, worked together, and cultivated the land to live in harmony together in Zheng State. They made a covenant that was honored for generations so that they counted on each other. Zheng says: 'If you do not betray me and my state, I will never get your merchandise by force or by extortion. If you are lucky enough to have precious goods, you don't have to tell me and I will not interfere.' Since they both stuck to the covenant unswervingly, they could rely on each other and coexist in peace and harmony."[34] This event happened during the period of 804 B.C. and 771 B.C., when Zheng Huangong made a covenant with the merchants out of political benefits. He promised to them that the government authorities would not intervene with normal trade and commercial activities by coercive measures; nor would the authorities seize the merchants' goods or property by force. They merchants, in turn, promised not to betray Zheng State to serve other countries. The validity of the covenant lasted for a long time and made a big contribution to the stability and peace of Zheng State, sustaining the merchants' normal trade and commercial activities in the State as well. Therefore, the true meaning and core of making a covenant lay in people rather than gods. In the latter periods, private contracts usually included expressions like "as valid as laws and decrees" as a form of promising to ghosts and gods to win mutual trust, which was the heritage and development of the covenant system. This point was also shown in *Contract of Xue (wife of Zhu Man) Buying Land in the Fourth Year of Xian Kang Period of Tsin Dynasty* (338 A.D.).[35]

---

[32]See footnote 11, pp. 107–108.

[33]*Legend of Spring and Autumn Century by Zuo Qiuming*. Year 27 of Xi Gong.

[34]*Legend of Spring and Autumn Century by Zuo Qiumig*. Year 16 of Zhao Gong.

[35]Cited from Zhang [16].

> In the February of the fourth year of Xian Kang Period of Tsin Dynasty, the late wife of Zhu Man has bought the land from the heaven and house from the earth, which was worthy of two million and the money was delivered immediately on the day. Anyone who covets Xue's land shall confront the gods of the heaven; anyone who covets Xue's house shall confront the guards of the Hades. All gods and spirits are the witnesses. This deed is as valid as laws and decrees from the emperor of heaven.

Judging from the covenant, obviously it was a contract of buying a graveyard instead of a normal business contract. Two points have to be noted here, first, this kind of contracts all followed the established structure and form of formal contracts of purchase and sale, and the clause of effectiveness as "This is as valid as laws and decrees" was added at the end of the contract. Second, the contract was viewed as something to win trust from ghosts, spirits and gods as well as a testimony to prove that Xue owned this land to build a tomb legally, preventing others from occupying the land. It seems that the latter is more practical and important than the first one.

The second aspect of demonstrating the validity of contract is through willingness and spontaneity, thus forbidding regret, which is the second phase of the development of private contract after that of winning the trust of ghosts and spirits. This is the symbol of the secularization and formalization of contract. Such clauses are derived from the tradition of winning trust from ghosts and spirits. They develop from emphasizing the witnessing, supervision, judgments, and punishments of ghosts and spirits to emphasizing the secular validity, that is, the validity of contracts to people. A contract is no longer a medium or carrier to get trust from ghosts and spirits, rather, it becomes the medium or carrier to get trust from both contractual parties as well as a tool to testify to the rights and obligations of the contract. A great number of private contracts unearthed in Dunhuang and Turpan showclearer and explicit description of the validity of contract compared to those in Han Dynasty. The following are examples:

> On January 26th, the first year of Qian Feng Period (666 A.D.), Zheng Haishi from Conghua village borrowed ten silver coins from Zuo Chongxi, with an interest of one silver coin and a half. The money should be paid back to Zuo when he requires it. If Zhen refuses to do so, then Zuo shall get the properties or belongings from Zheng's house worthy of the value. If nothing can be taken from Zheng, then his wife and children shall pay back the money for him. The authorities follow their policies and laws and common people private contracts. Two parties make a contract based on consensus and have the contract as the testimony …[36]

Again, in *Zhang Yiquan's House Sale Contract in the Fourth Year of Qian Ning Period (897 A.D.)*[37]:

> The establishment of contract must be completed on that day without either party owing or problems unsolved. The contract remains valid under any circumstances. Once signed, no party is entitled to go back. If one goes back on the contract, certain punishment is due. This contract is signed voluntarily by both parties. And it is used for further reference in case of unfaithfulness.

---

[36] *The Unearthed Documents in Turfan* (Book 4). *Documents of Tomb No. 1, Astana.*

[37] *Dunhuang Documents,* 5, *Contract Documents,* A.

And in *Shen Yanqing's Loan Contract*[38]:

> On April15th of Year Kuiwei, Shen Yanqing from Pingkang township signed a loan contract stating that by the end of August, Shen must repay with a piece of sheepskin. If not, interests will be generated monthly. No turning back on the contract once signed. If so, certain punishment is due (five Dou (a unit of volume) of wheat). This contract is signed for further reference in case of unfaithfulness.

To sum up the previous three contracts, both contracting parties had to reach consensus concerning the rights and obligations in the contract without being forced to. Meanwhile, the promises voluntarily made by both parties must be complied with; otherwise responsibilities for breach of the contract must be due. Besides, the validity of the contract could be decided by both parties so that the limitation and intervention from *jus cogens* would be diminished or offset. The contract itself was a loyal record of the agreement reached by consensus of both parties.

Thirdly, specific performance or clauses of execution. As Hobbes put, "Pledge cannot add binding force to contracts." Because pledge was made due to the fear of Gods. For the real protection of people's interests, conscientious fulfillment by both contracting parties would be necessary. When contractual obligations failed to be realized, the non-regretting party could seek remedies through private power to complete the realization process of contractual rights. For instance, in the aforementioned contacts, the obligee was entitled to take the household property from the obligor as pledges if the obligor could not fulfill the obligations under the contract when the time was due. The obligor would be in no position to raise objections. It is worth mentioning that in Tang Dynasty, set expressions like "private needs must comply with both parties" and "the government has policies and laws, and civilians follow private contracts" were very popular in contracts. On the one hand, it asserted the validity of civil contracts, but more importantly, it led civil contracts to form an enclosed validity system, namely, the validity of contracts would and could only be limited to contracting parties, rather than the third party or the state public power. This proved, from the opposite side, that the third party or the state public power was not legitimate to exert mandatory intervention and control on the contracting process and the relevant contractual clauses to weaken the validity of civil contracts. Therefore, the historic proposition of contractual freedom was realized. No changes or transformations were ever made throughout Tang Dynasty. From Song Dynasty, the intervention from the state government increased gradually. Contractual freedom was constrained by the mandatory regulations from the state so that the freedom declined drastically.

Fourthly, clauses of public remedy. When it is difficult for the power of gods and the private to fulfill contractual obligations, the state public power steps up to the historical stage as the last resort to ensure realizing the rights of the legitimate party and the justice of the contracts. This point will be further discussed later.

With respect to the confirmation of contractual validity from the civil customary law, one point that needs notice is that traditionally, Chinese society regarded marriages, land and debt as "trivial matters". The government empowered the civil

[38] *Dunhuang Documents,* 5, *Contract Documents*, D.

customary law the jurisdiction right to mediate such civil disputes. In essence, it was the "predetermine right" that forced the government to acknowledge the jurisdiction right of the civil society. Taking Ming and Qing Dynasties for example, the mediation of "trivial matters" such as marriages and land was granted to the elderly to operate in "Shenming Pavilion". In relevant policies concerning the pre-emption right of relatives and neighbors to immovable property, the civil customary law was finally adopted by the government and became the law because of its better efficiency than the government regulations. The predetermine right or priority right among family members was a unique feature of Chinese law culture and even more so an everlasting convention in Chinese contract culture. In Ming Dynasty, "*Zong Fan (The Family Regulations)*" in Xu family provided that: "If injustice happens among siblings, the leader of the house will make an inspection with fair judgment coming in the end. The leader of the family will take over if disputes occur based on the judgment. However, ten whips for each sibling will be conducted regardless before any in-depth investigations. After the whips, justice will then be given."[39] *Family Rules* of Family Zhu from Qing Dynasty provided that, "Disputes involving resentment, land and debt among family must be reported to the family leaders first in ancestral hall for mediation before reporting to the government. If not, the fine of five liang (taels) of silver will be conducted on the reporter."[40]

Improving Customs Through Rites: The Influence of Confucian Natural Law on Contracts

One of the prominent features of China's contract development was to depend on the civil strength to ensure and guarantee contract validity. The fundamental reason was that since Zhou Dynasty, the patriarchal clan system had continued with a deep and immovable root. However, it seemed a bit overwhelming to fulfill the contract simply by the family power itself or just one party's weak power, for contractual disputes among individuals such as mishandling or failure to achieve reconciliation were bound to ignite violence among individuals or more seriously, to start fights among families. This was intolerable for the gentry's class and the government. Therefore, apart from civil contract customary law, state statute law or judiciary and administration officials began to adopt "law" and "rite" as the norm to settle civil disputes since Zhou Dynasty, developing into a duality situation with civil customary law where they paralleled and overlapped with each other. They waxed through mutual reinforcement and restraint, compromised with and promoted the civil customary law. This process was called "improving the customs through rites (以礼正俗)", a process where Confucian natural law infiltrated and integrated into the civil customary law.

[39]Family and Clan Regulations in China. 1998. Edited by Fei Chengkang. citing from Xu [17].

[40]See footnote 39, citing from Wang Jiyou. *Family Rules of the Zhu in the District of Changgou, Piling*.

Joseph Needham inspected the differences between Chinese legalism and Confucian legal study, saying that "legalism only puts emphasis on solid law that simply reveals lawmakers' will". While conversely, Confucian law "abides by traditional conventions, routines and manners, which are deeply rooted in Chinese people's mind in all generations…This is the rite, which may be regarded as equal to natural law".[41] As was put in the preface, the fundamental feature of Chinese contracts is ethics. Just as American scholar P. Peernboom said, the theoretical principle of natural law was the emphasis on the necessary connection between law and ethics, meaning that a rule had to comply with ethics in the first place so as to become law.[42]

From the synchronic level, the influence of Confucian natural law on traditional contract culture was revealed from the following three aspects.

First, incorporating rites into laws—ethicization. The mutual complementarity of rites and laws were the fundamental pillar to sustain Chinese traditional society. It was the rites, rather than laws, that mediated civil legal relations. Mr. Zhai Tongzu believed that the core of Confucian rites were the family system and social identity.[43] The patriarchal clan system starting from Zhou Dynasty entitled the eldest son with various rights including those to preside over sacrifices, take charge of the property and manage family affairs. After the decline of the patriarchal clan system, family leaders and clan leaders became the basic units in politics and laws.[44] With the combination of families and the state, they not only took over the religious worship right, property management right and punishment right, they also became the preliminary judicial organ recognized by the state law. This predetermine right among families had a very prominent status in civil disputes. We could see this from relevant clan rules and family regulations. Wang Yanchou's *On Clan and Family Rules* once said: "If disputes occur within the family clan, the elderly are responsible for mediating and settling them. If disputes with another clan occur, they should be settled without going to the court unless they concern very important matters. If disputes with another clan concern only trivial things, the clan head would send someone who has a good rapport with the opposite side to mediate and settle them. If the impertinence lies in our family, an apology must be made by us; whereas if the impertinence lies in the opposite side, mediation and compromises should also be made by reporting to the local government."[45] The *Family Rules* revised during the reign of Emperor Kang Xi at the beginning of *The Genealogy Book of the Xu Clan in Daoguang Wuwei Chalin* read: "The disputes among the family members must be reported to the branch head (or clan head), who will gather other family members for discussion to give a fair judgment and punishment accordingly." *Family Regulations,* the first volume of *The Genealogy Book of the Ren Clan in Jingde during Guang Xu Period of Qing Dynasty*

[41] Joseph [18].

[42] P. Peerenboom. *Confucian Jurisprudence: Beyond Natural Law*. ibid. as in footnote 22.

[43] Qu [19].

[44] ibid., pp. 21–26.

[45] Predecessors' Rules of How to Behave Oneself (Volume 2). citing from Xu (1995). Zhonghua Book Company. The following clan regulations and family rules without indicating sources are all cited from Xu.

read: "The disputes among the family members should be settled by the head of the clan through discussion in the presence of other clan members to reach a fair judgment." The *Ancestral Rules*, the first volume of the *Genealogy Book of the Cui Clan in Ruxu in the Republic of China*, read: "When the juniors have disputes, they must resort to the senior clan leader to get a fair and reasonable judgment." What was worth mentioning here was that the priority rights enjoyed by the families were recognized and even awarded by the government, the violation of which would lead to certain punishments. The second volume of the *Datong Genealogy Book of the Chen Clan in Yimen in the Republic of China Division—Family Regulations* stipulated those during Qian Long Period: "The disputes, big or small, must be reported to the family or clan leaders in the first place. They can be reported to the government if they are too complicated. Those who report to the government without family judgment first will be subject to punishments." *Family Rules* at the beginning of the *Genealogy Book of the Wang Clan in Dongxi Chungu during Guang Xu Period of Qing Dynasty* wrote: "It must be reported to the ancestral hall when injustice occurs. Fair judgment would thus be yielded. Family members who report to the government directly without first getting the family judgment would be punished as a violation of family laws." The *Ancestral Rules* at the beginning of the *Genealogy Book of the Zou Clan in Yongding during Guang Xu Period of Qing Dynasty* wrote: "If one takes the liberty of reporting disputes to the government without informing the family leaders, the act will be seen as contempt to the elderly. Punishments will be conducted before judgments."

From Song Dynasty to the Republic of China, the priority rights of the family had become the first legal domain for the government to rule the society. Yet the paramount status of the family's priority rights on both the governmental and civil level stemmed from the "rites" that were constantly emphasized and honored by the Confucian natural law. This was clearly stated in *The Book of Rites·Da Zhuan*: "It is humane and moral for people to be close to their kinsfolks, therefore they respect their ancestors. Because they respect their ancestors, they honor and revere the clan as well. It is the sense of honor and reverence that unite the people of the same clan together." *Families and Clans*, the third volume of *Baihu General Sense*, showed a clearer inclination in its explanation of "clan": "The clan stays and unites as a group. The members of a clan experience love and misery, and share happiness and sorrow together." The moral value of rites in Confucianism emphasized the intimacy among family members. Its social value lay in getting together in love. Its social psychological basis was the family cohabitation decided by blood and geographical ties, and its ultimate goal was "Da Tong (大同 the Great Harmony)" where all mankind would care and love each other.

As an appendage of the monarchical power, the existence of clan power had its historic value and made corresponding historic contribution as well. However, when studying from the development of contracts, incorporating rites into laws by Confucian natural law (namely granting the clan power with legal status and enforcing it by the mandatory force of the state) had far worse side effects. Firstly, the patriarchal system and family or clan power overwhelmed individual rights and talents, so much so that the civil acts of civil subjects were largely constrained. Secondly, the statue laws of the past dynasties seldom adjusted civil contractual relations but assigned them entirely to family "discussions and judgments" and the "integrity" of the local government, resulting in the lack of a strong equitable mechanism for judicature and law enforcement. Thirdly, the principle of settling contractual disputes preferred ethics to justice, valued faith more than property, and emphasized harmony over interests, which obstructed the civil subjects' psychological motive to pursue interests.

Second, moral concern—the sense of human sentiment. Confucian natural law could be viewed as a paradox of two contradictory values: on the one hand, it stressed the "ethics" which honored the elderly and degraded the young, and advocated that the rich and noble enjoy higher social statuses than the poor and lowly. On the other hand, it also showed moral concern for the multitude as it was people-oriented. Although this moral concern was based on the ethics, Confucian law entitled people from the same social class the same rights and status to give prominence to "human sentiment". Investigating from the contractual aspect, for instance, the folk customary law and the state law both allowed the sale and purchase of humans and permitted them to be a means of debt guarantee. During the reign of Emperor Han Wu, "In Huainan area, it is common to sell one's sons and daughters to others as their servants, which were called "Zhui Zi (赘子)". If they are not redeemed within three years, they would remain servants."[46] During the reign of Emperor Guang Wu, a special "human sale-purchase law" was established.[47] It remained unchanged until Qing Dynasty. Interestingly, the law ensured the creditors' right of personal control over the debtors on the one hand, it also set up a large amount of amnesty policies to release the servants as the "Liang Ren (良人, ordinaries, or common people as opposed to servants of lowly status)"and meanwhile prevented the killing or damage of the lives and bodies of servants or tenant farmers on the other hand. It was even stricter in the prohibition of forcing the ordinaries to be servants to repay the debt. Based on *Law Code of Tang Dynasty*, "Those who force ordinaries to be servants shall all be punished as the third-level criminals; and those who are in the know but still commit the crime shall be punished as the second-level criminals."[48]In order to prevent the sale of ordinaries, a certain legal process was established regarding the sale and purchase of servants—"Guo Jian (过贱, transfer of servants)": "When selling and purchasing a servant, a certificate must be provided by the authorities and the servant must be examined by the county official to confirm his or her identity as the servant. This is called Guo Jian."[49] This was clearly stated in relevant contractual documents such as *Contract of Servant Purchase by Lady Xue Shiwu in the 20th Year of Kai Yuan Period in Tang Dynasty (732 A.D.)*.[50] This kind of servant purchase contract were very common in the documents unearthed in Turpan and Dunhuang, from which we could see that apart from the prerequisite that the servants should not be ordinaries, the sales had to

[46]*Book of Han Biography of Yanzhu. Yan Shigu's annotations of Ruchun.*

[47]*Book of Later Han Historical Records of Emperor Guang Wu* (Volume 1).

[48]*Law Code of Tang Dynasty Position Rules.*

[49]*The Collection of Edicts in Tang Dynasty.*

[50]Cheng [20].

be agreed by the servants themselves and verified by the government. As was stated in *Dunhuang Xingke Wang Xiuzhi's Sale Contract of Servant Hu*: "The identity of the servant has been verified by the government (in order to make sure the servant was not an ordinary). Moreover, this deal has been agreed by servant Hu Duobao."[51] From the perspective of judicial practice, it was common that the magistrates referred to laws and certain rules when conducting judicial acts, but it was also not unusual to judge a case by human sentiment. In other words, among "conforming to human sentiment", "conforming to law", and "conforming to reason", the first one proved to be the priority for local officials, gentry's class and family public discussions. American sinologist Wen-yen Tsao proposed the same idea in the 1960s and viewed it as a historical tradition for Chinese people, saying Chinese judicature attached the most importance to human sentiment in dispute settlement, followed by reason and lastly by law.[52] During Guang Xu Period, the Commissioner of Shanxi Fan Zengxiang showed the local officials' emphasis on "human sentiment" and their moral concern for the weak when dealing with a contractual dispute. Lady Wangzhao Shi sold her house to Li three years ago. However, they signed an agreement but no money was paid since it was not due yet. Afterwards Lady Wangzhao Shi sold the house to Jiao. The subordinate county government could not give a fair judgmentto the case, thus reporting it to Fan. Fan wrote[53]:

> Li Jishan bought the house from Lady Wangzhao Shi at the price of 760 Jin (a monetary unit). The agreement was signed but no money was paid since it was undue. Now Wangzhao Shi sold the house again to Jiao. Therefore, disputes occurred. The two buyers both insist that they bought the house before the other. The seller implored that she always hoped to sell the house to the higher bidder. Moreover, the seller is a woman who sold her house out of poverty, so it is understandable that she would breach the agreement and sell the house for better profits when Jiao offered to pay extra 100 Jin. In addition, it is not difficult for Li to purchase assets from elsewhere since he has no lack of money. Why bother messing up with a poor and muddled lady? The house is allowed to be sold to another buyer, and the former agreement is therefore invalid.

The interesting part of this case was that the imploration with human sentiment "beat" argument based on reason. Fan acknowledged Lady Wangzhao Shi's breach of the agreement "forgivable" though it was against the reasons due to the fact that she had to sell the house out of poverty. Therefore, her violation of the contract was understandable and valid. This was what D. F. Henderson called "didactic conciliation" rather than court verdict. The famous official assistant Wang Huizu in Qing Dynasty believed that a thorough understanding of law was absolutely necessary to be a successful official assistant; however, its application must be consistent with "human sentiment" with the complement of law to achieve the "co-existence" of both. His famous work *Zuo Zhi Yao Yan* put special emphasis on "human sentiment" by saying that "Understanding law is the essence of being a successful official assistant, and the elegance of its application lies in the observation of human sentiment. Customs vary from place to place. Therefore, it is of prior importance to

---

[51] *The Unearthed Documents in Turpan*. Book 4. *Documents of Tomb No.5, Astana.*

[52] Wen-en [21].

[53] *Fanshan Criticism* (Volume 8). "Presentations of Criticisms on Liu Luozhou".

learn modestly and make adjustments based on different situations before laws and decrees are adopted, thus coordination and reputation would be achieved. Otherwise resentment and slander would be generated." His *Xue Zhi Yi Shuo* also read: "Human sentiment and local customs differ from one place to another. When an official first takes office, it is vital not to be self-righteous … Every time he hears a case, he needs to summon some knowledgeable and sophisticated people to learn about the local customs. Afterwards a fair judgment shall be achieved with the consideration of both law and sentiment."[54] If the "human sentiment" in Fan's judgment laid emphasis on the improvement of the litigant's life and the rationality of her subjective motivation, then Wang expanded the scope of "human sentiment" to law making, judicature and law enforcement, drawing a gigantic and shining arc for traditional "human sentiment", thus exerting a huge influence on the traditional contractual development.

Third, "improving customs by rites"–regularization. The performance of ancient contracts, especially private commercial contracts, mainly relied on the power of the customary law, that was, "the customs and habits" that Wang Huizu repeatedly stressed. The power of the customary law was embodied in three kinds of powers, namely, those of clans, guilds and villages, which were the ultimate judicator and performer of contract validity. Sprenkel (Sybile Van Der Sprenkel) divided the Chinese legal institution into three levels: the first was the "informal mediation" that involved the mediation by a third party. The second was the "formal adjudication" conducted by non-governmental organizations such as clans, guilds and villages. The last one was the official trial. Among them, the second one exerted the greatest influence on Chinese judicial adjudication, namely, the power of customary law, which served as the "subordinate tribunals" approved by the government and was even granted "jurisdiction". The people who carried it out were mostly leaders of villages or localities, or social elites.[55] With respect to the contractual relations that involved issues like marriages, land and debt, the "predetermination right" of customary law was recognized by the government and was seen as "adaptation to local conditions". This predetermination right activated the sentiments and moral spirit of common people and formed a duality situation with official "judgment right" where mutual promotion and restriction coexisted. Hiroaki Terada believed that the Chinese traditional society featured "the state has its laws and statutes while the civil society has its private contracts". The "laws and statutes" expressed the political space under legislation, which was backed by the state mandatory power and took as the principle "the order from the heaven" with the ultimate goal of justice. On the other hand, "the private contracts", with contracts being the medium, demonstrated the economic living space of the civil society. Based on mutual trust, they were enforceable and took mutual benefits as the principle with the similar goal of achieving fair justice. Terada referred to "regional prohibitions" in *Yi Yan Heng Qiu* to prove his point: "The

[54]Wang [22].

[55]Sybile [23].

state has its laws while the local regions have their rules and prohibitions. Laws are used to govern the country while the prohibitions are used to regulate the region."[56]

While the government recognized the "predetermination right" of the customary law on contractual relations, it also deliberately wielded the state power to control and constrain the power of the customary law so as to maintain the effective order of private contractual relations. This was elaborated in *Xue Zhi Yi Shuo* by Wang Huizu, "to set up rules based on customs and to make adaptations to local conditions, preventing extremes", and in this way "the social order can be maintained, which would benefit all". This process was viewed by the government and the rulers as "improving customs through rites", which was demonstrated as follows: firstly, the government kept the final adjudication of civil contractual disputes. For instance, if one contracting party or both parties did not accept the "judgment" of the clans, guilds or tribes, it was allowed to report the case to the government, who would make the final adjudication concerning their rights and obligations. This was also acknowledged by folk customary law. Secondly, the procedures and formats of contracts were strictly stipulated, which would not be discussed in detail here. Thirdly, while the folk customary law was entitled "private remedy" in settling contractual disputes, reporting to the government and acquiring its admission was a must before "private remedy" was conducted. To put it straight, the ultimate execution of contracts was controlled by the government. Fourthly, the government enjoyed the authority to confirm and to judge in terms of the validity of the contracts. Whether a contract was valid or not normally depended on the joint agreement between two parties, on the level of the customary law, the premise of settling disputes was the validity of the contracts. Nonetheless, as the government kept and sustained the power of final adjudication of civil contractual disputes, the authority of confirming contract validity still belonged to the government. Taking the sale and purchase of servants in Han Dynasty as an example, in the first Year during the reign of Emperor Han Gaozu, famine swept the country. An imperial edict was issued allowing the famine victims to sell their sons and daughters as servants.[57] However, just after three years, the imperial court announced the sale and purchase contracts were invalid and the servants were remitted to be back to normal citizens.[58] At the beginning of Eastern Han Dynasty, the government also re-identified the sale and purchase of servants in the civil society. In the seventh year of Jian Wu Period, Emperor Guang Wu issued his imperial edict that those who were forced to be servants or became so due to famine were allowed to choose out of their free will to remain servants or not.[59] Though this act denied the validity of the contracts of servant sale and purchase in the civil society, it was a gesture of amnesty and mercy, promoting the stability of the society. Likewise, the acts of releasing servants as ordinaries in the society were approved by the government and the signing of "Servant Releasing Writ" was required. Based on the law in Tang Dynasty: "When releasing the servants as ordinaries, a writ must be

[56]Hiroaki [24].

[57]*Book of Han Record of National Economy.*

[58]*Book of Han Historical Records of Emperor Gao* (Volume 2).

[59]*Book of Later Han Historical Records of Emperor Guangwu.*

signed by the family leader and the first-born son and a copy of the writ has to be kept in the government."[60] A servant releasing writ from Tang Dynasty clearly reflected the profound influence of the government laws and decrees on the civil society[61]:

> I deeply recognized the hideousness of keeping servants. Therefore I decided to release those diligent and industrious servants as ordinaries who used to start to work very early in the mornings and toil till very late at nights. Those servants, together with their future decedents, have the freedom to choose their life. The government has laws and decrees. If this writ is violated, it will be reported to the government.

Apart from explicitly fulfilling the obligation of releasing the servants as ordinaries, this contract involved more of human concern and moral integrity in Confucian natural law. It was a typical model of abidance by law, which was advocated and encouraged constantly by the government.

Validity and Responsibilities of Contract

Zheng Yubo believed that the contractual validity should be divided into the validity of the contractual rights and that of the contractual obligations. The former one was reflected as the acceptance claiming power, execution power and sustaining power enjoyed by the obligee to the obligor's delivery, which was the premise of generating contractual responsibilities. The latter one involved the following obligations or responsibilities: (1) The obligor should render performance of the contractual obligations comprehensively, accurately and timely, (2) All the property of the obligor was the general guaranty of his/her obligatio; (3) The obligor should be condemned to the payment of damages by reason of incomplete, inaccurate or delayed performance of the obligations as often as he could not prove that such non-performance proceeded from a foreign cause which could not be imputed to him. Specific performance could also be resorted to when the obligations were still valid.[62] Based on Zheng, the validity of contracts served as the premise of contractual responsibilities while the latter was the reflection of the former.

The word "responsibility" has two sources in western languages. One is responsabilita from Latin "respondere", meaning that when the balance and order established by promises (spondere) is broken or violated, re-promises (respondere) is adopted to remedy the broken balance and order. Some scholars think that the core of contractual responsibilities is the remedial measures adopted regarding the balance and order achieved by promises. Therefore it is deduced that the essence of the civil legal responsibilities is the remedies granted by the law and backed up by the mandatory power of the state; when the civil rights are not breached, they serve as warnings to urge the involved parties to abide by laws and fulfill the legal obligations; when the civil rights are breached, they are manifested in the mandatory acquisition by

[60] *Law Code of Tang Dynasty Marriages.* Citing *Household Regulations* in Tang Dynasty.

[61] *Dunhuang Documents.* The 1st Series. p. 449, S4374.

[62] Zheng [25].

the victims from the infringers, meaning that the relationship between the victims and the infringers is seen as one between specific counterparts, which is the relation of "*obligatio*". The second source is also from the Latin word "obligato"—the obligations and responsibilities for other people. Yet "obligato" and "obligation" should share the same etymology with the meaning "to bind". Exactly because of this, Saint Jhomad Aguingas believed that the law was in nature to bind. To summarize, in western etymology, "responsibility" has two layers of meanings: one is the guaranty and remedy for a breached promise, namely, a contract of consensus; the other is the responsibilities and obligations of breaching contractual obligations. In other words, both contracting parties must be "bound" by contractual responsibilities and obligations; otherwise they must take on corresponding responsibilities and obligations.[63]

"Ze Ren (责任)" in Chinese etymology shares some interesting similarities with the "responsibility" or "obligation" in western languages. "Ze (责)", as a noun, means "zhai (债, *obligatio* or debt)". Its original semantic meaning is "zhai quan (债权, obligee's rights)"; when it is used as a verb, it means "ze qu (责取, claiming or demanding)", and that equals to the obligee's claiming right in today's civil law. "Ren (任)" has slightly complicated components with three layers of meanings that correspond to and interconnect with each other. The first one is "fu dan/cheng dan (负担/承担, to bear or to undertake)", namely the obligations that should be undertaken due to certain civil conducts. The second one is "dan bao/bao zheng (担保/保证, to guarantee or to ensure)", namely to guarantee by certain credibility or to ensure the performance of the obligation. "ren zhe (任者)" in Han Dynasty means the guarantor or warrantor in today's civil law. The third one is "ze ren/yi wu (责任/义务, responsibilities or obligations)", which connotes the moral duty of fulfillment or mandatory remedy obligation. Among them, "ze" in "ze ren" and "yi" in "yi wu" contain a huge amount of commercial moral routines of the society and have become the criteria for moral judgment of civil subjects' personalities. "ze" emphasizes that things "should" be done while "yi" highlights that things "must" be done. "ze" is an external power bound by contracts, its last resort being the counterpart's mandatory power and the state public power. "yi" is an internal personality status bound by customs and public opinions, itsmeans of remedy being moral self-discipline and judgment by public opinion.

The exploration of the etymology of "responsibility" in China and West aims to draw a clear line for contractual responsibilities. Currently the academic community has reached the consensus that contractual responsibilities mean the civil responsibilities generated by breach of contract. However, when it comes to the specific connotations or the essential features of contractual responsibilities, opinions are divided. There are mainly five kinds of theories: (1) The theory of guarantee. This has been proposed by the civil law scholars of the continental law system, who believe that the contractual responsibilities are those taken on when the obligor does not fulfill the contractual obligations. That is, the obligor's entire property is taken

[63]Zhang [26].

as the guarantee; and the obligee has to apply to the court for the mandatory enforcement of the obligor's entire property to realize his or her right.[64] (2) The theory of sanction. It is believed that the contractual responsibilities are the obligatory legal sanction based on the law or the agreement when the contractual parties fail to fulfill the obligations prescribed in the contract.[65] (3) The theory of the legal consequences. It regards the contractual responsibilities as the legal consequences that should be taken when the obligor fails to fulfill the agreed contractual obligations.[66] (4) The theory of remedy. It regards the contractual responsibilities as the remedy system for the obligee's rights when the obligor fails to fulfill the contract.[67] (5) The theory of compensation. It regards the contractual responsibilities as the compensation for the obligee's loss when the obligor fails to fulfill the contract.[68] To make a summary, apart from the first one which highlights the process of obligation fulfillment, the other four all define the essence of contractual responsibilities by their consequences and means, which is not appropriate since they do not involve the nature of contractual responsibilities. The establishment of the contractual responsibility system has two purposes: (1) to ensure the realization of the obligee's rights or the obtainment of certain compensation by means of agreement or law. (2) to force the obligor to fulfill the contractual obligations or to make certain compensation by means of agreement or law. Therefore, by using "the theory of rights realization" or "the theory of obligation fulfillment", it is easier to demonstrate the nature of contractual responsibilities and summarize the above five theories with less ambiguity.

Forms of Breach of Contract and the Remedies

The Roman law gives prominence to contractual responsibilities by uncovering the connotations of the obligor's performance act (solution) and defining the validity of the obligations and the contract. Article 1147 of *The French Civil Code*, article 1218 of *The Italian Civil Code* and article 415 of *The Japanese Civil Code* follow this way and they use "non-performance of the obligation" as the basic premise of the burden of contractual responsibilities. Article 280 and 325 of *The German Civil Code* and article 216 and 229 of *Civil Code of the Republic of China* specifically divide "non-performance" into "non-performance of the obligation" and "delay in performance (or execution)", and determine whether the party should assume contractual responsibilities and how according to actual conditions. The common law system uses "the breach of contract" to describe "non-performance of the contractual obligation" in the civil law system and classifies many kinds of breach acts into "anticipatory breach" and "actual breach", according to which contractual responsibilities are assigned.

[64] Huo [27].

[65] Zheng [28].

[66] Liu [29].

[67] Cui [30].

[68] Li [31].

By drawing lessons from the common law system, the current law making in mainland China has formed its own criteria and idea concerning forms of the breach of contract. The new *Contract Law* specifically provides *Chapter Seven* to dwell on "Liabilities for Breach of Contracts", defining it as "If a party fails to perform its obligations under a contract, or rendered non-conforming performance, it shall bear the liabilities for breach of contract by specific performance, cure of non-conforming performance or payment of damages, etc." (*Contract Law*, article 107). Meanwhile, it also categorizes the forms of breach into "anticipatory breach" (*Contract Law*, article 108) and "actual breach", laying down remedy measures corresponding to different kinds of breach acts. It is now a complete system with great feasibility and strong practicality.

The breach forms of Chinese ancient contracts were more complicated. Apart from the fact that the law or contract provided both parties must not breach the contract, normally the obligee's rights were safeguarded and protected through the realization of the legal or agreed guarantee clauses, and through punishments, compensation, deposits and penal sum. In general, the features of liabilities or responsibilities for the breach of contract in Chinese ancient society were listed as follows.

Firstly, the government and the civil society bore differences in terms of whether to take the defaulter's subjective fault or negligence as the premise of taking on contractual responsibilities. The fault or negligence here referred to the obligor's non-performance or performance of terms which were not in accord with the contract. This point was similar to the application principles of contractual responsibilities in Roman law. More specifically, it could be divided into two parts: one was that the government expressly stipulated that valid contracts must be fulfilled honestly and faithfully in the light of *ex aequo et bono*. Violations were regarded as illegal and breach of contract. Take Tang Dynasty as an example, according to *Law Code of Tang Dynasty*: "Those who buy servants, horses, cows and camels … if old illnesses are found in them after the contract is made, the buyer will be given three days to cancel or pull back from the deal. If the buyer cheats and no illnesses exist, the contract shall be fulfilled according to law. Otherwise 40 whippings will be imposed on the defaulter." *Discussion* by Zhangsun Wuji further elaborated: "If the buyer is not informed of the old illness, and finally finds out about it after the contract is made, he will be given three days to cancel or pull back from the contract. If the buyer lies about the illness just in order to cancel the deal, the contract shall be fulfilled according to law. Otherwise the party who breaches the contract will be beaten 40 whips."[69] It was worth mentioning here that as a special kind of movable property, the sale contract of servants and livestock should not be breached unless the subject matter was defective. Otherwise, breaching the contract by deception was not allowed. This determined the validity of contracts from the negative side, which meant, without negative evidence, i.e. the defects in the delivery of the subject matter by the seller, the buyer must not claim the contract invalid, breach the contract without performance or request return of the payment. Secondly, adding relevant clauses in the contract to aggravate the punishment of the breaching party and compensate the loss of the non-breaching

[69] *Law Code of Tang Dynasty Law of Trivia.*

party. This was commonly found in the documents unearthed in Dunhuang and Turpan. It in part rejected the clauses of the official laws, decrees and even imperial edicts of amnesty. In other words, the obligation performance clauses prescribed in the contract by both parties were of paramount validity. This was well demonstrated in many documents from *Ru Lv Ling (to enforce by law)* in Han and Jin Dynasties to the default clauses in Tang Dynasty. The following are examples of the contracts in Tang Dynasty:

> On January 20th in the year of tiger, Linghu sold the above-mentioned cow to Wu Guanghui from the same tribe for wheat in the time of famine. Wu paid nineteen Shi (a unit of volume) of wheat for the cow. The deal was completed on the day without any debt or overdue payment ... if the cow is found to be chronically ill and would not eat within three days after the contract is made, it is allowed to return the cow. After three days, the contract is established and no one shall regret or cancel it. The breaching party will be punished to give five Shi of wheat to the non-breaching party ...[70]
>
> In November of the year of chicken, Zhang Qinu borrowed six Shi of wheat from monk Haiqing in Tuling Temple. The same amount of wheat should be returned by August, the autumn of next year. If it is overdue, the amount of wheat that should be returned will be doubled. These things will be returned by the guarantor on behalf of the debtor. The creditor will be allowed to take away the debtor's property, bits and bobs, cows and other livestock ...[71]

The first example was a sale and purchase contract, which served as ample evidence showing the influence of lawmaking in *Law Code of Tang Dynasty* on private businesses. It also indicated that the breach of contract was not legitimate under valid circumstances. The second one was a loan contract. From this contract we could see that the contractual parties reached an agreement on the contractual responsibilities that must be taken on in case of delayed performance: (1) The burden of interests would be increased up to 200% when necessary, which was a double. (2) If the obligations were not performed within the due time, the guarantor, the debtor's family members or inheritors, managing agents would be held jointly liable. (3) According to the prescribed clauses in the contract, the creditor had the right to take away by force the debtor's assets and property to ensure the realization of his/her rights. Comparatively speaking, the governmental laws and decrees regarded the debtor's subjective fault or negligence as the condition of the breach while the private contracts paid less attention to this. The natural law theory of "tit for tat and repay when in debt" granted the creditors more initiatives. In tenancy and loan contracts, breach of the contract was caused when either party failed to perform the obligations in due time (putting aside the issues like "impossibility of performance"). In brief, the government legislation emphasized "subjective fault" and the corresponding objective consequences (non-performance or failure to perform as contracted) caused thereby in terms of the breach of contracts; yet private customary law stressed "objective standards", meaning that the debtor agreed that the objective fact of non-performance per se would cause responsibilities for the breach of

[70] *Dunhuang Documents* Five. *Contract Documents*. A.

[71] *Dunhuang Documents* Five. *Contract Documents*. D.

contract. It did not concern whether the non-performance or non-conforming performance resulted from the debtor's subjective fault. Moreover, the private contracts could even offset the validity of absolution from debts and obligations or that of prohibition on compound interests stipulated by the imperial edicts and government laws and decrees.

Secondly, there were different forms as regards the breach of contract in ancient China such as non-performance, delay in performance, incomplete performance and defective performance, which were similar to today's breach forms in mainland China.[72] In western civil law, non-performance of contracts was divided into repudiation and impossibility of performance. Observation of ancient Chinese contracts showed that refusal to perform the contractual obligations was subject to moral condemnation and enforcement of the social power, and could even lead to the mandatory intervention from the state. For example, Wan Yan Bo Jia, a circuit-judge in Jin State, gave a fair judgment and adjudication of the case: "A servant of Madam Jin State (the first lady of Jin State—the younger sister of Queen Xiao Yi) bought the lacquer without paying. Bo Jia put the several servants involved in the case into jail. Madam Jin State told Emperor Zhang Zong (son of Queen Xiao Yi) about it, and he replied: 'aunt, your servants would be released as long as you pay for the lacquer.' From then on, the privileged class did not dare to do that again."[73] In Liao, Jin and Yuan Dynasties, police patrol stations were set up to specially supervise "civil matters and supply and demand",[74] or to "administer the civil matters in the capital city".[75] The practice of Wan Yan Bo Jia could be described as strict and impartial, and Emperor Zhang Zong was also considered virtuous and open-minded in this matter. It was self-evident that they two exerted a great influence on stabilizing the contractual relations. When it came to impossibility of performance, there were no express terms concerning it in ancient Chinese and Japanese contracts. However, certain clues could be found in some specific judicial practices. The following were three most commonly seen situations: first, in cases of impossibility of performance due to force majeure, the obligor could be absolved from his obligations or debt. For example, in tenancy relationships, the obligee may generously remit rental grains or silver out of good will under circumstances of natural disasters such as flood or drought; or the obligor could be relieved of tax grains and rental silver according to state laws. This had been the common practice over past dynasties and was also acknowledged by the private customary law. Second, in cases of impossibility of performance due to accidents, the obligor could be exempted from all or part of the responsibilities. For instance, in contracts of sale, tenancy, brokerage, storage, etc., if burglary or robbery occurred, the obligor could be absolved from the obligations accordingly. Such regulations could be seen in *Wen Yuan Ying Hua* in Song Dynasty: "One who was robbed should be exempted…"[76] In Qing Dynasty, the pawn industry

[72]See footnote 63, p. 644.

[73]*History of Jin Biography of Wan Yan Bo Jia.*

[74]*History of Yuan Bai Guan Zhi.*

[75]*Records of the Unification of Yuan.*

[76]*Wen Yuan Ying Hua.* Volume 42.

as well developed. If the pledges were burned, pilfered or stolen, the pawnbroker should be responsible for compensation, which would be doubled particularly in case of theft. Yet if the pledges were robbed, the compensation responsibility would be reduced based on the circumstances.[77] Third, there was no doubt that both contractual parties should perform their obligations, but if the property was confiscated by the government due to their illegal acts, the obligee should not request the obligor to repay or fulfill other contractual obligations. In Tang Dynasty, Guifang business (柜坊, shops that kept or stored money and other valuables for others in Tang and Song Dynasties) was very prosperous. According to Zhang Zexian, as a place to keep money for people, Guifang appeared in the first year of Kai Yuan during the reign of Emperor Tang Xuanzong at the latest.[78] Its operation process was that the depositors deposited the money in Guifang, and Guifang would return the money duly. Butif the money being deposited was used for illegal purposes, then it should be confiscated as illicit money. If Guifang was in the know without reporting it to the government, it should bear joint responsibilities. In the second year of Qian Fu Period during the reign of Emperor Xi Zong in Tang Dynasty (875 A.D.), someone bought an official title with money. When the incident was revealed, the money was confiscated as illicit money and the official title was revoked. "The Guifang that kept the money was informed of the illicit act. However, it didn't report to the government. Therefore, all of its properties are confiscated with imposition of severe punishments. This serves as a warning to prevent future violations."[79] If Guifang knew nothing about it before, then it was exempt from the responsibility of repaying the confiscated property.

As for defective delivery, it is divided into defects of title and defects of quality. The defects of title in ancient Chinese contracts were mainly reflected in the following aspects: (1) Repetitive pawns. The transaction risk would be increased if the buyer was subject to recourse by the obligee. Therefore, express terms were found in contracts stipulating that if the pawner conducted repetitive pawns illegally, he or she should take the corresponding legal consequences. The laws and decrees in Qing Dynasty provided explicitly that: "If a pawned land is pawned again to another, the money gained shall be regarded as illicit money and the conduct shall be sentenced as larceny. The land or premises shall be returned to the original buyer or pawnee. If the pawner and the broker conduct repetitive pawn in the know, they would be punished as criminals, with money being confiscated. But if they are uninformed, they would not be punished."[80] This kind of legislative spirit dated back to the laws in Song Dynasty which forbade repetitive pawn. "In case of repetitive pawn of one's property, the original owner, the broker, the neighbors and those who signed on the contract should all be punished as committing larceny according to their respective amount of money gained from cheating. For those who did not share the illicit money,

---

[77] Wei [32].

[78] Zhang [33].

[79] *Quan Tang Wen (The Collection of Essays in Tang and the Five Dynasties)*. Volume 89. *Nan Jiao She Wen*. See also in *The Collection of Edicts in Dang Dynasty* volume 72. *Nan Jiao She Wen in the Second Year of Qian Fu Period.*

[80] *Law Code of Qing Dynasty Household Regulations Sale and Pawn of Land and Premises.*

their punishment would be reduced by three levels, but they would still be fined to compensate the person being deceived. If the fines and compensatory money on the pawner are still not enough, the broker and neighbors who signed should also be fined together to make up for the loss. The property should be returned to its legal owner."[81] In judicial practices, the local magistrates would usually decide that the first buyer or pawnee be the legal owner of the property. The pawner, the informed second pawnee and the broker should all assume responsibilities for breaching the contract and receive punishments. A typical case judged by Weng Haotang was recorded in*Law Reports of Southern Song Dynasty*: Wang Yizhi first pawned his house and premises to Xu Kejian, after which Wang pawned them again to Shu Yuanxiu. Weng Haotang decided that the business with Shu was illegal and that the house and premises must be returned to the original pawnee Xu; and he sentenced that both the pawner Wang Yizhi and the broker Chen Sicong "to 100 floggings"[82] based on the law "anyone who pawns his or her premises to more than one pawnee should be flogged 100 times, and the knowing broker should be punished the same way". Thanks to the emphasis by the government, the clause of "no repetitive dealings" were commonly found in private contracts, which served both as the guarantee and as the default clause. For example, *The Land Sale Contract of Wu Qifu in Xiuning County* in the seventh year of Shun Zhi Period in Qing Dynasty (1650 A.D.): "The land was not sold before and no repetitive selling's were ever conducted." *The Land Sale Contract of Xu Zhenyuan in Xiuning County with Official Red Seal* in the nineteenth year under the reign of Emperor Kang Xi (1680 A.D.): "No repetitive dealings with others were ever conducted." *The Cropland Sale Contract of Sun Qianxiu in Xiuning County* in the thirty-second year under the reign of Emperor Qian Long (1767 A.D.): "The cropland was not sold before, and no pawns or other unclear dealings were ever conducted. If so, I will take on all the legal consequences. The buyer shall not be involved."[83] The contracts dating back to Han and Tang Dynasties were also the same. *The Land Purchase Contract of Fan Lijia in the Seventh Year during Guang He Period of Han Dynasty (184 A.D.)* stipulated that if anyone other than the owner and the buyer claimed rights over the subject matter, then the owner should take full responsibilities. Such clauses were prevalent in contracts of Tang Dynasty, as in the *Horse Purchase Contract of Shi Randian in the 21st Year of Kai Yuan Period* (733 A.D.)[84]:

> On January the fifth (Chinese lunar calendar) in the 21st year of Kai Yuan Period, Xizhou citizen Shi Randian bought a horse from Kang Sili with eighteen Pi (a unit of length, especially for cloth) of silk cloth in Xizhou city. The payment was completed on delivery of the horse on that day without any debt or delay. If further disputes (He Dao Shi Ren 寒盗识认) occur concerning the dealing or ownership of the horse, the seller should take the responsibilities without involving the buyer. This contract is made and signed by both parties to prevent bad faith …"

---

[81] *Criminal Code of Song Dynasty* volume 13.

[82] *Law Reports of Southern Song Dynasty Illegal Trade.*

[83] *The Collection and Annotations of Contracts in Chinese History.* Book 2, p. 1134, p. 1162, p. 1170.

[84] Cited from Wang [34].

"He Dao Shi Ren (寒盗识认 or 认识)" was a very common usage in the contracts in Tang Dynasty with two layers of meanings: First, the subject matter was later alleged to be stolen. "寒 (He)" here meant "诃" (scold) and "盗 (Dao)" meant steal; second, the subject matter was stolen and sold behind the back of the original legal owner. Whatever the situation was, the seller would be fully responsible for the mediation. If the subject matter needed to be returned to the original owner, the seller should pay back the money to the later buyer and provide compensation.

(1) The sale of goods or property by the humble juniors without authorization in a family. Both the official and the private customary law strictly prohibited the humble and young from selling family property without authorization. The laws in Tang Dynasty provided: "If the humble juniors sell the property worthy of ten Pi without authorization, the punishment of ten whippings will be imposed. Every ten Pi of worth would increase one level of punishment up to a hundred floggings at most."[85] Zhangsun Wuji explained its legislative intent: "There must be a senior within a family, thus the descendants have no right to deal with the property since the senior is in charge." Laws of the dynasties after Song all followed this legislative spirit. If the buyer to whom the humble juniors sold or pawned the property was not in the know, he or she could get the money back while the contract would be declared invalid. If the buyer still conducted such act knowingly, then he or she would lose both the money and property, and meanwhile be penalized by whippings, floggings or exile.[86]
(2) Infringement on the pre-emption right of relatives and neighbors in the sale and pawn of real estate property. The pre-emption right of relatives and neighbors, to a great extent, exemplified the relevant mechanism and internal spirit of the sale of real estate property in ancient Chinese society. Therefore, it was necessary to make an explanation here. The "real estate property (物业 wu ye)" included such immovable properties as land, premises and graveyards. "Sale and pawn (典卖 dian mai)" included two kinds of civil acts—"sale" and "pawn", which bore similarities in the legal procedures, thus they were usually collocated together in ancient China and are discussed together here. "Relatives and neighbors (亲邻 qin lin)" here referred to "family members of the clan" and "neighbors". The so-called pre-emption right of relatives and neighbors meant that when the owner sold his or her real estate property, his or her relatives and neighbors enjoyed the priority to buy it under the same conditions with others; when the property was redeemed, they still had the priority to do so.

Immovable properties were the materialized power to maintain the families and the society in ancient China, and two elements were essential for their dealings: free will (合心 he xin) and lawfulness (合法 he fa). Free will involve the owner's absolute control over his or her own properties; lawfulness denoted the protection and limits on the dealings of immovable properties from the state in order to safeguard the stability and safety of commodity circulation. *Law Reports of Southern Song*

[85]*Law Code of Tang Dynasty.* Volume 12. *Marriages.*

[86]Refer to *Law Reports of Southern Song Dynasty Illegal Trade No Deals on Common Property.*

Dynasty Qu Shu (Redemption) read: "In general, it is very important to purchase land and properties based on the principles of free will and lawfulness. Lawfulness helps prevent disputes while free will protects the descendants." The priority right of relatives and neighbors in the sale and pawn of properties approved by the ancient Chinese government was a typical example.

The relation in the sale and pawn of property concerned three types of legal subjects: the proprietor or owner of the property, the buyer or the pawnee, and the relatives and neighbors related to the property. Among them, the first and the second were the direct parties in property sale and pawn. Yet relatives and neighbors were the important factor that had a direct impact on the validity of the dealing.

First of all, we would discuss the order and scope of the pre-emption right of relatives and neighbors. Taking Song Dynasty as an example, Volume 13 of *Criminal Code of Song Dynasty* stipulated: "Whenever one sells or pawns his or her real estate property, his or her close relatives shall be asked first whether they want to buy it or not, then the neighbors, then non-relatives and non-neighbors. If the relatives cannot afford it or cannot reach an agreement on the price with the owner, then the owner is allowed to sell it to the highest bidder. If the owner and the middleman deceive the relatives and neighbors by lifting the price, or if the relatives and neighbors hinder normal dealing by under pricing the property, they shall be punished according to the severity of their conducts and the situation." In summary, we could see that (A) the relatives and neighbors had to be considered and asked first in dealings of real estate property; (B) If the relatives and neighbors refused to buy it under the same conditions with others, or they offered a price lower than that required by the owner, then the owner would be free to deal with others; (C) If the relatives and neighbors deliberately lowered the price to hinder the deal, or if the owner or broker colluded to raise the price to deceive the relatives and neighbors, they should all assume corresponding legal responsibilities.

In the second year of Kai Bao Period (969 A.D.), the imperial court further confirmed the order and range of relatives and neighbors: "Family members shall be considered and asked before the neighbors when one sells or pawns the real estate property. The order of precedence of the neighbors are based on their residential locations—first those living in the east and the south, and then the west and the north. If all of them would not buy it, then the seller will be free to deal with non-relatives and non-neighbors."[87] The stipulation was revised in the first year of Shao Sheng Period under the reign of Emperor Zhao Xi (1094 A.D.), which was: "When one sells or pawns his or her real estate property, the people to be considered and asked first shall be those clan members who are closely related to the owner and meanwhile, whose graveyards are within a hundred steps from the land for sale."[88]

Yuan Dynasty inherited this spirit in property sale and purchase. In the sixth year of Zhi Yuan Period, the Central Secretariat (Chung-shu Sheng) Tai Yuanlu reiterated the order and range of relatives and neighbors when he, based on "old practice", dealt with disputes related to sale and pawn of real estate property (such as deceits,

[87] *The Compilation of Song Dynasty National Economy.*

[88] *A Review of Laws and Regulations* volume 5.

manipulation of prices and extortion of valuables): "When selling or pawning land and premises, family members (from close ones to distant ones) should be asked first, then the neighbors, and at last non-relatives and non-neighbors."[89]

Judging from what has been mentioned above, it is clear that relatives weighed more heavily than neighbors in the order of precedence. Relatives fell into five classes (五服, Wu Fu) according to their intimacy level, and neighbors were categorized by their residential locations—those living in the east and west came before those in the south and north. Whether or not the pawnee or buyer was able to realize the purchase right and complete the deal successfully depended on whether or not the relatives and neighbors wielded their pre-emption rights. This custom was followed till Ming and Qing Dynasties and even till today's civil society. In June of the 30th year in Jia Jing Period, Ming Dynasty, *Contract* of *Wei Fuqing Selling Land* provided: "The city dweller Wei Fuqing bought two Mu of land … now the land needs to be sold for some reasons, so he entrusted a broker to sell it for him. The family members and neighbors were considered as prioritized buyers before others. Since they gave up the right to buy it, the broker then sold it to another man in the county Deng Fading."[90] In May of the 9th year in Qian Long Period, Qing Dynasty, *Contract* of *Ye Linjuan Selling Land* provided: "Ye Linjuan received a piece of land from his brother … Due to a lack of money, Ye decided to entrust a broker to sell the land. Close relatives including uncles and brothers were asked in the first place. Since they gave up the right to buy it, the broker then sold the land to Yang Shizhao of Dakang Wenxue Fang."[91] The aforementioned two examples aim to illustrate that the pre-emption right of relatives and neighbors in the sale and pawn of real estate property was a mandatory provision approved by law in Song and Yuan Dynasties. Not only "willingness" (free will) but also lawfulness was needed in the success of property transactions. In Ming Dynasty at the latest, the pre-emption right of relatives and neighbors had become a very powerful contracting clause. The civil society absorbed the state laws and decrees into contracts as essential contract terms to ensure the validity of them. Dating back to Dynasties of Han, Wei, Six Dynasties, Sui and Tang, such regulations were not uncommon. Yet at that time, the priority right was indirectly realized by the mutual agreement in the contract to exempt the buyer from responsibilities. This was clearly exemplified in *Du Gezi Land Selling Contract* in September of the 7th year in Guang He Period in Han Dynasty: "Once the land is owned by others, Gezi should be exempted."[92] Another example was *Zhang Yiquan House Selling Contract* in the 4th year of Qian Ning Period under the reign of Emperor Zhao Zong: "If there are other people such as brothers-in-law claiming ownership of the house after it is sold, the original owner Zhang Yiquan and his sons should bear the responsibilities. The buyer has nothing to do with it."[93] Though such

[89] *Laws and Decrees of Yuan Dynasty* volume 19. *The Ministry of Revenue,* "Selling and Pawning Relatives Must Be Informed".

[90] Fu [35].

[91] Yang [36].

[92] Niida [37].

[93] See footnote 92.

rights guarantee clauses seemed very solemn, it was uneasy to take effect mostly because of the priority right of relatives and neighbors, thus jeopardizing the buyers' interests. As a result, laws and decrees since Song Dynasty had clearly stipulated that the relatives and neighbors must be considered and asked first in the sale and pawn of property. This practice extended to the successive generations with more delicacy. Taking such priority right as one of the contract clauses seemed to increase the transaction cost, but it actually won the security of the transaction.

The pre-emption right of relatives and neighbors had not always been invincible in real estate transactions. It was still subject to multiple restrictions, which were designed to balance the risk burden and transaction costs between relatives/neighbors and buyers. To be more specific, the restrictions on the priority right were reflected in the three aspects of people (blood proximity), geographical location and time. According to the law in Song Dynasty: "The so-called relatives and neighbors who shall be asked first refer to those who both are related and live close to the owner. Relatives living far away and non-related neighbors are not included in the consideration." Again, based on the regulations inthe same dynasty: "Neighbors who enjoy kinship closer than Si Ma (缌麻)** with the owner must be considered and asked first as the prioritized buyers in the sale and pawn of real estate property. Other households parted by fields, except that the fields or rivers have long existed from old times or served as ways to connect people, are not regarded as neighbors."[94] Such laws and decrees set certain limitations on people and their locations, that was to say, only close family members with their land or houses adjacent to those of the seller were entitled to such pre-emption right. It was the combination of both blood ties and geographical proximity that generated the pre-emption right of relatives and neighbors in property sale and pawn, the pre-emption buyer lacking either one would be deemed as "Wang Zhi Qin Lin (妄执亲邻)" ***, which would be investigated and interrogated by the government.[95] The case of Chen Ziwan in *Law Reports of Southern Song Dynasty* was an ample illustration that such limitation was already valued by the government in Song Dynasty: When Chen Ziwan was broke, he conspired with Yang Shirong and took advantage of the priority right of relatives and neighbors to redeem the land sold thirty years ago. Afterwards, they were both sentenced to "Wang Zhi Qin Lin" and "100 floggings".[96] As for the restriction of time, there were three types: (1) The pre-emption right could be exercised within three years after the date of sale or pawn, that was, legal proceedings could be initiated to ask for the realization of such pre-emption right within three years from the date of sale or pawn, exceeding which the right would terminate[97]; (2) If the relatives with the pre-emption right wanted to redeem the property of the original owner when he or she (party to the contract) had been dead for more than 30 years, the government would not accept the case[98]; (3) The relatives and neighbors, when being asked by the seller, must respond within

[94] *Law Reports of Southern Song Dynasty Redeeming.*

[95] see *LawReports of Southern Song Dynasty.*

[96] See footnote 95.

[97] See footnote 95.

[98] See footnote 95.

legal limits of time as to whether or not to buy the property: "If they are unwilling to buy the property, they need to respond to the seller within three days. If they intend to buy it, they will be given 5 days to offer the price. If the price offered is not fair and the buyer violates the time limit in the meantime, the property sale will be at the seller's disposal. Anyone who forcibly occupies the property within the time limits is in no position to buy the property."[99] These three time limitations not only guaranteed the interests of both sellers and buyers, but also urged those pre-emption buyers to actively wield their right so as to avoid further disputes and secure the transaction. Besides, the time limit for redemption was 100 days in Yuan Dynasty, and the government would not provide protection after 100 days; however, if the pawnee deceived the relatives and neighbors, the property could still "be redeemed by its price" even after 100 days.[100] This regulation could be seen as a restriction on the pre-emption right. Meanwhile, it was also a legal remedy for the right.

Another two restrictions on the pre-emption right of relatives and neighbors were the two principles of "Gui Jiu Bu Wen (归就不问: property transfer between close clan members was prioritized)" and "Mu Tian Wei Shang (墓田为上: the graveyard came first)". The so-called "Gui Jiu (归就)" referred to the paid transfer of real estate property rights among close clan members.[101] On this occasion, other relatives and neighbors were not allowed to claim the pre-emption right. In *Law Reports of Southern Song Dynasty Households and Marriages*, Huang Zizhen defended himself: "When I sold the land property to a close member of the same clan, I did not need to ask other relatives or neighbors because that was our ancestral property." Obviously, what he said was based upon the stipulations about Gui Jiu at that time. As for "Mu Tian Wei Shang (墓田为上: the graveyard came first)", it stemmed from the ancient Chinese feudal clan system, which, for thousands of years, had considered as the top priority in life governing the world with "filial piety" and respecting and honoring the ancestors. "It is humane and moral for people to be close to their kinsfolks, therefore they respect their ancestors. Because they respect their ancestors, they honor and revere the clan as well. It is the honor and reverence that unite the people of the same clan together."[102] Graveyards (the symbol of the clan's prosperity) represented the mysterious material energy of the trinity of the clan, the state and society, while ancestral halls (the symbol of ancestors) represented the spiritual bond. Therefore, whenever the sale or pawn of real estate property concerned graveyards, the parties to the contract as well as the government were all very meticulous and rigorous in fear of corrupting social morals and indoctrination. If the graveyard owner's interests were in conflict with the pre-emption right of relatives and neighbors, the former should

---

[99] *Laws and Decrees of Yuan Dynasty* volume 19. *Tax Limits on Sale and Pawn.*

[100] *Laws and Decrees of Yuan Dynasty* volume 19. *Tax Limits on Sale and Pawn.*

**Translator's annotation: there were five levels to classify relatives based on the intimacy degree in ancient China. Si Ma (缌麻) referred to the most distant one of the five.

***Translator's annotation: Wang Zhi Qin Lin (妄执亲邻): one falsely claimed that he or she did not exercise the pre-emption right of relatives and neighbors, thus asking for redemption of the property that had already been sold or pawned.

[101] Zhang [38].

[102] *The Book of Rites Etiquette Rules.*

be put above everything else. In the case of Huang Zizhen, Fan Xitang's judgment was clear enough: "We should be really careful when it comes to the graveyard and the pre-emption right. Those who want to realize the pre-emption right aim to get the real estate property; while those who want to keep the graveyard aim to honor the ancestors. If we support the former and give up protection of the graveyard, it is just like putting the cart before the horse, which completely violates the law."[103] Whenever it concerned the transfer of graveyards, the pre-emption right of relatives and neighbors should be limited. Even if the buyer had completed the purchase and begun to use it, the land-use rights were still strictly limited. A prominent feature was that "Yin (阴)" or "Yang (阳)" should be clearly stated in ancient land titles. If a land title did not stipulate clearly "including use for both Yin and Yang", then the buyer was only allowed to cultivate the land and must not use it to bury the dead.[104] This could be seen as another example of the principle of "the graveyard came first". Moreover, the judicial practice of "the land can be taken away but the graveyard must not"[105] also lasted from Song Dynasty to the Republic of China.

The fact that the pre-emption right of relatives and neighbors was recognized and protected by the law generated multiple subjects in property sale and pawn. The rights and obligations among the three types of legal subjects mentioned in the previous section constituted the main content of the pre-emption right of relatives and neighbors. To be specific, the seller or the pawner enjoyed the following rights: (1) The disposal right to one's own real estate property. One could decide whether to sell or pawn the property based on one's own will. This was an absolute right similar to today's real right. (2) The right to demand consideration. The premise of selling or pawning one's property was that one must obtain an equal consideration. The consideration (or the price) should be negotiated only between both parties. After the property was sold or pawned, the seller would be exempt from the corresponding tax burden. The obligations of the seller (also the property owner) were reflected in the following three aspects: (1) The property sold or pawned must be owned by the seller. That was, from the source of the property right, the seller was in actual possession of the property, and his or her management, control and disposal of the property must have legal basis. (2) Guarantee for defects of right. If disputes were incurred over the ownership and the right to use concerning the property sold or pawned, the seller had to bear the loss caused by defects of title for the counterpart and be penalized by the government. (3) The obligation to inform. This obligation was closely relevant to the pre-emption right of relatives and neighbors, which would be elaborated later.

For those who enjoyed the pre-emption right of relatives and neighbors, their rights and obligations were as follows: (1) Request to exercise the pre-emption right. If the relatives and neighbors had blood and geographical proximity with the property for sale or pawn, they were allowed to, in accordance with the law or contract (as

[103] *Law Reports of Southern Song Dynasty Households and Marriages Fight over Property.*

[104] *Research Report on Civil and Commercial Cases and Customs.* 1969. Taipei Jinxue Publishing House, p. 599.

[105] *Law Reports of Southern Song Dynasty Tombs Fight over Hills and Tomb Prohibitions.*

mentioned above, the pre-emption right of relatives and neighbors had since been included in the terms of the contract and become the mutual obligation of both parties), make a request to the property owner or the government to exercise their pre-emption right. (2) Respond to the seller or offer the price within the time limits. After the pre-emption buyers were informed of the sale or pawn, they must make clear whether to buy or accept the pawn of the property within the time limits (The author has not yet found clear regulations of the time limits in Song Dynasty. In Yuan Dynasty, as mentioned above, the time limit for response was within 3 days while for offering price, 5 days). In case of deciding to buy it, they must also conduct further negotiation about the price with the seller in time. As for buyers or pawnees, they were obliged to abide by the laws and must not conspire with brokers and sellers to deceive the relatives and neighbors who possessed such pre-emption right.

More precisely, the pre-emption right of relatives and neighbors in Song and Yuan Dynasties were realized and protected through the following means: firstly, the owner/seller's obligation to inform. The owner must fulfill this obligation if he or she intended to sell or pawn his or her real estate property. In Song Dynasty, it was stipulated that: "When one sells or pawns the real estate property, Neighbors who enjoy kinship closer than Si Ma with the owner and whose graveyards are within a hundred steps from the land for sale, must be informed first as the prioritized buyers."[106] The relevant stipulations in Yuan Dynasty were already discussed above. Two reasons accounted for the obligation to inform: (1) To protect the pre-emption right and avoid disputes; (2) To protect the bona fide counterparts. In pawns, close family members and neighbors also had the pre-emption right to be pawnees. If they "could not afford it, then the owner is allowed to pledge the property to the highest bidder".[107] If the seller had not informed the relatives and neighbors of the sale or pawn when he or she should have, or even colluded with the broker or others to deceive the relatives and neighbors, then they had to bear corresponding civil and criminal responsibilities and the contract would also be invalid. This kind of practice has been preserved till now and followed by many ethnic minorities. When Zhuang people sell the land, the seller should find a broker and inform the relatives in the same clan first. If the relatives cannot afford it, then the land can be sold to other clans. For Miao people, the relatives' pre-emption right is more obvious. Even if the seller and the buyer of other clans have already agreed on the price of the land, the relatives in the same clan should still be the prioritized buyer as long as they offer a price not lower than that of the buyer of other clans. The same is true of pawns. Relatives in the same clan have prioritized pawn right over others. Only when the relatives and neighbors offer a lower price than other people can the owner pawn the property to others. Besides, the pawn contract between the pawnee and the owner must be witnessed and examined by both parties' families to avoid further disputes.[108]

[106]See *Law Reports of Southern Song Dynasty Households and Marriages Fight over Property.* The item *The Tomb* is cited from the judgment of Hu Shibi.

[107]*Criminal Code of Song Dynasty.* Volume 13. *Marriages Sales and Pawns.*

[108]Gao [39].

Secondly, contracting. Chinese contract documents fell into the set pattern very early. Daily transactions took bonds, contracts and the like as the basis for determining the rights and obligations of both parties. From the author's point of view, the inclusion of the priority right of relatives and neighbors into contracts as required by the government started in Zhao Fu's written petition in the 8th year of Tai Ping Xing Guo Period of Song Dynasty (983 A. D.): "There are many disputes in real estate sales and pawns. They all result from privately composed contracts by different people without official standards, thus deceptions and cheatings are widespread, increasing disputes and litigations. Therefore, I sincerely propose that the central government, local authorities and the Bureau of Commercial Tax should gather people together and set up respectively a standard contract sample of sale and pawn, so that the public can follow."[109] But after a long lapse of time, "The relatives and neighbors all fight over the real estate property as the pawnee or buyer lost the contract. The Bureau of Commercial Tax could not find it, either." Based on this, in the 1st year of Qian Xing Period under the reign of Emperor Song Zhen in Song Dynasty (1022 A.D.), it was announced to the public that: "When selling, pawning or pledging one's real estate properties, the contract must be in quadruplicate. One is kept by the buyer/pledge/pawnee, one by the owner or seller, one by the Bureau of Commercial Tax and one by the county government."[110] In judicial practices, the government also judged the cases with the contracts being the main evidence. Expressions like "The pawn of real estate property has to be based on the contract. Each party of the contract would keep one copy. This is the common practice known to the public" were commonly seen in *Law Reports of Southern Song Dynasty.* It showed that it was difficult to win a case without a contract. Meanwhile, the contract would not be valid if it was simply agreed by both contractual parties. Within a certain period of time after the establishment of the contract, "the government must review and inspect the contract in the presence of the owner, the relatives and neighbors, the broker, and the contract writer. And they must also bring a complete copy of the contract to the government to confirm the acreage and tax situation of the land".[111] Only after it was confirmed by the careful inspection of the government and the deed tax was paid, the government "would authorize the deal and give an official certificate to the pawnee or buyer".[112] Then the government would wait until after the original tax, rent and labor fees were transferred to the buyer to seal the contract. At this point, the contract was officially established and became legally binding. These procedures were called "authorizing and sealing by the government". It was worth noting that requiring the presence of the owner, the relatives and neighbors, the broker and the contract writer was to ensure the authenticity of the contract. If further disputes occurred, the above-mentioned subjects would assume joint liabilities. Meanwhile, the presence of the relatives and neighbors (only those entitled to the priority right) was to make sure they gave up the priority right officially. According to the second volume of *The*

[109] *Annals of Northern Song Dynasty*. Volume 24. The item of "the 8th year of the Taiping Xingguo".
[110] *The Compilation of Song Dynasty National Economy.* 61–62.
[111] ibid., 61–26.
[112] ibid., 37-1.

Governance of States and Counties in Song Dynasty: "In the sale and pawn of land, the certificate with the official seal is the prerequisite for transference. If the money has already been paid but the certificate is not sealed, the transference process is still not completed and the deal invalid." Therefore, when the government judged the cases of property sale and pawn, it would take the officially sealed contract (not the private one) and the completed transference to the buyer as the basic legal evidence and also as the standard to judge whether or not the relatives and neighbors waived their priority right. This was called "the topmost basis for settling the case is the officially sealed contract".

Thirdly, signing and marking. The validity of contract would be ensured without future disputes after the relatives' and neighbors' signing. The signing of names or marking of fingerprints by relatives and neighbors on the transfer contract of the owner's real estate property was called "zhi ya (知押)" in Song Dynasty. In the case of Mo Rushan suing Mo Rujiang in *Law Reports of Southern Song Dynasty Households and Marriages Property Disputes*, Mo Rushan sued Mo Rujiang due to the absence of his signature in the latter's contract. The signing of the relatives and neighbors as well as that of the broker functioned as both evidence and guarantee. Yet the former had one more implicit function, that was, for those informed of the sale or pawn (meaning those entitled to the pre-emption right), their signatures implied that they waived their right and acknowledged the owner's disposal of the property. Nowadays in Tu people' customary law, the buyer has to prepare other three shares of money except for the money to buy the land: one for the broker, one for the contract writer and one for the close relatives of the seller. This is because the local customary law requires that the contract of real estate sale must be signed by the close relatives of the seller to be effective and valid.[113]

Fourthly, public notification and credibility. From ancient times to the present, the completion of real estate transactions has always been marked by certain procedures. In fact, the wine drinking in ancient times and feasting others today are all typical ways to publicly notify others of the property sale or pawn. The official seal, to some extent, could only prove the establishment and validity of contract. Yet, as far as the pre-emption right of relatives and neighbors was concerned, wine drinking and feasting gained more publicity of the real right and credibility. In Shuzo Shiga's discussion of the functions of the "broker", he proposed that the feast for thanking the broker was essentially to publicly notify others or make an announcement.[114] Hugh T. Scogin also discussed the role of the "witnesses" (brokers) in ancient Chinese contracts and expounded they were in nature to witness. He further proposed that "the openness of the procedures and the emphasis on witnesses and documents have enabled the evidence to prove in actual practice", and that the rituals or ceremonies of contract completion like wine drinking and feasting were the same as those of making a covenant in ancient times, "they are both morally binding and religiously

---

[113]See footnote 20, pp. 331–333.

[114]Shuzo [40].

binding".[115] In modern times, these rituals and ceremonies have been preserved among the ethnic groups in China. Minorities including Zhuang, Miao, Zang, Yi, Tu and Dong people have still kept feasting as the ceremony to publicly notify others of the completion of the deal. In particular, Miao people have the customs of "feasting the broker" and "giving grains to relatives". "Feasting the broker" means that the buyer invites the relatives of both parties, head of the village and the broker to a feast. "Giving grains to relatives" means that the buyer gives each of the seller's uncles and brothers five kilograms of grains, and meanwhile the buyer and the seller would both reward the broker with ten kilograms of grains or four or five Jiao Qian (角钱, a name of ancient coins). Finishing the above ceremonies marks the formal establishment or completion of the deal. If anyone goes back on his or her words, all the people present at "feasting the broker" are obliged to testify.[116] It should be particularly noted that the ceremonies in property sales and pawns are not simply about rewarding brokers, but more about public notification to enhance the credibility of the validity and effectiveness of the deal. At the same time, the reason why the buyer is willing to spend money to feast others or reward the seller's relatives in addition to paying the price of the property is not only that they would be obliged to testify in the future, but also that the buyer could take this opportunity to make sure the relatives and neighbors of the seller have given up their pre-emption right. In this way, the ceremonies achieve these three goals simultaneously and are utilized to the fullest.

Fifthly, remedies. The pre-emption right of relatives and neighbors was violated when the owner/seller failed to fulfill the obligation to inform, arbitrarily established the contract to sell the property to others, or colluded with the buyer or pawnee to deceive the relatives and neighbors. Such conducts were "illegal deals" in Song Dynasty. The relatives and neighbors could realize their pre-emption right through the government in the following two ways: one was to ask the government to issue a document to recover the property according to the law, which was, to determine that the property transaction contract was invalid and that both parties got their things/money back. Then those who were entitled to the pre-emption right could buy the recovered property. The other was to redeem the pawned property at the original price based on the pre-emption right. In those "illegal deals", if the buyer still proceeded with the deal even though he or she knew that the seller/owner did not ask the relatives and neighbors in the first place, then both parties would bear joint liabilities and be penalized by floggings with the property recovered and money confiscated by the government. In Yuan Dynasty, there were express stipulations concerning the right of relatives and neighbors to be informed or the seller's obligation to inform as follows: (1) To show truthfully whether the owner had informed the relatives and neighbors by their response of "giving up the right to buy" or "offering the price". (2) If people entitled to the pre-emption right did not reside in the local area, then the owner should send a person to go there to ask about their intentions. (3) If the owner

[115]Hugh T. Scogin. *Between Heaven and Man: Contract and the State in Han Dynasty*. Cited from the same source as in footnote 22.

[116]See footnote 20, pp. 331–332.

failed to fulfill the obligation to inform and sold the property privately, the prioritized buyers could redeem the property at the original price within 100 days. (4) If the owner fulfilled the obligation to inform but deliberately raised the price, preventing the relatives and neighbors from exercising their pre-emption, then sold the property to a third person privately at a lower price, the prioritized buyers were allowed to redeem the property at the selling price within 100 days under this circumstance. (5) If the owner and the buyer conspired together or deliberately delayed the time to deceive the relatives and neighbors, then the prioritized ones were still allowed to redeem the property at the selling price even after 100 days.[117]

The adoption and development of the pre-emption right of relatives and neighbors in property sale and pawn in ancient China indicated its rationality and effectiveness. In Song Dynasty, the law required that those entitled to the pre-emption right had to be both relatives and neighbors at the same time; whereas in Yuan Dynasty, either relatives or neighbors could enjoy this pre-emption.[118] By now ties of consanguinity have ceased to play a role at the legal level, yet they were still popular as a kind of "custom" or "practice" in civil transactions and dealings. Though the pre-emption right of neighbors as regards the geographical relations was somehow different, its spiritual essence remained the same. Japanese scholars Tomoo Uchida and Amano Motonosuke believed that the "pre-emption right" dated back to the common ownership of the ancient clan system. Yet Kishimoto Mio held that the pre-emption right "is an institutional device formed by people at the civil level to deal with the risks brought by the free circulation of land",[119] which just hit the nail on the head. Butin Kishimoto Mio's view, the pre-emption right of relatives and neighbors was only limited to the level of civil society. That is true in today's society, but not the case in ancient times.

After outlining the institution of the pre-emption right of relatives and neighbors, it is necessary to sort out its essence and value. According to the author, the historical value of this institution is listed as follows.

First, the pre-emption right of relatives and neighbors in property sale and pawn was an inevitable outcome of the Chinese clan system and an effective institution to maintain the stability of families and social economy as well. Common ownership of the clan and prohibition of private accumulation of property by the humble juniors had been the long-term traditions in Chinese families, which fundamentally rejected the individual's independent disposal of property. Thus family interests must be prioritized over individual interests in the dealings and transactions of property. The combination of the economic structure built on clan consanguinity and the family structure based on living together and common ownership directly gave rise to the pre-emption right of relatives and neighbors; and the village-based geographical structure featured by the same clans living together indirectly stimulated its development, maturity and finally fixed the pattern of this institution. To put it straight, any economic system or legal system aimed to seek a balance of interests, otherwise

---

[117]Huo [41].

[118]ibid.

[119]Kishimoto Mio. *Contractual Documents in Ming and Qing Dynasties*. See footnote 56, p. 301.

it would lose the foundation of its existence. On the surface, the pre-emption right tried to protect the feudal closed trading system of "real estate stays within the clan" and "the family property never goes to outsiders". Just as Mr. Liang Zhiping once criticized: "The pre-emption right of relatives has always been an obstacle to the free transfer of land." He further criticized that it led to the uncertainty of transactions and hindered free transfer of land. However, his comments were a huge mistake. On the one hand, the pre-emption right was relative and limited rather than absolute and unconditional. On the other hand, although there were some families that had lived together and commonly owned their property for near 700 years in history, the more common occurrence was the dispersion and reunion of clans and families. Thus normal transactions still accounted for the main part except for natural disasters and man-made accidents. During the reign of Emperor Kang Xi, it was common in Jiangsu that "a land had been transferred many times to different people within 100 years". During the reign of Emperor Qian Long, "a land had been traded several times within ten years" in Suzhou. Such was the case in the heydays of Kang Xi and Qian Long Periods, not to mention the situation in war times. Therefore, it was not the pre-emption right that obstructed the free transfer of land. The author believes that the real reason behind it lay in the mindset that "to get rich by doing business and to keep the fortune by buying land and doing agriculture".[120] The true essence of the pre-emption right was family mutual assistance of the rich and strong helping the poor and weak so as to maintain the stability of the families and even the stability of the society. Japanese scholar Uhmno Yoshitaro held that the west emphasized individualism and antagonism, whereas Chinese villages (which were, in fact, formed by families of the same clan living together) had an affinity of mutual cooperation. Naito Konan believed that "the Chinese society is built on the progressive clan system featured by common ownership".[121] Sun Yat-sen, as the pioneer of democratic revolution, proposed the social evolution model of "from patriarchal clans to the national clan".[122] These showed that the pre-emption right of relatives and neighbors had its own social roots.

Second, the pre-emption right had maintained the stability of the property and indirectly saved the social cost. The procedures of real estate transfer within the clan were simple, which greatly reduced transaction costs. Prioritizing relatives and neighbors under the same conditions was a win–win in that it not only enabled the owner to get the same profits, but also sped up financing and diversified the use of idle money within the clan. More importantly, the pre-emption right could effectively eliminate cheatings and deceits in property sale and pawn, which stabilized the value of the property and reduced the unnecessary cost of litigation.

Third, the pre-emption right was also a necessary means for clans to protect their interests. Chinese society had existed in the form of clans for thousands of years. The properties of a family or a clan were mainly public, similar to today's common ownership, except that the decision-making power was in the hands of the patriarchs,

---

[120] Ye [42], Fu [43].

[121] Kishimoto Mio. *Civil Society and China*.

[122] *Collected Works of Sun Yat-sen*. 1981 volume 8. People's Publishing House, p. 238.

branch heads and the elders. Even in the late 1920s, the clan of He Chuiyu in Hexi Village, Nanhai County of Guangdong province was still imitating the spirit of the western constitution to safeguard its common ownership. That was done in the name of clan referendum, but the opinions of the patriarchs and leaders were important enough to influence or even decide the will of the clan members.[123] When examining Meifa Village in the economic and cultural districts of the southeastern coastal areas of Xiamen, Zhangzhou and Quanzhou, Mr. Wang Mingming, based on the facts, also argued for the revival of traditional family and clan consciousness and the return of clan authority after 1979.[124] It appeared that the pre-emption right stressed the blood ties and the geographical proximity of relatives and neighbors. In reality, it aimed to protect the common interests of families and clans from damages. An example in the customary law concerning creditor's rights could be cited here to prove that the clans had to promote the pre-emption right so as to protect their common property. For Wa people, families of the same surname should bear joint obligations to pay off outside debts. If the debtor failed to repay the debt in time, it would be legitimate for the creditor to search any house owned by people with the same surname or in the same clan and confiscated their property, take by force their livestock and even people. Such custom of "the father and son share weal and woe, and the same surname brings the same liabilities" had been deeply rooted in people's mind, which was equivalent to laws. People of the same surname had to be united to prevent the interests of other clan members from being infringed upon. Similarly, people of the same surname should also be united to exercise reasonable claims. Under such circumstance, if the debtor was allowed to dispose of the property freely, the consequences would eventually affect the interests of other clan members. Therefore, the pre-emption right safeguarded the real estate property of the clan, in case it was occupied by people of other clans, which could even lead to litigations and fights. Also, the pre-emption allowed the debtor to redeem the property after he or she paid off the debt. The interesting thing about Wa people was that if they wanted to sell people to repay the debt, clan members of the same surname still enjoyed the pre-emption right. Only when they gave up the right could the people be sold to other clans. In these cases, people themselves were also viewed as the common property, to which people of the same surname had the pre-emption right. The real motivation behind this was to protect the productivity resources of the clan.[125]

Forth, the author believed, just opposite to what Mr. Liang Zhiping argued, the pre-emption right actually enhanced the certainty of transactions. The institution of the pre-emption right was originally intended to balance the costs and risks of transactions between buyers and relatives. As was mentioned before, the pre-emption right was the important material basis for maintaining the stability of families, society and

---

[123] *The Family Regulations of the Clan of He Chuiyu in Hexi County, Nan Hai*: "when it comes to the disposition of the real estate property, 7/10 of the family members have to be present for the initial vote; and 7/10 of the present members have to vote to support the initiative so that it can be granted valid, otherwise it is not." Cited from the same source as in footnote 39.

[124] Wang [44].

[125] See footnote 20, p. 348.

the country. The law had its clear stipulations and people had their private contracts, which was an objective historical fact that could not be changed. The pre-emption right seemed to indeed attach the most importance to protecting the interests of relatives and neighbors. In the meantime, it undeniably and greatly reduced the transaction risks though it increased the transaction costs on the part of buyers or pawnees. The legitimacy, validity and rationality of the transactions based on the official laws and private contracts could save the buyers and pawnees from unnecessary litigation costs and even property confiscation. As a result, the pre-emption right also served to protects the interests of buyers and pawnees apart from ensuring the interests of relatives and neighbors in the first place.

"The fundamental spirit of law is property right."[126] An overview of the pre-emption right in ancient Chinese society not only helped us to confirm the objective and widespread existence of this institution, but also showed the mutual recognition of it both by the government and the common people. What's more, we could see its historical contribution to maintaining the stability of the traditional Chinese society and families. Besides, it was not difficult to find out a series of mature techniques in its legislation and judicature. Mr. Su Li held that the customs and common practices of ancient China were more convenient and effective than the statutory law in a simple society, because they could lower the transaction costs as well as establish expected regulated behaviors.[127] It was fair to say that the pre-emption right, as a kind of reasonable local resource, had played such a role.

Fifth, the arbitrary disposal of the common property by co-owners. It was legitimate for the co-owner to deal with his or her share of property. But if the property was the undivided "common property (众业, zhong ye)" or "public property (公产, gong chan)", then it was jointly owned by a certain group of a common identity or a social organization. The arbitrary disposal of it by one or some of the co-owners would be sued for recourse by other co-owners. The government also took an active part in protecting the integrity of the ownership of all co-owners to ensure social stability. If the common property was sold without the consent from other co-owners or without informing them, then it would be hard for the buyer to obtain ownership. If the buyer was in the know but still continued with the deal, then he or she must bear the risk of losing the property and be penalized by the government. In view of this, the buyer would require guarantee of the right from the seller or pawner at the initial stage of making the contract, which was, if any defects of title occurred to obstruct the realization of the buyer's ownership, the seller or pawner would be liable for breach of contract. Unfortunately, fulfilling such default clauses when it concerned common properties was not easy. It was usually the buyer who suffered the loss of property and money. The common property in ancient China could be generally divided into three categories: family "common property" or "equal property (均产, jun chan)", "public property" of the clan and "Buddhist property (佛产, fo chan)" in temples. (1) Common property or equal property referred to the properties that were specially reserved or hard to be divided within a family. It was usually real estate property

[126] *Karl Marx and Frederick Engels* volume 26. People's Publishing House, p. 368.
[127] Su [45].

or immovable property. For example, *Regulations* that recorded the division of the common property of a family in Huizhou in the 10th year of Chong Zhen Period in Ming Dynasty (1637 A.D.) provided that: "For long the mountains and land should not be divided. They should be maintained by the whole family without parsimony or abuse. Profits gained from the land should also be the common property, which would never be divided. No disputes shall arise. Anyone harming the common interests for private gains would be punished as unfilial crime;" and "The mountains and land are all the equal property of the family. Some of the land is rich and fertile whereas some is barren and infertile. Some borders the real estate of other families with potential external problems. But they are all the family equal property. Every family member should make concerted efforts to pay the taxes of the land, and cultivate it well without making excuses. Violations of the regulation would be considered as unfilial crime."[128] Since such family common property was also a burden of taxes, it would "never be divided" so that no one would shirk the responsibilities. Besides, it could only be increased, but not reduced. The reason why it was called "equal property" was because of the following two considerations: one was that the quality or soil fertility of the land in various places was quite different, making equitable distribution of the land rather difficult, so it was regarded as the common property and all descendants would have the equal right to enjoy their interests. The other was that disputes might arise concerning the land bordering that of other families', which would be really hard for one single person to cope with. In this case, it was preserved as the equal property to be protected by all the male members of the family from outside invasion. The sale and pawn of the common property or equal property of the family had to be consented to by all the family members, otherwise the deal was invalid. This was the common practice recognized by the government in traditional Chinese society. At the civil level, living together and sharing the property had become the main mode of Chinese family life since Qin Dynasty. The property was publicly owned within a family, and no one was allowed to dispose of the property without the permission of the family leader. If the leader passed away, the common/equal property would still be inherited and managed together by the younger generation. A case of Liang Huai and his two nephews Liang Shunlao and Liang Huilao in *Law Reports of Southern Song Dynasty* could well illustrate this tradition: Liang Huai and his two brothers had already divided the ancestral property and got their portions. However, a piece of land next to Ling Yao Temple was maintained for it was clearly stipulated that the land was the "common property" of the family that should not be divided. Liang Huilao secretly divided the land into three portions and sold two of them to the neighbor Gong Chengzhi, who then started digging and building on it. The government judged the case as follows: "Liang Huilao refused to consider his uncle, cared nothing about the common property of the family and secretly sold it to Gong. This is cheating the elderly and conducting arbitrary deals. Does he not know that it is illegal? Moreover, as Gong Chengzhi's land is adjacent to Liang Huai's, how could he not know that the

[128]Cited from Zhang Youyi. *Selected Documents of Household Division and Inheritance of Landlords in Huizhou in Ming and Qing Dynasties*. As in Collected Papers of Institute of Economics, Chinese Academy of Social Sciences (Series 9).

property is the common property of the family? Thus Gong lured Liang Huilao into making the contract. Both Gong and Liang are guilty in that Gong committed the crime of illegal buying and Liang committed illegal selling. Therefore, according to the regulations, the money involved in the deal shall be confiscated by the government and the property shall be returned to the owner."[129] In this case, Liang Huilao secretly divided the land into three portions and sold two without getting permission from his uncle. Such conduct was defined by the government as "illegal selling" for the following two reasons: one was that dividing the common property was strictly prohibited, not to mention selling or pawning it. The other was that Liang Huilao secretly sold the property without informing his uncle nor getting his permission. The government's judgment cited certain regulations as the basis for determining the punishment, showing that explicit regulations had already been established in Song Dynasty. The same was true of Tang Dynasty. According to *Law Code of Tang Dynasty*: "Whenever the humble juniors in a family secretly dispose of the common property, they would be penalized by a maximum of 100 whippings."[130] Yet the emphasis of *Law Code of Tang Dynasty* was put on prohibiting the humble juniors from secretly disposing of the common property whereas the case cited in *Law Reports of Southern Song Dynasty* obviously aimed to protect the common property. The reason why Gong Chengzhi had to return the property and hand in the money for the deal was that he insisted on buying it even when he knew that it was the "common property". Thus he had to bear the transaction risks himself. (2) "Public property" of the clan. G. P. Murdock, in his book *Social Structure*, proposed that "united by reciprocal relationships and bound by a common culture, the members of a 'community' form an 'ingroup'. Since they assist one another in the activities which gratify basic drives, and provide one another with certain derivative satisfactions obtainable only in social life, there develops among them a collective sentiment of group solidarity and loyalty, which has been variously termed syngenism, we-feeling, esprit de corps, and consciousness of kind".[131] The evolution of Chinese family system started from the patriarchal clan system before the Spring and Autumn Period to the aristocratic extended family system in the Middle Ages and finally evolved into the clan authority system after Song Dynasty. Especially since Song Dynasty, the family system had embodied typical Chinese characteristics in its cultural reconstruction, where there were three interrelated ways: building ancestral halls to honor the forefathers and ancestors, purchasing/donating ancestral lands to take in family members and establishing the pedigree book to verify the blood ties.[132] It was noteworthy that the most important function of the pedigree of a clan was not so much of what Fang Xiaoru (a famous scholar in Ming Dynasty) defined as "to record the names, eras, and the like of all the forefathers",[133] but to serve as a kind of "cultural identification" to prevent

[129] *Law Reports of Southern Song Dynasty Households and Marriages Illegal Trade.* "No Deals on Common Property".

[130] *Law Code of Tang Dynasty* volume 12. *Households and Marriages.*

[131] Murdoch [46].

[132] Xu [47].

[133] Fang Xiaoru. *Xun Zhi Zhai Ji.* Volume 13. *Zu Pu Xu (Pedigree of the Family).*

family disorders and disintegration, and also to provide an objective and reliable basis for mutual assistance in economic and social life. This was the fundamental reason why the Pang clan in Nanhai district forbade the descendants to engage in industry and commerce. According to *Family Instructions of the Pang*: "(The Pang clan in Nanhai district) they have lived in the countryside for generations and have already accumulated our real estate. The descendants shall not move to the provincial capital. Otherwise the agricultural business of our clan will be forgotten in three years and the clan and family branches will disintegrate in ten years. People are easily changed by the local customs. Few people are able to extricate themselves from the bad influence such as extravagance and idleness."[134] Family instructions of the Ding clan in the city of Changshu even required that living at home be the precondition if one wanted to get help from the clan, "One who goes out and does not live at home shall not get his or her supply of rice. Only when he or she returns will the rice supply resume but without replenishment of the rice during absence." Its management of rice supply was quite advanced as well, "People who apply for the rice have to register and be examined. Then they will get the stamped rice tickets which will expire and should be renewed at the end of the year. It is necessary that they go to claim the rice in person with the stamped rice tickets. If one mortgages the rice tickets or if one's rice is not delivered back home after being claimed, his or her supply of rice will be cut off for a quarter. If one loses the rice, the supply of rice will be cut off for a month."[135] In the meantime, in order to strengthen the management of the clan, the most serious punishment would be imposed upon those who severely harmed the clan's interests and tarnished the clan's reputation, i.e., "erasing the name from the pedigree book". Once a person's name was erased from the pedigree, his or her economic and cultural connection to the clan was erased at the same time. In economic and social life, public property of the clan was closely related to the ancient contractual liability system. Because it was "public", descendants with the same surname must defend it together. The public property of the clan often included Ji Tian (祭田, the land set apart for annual sacrifices), Yi Tian (义田, the land to provide for clansmen or the poor), and Xue Tian (学田, the land to build schools whose fund was based on the income of the land), to which all clan members enjoyed equal rights and obligations without exceptions. These kinds of land were to worship the ancestors, support the clan, set up schools and hold charitable activities. Clans of all dynasties had been extremely cautious in dealing with their public property and exhorted their descendants with strict words and admonitions. For example, the pedigree book of the Hong clan in Feishan during the Republic of China provided that: "All the public property of the clan … is used to cover sacrificial expenses. Anyone who secretly sell seven one inch of the property shall be expelled and erased from the clan forever apart from making compensation."[136] The Huang clan in Huanfeng, Jiangxia district also stipulated that

[134] *Lingnan Yishu* volume 31. Pang Shangpeng. *Family Instructions of the Pang.*

[135] *Regulations of Ding Family in Changshu Regulations of Purchasing Land* cited from the same as footnote 20.

[136] *The Pedigree of Family Hong in Feishan, the Republic of China* volume 1. *Regulations of the Ancestral Hall.*

"invasion, sale and pawn of Ji Tian were strictly prohibited".[137] The pedigree book of the Ji clan in Gaolu, Pucheng provided "Ji Tian is the gift from the ancestors to benefit the descendants…Whoever sells the land secretly will be sued by the whole clan and be reported to the ancestors. Moreover, he or she will be expelled from the sacrificial activities and his or her name be erased from the pedigree book".[138] The Wu clan specified more clearly: "People who steal and sell Yi Tian will be penalized by the government and the land will be returned to the clan."[139] To protect the public property, many clans submitted their public property certificates to the government to get official stamps and signatures, which aimed to enhance the public credibility of the certificates so as to prevent stealing and selling. The Zheng clan in Pujiang lived together for up to 332 years from the 3rd year of Bao Qing Period in Southern Song Dynasty (1127 A.D.) to the 3rd year of Tian Shun Period in Ming Dynasty (1459 A.D.). They were separated later due to natural disasters rather than divided opinions. *The Regulations* of this righteous clan stipulated: "The certificates and credentials of the family property are marked by words like 'family property of the Zheng that the descendants shall keep forever'. We still need to establish formal certificates of the property which clearly record the area and boundaries of the land, and submit them to the government to get official stamps and signatures. Newly-bought family property should also follow this rule. Then the clan leader shall seal those official certificates up for storage in front of all the clan members. No one shall unseal them without authorization. Nobody, old or young, shall suggest pawn or sale of the property. Otherwise he or she will be punished as being unfilial." This was "submitting to the government to get official stamps and signatures" by the Zheng clan. The aforementioned Huang clan followed another way of "submitting to the government to register". As long as the public property was registered and stamped by the government, the stealing and selling of it by the clan members would be strictly prohibited. Meanwhile, no one of other clans was allowed to secretly buy it. In many cases, even if the buyer was not informed or got a written guarantee from the seller, the property would still be recovered by the government and it would be difficult to hold the seller liable for breach of contract. According to the laws in Qing Dynasty, once registered and filed by the government, Yi Tian would be categorized as public property that was not allowed to be sold. "Any unfilial descendant who secretly sells Ji Tian or Yi Tian will be penalized. If the area of the land sold is between one Mu (a unit of area) to ten Mu, the seller will be punished by 100 floggings and spending one month in pillories. If the area is over ten Mu, then the seller will be banished"; and the buyer would be regarded as "having committed the same crime as the seller had. The land should be returned to the clan and the money spent to buy it confiscated".[140] The high

[137]*The Pedigree of Family Huang in Huanfeng, Jiangxia, the Republic of China*. Preface. *General Notes*.

[138]*The Pedigree of Family Ji in Gaolu, Pucheng, the Republic of China* volume 1. *Regulations*.

[139]Li Weizhen. *Collected Works of Da Bi Mountain*. Volume 56. *Records of Yi Tian (the Charitable Land) of Family Wu*.

[140]*Records of Cases, Laws and Systems of Qing Dynasty* in Guang Xu Period. Volume 755. *Hu Lv (Households Decrees) Stealing and Selling Land and Premises*.

consistency between the civil society and the government in terms of public property of clans highlighted the importance of public property. However, it was a serious infringement on the right of a bona fide third party to ask for compensation based on liabilities for breach of contract. (3) Buddhist property. Buddhist property or the property of temples had become another important factor in the civil economic life since the introduction of Buddhism into the East. The government and temples had always imposed strict restrictions upon Buddhist property to maintain the normal temple life, among which the most important measure was to preserve Buddhist property as the public property and prohibit private sale and pawn of it by anyone. *Dunhuang Documents* numbered P2187 recorded in detail the special protection of the Buddhist property in Tang Dynasty: "The land, buildings and all the other property … as long as they belong to the temple … are not allowed to be invaded, sold or pawned. Anyone who violates this rule shall be reported to the government by the temple based on its certificates and be severely penalized. The property sold or pawned shall be returned to the temple and the buyer or pawnee would suffer the losses themselves."[141] Two points were worth noting here: one was that the temple could "report to the government based on its certificates". The "certificates" might be some kind of property certificates or the certificates of title issued by the government granting special protection. Either way, the indisputable fact was that the temple property was specially protected by the government. The other was that "the buyer or pawnee would suffer the losses themselves", which was not appropriate because even if the buyer bought the property out of good intentions, still he or she could not claim the remedy for breach of contract, and would even lose both the property and the money. This document showed that there must be special laws and regulations on the protection of temple property in Tang Dynasty. No matter whether the buyer was subjectively at fault or not, or whether there were negligent acts or not, one would be subject to risks of losing both the property and money as long as the deal involved temple property. In addition to the above three kinds of public property, the guilds, business groups, and townsmen associations in different regions had also adopted the way of "submitting to the government to get official stamps and signatures" since Ming and Qing Dynasties so that their public property could be protected by the public power of the state. The details of this would not be discussed here due to the limit of space.

As for defects of quality, there was no lack of relevant stipulations in ancient contracts. In *Shounu's Contract of Selling Land in Han Dynasty*, it provided that if (after measurement) the area of the delivered land was found to be smaller than that stipulated in the contract, then the seller had to pay back a certain amount of money according to the are age of the missing part. The tenancy contracts in the documents unearthed in Astana, Turpan stipulated in detail the quality of wheat handed in by tenants as the rent. For instance, in *Contract of Zhao Huaiman Renting Land in the 17th Year of Zhen Guan Period* (643 A.D.), "Measure the wheat with Gao Chang

[141] *Documents of the Temples of Dunhuang*, p. 2187. Cited from Li Delong.1995. "Property Secularization of the Temples and Monks Reflected in Dunhuang Documents", *Journal of Shanxi University (Philosophy and Social Science Edition)*, (2).

Hu Dou (a kind of ancient measuring vessel) in order to get good, clean and plump grains. If the wheat is not good, it would be laid out to the windward direction so that the wheat of bad quality would be blown away by the wind, thus leaving the good to pay for the rent."[142] *Contract of Suo Shannu Renting Land in the 22nd Year of Zhen Guan Period* (648 A.D.) also provided: "In autumn, harvest the wheat and measure it with Gao Chang Jiu Gu Ping Yuan Hu (also a kind of standard ancient measuring vessel). The landlord would get the clean and good wheat. If the wheat is not good, it would be laid out to the windward direction so that the wheat of bad quality would be blown away by the wind, thus leaving the good to pay for the rent."[143] "Clean and good" in these two contracts was the standard for the landlord to collect wheat, which meant the wheat should be clean, pure, full and plump. Generally speaking, the subject matter of rights and obligations in ancient contracts was the movable or immovable property as "objects". But in contracts of mortgage, buying and selling, and employment, a person also became the "object". The defects of quality concerning the "person" in these contracts were mainly embodied in the requirement of the person's diligence, loyalty and good health. Violation of this standard would cause liabilities for breach of contract. Taking employment contracts as an example, when people in Tang Dynasty hired laborers, both parties were bound by certain rights and obligations as in *Contract of Dou Boti Hiring the Laborer inthe 10th Year of Zhen Yuan Period (794 A.D.):*

> This contract is made on January 1st, Jia Shu Year on Chinese Lunar Calendar. Dou Boti from Cihui Township, due to a lack of labor in his family, has hired Yan Shou, son of Deng Naerbo from Longle Township, to work for him for a year. From January to the end of September, the employee's monthly salary shall include one Duo**** of grains, a pair of spring clothes, a shirt, a strip of clothes and a pair of leather shoes. Since the employment, the employee is obliged to work hard. Absence from work for a month is not allowed. If the employee is absent from work for one day during busy farming seasons, then two Dou***** of grains will be reduced from his salary. If he is absent for one day during slack seasons, one Dou of grains will be reduced. When the employee is using farming tools such as cages, sickles and hooks in the fields, he shall take the full responsibility if the tools are broken or damaged, which has nothing to do with the employer. But when the tools are at home, it is the employer that should take the full responsibility for them. If the employee is caught stealing other people's vegetables, fruits, livestock or other things, he himself shall be held liable. If he gets sick, his salary will be cut down according to the number of days of his sick leave. If he is wounded by thieves or robbers, the situation will be dealt with based on common practices. Both parties to the contract have discussed and reached an agreement on these rules that shall not be violated by anyone. In case of breach of contract, the breaching party shall be fined ten Duo of grains and give it to the non-breaching party. This private contract is thus established as evidence to avoid further disputes …[144]

---

[142]The *Unearthed Documents in Turpan.* Book 4. *Documents of Tomb No. 301, Astana.*

[143]ibid. Book 5. *Documents of Tomb No.24, Astana.*

[144]*Dunhuang Documents.* 5. *Contract Documents.* C.

*****Translator's annotation: Duo was a unit of measurement for grains used in Dunhuang region in Five.*

Dynasties. One Duo equaled about 200 liters.

******Translator's annotation: Dou was a unit of measurement for grains. One Dou equaled ten liters.*

According to the stipulations in this contract, the employee should undertake the following obligations, otherwise he would bear liabilities for breach of contract: (1) He should work conscientiously without absenteeism, or his salary would be cut down. (2) He should manage the farming tools well and give them back to the owner in time, or he should make compensations for the loss and damage. (3) He was not allowed to steal other people's property. If he got caught, he should take full responsibility and the employer would not be jointly and severally liable. (4) He should be in good health. If he got sick and could not labor, his salary would be cut down according to the number of days absent from work. (5) If he was wounded by thieves or robbers, the situation would be handled based on common practices. And if he hurt himself without being involved in an accident, the employer would not be responsible for it and he was allowed to cut down the salary or even rescind the employment contract.

Sixth, the ways to undertake the responsibilities reflected different features. In ancient Rome, the relation of *obligatio* was seen as a sort of personal relation (*raporti personali*). The obligee established a relation of *obligatio* with the obligor out of trust (*finucia*), and the obligor voluntarily accepted being bound by the *obligatio*, pledging himself as the guarantee. This kind of *obligatio* embodied the relation between the persons and trust. Cheating or betraying the trust was considered as "fraud" (*dolus*), i.e., the responsibilities that the cheaters bore were only reputational and moral punishments. Later, the principle of interests was added to the contract and became the standard to judge whether or not to undertake the contractual liabilities. Thus the scope of human contractual relationships was greatly expanded, and contractual liabilities evolved from personal liabilities to property liabilities.[145] The nexum in Rome Law was a typical debt bondage (*obligatio*) contract that pledged the person as collateral. If the obligor defaulted on his/her loan, the obligee was allowed to capture him/her, bring him/her to the magistrate and declare that the obligor was detained. If no guarantor came forward to free the obligor from detention, then the law enforcer would award him/her to the obligee.[146] The obligee regarded the obligor as an *obligatio* slave (nexus), except that this slave identity was just a "quasi-slave".[147] The obligee enjoyed many powers over the obligor including selling him/her to countries farther than Tiber or even putting him/her to death. When the obligors were in the majority, the obligees could even divide the obligors' bodies and distribute them among the obligees.[148] By 326 B.C., *Lex Poetelia* eventually replaced personal liabilities with property liabilities and regarded *obligatio* as a simple property relationship where the obligor's property was used as the guarantee of the *obligatio.*[149] As for the order of compensation, actual fulfillment of obligations came before compensation

[145]Ding [48].

[146]Giuseppe [49].

[147]Pietro [50].

[148]Law of the Twelve Tables. Volume 3. "Enforcement". Cited from Zhou [51].

[149]See footnote 147, p. 354.

for losses.[150] There were two ways for obligees to obtain compensation: litigation and negotiation. In comparison, the latter took precedence over the former. But no matter what kind of compensation it was, monetary compensation was the principle (*omnis condemnatio pecuniaria*).[151]

The thing that remained unchanged concerning the contractual liabilities in ancient China was that the personal liabilities overlapped property liabilities. Their orders and the ways to realize the obligee's rights also had unique characteristics, which are discussed as follows.

1. The forms of contractual liabilities. The ideas of contracts in China was driven by ethical justice, so civil ethics like good faith and honesty had exerted great influence on the ways to undertake contractual liabilities. Generally speaking, it was reflected in the following aspects. Firstly, physical punishment was considered as a natural way of undertaking contractual liabilities, as criminal law and civil law being integrated and mixed with each other was still a feature of Chinese contract spirit. The physical punishment to the obligor not only meant to punish, more importantly, it aimed to tarnish the obligor's reputation with punishments like whippings, floggings, penal servitude and exile so as to warn other people to guard against this person to avoid loss of property. This point could be illustrated by the case recorded in the inscriptions on *Zhen Yi* (a bronze ware in the shape of a washbasin with a tubular handle) of Western Zhou Dynasty, which showed how the government official Bo Yangfu dealt with the contract dispute between a mentor and his student. Mu Niu once swore to his mentor that he would pay a certain amount of money to his mentor, but later he broke the promise. When they both went to the court, Mu Niu swore again and pledged the value more than Wufu as the collateral of the debt. According to the judgment in the inscriptions, there were two ways to punish Mu Niu for his default in line with the laws of Zhou Dynasty: 1000 whippings or tattooing and inking on the face. Bo Yangfu, as the magistrate, cut down 500 whippings and cancelled the tattooing and inking on condition that Mu Niu had to hand in a fine of 300 Huan (a unit of weight in ancient China) and apologize to his mentor to restore peace. Moreover, he had to ensure that if he breached the contract again, he would be punished by both whippings and tattooing and inking. Mu Niu swore in court that he accepted the judgment.[152] From Qin Dynasty to Qing Dynasty, though liabilities for breach of contract were mainly based on property liabilities, physical punishment never stopped. For example, *Law Code of Tang Dynasty* stipulated: "If one takes the liberty of using others' property that was entrusted to him/her without permission, he/she shall be penalized as committing corruption, the punishment being one level less than that of corruption. If one fraudulently claims the death or loss of the entrusted property (such as livestock or other property) in order to embezzle it, then he/she shall be penalized as committing the crime of fraud, the

[150] *Corporis Iuris Civilis Fragmenta Selecta IV 1* 1994. Trans. by Ding Mei. China University of Political Science and Law Press, pp. 74–75.

[151] See footnote 145, pp. 90–91.

[152] Cited from Kong and Hu [52].

punishment being one level less than that of fraud." Zhangsun Wuji wrote in *Law Code of Tang Dynasty*: "If one takes the liberty of using others' property that was entrusted to him/her without permission, he/she shall be penalized as committing corruption, the punishment being one level less than that of corruption in law. Secret use of the property worthy of one Chi (a unit of length to measure cloth) results in ten whippings. The punishment will be raised by one level with every additional worth of Pi (a bolt of cloth); and ten Pi, 100 floggings with a maximum prison sentence of two years and a half. If one fraudulently claims the death or loss of the entrusted property such as livestock or other property, he/she shall be penalized as committing the crime of fraud, the punishment being one level less than that of fraud in law. Illegal possession of the property worthy of one Chi results in 50 whippings, which will also be raised by one level with every additional worth of Pi; and if it reaches five Pi, then 100 floggings, which will be raised by one level with every five Pi."[153] Entrusting property to others was essentially a matter of personal credit. It would be hard to protect the interests of the original owner if the trustee invaded or embezzled it. That was why the law expressly stipulated that those who illegally disposed of the entrusted property were subject to criminal liabilities. The following case in *Law Reports of Southern Song Dynasty* was a typical contract dispute concerning entrusted property. Yan Wenlong engaged in trade and deposited his silver and money inbroker Li's family. "They made the contract as the proof". But later the father and son of Li family intended to "misappropriate" his money and did not want to give it back. When they went to court, the Lis claimed that Yan was in arrears with his taxes, and cheated and bullied common people. The local magistrate investigated the case and decided: "Arrears is a minor crime whereas fraud is a major crime. Li Qiwu and Li Si should be punished with 100 floggings before being sent out of the town and also should pay back the money and silver."[154] In this case, the father and son of Li family were not only held responsible for breach of contract and returned the property, but also underwent criminal punishment, which was a typical example of mixing criminal law with civil law. In ancient China, people who committed crimes out of subjective intent or subjective fault were generally subject to criminal penalties as a way to eliminate fraud and corruption in civil economic life. What's more, property liability was the main form of contractual liabilities in ancient times. It could be categorized as follows: the first was liquidated damages–a certain amount of money agreed by both parties to the contract to be paid by the defaulting party to the non-defaulting party as compensation in case of breach of contract. It should be noted that most of the clauses of liquidated damages in ancient contracts were punitive. Take as an example *The Land Tenancy Contract of Zhang Hailong in the 3rd Year of Long Shuo Period of Tang Dynasty (663 A.D.)*:

[153] *Law Code of Tang Dynasty* volume 26. *Law of Trivia.*

[154] *Law Reports of Southern Song Dynasty* volume 26. *Law of Trivia.*

> On September 12th, the 3rd Year of Long Shuo Period, Zhang Hailong, a villager of Wucheng township, rented two Mu of land in Bei Qukou of Wucheng from villager Zhao Ahuanren. They both agreed to cultivate the land for livelihood. Hailong should provide wheat seeds and cattle for planting and ploughing. In autumn, Hailong and Ahuanren should divide the wheat that is harvested equally. If Ahuanren does not allow Hailong to cultivate the land within the prescribed period of time, Ahuanren should pay fifty Wen (a quantifier of ancient coins) to Hailong as a fine. If Hailong does not farm the land as prescribed, he should pay fifty Wen together with some fodder to Ahuanren.[155]

In this tenancy contract, the land was provided by the landowner Zhao Ahuanren and cattle and wheat seeds by Zhang Hailong. The harvest would be divided equally between the two. The default clauses were quite clear: Zhao must provide the land to Zhang for farming during the prescribed period of time, otherwise Zhao should be fined fifty Wen as liquidated damages. Similarly, Zhang must contribute cattle, wheat seeds, and labor to cultivate the land, otherwise he should also be fined fifty Wen and hand in some fodder as liquidated damages. Judging from the contracts in Tang Dynasty, the sum of liquidated damages were mostly "twice the contract price". In *Contract of Zhang Yuchui Hiring the Person to Guard the Beacon Tower in Wucheng Township, Gaochang County, Xi State in Tang Dynasty*, Zhang hired a person to guard the beacon tower for him with eight Wen of silver coins and made clear that breach of contract was not allowed, "the defaulting party should pay twice the price to the non-defaulting party".[156] Similar stipulations also appeared in *Contract of Zuo Chongxi Renting the Vegetable Farm in the 3rd Year of Zong Zhang Period (670 A.D.) in Tang Dynasty*.[157] The second was the deposit penalty. In ancient contracts, a deposit served as an advance payment to certify and ensure the fulfillment of the contract. The deposit penalty, similar to that nowadays, meant that the deposit payer would lose the deposit if he/she violated the contract; and the deposit receiver had to pay back twice the sum of the deposit if the violation was on his/her part. Some old customs were followed in regions like Haiyang County, Shandong Province, which was, if the buyer had already delivered the deposit to the seller, he/she must not abandon the deposit and propose to terminate the contract in the early stage of contract fulfillment; at the same time, the seller was not allowed to return the deposit.[158] This custom was rarely found in the civil society, it was not hard to notice that the deposit here played more of a role to certify rather than to guarantee. *Jiangnan Sideline Business Report* in 1937 recorded that when the rural households had no money to buy raw silk, the middleman guaranteed to the silk firm to help them get raw silk unconditionally. When the silk fabrics were produced, the middleman bought them with his own money. Then the households could not only pay back the money that should have been paid to buy raw silk, but also get silk fabrics, "They

[155] *The Unearthed Documents in Turpan* Volume 5.

[156] See footnote 155.

[157] ibid. Volume 6. *Documents of Tomb No.4, Astana.*

[158] *The Survey on Civil Practices* (Book 2). 2000. Edited by Former Judicial Administration Department of Nanjing National Government. Proofread by Hu Xusheng et. al. China University of Political science and Law Press, p. 470.

were really happy and there was no difficulty".[159] Here the fact that the middleman guaranteed to the silk firm to help the rural households get raw silk without paying was in nature purchase on credit. The households did not need to pay in advance, but they must sell their silk products to the appointed middleman who was fully in charge of selling those in order to make intermediate profits. What the middleman did was nothing but restricting the operation of the households with goods (raw silk), which was in the nature of deposit. Although his purchase on credit solved the problem of money and goods shortage for the households, the raw silk they got without paying actually resembled the deposit very much, blocking the free circulation of their businesses. The third was damages or compensation. It was a historical progress of civil law that the defaulting party should pay damages in compensation for the interests of the counterpart in lieu of taking personal liabilities. In *Law Code of Tang Dynasty,* if the property or livestock entrusted to another person was actually dead or lost, whether or not to compensate should be decided in accordance with the relevant provisions. "Whoever loses the public property or private property shall make compensation in full; but those who are robbed of the property shall not be liable for compensation." "Whoever loses the property that was entrusted to him/her by others not in the cases of robbery or plunder shall take the full responsibility for the loss. As for livestock, no compensation shall be paid if it dies by natural causes; otherwise the keeper shall make appropriate compensation in compliance with relevant laws."[160] Compensation could be divided into compensation for vested or lost interests and that for prospect interests. The preceding examples in *Law Code of Tang Dynasty* were all about compensation for lost interests. However, in many contracts especially in the default clauses, the compensatory terms or punitive terms were commonly seen, which actually the compensation for prospect interests were. These provisions were more easily found in contracts of Tang Dynasty than in those of Yuan, Ming, and Qing Dynasties and since. The reason behind was that the civil contract disputes in Tang Dynasty relied mostly on private remedies without active intervention from the government. But contracts in subsequent dynasties replaced the clear and specified compensatory terms with expressions like "leave it to official judgment", showing that the government gradually strengthened its management of private contracts and that there were detailed and specific provisions regarding contractual liabilities in official laws and juridical practices at that time. The fourth was repayment of debts with labor or livestock labor. Such liabilities for breach of contract appeared to guarantee the debt with the person, but as a matter of fact, it had completely deviated from the historical way of "serving as a slave" and evolved into a civilized form in which debts could be paid off with the labor of the person or of the livestock. There was a story about Dong Yong who sold himself as a slave in Han Dynasty: "In the early Han Dynasty, Dong Yong, who had lost his mother at a very young age, supported his father on his own. When his father died, Dong Yong had no money to bury him. So he borrowed ten thousand coins from another person and told him: 'If I don't have enough money to pay you back in the future, I will serve

[159]Fan [53].

[160]*Law Code of Tang Dynasty* volume 26. *Law of Trivia.*

you as a slave.'".[161] Although cases of this kind were prohibited by the government from Han Dynasty to Tang Dynasty, the folks kept on doing so. Mr. Li Zhimin has incisive and detailed exposition on this point, which is available for reference.[162] There were three ways to repay the debt with labor: to repay with one's own labor or others' labor, to repay with the labor of one's slaves, and to repay with the labor of one's livestock. This form of liabilities for breach of contract was widely applied and affirmed by the official laws as far back as Qin Dynasty.[163]

2. The order of the ways to realize contractual liabilities. The realization of contractual liabilities in traditional Chinese society mainly relied on private remedies and public remedies with the former preceding the latter. That was to say, the realization of contractual liabilities in official laws and civil customary laws depended on the principle of mutual agreement by both parties to the contract, similar to today's negotiation style. If the two parties failed to reach an agreement, then relevant social groups such as clans (bound by clan regulations) and guilds (bound by guild regulations) would mediate between them with the aim of settling disputes fairly. For instance, the industry and business associations first appeared during Wan Li Period in Ming Dynasty.[164] One of their major functions was to coordinate the interests of businessmen, seek common benefits and suppress disputes. In the 51st Year of Kang Xi Period in Qing Dynasty, Xiancheng Association was established by businessmen in Guangzhou. Ma Shibo, the chief of the association, said the purpose of establishing it was not for the profits but "for the righteousness": "If the businessmen all pursue their own interests and never get united to seek common good, they would become selfish, invade others' property and obstruct the development of the industry. So everyone pursuing their own profits results in everyone getting no profits."[165] Thus Ma initiated the business association in order to uphold righteousness, mediate disputes and seek common profits. In Dao Guang Period, businessmen from the city of Shaoxing ran more than 100 cd shops in the city of Suzhou. They established Dongyue Association to unite together, make more achievements and foster relationships as fellow-townsmen. "The pricing of the commodities should be unified. No one is allowed to arbitrarily increase or reduce the price. In case of unfairness, the people involved should meet the chief in the guildhall, discuss and make rules to settle the disputes."[166] Thus it was no wonder that all kinds of guilds, clubs, associations and academies were called "specialized communities" by the scholars

[161] *Tai Ping Yu Lan (Taiping Imperial Encyclopaedia)* volume 411. *The Personnel Section The Sense of Filial Piety.*

[162] Li [54].

[163] *Bamboo Slips Unearthed from the Qin Tombs in Shui Hu Di, Hubei.* 1978. Wenwu Publishing House, pp. 84–87.

[164] Zhang [55].

[165] *Collections of the Documents of Townsmen Associations in Industry and Commerce in Beijing Since Ming and Qing Dynasties, Establishment of Huangpi Hutong Xiancheng Association.*

[166] *The Selection of Inscription Materials in Jiangsu Province Since Ming and Qing Dynasties.* 1959. SDX Joint Publishing Company, p. 217.

for they actually served that certain function.[167] In Qing Dynasty, many Nan Hua Palaces were set up in Sichuan as the guildhalls or clubhouses for businessmen from different provinces. "If people like shop owners and other residents are involved in conflicts, they should meet the chiefs of their associations and guilds to figure things out."[168] It was even expressly stipulated in some places that civil economic disputes "have to be reported to the leaders of local conventions, chiefs and branch heads of the associations or guilds to be discussed and judged".[169] If neither both parties to the contract nor the relevant social groups were able to settle the disputes, they would resort to the public power of the government. Another two ways of implementing contractual liabilities were specific performance and compensation for losses, and again, the former preceded the latter. Since the motivation behind making a contract was mutual benefits for both sides, the default of one party would inevitably lead to losses of the other party. Thus specific performance and compensation for losses existed in both Chinese and Western contract theory as remedies. The defaulting party would be forced to fulfill his/her obligations when it was possible and necessary; otherwise the losses of the other party should be compensated in the form of damages. In ancient China, specific performance could be enforced by people, or by the government or both. For example, the obligee could stipulate in the contract that if the obligor defaulted on the delivery, the obligee would be empowered to enforce the fulfillment by compulsory means, as in *The Contract of Tian Poji Buying Trees in the 2nd Year of Yan Shou Period under the Reign of Gao Chang Kingdom*[170]:

> On March the 2nd in the 2nd Year of Yan Shou Period, Gao Chang Kingdom, Tian Poji bought trees … from Zhao Minger. She should pay eight Wen of silver coins by June 15th … If the payment is not made in time, the sum of money that shall be paid would be increased. If the payment is still overdue, the creditor will be entitled to take away the debtor's family property to satisfy the debt … (the rest is omitted)

This was a contract of buying trees, and both parties agreed that the buyer would pay for the trees in time. In case of default, the creditor was allowed to take away the debtor's family property to satisfy his debt. Expressions like "be entitled to take away one's family property" and "be allowed to take away one's family assets" served as the general formula in contracts of sale, loan and pledge in Tang Dynasty. It could be seen that the contractual responsibilities were compulsorily enforced by private power. There were also express provisions in *Law Code of Tang Dynasty* that regulated the practice of compulsory enforcement in civil society: "In case of default on debt, the creditor should report it to the government for judgment even though he/she is allowed to take away the debtor's property to satisfy the debt. If the creditor, without reporting to the government, invades the debtor's property and takes away things that are valued more than the debt, he/she will be punished as

[167] Zhang [56].

[168] The Republic of China *Annals of Qionglai County*. Volume 2. *Jian Zhi*.

[169] The Republic of China *Annals of Qianwei County Residents*.

[170] *The Unearthed Documents in Turpan*. Book 5.

committing corruption."[171] Two things could be inferred from this clause: one was that many people forcibly took away the debtors' family assets without permission from the government at that time when it concerned overdue debt. The other was that if the creditor took away things that were worth no more than the debt, he/she would not be punished even if he/she did not report to the government. This meant that the government acquiesced in their private remedies, and would step in to ensure the realization of creditor's rights when private remedies were insufficient.

3. Ways to realize contractual liabilities. There were two ways to realize contractual liabilities in Roman law: litigation compensation and agreement compensation. The latter came before the former in terms of the order.[172] In ancient China, private negotiation and mediation always played a dominant role as advocated by the government. The pre-determining right discussed in previous sections was a good illustration of it. Moreover, two points needed to be mentioned here: the first was the institution of local conventions (乡约, xiang yue: an institution where people living in the same village or township abided by the same set of rules and regulations, dealt with problems in different aspects and assisted each other to ensure the harmonious life and development in the region) started to prevail since Zheng De Period in Ming Dynasty.[173] It was of great benefits to inspire people and re-establish justice and righteousness in a time of moral degradation and indifference. The local convention was in nature community autonomy that excluded official intervention at the beginning. For instance, the second volume *Xiang Yue* of *Tai Quan Xiang Li* written by Huang Zuo in Ming Dynasty recorded: "The villagers elect by themselves the smart, honest and respectable ones to be the leader and vice leader without intervention from the government. Once a local convention is established, the public granaries, the local household registration system and sacrifice activities would all be set up accordingly by the local people, and the government should not send over officials to inspect in order to avoid disputes. In addition, it is not necessary to inform the government of the leaders' names." From this point of view, the autonomy by local people properly ruled out the effectiveness of official laws in that matters like marriages, land, and debts were governed as internal affairs in the community. In dispute settlements, the local convention stressed negotiation, public discussion and mutual agreement as the most important ways. After Qing Dynasty, the gentry class became active. They "joined hands and sought local autonomy of the community" with the government. By setting up "gentry area", they made a great contribution to the protection of the country and its people, dispute settlements, problem resolution and charity. In *Ben Shu* of Feng Yu Charitable Farmstead******, the power of the gentry class was recorded and discussed: "Now the social atmosphere in Wu State is getting worse. Things like affray, arson and robbery are frequent occurrences that have to be prohibited. These problems can only be solved by the concerted efforts of the gentry and the government. Gentry can observe what is happening

[171] *Law Code of Tang Dynasty*. Volume 26. *Law of Trivia*.

[172] See footnote 135, p. 90.

[173] Cao [57].

around and present complaints to the government, which the officials would pay special attention to and submit to the county magistrate without slight."[174] Some scholars said the gentry remedies was not only a charitable act, but also a means of social control.[175] The second was that the government expressly advocated that people had better settle disputes of private contracts by themselves, which provided a broad space for agreement compensation in the civil society. For example, it was stipulated in the 6th year of Yong Zheng Period in Qing Dynasty that "Disputes over minor matters like marriage, land, debt, affray, and gambling should be coped with by the officials of the place where the offence took place. It is not allowed to report to the state or county where the plaintiff resides"; "As for the minor disputes over money, debt and land, there is no charge to be filed. The cases should be adjudicated by the local government. Submitting all the cases to the capital is prohibited". In the 34th year of Qian Long Period, it was further stipulated that "The cases of minor matters like marriage and land shall be returned to the local government for settlement and judgement. Those who filed the cases to the central government would still be punished for leapfrog appeal".[176] The legislative spirit reflected by these stipulations lied in the concept that national affairs were of supreme importance. Xue Yunsheng commented: "Common people from other provinces, prefectures and counties who dare to file a case concerning minor matters like marriage and land to the central government in the capital must be restless ones. Their cases are to be returned…and they will also be punished."[177] These stipulations manifested typical traits of the laws in Qing Dynasty. As a consequence, contract disputes, including the realization of contractual liabilities, were all entrusted to the force of folk customary law and local grass-roots governments, which in turn judged cases by folk customary law (common practices). This interactive influence contributed to the maturity and development of folk customary law, and other social forces including clans, guilds and local conventions made their own rules to manage the businesses in their respective places. Zhang Haishan in Qing Dynasty said: "Disputes over minor matters like marriage and land should be dealt with by the head or vice head of the clan. Only important matters can be reported to the government."[178] This idea chimed in with the pre-determining right of clans in the civil society. Therefore, the system of agreement compensation finally developed into the trifecta of negotiation between the two parties, mediation by a third party and dissuasion from litigation by the local official. Except for a very few major cases, the way of fulfilling contractual liabilities by the civil society and the government

---

[174] *Annals of Wu County in the Republic of China.* Volume 31. *Feng Yu Zhuang Ben Shu.* printing copy in the 22th year in the Republic of China.

[175] Yu [58].

******Translator's annotation: Feng Yu Charitable Farmstead (丰豫义庄) was a charitable institution built by one of the gentry Pan Zengyi in his hometown Suzhou aiming to help the people in the community.

[176] *Law Code of Qing Dynasty.* Volume 3. *Criminal Law Lawsuits Overstepping Indictment.*

[177] Xue Yunsheng. *Cases and Questions* volume 39.

[178] See footnote 63, pp. 655–656.

basically entered a one-way road—mediation and negotiation, dissuasion from litigation and pacifying the people. Traditional ethical justice covered contractual justice, which marked the basic orientation and unique symbol of the development of ancient Chinese contract law.

Contract Risk and Exemptions

The essence of contract risk is to share the unexpected risks among the contracting parties, i.e. the consequences of interest losses taken by one or both parties, which are caused by the fault of neither party. The risk system aims to determine whether one party has the right to pass the losses to the counterpart or to obtain compensation from the counterpart when he/she suffers losses from the risk, so as to balance his/her interests and losses and to seek contractual justice and fairness. In accordance with the spirit of Roman law, risks and interests go hand in hand, that is, those who enjoy the interests should naturally bear the risks caused by those interests. Risk mainly comes from two sources: objective responsibilities (responsabilita obbiettiva) and subjective responsibilities (responsabilita soggettiva), and the risk that incur contractual liabilities mainly belongs to the subjective ones—causes (causus), which can be divided into "accident incidents" (causus fortuitus) and "force majeure" (vis maior). The former refers to incidents that are avoidable but unforeseeable by ordinary people and to which the obligor is unable to respond effectively and promptly; the latter refers to those foreseeable but cannot be overcome by the power of ordinary people especially that of the obligor. In Justinian Period, if the risk in the relation of *obligatio* was the sudden impossibility of performance caused by an accident or force majeure, then the obligor was not responsible for the consequences therefrom. That was the famous principle of "the incident does not incur contractual liabilities". However, this principle must be supplemented by that of "the accident is no fault" proposed by the famous Roman jurist Alfven, meaning accidents and force majeure only referred to those incidents caused by external rather than internal reasons, that was, the obligor would not be held responsible for the incident on the premise that there was no fault on his/her part.

As for the risk burden, it should be provided for by law or by mutual agreement of the two parties if neither one was at fault; but if there was fault on the part of either party, the risk would be passed to the side at fault. The contractual liability system of Justinian adopted the doctrine of risk on the part of the obligee (periculum emptoris). Paul remarked in his discussion on risk burden of the sale contract: "Once the sale contract is concluded, the benefits brought by the increase of land or the losses incurred by the reduction of land due to the impact of rivers were passed to the buyer. Because the buyer would still bear the risk even if all the land is submerged by the river, there is no doubt that the benefits obtained accrue to the buyer."[179] The "risk" herein referred to natural risks (rishio naturale). Based on Roman law, whoever enjoyed interests bore the risks, which was developed into the rule of "natural risks

[179] See footnote 150, p. 47, cited from Paul, *On Sabin* (5th ed.).

borne by the obligee". Contractual risks (rischio contratuale), on the other hand, were assumed by the obligor, meaning the obligor must bear contractual liabilities for the risks due to his/her fault. "The principle of the obligee bearing risks" found its inheritance in the *Code Napoléon*. By contrast, "the principle of delivery" (res perit domino) adopted in countries like Germany, Italy and China marks delivery as the boundary for passing of risk. Section 446 of *German Civil Code* expressly stipulates the passing of risk and of charges: "The risk of accidental destruction and accidental deterioration passes to the buyer upon the delivery of the thing sold. From the time of delivery the emoluments of the thing accrue to the buyer and he bears the charges on it." *Italian Civil Code* also provides for the liability for risks in contracts of sale, lease and transport.[180] Article 142 of Contract Law of the People's Republic of China provides that "The risk of damage to or loss of the subject matter is borne by the seller prior to delivery, and by the buyer after delivery, except otherwise provided by law or agreed by the parties."

There was no complete theoretical system concerning the contract risk in ancient China. It can only be sorted out from the relevant laws, precedents and habits. The general characteristics of the contract risk system in ancient China are listed as follows.

Firstly, subjective fault or negligence was an important basis for determining risk burden. The principle of "liability for fault", which meant the liability for the losses caused by the inability to perform due to the subjective fault of one or both parties, was widely applied to all kinds of contracts in ancient times. Taking the pawn industry in Qing Dynasty as an example, the pawnbroker should be liable and compensate for the losses if the pledge was burnt, stolen or robbed: "If the pledge is burnt up in a fire caused by the pawnbroker, the pawnbroker shall pay half the original pawn price to the pawner as compensation. If the fire started in the neighborhood and spread to the pawnbroker's shop, the compensation money can be cut down by two tenths and the interest can be deducted monthly … If a dye shop is burnt, the shop owner shall make a list of the things burnt and report it to the local government for evaluation. If the fire is caused by the shop owner, the official shall order the shop owner to pay half the evaluated price to the party that suffers the loss as the compensation. If the fire started in the neighborhood and spread to the dye shop, the sum of compensation will be reduced to three tenths of the evaluated price. The payment shall be made within a month." "If the pawnshop is stolen, the shop owners shall compensate for all goods, whether it be clothes, rice and beans, silk floss, carpentry, paintings and calligraphy, gold and silver, pearls and jades, copper and iron, lead and tin. Two Liang (a unit of weight for ancient coins) of silver shall be paid by the owner, one for the pledge and the other for compensation. If the pawnshop is robbed, the compensation will be five Qian."[181] It could be seen from the above that the liability of compensation for losses due to the shop owner's fault or negligence was greater than that due to other people's fault or negligence. That was because starting a fire and being stolen

---

[180]Codice Civile Italiano. Clause 1523, 1588, 1693.

[181]*Huang Chao Zheng Dian Lei Zuan (Laws and Systemsof the Dynasties)* volume 380. *Criminal Law 12 Household Law Law of Lands and Houses.*

resulted from the shop owner's fault and negligence, whereas being involved in a fire and being robbed were things beyond the control of the owner. Therefore, the liability for fault was justified as the important standard for determining risk burden.

Secondly, the liabilities were shared on a fair and reasonable basis. In light of law, no fault led to no liability. In ancient China, however, the priorities were reason, sentiments, righteousness and morality. Hence the contract risk would be shared between the two parties on a fair and reasonable basis if the losses were caused by accidents or natural disasters out of no one's fault. A case in Song Dynasty was quite intriguing: "A villager went to his neighbor's house to borrow a pot, but he broke it before leaving the house. The owner demanded compensation, and the borrower refused on the grounds that he had not stepped out of the owner's house." The case went to the local court and the magistrate judged "it is appropriate that each pay half the price of the pot".[182] According to common sense, when the subject matter was already delivered to the borrower, then the risk burden should be borne by him. Nevertheless, the borrower defended that he did not even leave the lender's house and the magistrate unexpectedly decided that the two parties should share the responsibilities and risk. The custom of "a fallen house results in a bad bargain" in traditional pawn contracts further showed the fairness in bearing risk burden. If the pawner pledged the house to the pawnee, he/she was only able to recover the original land, residual wood and stone materials when the house was unfortunately damaged by flood or fire or just collapsed naturally before redemption. The pawner was not allowed to make a claim for compensation with the pawnee and the latter should not pay back the pawn price to the pawner either.[183]

In general, contractual liabilities would be exempted under the following circumstances in ancient times.

Firstly, force majeure. The etymology of force majeure lies in the Vis Casus in Roman Law. According to some research, Vis means natural or human, with the connotation of being external and inevitable, and Casus refers to unforeseeable events.[184] Gaius once commented on force majeure: "Force majeure is what the Greeks call ΙΟΣΟγβ Ιαγ, i.e., the power of god. If these natural forces are unavoidable, the lessee should not be liable for the losses incurred".[185] There were also relatively sophisticated provisions regarding *fore majeure* in the laws and decrees of Tang Dynasty: "If the flood or fire that leads to losses results from someone's fault, then he/she shall be penalized and make compensations. If the losses are caused by inevitable events, no one will be held liable."[186] This meant that the losses incurred by accidents due to no one's fault or negligence, which was regarded as force majeure, would not be compensated for. In addition, in tenancy contracts, if there was no harvest of grains in case of drought or flood, the tenant was allowed to request the

[182] *Wen Yuan Ying Hua* volume 543.

[183] See footnote 158, pp. 40, 144.

[184] See footnote 63, p. 674.

[185] See footnote 150, p. 161, cited from Gaius.

[186] *Law Code of Tang Dynasty* volume 26. *Law of Trivi*a.

landlord for a reduction or exemption of rent. Likewise, the landlord could also voluntarily exempt the tenant from performing the obligations without compensation. This was one typical example of exemption from liability due to force majeure.

Secondly, accidents. According to *Law Code of Tang Dynasty*, contractual liabilities caused by unpredictable situations where timely effective response was difficult, known as today's "accidents", could be exempted. For instance, "Whoever discards, loses, or destroys others' property, be it public or private, must make compensation accordingly. However, if the property is robbed from the keeper, he/she shall be exempted from being punished and making compensation." It meant that if one kept the property for the government or other individuals but intentionally destroyed or lost it, he/she must compensate for it; but in case of robbery, no compensation was demanded. This provision was slightly different from that of Roman law where the obligor bore unlimited risk liability in the brokerage contract, i.e., the recipient (accipiens) could not be exempted from the liability of returning the subject matter or the sum of money equal to the value of the subject matter whether it be accidents or force majeure. Ulpianus remarked in his discussion of brokerage contracts: "In a brokerage contract, the risk of subject matter are upon the recipient. In that sense, he either returns the subject matter intact or pays the price equal to the value of the subject matter as compensation."[187] In Tang Dynasty, the consignment business throve, where people sold goods on consignment. The novel *The Biography of Huo Xiaoyu* written in Tang described how Huo, the heroine, sent her maids to entrust her utensils and gadgets to Hou Jingxian's shop to be sold on consignment when she suffered from poverty.[188] If the consignment shop was robbed, its liability for compensation could be reduced or exempted, which was quite different from that of the Roman law. This could be explained by the fact that the Roman law put emphasis on the objective state of actual administrative control, while *Law Code of Tang Dynasty* focused on where there was fault or negligence. In short, Roman law typically embodied the objective liabilities whereas *Law Code of Tang Dynasty* the subjective liabilities.

Thirdly, evictio by public power. When the subject matter was prohibited by law, the contract liability was generally exempted if non-performance or other legal consequences of the contract were incurred by evictio by public power. *Law Code of Tang Dynasty* had detailed record of such issues:

> Question: If someone steals property and immediately sells or lends it to other people so as to make a profit. Is it justifiable that he gets the profits? The stolen goods could include people and livestock and be traded to different households many times, among whom some may be in the know and others are not. Then how to deal with the profits incurred in this kind of situation?
>
> Answer: As stipulated in the law, it should be decided according to the ways of getting profits. If the profits are gained from the business or lending activities due to the efforts of the subsequent owner rather than the original one, then they are not fruits of the property and should be taken by the subsequent owner. If the stolen goods are traded many times

[187] See footnote 150, p. 68, cited from Ulpianus, *On the Edict* (32th).

[188] *Tai Ping Guang Ji* volume 487. *Legend of Huo Xiaoyu.*

> among different people, the subsequent owner in the know should return both the thing and the profits to the original owner, and he/she who is not in the know should return the thing and keep the profits.[189]

On the surface, this concerned the ownership of stolen goods and unjust enrichment. In fact, once the subject matter in the contract of sale and pledge was found to be stolen goods, it would be immediately recovered by the government and returned to the original owner. If the buyer in the deal knew that it was stolen goods but still completed the deal, then the profits generated were deemed as unjust enrichment. Otherwise, the buyer should only return the property without giving back the profits. Simply put, the government would definitely recover the subject matter in the sale contract whether the buyer knew it was stole nor not. At this time, the buyer should not require the seller to continue to perform or to assume the liabilities for breach of contract. The slight difference was that if the buyer was informed, he/she should be responsible for returning both the property and profits; if not, he/she could keep the profits while returning the property only.

Fourthly, amnesty. Traditional Chinese society valued benevolent administration as the core. Back then, rulers often issued merciful imperial orders and decrees of amnesty to relieve people of both public and private debts. Qualified debtors would be exempt from all the contractual liabilities and the creditor was not allowed to require specific performance through either public or private power. When Song Guangzong ascended the throne in the 16th Year of Chun Xi Period of Southern Song Dynasty (1189 A.D.): "All the debts in the society are forgiven regardless of their duration and sum. Some people do not think highly of this edict since they just lent out their money ten days ago and thus lost both their capital and interest. He Dan, a senior official at that time, talked about this with Song, who then decided that debtors should pay the capital back…In July, the 5th Year of Shao Xi Period, another edict was issued to pardoned people's debts, but only the debts owed three years ago."[190] The reason why a debt pardon was issued again in the 5th Year of Shao Xi Period (1194 A.D.) was because emperor Song Ningzong ascended the throne that year. Two pardons of public and private debts within merely five years were intended to show the keen intelligence and benevolence of the ruler. Debtors were more than happy to be pardoned whereas for creditors, it was nothing but a great blow. They would usually lose both the capital and profits and some even become homeless and insolvent unless the debtors voluntarily paid off the debts. In contrast, the pardons and amnesty edicts in Tang Dynasty were more reasonable, which were already explained before. However, in any case, the disadvantages of the government's intervention with private contractual relationships by administrative or judicial means far outweighed its minor advantages for it did disrupt the normal economic order in the civil society. Therefore, it was for a good and understandable reason that specific terms excluding the validity of amnesties and pardons from the government were commonly found in private contracts.

---

[189] *Law Code of Tang Dynasty* volume 4. *Ming Li.*

[190] Hong Mai. *Rong Zhai San Bi* volume 9. "Pardons of Debts".

Fifthly, prescription. The system of prescription was the most reasonable one among all kinds of exemption conditions. The purpose of setting prescription was to urge creditors to actively claim and realize their rights. If they neglected to do so, their creditors' rights would expire after a certain period of time, and then it would be difficult to get the recognition and remedies from the government except for private remedy. The system of prescription was twofold in ancient times: one was acquisitive prescription or positive prescription and the other extinctive prescription or negative prescription. Both were widely used in contractual relationships. The former referred to the legally prescribed period of time of continuous occupation of the property that was needed to acquire the property ownership from the original owner. For example, the imperial edict of the 3rd Year of Jiang Long Period during the reign of Emperor Song Taizu: "If the pawnee keeps the pledge for 30 years, and the original pawner has no written contract or the authenticity of the contract is hard to distinguish, then the pawnee is able to acquire the ownership of the pledge legally based on this edict."[191] Similar rules also existed in the 18th year of Qian Long Period in Qing Dynasty (1753 A.D.): "After 30 years, the property is not allowed to be redeemed if the name of the redeemer was not clearly indicated in the contract even though it was not stipulated 'never to be redeemed'."[192] In the two cases above, the pawner was not allowed to redeem the property and reclaim his ownership based on the contract, neither would the pawnee be liable for breach of contract. Extinctive prescription was also quite common in ancient Chinese contracts. As far back as Western Zhou Dynasty, the government provided for the extinctive prescription: "Litigations concerning the contract of sale shall be submitted within the prescribed period of time, or they will not be accepted. The limitation is stipulated according to the region of the litigant."[193] Zheng Xuan once remarked: "Since the cases are not accepted after the prescribed period of time, people have become less litigious than before." The protection time period for creditors' rights was 30 years in Tang and Song Dynasties. *Criminal Code of Song Dynasty* cited the regulations in the 4th year of Chang Qing Period of Tang Dynasty and stipulated: "Contracts without clear and detailed provisions lead to disputes, let alone those made many years ago. It would be hard to distinguish right from wrong and judge the case after so many years, thus leaving many disadvantages. There were people who went to Taizhou County to file a lawsuit concerning their debt long ago. The debtor fled 30 years ago, leaving no evidence but the contract. This case was not accepted."[194] Besides, the prescribed limitation of action for inheritance disputes in Song Dynasty was three years, for trade disputes 20 years, and for disputes over ambiguous or unclear contracts 20 years.[195]

---

[191] *Criminal Code of Song Dynasty* volume 13.

[192] *Law Code of Qing Dynasty* volume 9. *Household Law Pawn and Sale of Land and Houses.*

[193] *Rites of Zhou Di Guan Zhi Ren.*

[194] *Criminal Code of Song Dynasty* volume 26.

[195] Refer to *Law Reports of Southern Song Dynasty.*

References

1. Malinowski, B.K. 1926. *Crime and Custom in Savage Society*, 25. London: Reutledge.
2. Hobel, E. Edamson. 1993. *The Law of Primitive Man*. Translated by Zhou Yong. China Social Sciences Press.
3. Liang, Zhiping. 1992. *Fa Bian*, 57–58. Guizhou People's Publishing Press.
4. Zhang, Naigen. 1996. The essence of western law. *Journal of Comparative Law* (1).
5. Yin, Tian. 1995. *Droit Contemporain des Contrats en France*, 241. Law Press China.
6. George, H. Sabine. 1986. *A History of Political Theory*, 487–488. Translated by Liu Shan et al. The Commercial Press.
7. Thomas, Hobbes. 1985. *Leviathan*, 99, 103, 104, 108–109. Translated by Li Sifu and Li Yanbi. The Commercial Press.
8. Kong, Qingming, Liuyuan Hu, et al. 1996. *The History of Chinese Civil Law*, 281. Jilin Publishing Group.
9. Gao, Qicai. 1995. *Chinese Customary Law*, 404, 422. Hunan (Education) Publishing House.
10. Yintian. 1995. *Droit Contemporain des Contrats en France*, 241. Law Press China.
11. Laura, A. Skosey. 1994. Recent American academic writings on traditional Chinese law. In *American Scholars' Comments on Chinese Legal Traditions*, ed. Gao Daoyun (Karen Turner), Gao Hongjun and He Weifang, 98–99. China University of Political Science and Law Press.
12. Zhang, Erguo. 1995. The alliance issues in Pre-Qin Period. *History Quarterly* (1).
13. Chen, Mengjia. 1966. Oaths of alliance and unearthed books of Eastern Zhou dynasty. *Archaeology* (5).
14. Dobson, W.A.C.H. 1968. Some legal instruments of ancient China: The Ming and the Meng" In *Studies in the Chinese Humanities CM*, ed. Chow Tse-tsung, 269–282. Iwaukee: University of Winsconsin.
15. Li, Li. 1995. Changes in the covenants of Eastern Zhou Dynasty and those in the legal system of spring and autumn and warring states period. *Chinese Journal of Law* (4).
16. Zhang, Chuanxi. 1995. *A Study of the Problems in Qin and Han Dynasties*. Peking University Press.
17. Xu, Zichu. 1998. *Rules and Regulations of the Clan Xu in Yuyao County, Jiangnan Region*. Shanghai: Shanghai Academy of Social Sciences Press.
18. Joseph, Needham. 1956. *Science and Civilization in China*, vol. 2, 544. Cambridge University Press,.
19. Qu, Tongzu. 1981. *Chinese Law and Chinese Society*, 326. Zhonghua Book Company.
20. Cheng, Chalin. 1986. The economical documents on public inspection and past case records in Tang Dynasty. *The Journal of Chinese Social and Economic History* (2).
21. Wen-en Tsao. 1962. Equity in Chinese customary law. In *Essays in Jurisprudence in Honor of Roscoe Pound*, 21–43. Indianapolis/New York: Bobbsmerrill.
22. Wang, Huizu. 1991. *Records of Ruling. The Collection of Economic Articles in Qing Dynasty*, vol 22. Zhonghua Book Company.
23. Sybile, Van Der Sprenkel. 1962. *Legal Institutions in Manchu China: A sociological Analysis*, 102. University of London, Athlone Press.
24. Hiroaki, Terada. 1998. The nature of "agreement" in law orders in Ming and Qing Dynasties. In *The Civil Trails and Civil Contracts in Ming and Qing Dynasties*, ed Wang Yaxin, and Liang Zhiping, 141–157. Law Press China.
25. Zheng, Yubo. 1981. On the validity of obligations and general guarantee. *China Law Journal* (14).
26. Zhang, Lihong. 1996. The contractual responsibilities of roman law and its development in modern China. In *Civil and Commercial Law Review*, vol. 5. Law Press China.
27. Huo, Jianyuan. 1992. *Research on Contractual Responsibilities*. Jilin University Press.
28. Zheng, Yubo. 1984. Analysis on civil responsibilities. In *Essays on Civil Law and Civil Obligations*, 60. Taiwan Wu-Nan Book Inc.
29. Liu, Jingwei. 1988. On mandatory specific performance and money compensation. In *Essays on Civil Law*, 411. Qunzhong Publishing House.

30. Cui, Jianyuan. 1992. *Research on Contractual Obligations*, 55–56. Jilin University Press.
31. Li, Rongsheng.1983. *Introduction of Economic Contract Law*, 168. Heilongjiang People's Publishing House.
32. Wei, Qingyuan. 1995. *New Analysis of Ming and Qing History The Social Functions of the Pawn Business in Qing Dynasty*, 450. China Social Sciences Press.
33. Zhang, Zexian. 1995. *Industrial and Commercial Businesses in Tang Dynasty*, 338. China Social Sciences Press.
34. Wang, Zhongrong. 1975. Attempting explanations of the tang documents on property unearthed in Turpan. *Cultural Relics* (7).
35. Fu, Yiling. 1941. Investigation on the tenancy traditions in Fujian in Ming and Qing Dynasties. *Fujian Cultural Journal* 1 (1).
36. Yang, Guozhen. 1992. Selected works of land documents in Qing Dynasty. *The Journal of Chinese Social and Economic History* (1).
37. Niida, Noboru. *History of Chinese Legal System Land Law*. Zhang, Chuanxi. *Studies on Qin and Han Problems.*
38. Zhang, Jinfan. 1998. *An Overview of Civil Law in Qing Dynasty*, 142. China University of Political Science and Law Press.
39. Gao, Qicai. 1995. *On Chinese Customary Law*, 331–333. Hunan Publishing House.
40. Shuzo, Shiga. 1984. *The Judgments of Four Laws in Qing Dynasty of China.* Sobunsha Press.
41. Huo, Cunfu. 1995. On the sale and purchase procedures of real estate property.*Chinese Journal of Law* (6).
42. Ye, Xianen. 1985. *Studies on the Economic Structure of Chinese Feudal Society*, 154–155. China Social Sciences Press.
43. Fu, Yiling. 1956. *Merchants and Commercial Capitals in Ming and Qing Dynasties*, 35, 80. People's Publishing House.
44. Wang, Mingming. 1997. *The Culture and Power in the View of the Village*, 10. SDX Joint Publishing Company.
45. Su, Li. 1996. *Rule of Law and Its Local Resources*, 8–9. China University of Political Science and Law Press.
46. Murdoch, G.P. 1949. *Social Structure*, 83. New York.
47. Xu, Yangjie. 1995. *Historical Comments on the Family Systems in Song and Ming Dynasties*, 12. Zhonghua Book Company.
48. Ding, Mei. 1998. *Contract Liabilities in Rome Law*, 42–43. China University of Political Science and Law Press.
49. Giuseppe, Grosso. 1994. *Storia Del Diritto Romano (The History of Roman Law)*, 123. Translated by Huang Feng. China University of Political Science and Law Press.
50. Pietro, Bonfante. 1992. *Istituzioni Di Diritto Romano*, 353. Translated by Huang Feng. China University of Political science and Law Press.
51. Zhou, Nan. 1994. *Theory of Roman Law*, 933–934. The Commercial Press.
52. Kong, Qingming, & Liuyuan, Hu. 1996. *History of Chinese Civil Law*, 25. Jilin People's Publishing House, p.25.
53. Fan, Shuzhi. 1997. The market mechanism of the towns in Jiangnan Region. *Researches in Chinese Economic History* (2).
54. Li, Zhimin. 1988. *Civil Law in Ancient China*, 104. Law Press China.
55. Zhang, Mingfu. 1997. Discussion on the Reasons of the emergence of Townsmen Associations in Ming and Qing Dynasties. *Journal of Northeast Normal University (Philosophy and Social Sciences)* (1).
56. Zhang, Yan. 1997. On the Communities in Qing Dynasty. *The Qing History Journal* (2).
57. Cao, Guoqing. 1997. Characteristics of conventions in Ming Dynasty. *Chinese Culture Research* (1).
58. Yu, Xinzhong. 1997. Social relief of squires in the middle of Qing Dynasty. *Journal of Nankai University (Philosophy, and Social Science Edition)*

Chapter 5
Rationality: The Fulcrum of Balancing Interests-Principles of Contract

Karl Theodor Jaspers' theories about civilization have enjoyed great popularity among scholars including a number of Chinese scholars and researchers in the field of philosophy and history in recent years. According to Jaspers' view, human civilization has undergone four phases—the prehistoric civilization, the ancient civilization, the axial age, and the technological age. Different forms of civilizations are also implicated in the integration and transformation of these four major civilizations. During the axial age (800 B.C.–200 B.C.), the civilizations of China and India coexisted with those of the West, adding color to each other. Then Jaspers argued that when the eastern civilization began to decline at the beginning of technological civilization (15th–20th century), the western civilization started to make a full breakthrough since the year of 1500. Jaspers had no apparent preference for the European culture, but his "historical conclusion" led to the notion that Western civilization (and of course, European civilization) had been the mainstream culture of the world since the 16th century, while the East, represented by China and India, gradually faded and became a kind of "sunset culture". They had a glorious past, but it was difficult for them to have the brightness of a sunrise again. Undeniably, Jaspers' sense of superiority about his own culture was more gentlemanly than Emile Durkheim and Max Weber, whose teachings and theories were European-culture centered. Moreover, Jaspers' theory explored the development of history per se through the transformation and progression of history. According to him, the reason why west civilization became the mainstream of technological civilization was that it not only boasted abundant resources but also cultivated highly effective ways to utilize them. These ways were shown mainly in six aspects: (1) The thoughts of political liberty had existed in the western world since ancient Greece; (2) openness, incessant introspection and spirit became the standard of the pursuit of reason in the west; (3) the west achieved complete self-centered awareness; (4) they faced the reality and searched for living space; (5) they were open-minded and tolerant; (6) they were in infinite pursuit of religious truth.[1] By inducing Jaspers' theory, it could be easy to find that he believed

[1]Jaspers [1].

Y. Liu, *The History of the Contractual Thoughts in Ancient China*,
https://doi.org/10.1007/978-981-15-5768-2_5

an ideal civilization, or the existing and reasonable form of civilization should have the following qualities: democratic politics, liberal economy, independent personality and colonial expansion (as long as it was the expansion beneficial for the living space, the means of expansion would not matter because the development of history seemed to accept the natural selection of "the winner takes it all"). Undoubtedly, Jaspers' comments of west civilization were keen, insightful and profound. However, the "evolutionary standard" or the form of development concluded and extracted from one's own culture could be considered as a tool to reflect on one's own history instead of the criteria to judge or measure other culture. Every culture has its unique core, which is compose of "traditional thinking", "related values" and various systems derived from them.[2] Leslie White's idea is also worth learning: it is not man that dominates culture, rather, it is culture that restricts and defines man as well as creates culture itself.[3] Therefore, culture constructs a certain kind of social institution instead of being established by it.

The development of Chinese contract culture conforms to the reason of history, which connects different kinds of culture, resulting in the similarities and integration among them. On the other hand, the differences and distinctiveness of various cultures serve as the internal impetus of their independent existence and development, the loss of which would lead to the loss of value of the culture itself. The universal culture seems like only a hypothesis or fantasy. It is an objective fact that the independence and distinctiveness of every culture coexist and blend, thus raising a serious task for the people or the society—the subjects of culture, that is, the task of appreciation and transformation instead of discard or destruction. Only by studying the development of Chinese ancient contracts from this perspective can we grasp the nature and rationale of it through those ancient classics and long-lasting traditional practices.

Contracts are not only the product of human reason and wisdom but also the reliable record of human civilization. Its existing basis or validity is determined by three factors: Firstly, free will. The contract made by both parties out of their own desires is mutually binding and must be complied with. Secondly, lawfulness. That is, after the emergence of private ownership and the country, the private contract is affected and restricted by public power, so that it manages to satisfy the interests of contractual parties without harming the public interests of the government and society. Thirdly, rationality. It is a flexible control valve that manifests the goodwill and forced adjustment of the private customary contract itself. It also further serves as a balanced evaluation of the contractual relationship regulated by public power, sustaining a state of unbiased neutrality. The criteria of rationality are illusory and empty but yet concrete and operational. The mentioned three elements run through the whole development process of ancient Chinese contract law. Judging from the synchronic level, free will and lawfulness are always the two major rules for regulating contracts. The function of free will is to stimulate the contracting parties to pursue interests and rights as well as satisfy their own actual desires; while the function of lawfulness is to place the freewill contractual behaviors under the control

[2]Kluckhohn et al. [2].

[3]White [3].

of public power, so as to (1) achieve a balance of interests between contractual parties; (2) adjust the interests of contractual parties to those of the whole society (the interest among all the equal civil rights); (3) demonstrate the constraints and regulation of public power on private contracts, conforming them to the fundamental interests of the country or the society, in order to reflect the capacity of public power per se and to obtain ruling resources both politically and economically such as the regulation of contract clauses and procedures and the collection of contract tax. "Rationality" is a humanistic and ethical point that exists between the two poles of "free will" and "lawfulness". It is the original motivation as well as the direct result of the interplay between "contract justice" ("free will") and "social justice" ("lawfulness"). This chapter examines the concrete manifestation and the functions of "rationality"—the humanistic ethical criterion—in the development of contracts from the diachronic level. It aims to explain the value orientation and culture of the development of Chinese contract spirit, in an attempt to prove the rationality and reality of the existence of Chinese ancient civilization or culture.

Rationality—The Threshold of Ethical Justice

The "rationality" in western contract culture embodies the legal philosophical concepts such as "justice" and "freedom", the "equity" in judicial practices, the neutral attitude of state organs and the limited intervention policy. The essence of pursuing "rationality" in China is to achieve value goals such as "justice" as well, only in a different way from the west. Instead of relying solely on external things like "laws" or the "contract" relationship between the parties to achieve "justice" or realize rights, it also puts great emphasis on "rites", "sentiments", and "virtues", which are inherent characteristics in Chinese culture. Before we further explain the ways of realizing "rationality", one concept must be clarified: what is "rationality"?

"Rationality" is not "free will" in that "free will" refers to the process of interests offering and attraction, interest convergence and finally resulting in an exchange of interests based on the desires of the contractual parties. Nor is it "lawfulness" in that "lawfulness" indicates the intervention with and restrictions on "free will" by public power, that is, inserting social interests, precisely the interests of the ruling class or the privileged class, into individual interests. This shows a relatively high degree of "socialization" of ancient Chinese contracts, and the fundamental goal of its "socialization" is to maintain the stability and wealth of the society so as to ensure the interests of the contractual parties and those of other parties are all balanced. This is the same goal as that of contract "socialization" in the west in the 20th century, but a slight difference is that the priority concern of the "socialization" of ancient China contracts is to protect the privileged interests of the privileged class as a way to maintain the stability and continuity of the state power, and to obtain political power in the name of "social interests". Therefore, the interests of the contractual parties and those of other members of society would come as second or even be ignored.

So, what exactly is "rationality"? "Rationality" that has dominated the evolutionary history of Chinese contracts for thousands of years actually represents an idea, referring to the fulcrum for equalizing the interests of the contractual parties and those of other social subjects. In nature, it is a kind of abstract "ethical justice" and a "neutral" state of interests. The main culture or elite culture from pre-Qin philosophers (Qin is the first feudal dynasty of ancient China) to the late Qing Dynasty (the last feudal dynasty of ancient China) always pursued the beauty of "neutrality", making it not only a standard of artistic aesthetics but also one of legal cultural. To be specific, rationality, as a kind of ethical justice, implies the following essence and foundation legal philosophy: (1) Equality. Equality means the equal status and personality among all social subjects without any distinction. At the same time, the application of laws should also be equal and should not be different. This idea embodied primitive democracy in the early Confucianism and many other philosophies, but with the establishment of an orthodox monarchy and the flourishing of the family system, this "equality" has evolved into something similar to Aristotle's "distributive justice", i.e., the equality based on "ethical principles". People of equal social status are entitled to equal rights. This kind of ethical equality first recognizes an ethical arithmetic sequence where social subjects are deliberately divided into different ranks, and the rights and resources contained in this justice are evenly distributed in the same sequence, thus being called "rationality", which later evolved into a "rites and law" culture of institutional form. (2) Fairness. Fairness, based on "ethical equality", is a kind of social theory formulated by ancient Chinese elites, requiring that "Sheng Ren" (the sage) and "Wang Zhe" (the king) should be impartial and even-handed in law making. It is also regarded as a standard to balance the conflicts of interests among different social classes and to realize mutual benefits and stability of the society, so as to seek "Huang Tu Yong Gu" (everlasting ruling) and "Guo Tai Min An" (a secure and well-off country), and finally reach the goal of "Sheng Ren Zhi Zhi" (sage governing). This is another layer of "rationality". Shang Yang (a reformer of Qin State in the Warring States Period), advocated that "all men be equal before punishments without any distinctions".[4] Han Fei (a representative of Legalism in the late Warring State Period), claimed that "law should not protect the privileged".[5] Guan Zhong (a famous politician in the Spring and Autumn Period), required that "the state be ruled by law" and "all the people regardless of their social statuses should obey the law".[6] Zhang Shizhi, a famous judicial officer in Han Dynasty, held that "both the emperors and his citizens should abide by the law".[7] Li Shimin, Emperor Taizong of Tang Dynasty, honestly stated that "the law is not the law of mine but the law of all the people" and "justice should be upheld and law offenders must be punished by law".[8] Nurhachi, Emperor Taizu of Qing Dynasty, concluded that the decline of the late Ming Dynasty resulted from "loose and unfair

[4] *Shang Jun Shu · Shang Xing (Rewards and Punishments).*

[5] *Han Fei Zi · You Du (Moderation).*

[6] *Guan Zi · Ren Fa.*

[7] *Book of Han · the Biography of Zhang Shizhi.*

[8] *Zhen Guan · Zhengyao Gongping (Justice).*

laws".[9] It should be noted that the original rationale or internal source of the concepts of ethical justice including "fairness" and "equality" is slightly akin to the western philosophy of natural law, i.e., a neutral state between the "Tian Li (天理, heavenly principles)" and "human desires"—the state of "stand to reason", later called "rationality". Without this standard of value mentioned above, laws and decrees would be empty and unenforceable. Shen Dao (one of the founders of legalism in the State of Zhao, who once pursued Daoism), said that "the law comes neither from the heaven nor from the earth, but it comes from the people and is accepted by people's hearts".[10] Guan Zhong also asserted that "laws should conform to people's needs".[11] Shang Yang further emphasized that "laws will not come through if they are enacted without considering the people and national conditions".[12] Yin Wen (a famous philosopher of the State of Qi in the Warring State Period), earlier integrated the Dao of Heaven with humanity, saying that "the Dao of Heaven should accord with human feelings".[13] The natural law philosophy of the pre-Qin philosophers was included in the category of Confucian philosophy of law in the Han Dynasty and was interpreted by the Confucian master Dong Zhongshu as Confucian Jurisprudence of the "Doctrine of the Mean": "It is common and natural that people who are excessively rich will become conceited to commit atrocity while people who are extremely poor will get desperate and become thieves. The saint can foresee the root causes of social turbulence through this phenomenon. As a result, he would govern the country and regulate people's behaviors according to their statuses, so as to make the rich satisfied with their wealth without getting conceited and help the poor earn their living without getting desperate. In this way, a balanced harmony of the society would be achieved without a loss of wealth, and it would be easier to govern the nation."[14] Dong Zhongshu had already been keenly aware that social instability was not due to the inequalities in the social hierarchy, but rather to the imbalance in the distribution of social resources and the disparity between the rich and the poor. He therefore advocated to coordinate the distribution of interests among the social strata starting from human nature per se as the means to govern the world, the ultimate goal of which was to reach the state of "stand to reason". This kind of conflation from the means to the goal was precisely the premise to recognize and obey the identity of the "ruler" for a civil society, mainly the lower ranks. The endurance and rationality of the Confucian philosophy of law is well reflected in this point, that is, the original form of "heavenly principles and human nature" is drawn from instrumental value to objective value, finally making "reason" the most powerful control tool for neutralizing interest and making it the highest goal of interest pursuit.

---

[9] *Old Records in the language of Manchu · Emperor Tai Zu.* Volume 3, item "the Lunar February in the Year of Gui Chou".

[10] *Shen Zi · Yi Wen (the Lost Articles).*

[11] *Guan Zi · Mu Min (To Govern People).*

[12] *Shang Jun Shu · Yi Yan (Concentration).*

[13] *Shen Zi · Abidance. Cited from Yin Wenzi.*

[14] *Chun Qiu Fan Lu · Du Zhi (Law and Regulations).*

From the perspective of social history, the "rationality" of ethical justice could be decomposed into three levels:

First, "sentiment and reason (情理, Qing Li)". It is listed as the first level because the civil society regards this seemingly "empty" social category as the premise and goal of the existence of social contracts and private contracts, i.e., "being reasonable and sensible" is the highest social goal of contracts and the fulcrum that balances interests as well. People are born with desires, which are called "sentiments (情, Qing)". The process of acknowledging others' "sentiments" and "desires (欲, Yu)", controlling those of one's own, and finally striking a balance of interests between oneself and others is considered as "reason (理, Li)". "Sentiment" favor oneself whereas "reason" benefits others. Only when one benefits others can one benefits oneself and this is the "unity of sentiment and reason", or the "harmony of sentiment and reason". The absence of "reason" would inevitably lead to its decay or exclusion by other interest subject; while the deficiency of "sentiment" would necessarily cause a loss of psychological motivation of performance. This point is consistent with Darwin's idea of the balance between "egoism" and "altruism",[15] and also echoes with Hobbes's view about two major principles ("desires" and "reason") of human nature.[16] More details about this will be elaborated in the following part.

Second, "rites and laws (礼法, Li Fa)". If we simply rely on "heavenly principles", "senses", or even "conscience" or the so-called "reason" in the west, it is difficult and unrealistic to curb "human desires" and prevent their damage to others' interest. Therefore, rites and laws came into being. The part of laws will not be elaborated here since there have been already many functionalists of law. As for "rites", its influence on Chinese civil society is far greater than that of law. In many occasions, especially in contractual social relations, the regulating function of rites also shows its strong side. According to the original Confucian teachings, "rites" is not only a kind of ritual but also a concept or belief. Its essence lies in "abstinence (节欲, Jie Yu)—to restrain your desires", i.e., a kind of social norm regulating human nature and emotions. Confucius's sagacious statements illustrated the genuine social functions of rites: "People who are poor will become desperate, while those who are rich will get conceited. People living in poverty tend to steal while conceited ones would riot and rebel. Therefore, rites are set up according to human nature and emotions to regulate them, as a way to maintain the social order." Confucius also stated that the true value of human nature rested in "being happy in poverty, and being courteous and ritual in riches".[17] It is evident that there is an overlap between Dong Zhongshu's philosophy of law and Confucian ideas of "rites". They both coordinated and neutralized the interests among different social classes, restraining the desires of the poor and the rich in an attempt to facilitate their learning of "rites". The idea was later internalized as an ethical philosophy of Confucianism and was finally developed into the philosophical basis on which the "ruler" taught the people to achieve moral self-discipline. At the same time, it could not be ignored that the rites were also

[15]Charles Darwin. *Principles of Sociology*. More details see in Kardiner and Prable [4].

[16]Hsabine [5].

[17]*The Book of Rites · Fang Ji.*

externalized into a kind of social norm that prevailed in the country while being internalized into moral self-discipline. This social norm was accepted and defended by the social elites such as the intellectuals and bureaucrats and finally became a most important tool for maintaining Chinese society and its traditional culture, exerting strong influence on the development of contracts.

Third, "virtues (德性, De Xing)". "Virtues" were included into the category of morality in the Spring and Autumn Period,[18] and its ethical philosophical basis was what Mencius, the saint of Confucianism, advocated as the goodness of human nature, which, as the symbol that distinguished "human" from "non-human" or "beasts", added the meaning of "righteousness" into the Confucian philosophy of "benevolence". Different from rites and laws, "virtues" belong to a pure moral category, signaling the inherent power of personality. At the private level, it is often referred to as "friendship" or "bonds". "Friendship" usually means the friendliness to people without ties of blood, business interaction or friendly relations whereas "bonds" mostly come from a certain range of social interactions. But both of them have a revered moral quality as well as a powerful and long-lasting moral force, which have long been followed and finally accepted by the civil society and promoted by the folk customary law. Dating back to the pre-Qin times, Confucius paid particular attention to the highly self-disciplinary moral philosophy of "virtues" and persuaded the "ruler" to arouse people's kindness in order to obtain the political effects of peacefulness and stability of the society: "teach people with virtues, regulate them with rites, and then they would have righteous hearts; teach people with politics, regulate them with punishments, and then they would have rebellious hearts."[19] Among all the four governing strategies of "virtues", "rites", "politics" and "punishments", Confucius listed the self-disciplinary "virtues" as the top priority. The greatest optimization effect of Chinese culture comes from the "virtues" or "friendship".

Sentiment and reason, rites and laws, and virtues run parallel with each other and constitute a very special concept of "justice" in Chinese ancient contract law, namely "rationality".

The next question is: through what kind of power or channel is this seemingly abstract and yet specific concept of ethical justice adopted and realized? In western civil law systems, codes of written law and discretion of judges are the social lever to safeguard the concept of justice. In common law or case law systems, the "evaluation system of evidence through inner conviction" of codes and judges forms a set of detailed and specific operating procedures, thus realizing the ideal of "justice" represented by philosophers and jurists. The U.S. *Uniform Commercial Code* stipulates that "if the court as a matter of law finds the contract or any clause of the contract to have been unconscionable at the time it was made the court may refuse to enforce the contract".[20] The Principles of European Contract Law, revised in July 1998, also puts special emphasis on "Good Faith and Fair Dealing", requiring that

[18] Ba [6].

[19] *The Book of Rites · Xiang Yi.*

[20] Uniform Commercial Code, §2-302.

the parties may not exclude or limit this duty.[21] In ancient China, the "rationality" of ethical justice was popularized by two kinds of forces—the customary power of the people and the political ideology of the Confucian "ruler".

The customary power of the civil society was the primary driving force for the principle of "rationality". The official laws and the ethical rites of the elites class were produced in conformity with the people's needs and aspirations. Kishimoto Mio holds that the relationships in private law were not regulated by national laws in old China, instead, they were left to the public to freely form such relations.[22] Hiroaki Terada believes that China's civil order is built on a kind of contract and competition, which is similar to that of the west. However, its civil regulations were "almost entirely a kind of spontaneous civil order. The state has neither actively provided any order framework to the society nor provided sufficient guarantee for the normative order that has been formed".[23] It should be said that the first half of Terada's conclusion is correct, that is, the dominant force (not necessarily the only force) that promotes the entire ancient contract ethics is the civil habit of self-survival and the resulting civil order. However, it is against the historical facts if we think that the state or government did not respond positively to the recognition and promotion of civil customary law and to the stabilization of the civil transaction order. In fact, the construction of many ethical systems and contract culture systems in traditional Chinese society were generated among the people and ultimately were recognized and protected by the government. Among them, the most powerful social force was the elite class, namely the Confucian bureaucrats and gentry who regarded themselves as the Confucian "ruler". As Kishimoto says, the Chinese bureaucratic class was not a professional group that was separated from the society in terms of functions, but a social group that were qualified to be the "ruler" due to their outstanding personality and ethical conduct.[24] R. M. Unger believes that Chinese law has evolved from customary law to bureaucratic law, and he classifies the evolutionary forms of law into customary law, bureaucratic law and legal order.[25] Professor Shuzo Shiga proposes that the concept of "sentiment and reason" in China's legal order is a kind of "Chinese-style sense of justice and equity", and it is the value judgment criterion of common law, which is similar to Unger's idea about "customary law".[26] On another occasion, Shiga profoundly analyzes the statuses and interaction between "sentiment and reason" and law in Chinese traditional society. He holds that "sentiment and reason" is the value judgment of a sound social life, giving people a kind of "equitable" feeling in particular, and thus making heavenly principles, human sentiments, and national

---

[21] The Principles of European Contract Law, §1-201. Trans. by Han Shiyuan. 1999. *Classic Journal of Foreign Law* (1).

[22] Kishimoto Mio. Contracts in Ming and Qing Dynasties in China. See in [7].

[23] Hiroaki Terada. *Rights and Grievances: The Litigation and Civil Procedures in the Qing Dynasty*. See footnote 22, p. 273.

[24] Kishimoto Mio *"Civil Society Theory" and China*. See footnote 22, p. 382.

[25] Unger [8]. Cited from Liang Zhiping. 1996. *Customary Law in Qing Dynasty: Society and the State*. China University of Political Science and Law Press, p. 4.

[26] Shuzo Shiga. *A Survey of Chinese Legal Culture: Based on Litigation Forms*. See footnote 22, p. 14.

law the legal source of China's hearing system and a universal judgment standard as well.[27] From the historical materials of the numerous customary laws and the documents printed officially and privately of the Confucian "ruler", we can see that the folk customary forces and the benevolent ideology of the "ruler" were the two major social forces that adjusted social interests and eventually made them equitable, so that the civil order was maintained with "rationality" and the "ruler" was welcomed as "righteous and honest". This is a shining part of Chinese civilization over thousands of years and also the social psychological soil in which grows the tree of ancient Chinese contracts.

The Principles of Contract: The Guarantee of "Rational" Interests

Two sources of power—folk customary power and the benevolent governance of the Confucius "ruler"—contribute to the realization of "rationality" of ancient contracts and directly impact the national law making, law enforcement and judicial procedures. There are two ways to realize the value of "rationality": first, the principles of contract as the guarantee of rational interests; second, contractual liabilities as the remedy for rational interests.

The abstractness of the principle of the contract originates from its generalization for it regulates contractual behaviors by general rules so as to achieve free will, lawfulness and rationality, ensuring the deserved interests of both parties instead of infringing on those of others and the society. The reason why the principle of the contract becomes a strong guarantee of rational interests is that folk customary power and judicial authorities would regulate irrational contractual behaviors based on accepted trading principles, thus enjoying much discretion and balancing interests of different parties through this.

The principle of protecting rational interests has to be rational and reasonable in the very first place, which, as the premise for the legal effect of the principle of the contract, is also the prerequisite of making up for legal loopholes and making laws. On the surface, the "rationality" of the "rational" principle of the contract is decided and expressed in legal provisions; whereas in reality, it is the recognition and generalization of ethical justice rules in folk trading. The explanations are as follows:

First, the principle of voluntariness. The voluntariness is the embodiment of the value of legal freedom. John Locke, the leading figure of the natural law school in the United Kingdom, believes that in a natural state all people are equal and independent, and everyone has a natural right to defend his "Life, Health, Liberty, or Possessions". Based on this, Locke proposes that "people's interest is supreme law", for the law itself is the "consented social norms" by all members of the society. The true meaning

[27] Shuzo Shiga. A *General Survey of the Civil Law Sources of the Litigation System in Qing Dynasty*. See footnote 22, pp. 20, 24, 34.

and goal of the law is to "guide a free and wise person to pursue legitimate interests" rather than to abolish or limit freedom.[28] A famous quote from Dante is "the first principle of freedom is the freedom of will". This value of "freedom" has been demonstrated later in the theory of contractual liberalism. P. S. Atiyah holds that the binding power of the contract stems from the "consensus" of the contractual parties on the premise that the making of the contract is the result of free choice without external intervention or regulation.[29] The connotation of the freedom of contract includes four aspects, namely, whether or not to sign a contract, whom to contract with, the contents of the contract and the choice of the contractual form.[30] The historical value of contractual liberalism lies in the fact that the contract breaks away from the limitation of identity, freeing the contract bodies to participate in the market competition, thus consolidating the humanistic ethical concept and directly leading to the rapid development of the western capitalist economy.

The principle of voluntariness in ancient Chinese contracts is embodied in the fact that "everything should be agreed by both parties", that is to say, the premise of a contract is the "consensus" by both parties. During the period from Western Zhou Dynasty to late Qing Dynasty, buying or selling by force was strictly forbidden by all ordinances and laws. In terms of folk trading, consensus by both parties was the criterion of folk customary law as well as the principle prescribed by law. As was stated in the ancient Chinese classic book *The Book of Changes*, "harmony brings benefits",[31] and inharmony would result in an imbalance of interests, thus leading to a failure to realize the principle of fairness. Therefore, this was explicitly prohibited by law. Taking Song Dynasty as an example, the authorities took a very strong attitude towards those who purchase things by force:

> According to the record of Kai Fengfu, when the crops grew ripe in the capital, people from Xiangzhuang would ship those firewood to town to sell. Then many middlemen would go to buy those and make an agreement on the price and quantity with the sellers, leaving the deposits. But unexpectedly, the middlemen pulled the sellers' bullock carts by force and got more cargo and money than the previously arranged price. Before the cargo was sold out, the middlemen gave short weight in order to reduce the cost of the cargo, and delayed the bullock carts of the sellers, wasting their travelling expenses. Although the authorities issued a proclamation to regulate this bad phenomenon, it did not stop. Then some officials were specially assigned to control and stop this. If someone broke the rules, the authorities would judge and punish. Then the firewood would be sold by the sellers on their own while officials on patrol would observe and send those who violated the rules to the authorities.[32]

These were the prohibitive regulations approved by the central government to prevent purchase by force. In Song Dynasty, purchase by force and selling afterwards were quite common phenomena. At that time, the market economy was well-developed, with different Ya Hang* scattered in the capital. Taking the fish market

---

[28] Li [9].

[29] Atiyah [10].

[30] Su [11].

[31] *The Book of Changes · Xi Ci (B).*

[32] *The Compilation of Song Dynasty · National Economy*, 55–31. "March, the 8th Year of Tian Sheng".

as an example, the middlemen's buying and selling by force was deeply hated by the local authorities: "These middlemen go about by tens and hundreds, covering up for each other. When the villagers want to sell something without letting them know, they would jointly beat those villagers with fists. The beating style "She Jia Quan" was the most unscrupulous one."[33] A case in Song Dynasty could well demonstrate how the local authorities protected people's property rights: Zhao Hong lived in An Qing and bought a piece of land in Yi Huang. Because of the long distance between the two places, he entrusted his land in Yi Huang to his younger brother Zhao Huan. Then Zhao Huan took Zhao Hong's property as his own business and donated it to the county school, and later donated it to another educational institution. After that, Zhao Yong, Zhao Hong's son, requested the return of the real property. Fan Xitang's judgement went as follows: "(Zhao Hong) entrusted his younger brother to take charge of his land, and this is very reasonable… (Zhao Huan) violated the other's rights and went against the intent of the owner of the land, which cannot be described as legal. According to the office, it is clear that the land should be inherited to Zhao Yong. So the authorities would give back (Zhao Yong) his family property and it is just and reasonable."[34] Judging from it, Fan Xitang's criteria for judging the case were: first, it accorded with "human sentiments" to entrust the property to one's younger brother; second, it was presumed that the younger brother dealt with the land without the consent of the elder brother, and this was illegal; third, he agreed with the ruling of the original trial to return the land to the legal heir of the original owner, thus the entire ruling process was properly applied with rationality.

In the trading between civil subjects and officials, the positions of the government and the civil subjects should be equal. The officials should not bully common people in their trading. With great emphasis on "harmonious purchase by appropriate means", it was forbidden to exploit people and violate their interests. Emperor Song Wu (Liu Yu) once made an announcement to the country in the first year of Yong Fu Period (420 A.D.): "In the case where the government needs to procure something, it should send a special official to purchase from the civilians and pay for it at a reasonable price in proper ways without taking advantage of their positions."[35] Emperor Qi Wu announced in the fifth year during the reign of Yong Ming Period (487 A.D.): "The central government and the local authorities paid hundreds of millions to buy grain, silk, brocade and the like, and the price paid was in the interest of the common people…The goods bought must be things that were needed by the government, who should reach an agreement on the price with sellers and not default on the payment."[36] In Tang and Song Dynasties, the policies of "harmonious purchase by appropriate means" and "consensual and fair trade" became more

[33] *Law Reports of Southern Song Dynasty. Volume 14.* Item "The Brawl Between Fish Sellers".

[34] *Law Reports of Southern Song Dynasty · Household Marriages · Property Rights.*

[35] *Book of Song.* Volume 3. *Biography of Emperor Wu* (B).

[36] *Book of Qi.* Volume 3. *Biography of Emperor Wu.*

*Translator's annotation: Ya Hang (牙行), the name of the agency of middlemen that intermediated transactions between buyers and sellers after Song Dynasty.

formalized to curb bad behaviors and unfairness in trading between the government and civilians.

In terms of market regulations, a study of the current historical records shows that the norms in Tang Dynasty were very strict with the law explicitly prohibiting misconducts including “extortion (乞索, qi suo)”, “monopoly (较固, jiao gu)”, capitalizing on others’ precarious situations or difficulties, cheating and counterfeiting. *Law Code of Tang Dynasty* stipulated: “Acquisition of property by inappropriate means is just like extorting, and the property illegally obtained shall be returned to the original owner.” Zhangsun Wuji explained: “Acquisition of property by inappropriate means is nothing less than the misconducts including threatening, cheating, buying and selling by force for a great profit, plundering, etc.” There were two types of “extortion”. One was “forced extortion”, meaning buying and selling by force; and the other was “peaceful extortion”, that was, trading through fraud. Both of the two types violated the true will of one party to the contract. Therefore, Zhangsun Wuji also provided for the situations of “extortion, cheating and betrayal” in *Law Code of Tang Dynasty*: “Acquisition by inappropriate means is extortion…and cheating…the situations where the misconduct goes beyond the time limit of the decree for pardon or the cheater does not turn himself or herself in during a certain period of time all fall into this category and the punishment will be decided accordingly.”[37] Emperor Tang Xuanzong, in the eleventh year of Tian Bao Period in Tang Dynasty (752 A.D.) enacted an edict to prohibit high-ranking officials and the rich from violating others’ property: “The privileged class recklessly plundered civilians’ land regardless of the law. They bought and sold people’s property illegally, and sometimes change the deeds at will or enslave them, rendering the folks homeless.”[38] The laws in Ming Dynasty stipulated: “Purchase and sale by force are considered breaking the law. The goods being sold by force shall be taken away by the government and the money shall go back to its original owner; meanwhile the goods being purchased by force shall be returned to its original owner and the money paid shall be handed into the government.”[39] *Law Code of Qing Dynasty* stipulated that the market transactions must be subject to mutual consent, “In dealings and transactions, those who manipulate the market to make a profit and the sellers who gang up with middlemen to control the market price intentionally shall be whipped with bamboo strips eighty times. Those who bid up price in a sale deliberately to cheat others so as to make a profit shall be whipped with bamboo strips forty times. The things illegally obtained by these means are considered as stolen goods, and in serious cases the misconduct will be punished as larceny.”[40] This provision originated from “monopoly” and “manipulation of price (by bidding up or down the price) (参市, can shi)” that were forbidden by *Law Code of Tang Dynasty*. The illegality of the two types of behaviors lied in the use of forced means and fraudulent means to mislead people to trade in an involuntary state. According to *Law Code of Tang Dynasty*, “monopoly (jiao gu)” means: “The

---

[37] *Law Code of Tang Dynasty*. Volume 4. *General Definitions and Rules.*

[38] *Ce Fu Yuan Gui.* Volume 495. *Land System.*

[39] *Annotations of Law Code of Ming Dynasty.*

[40] *Law Code of Qing Dynasty.* Volume 15. *Hulv · Shichan.*

sellers or the buyers, without reaching an agreement, try to control and manipulate the market, preventing outsiders from buying the goods. Note '*jiao* means extorting others' benefits while *gu* means blocking or controlling the market'. The vendors act evilly in collusion with each other to sell cheap goods at an expensive price while purchase expensive goods at a cheap price, in an attempt to perplex people and control the market." As for "manipulation of price (can shi)", it was stipulated in *Law Code of Tang Dynasty*: "Vendors who act illegally in collusion with others to sell shoddy goods for a high price so as to make a profit while perplexing people or outsiders shall be whipped with bamboo strips eighty times. In a more serious case those who committed the crime shall be whipped ninety times. And the case will be judged as larceny where the goods or money shall be returned to the original owner."[41]

Second, the principle of honesty and good faith (诚实信用, cheng shi xin yong). In ancient Rome, foreign magistrates had confirmed the principle of "fides bona" as having a normative significance. *Napoleonic Code* clearly stated for the first time that the fulfillment of the contract must follow the principle of good faith. Article 2, paragraph 1 of *German Civil Code* stipulates that "any person must abide by the principle of good faith when exercising his rights or performing his duties".[42] The U.S. *Uniform Commercial Code* defines "honesty and credibility" as: "honesty and credibility requires the trader to be completely honest in transactions and to conduct fair transactions based on reasonable commercial standards." *The Restatement (Second) of Contracts* (1980) regards interdependence as the axis of the contract system.[43] The Japanese scholar Wagatsuma Sakae (わがつまさかえ) explains the following ideas in *General Introduction to the Rights in Obligatio*: Contract is a "coordinated body governed by the principle of good faith". And in *General Principles of Civil Law*, he believes that "the violation of the principle of good faith in exercising rights constitutes the abuse of rights".[44] The real purpose of enumerating the historical materials mentioned above is to illustrate that the principle of good faith was formed earlier in the west, but it was not until the end of the 19th century that it became the principle to regulate contract behaviors. And since the middle of the 20th century, it has evolved into the basic clause of the contract and expanded from the legal mechanism of the civil law system to a universal contract principle.

In terms of the etymology of "honesty and good faith (诚实信用)", it is "Bona Fide" in Latin, "Bonne Foi" in French and "Good Faith" in English. They can all be transliterated as "Shan Yi (善意, good faith)", whereas in German "Treu und Glauben" contains two layers of meaning: loyalty and faith, which is translated into "faith and honesty" in Japanese.[45] In Chinese etymology, "honesty (诚, cheng)" and "faith (信, xin)" are closely related. "Honesty" is the premise of "faith" while "faith" is the expression of "honesty". "Honesty" and "faith" combined constitute

[41] *Law Code of Tang Dynasty*. Volume 26. *Law of Trivia*.

[42] Tsunoshi [12].

[43] Fu [13].

[44] Takashi [14].

[45] *Science of Civil Law*. 1994. Edited by Peng Wanlin. China University of Political Science and Law Press, p. 38.

a kind of noble personality trait as well as commercial norms, that is "honesty and faith (信义, xin yi)". The contracts in Han Dynasty were the direct consequence of the commodity economy and this period also marked the germination of individual rights. In the discussion of relevant scholars, we can see their emphasis and advocacy of honesty and good faith as important contractual obligations. Ban Gu, the famous historian in Eastern Han Dynasty, said in his classic work *Baihu General Sense*: "Honesty is the same as faith, that is, the unswerving commitment."[46] This is an etymological interpretation but is more of a value judgment. The external sincerity is the expression of inner honesty, which is a moral character unique to human beings. *Huai-Nan Tzu*, which was written earlier than *Baihu General Sense*, directly associated "faith" with "commitment", regarding it as a basic character that elite people should possess: "One who keeps his or her promise, abides by his or her contract and acts in a lawful manner is a person of honor."[47] Dating back to the Western Zhou Dynasty, *the Rites of Zhou*, as a social norm equivalent to the law, stated that the real function of the contract is to "close the case honestly".[48] That is to say, the contract was a means of making commitment as well as the documentary evidence that prompted the parties to honestly perform the contractual obligations. This materialization function of contracts was the result of emphasizing the social and moral obligations of contracts. In *Interpretation Dictionary of Chinese Characters*, "faith" and "honesty" were synonyms,[49] representing their moralization; whereas Yang Xiong held that "faith" also meant "evidence",[50] representing the growth of social obligations in the course of contractual materialization.

An important fact should not be overlooked here: during the development of the Chinese contract, the public power always showed great enthusiasm in private contracts, whose legislative basis and judicial guidelines were based more on the moral obligation of "honesty and good faith" to require both parties to perform their duties honestly rather than based on the law. Because the legislation of contracts was the recognition and promotion of relevant commercial ethics and professional norms in private trading, and was eventually abstracted by scholars as a kind of ethical justice theory that included social obligations and moral obligations. Hugh T. Scogin, Jr. believed that until Han Dynasty, the specific performance of private contracts regulated by the national law still existed, which established "faith" as the moral obligation and deprived unfaithful people of their "dishonest" property as the punishment. Therefore, the "fulfillment of the contract" in Han Dynasty was in the moral sense, i.e., individual behaviors were subject to social obligations and etiquette obligations.[51] Scogin's idea was exact in Han, but one point has to be noted: From Western Zhou Dynasty to late Qing Dynasty, the state law or public power had always regarded "honesty and good faith" as the basis for the making and

---

[46]*Baihu General Sense · Qing Xing.*

[47]*Huai Nan Tzu · Tai Zu.*

[48]*Rites of Zhou · Si Tu · Si Shi.*

[49]*Interpretation Dictionary of Chinese Characters · Yan Bu.*

[50]*Fa Yan · Self-cultivation.*

[51]Scogin [15].

performance of contracts and the national power as the guarantee, which meant that the overlapping of commercial obligations, ethical obligations and legal obligations underlay the development of Chinese contracts. At the same time, it also showed explicitly that the emphasis on the principle of "honesty and good faith" by the state law and folk customs was to guarantee the realization of individual rights that accorded with morality and law, but its ultimate goal or the highest pursuit was to strike a balance between social stability and individual rights, making them lawful, fair and reasonable. Thus there were two channels for the implementation of the principle of honesty and good faith: first, the enforcement of the law; second, the regulation of morality. These two opposing sides constituted the unique contract culture of traditional Chinese society.

At the level of the law, "honesty" was attached the most importance to, which meant, it was a legal obligation to engage in business conduct with goodwill and diligence, and offenders must be financially punished, or even worse, be educated and physically punished (corporal punishment or penal servitude). The *Book of Rites* stressed that "goods such as equipments, chariots and textiles that do not meet the standard" must not be sold in the market.[52] In Qin Dynasty, the national standards for various products were specified in details. Take Qian (coins) and Bu (cloths)** as an example: "One standard Bu is eight Chi (a unit of length) in length and 2 Chi and 5 Cun (a unit of length) in width. Those that are of poor quality or do not meet the standard must not be circulated", "The merchants and government officials in the market are not allowed to select between the two currencies of Qian and Bu; if the administrators know such misconduct without reporting, or the supervisors sit loose on these illegal actions, they will all be judged guilty".[53] Tang Dynasty, the peak period of commodity economy, severely punished dishonest trading. The ban and punishments of substandard or shoddy products (in Chinese "行滥", Xing Lan) also served as a warning to others. *Law Code of Tang Dynasty* stipulated: "Those who manufacture or sell substandard products of poor quality such as Bu, equipments and others must be whipped with bamboo strips sixty times", and the goods should be confisticated. "Substandard" meant "shoddy or of bad quality ('行滥', Xing Lan)",[54] which was the same as the counterfeits or inferior products today. Emperor Tang Zhongzong decreed in the first year of Jing Long Period (707 A.D.): "All goods that are inferior and shoddy shall be confisticated."[55] And also in Tang Dynasty, certain officials were in charge of "supervising and sorting out inferior and shoddy products"[56] so as to prevent cheating and frauds. Song Dynasty witnessed even more strict regulations on market dealings in accordance with the principle of honesty and

[52] *The Book of Rites · Wang Zhi.*

**Translator's annotation: In ancient times, Qian (钱) and Bu (布) were different forms of currency. According to the law, 11 Qian equaled 1 Bu.

[53] *Shui Hu Di Qin Mu Zhu Jian (Bamboo Slips of Qin Dynasty Unearthed in Shuihudi) · Eighteen Categories of Qin Laws · Jinbulv.*

[54] *Law Code of Tang Dynasty.* Volume 26. *Law of Trivia.*

[55] *Institutional History of Tang Dynasty.* Volume 86.

[56] *Wen Yuan Ying Hua.* Volume 53.

good faith. *Criminal Code of Song Dynasty* stipulated that the profits obtained from selling, reselling and manufacturing inferior and shoddy products were treated as those obtained from "larceny". The greater the profits, the heavier the crime. Officials who knew the misconduct without reporting and dealing with it would be regarded as committing the same crime, and they would "be punished in the same way as those accused of larceny".[57] In Southern Song Dynasty, people were overwhelmed with counterfeits and inferior goods. In the city of Hangzhou, "Vendors sell fake goods at high prices as if they are real ones, going so far as to sell paper as clothes, copper and lead as gold and silver, and even soil and wood as perfumes and aromatic drugs". The intellectuals and civilians suffered so much that they called them "day time frauds (cheaters who pretended to be vendors)".[58] *Dongjing Menghualu* also recorded such scenes in the streets of Kaifeng city "at dawn…vendors start to take to the streets, selling and buying commodities…at dusk, they begin to sell fake and inferior products (He Lou) including headwears, daily utensils and curios".[59] He Lou (Chinese "何楼", also written as "河楼") also referred to fake and inferior products, and its etymology was discussed by Ruan Yue in his work: "At the beginning of the Dynasty, there was a building (a building is called "Lou, 楼" in Chinese) named "He" in the capital. The products sold in the "He building" were all fake and inferior. So people started to use He Lou to refer to those bad products. Now the building has already been obsolete but the wording remains."[60] In my humble opinion, Ruan's idea still needs further exploration, because "He Lou" was a name in Song Dynasty whereas the wording "Xing Lan (行滥)" already prevailed in Tang Dynasty. I hold that He Lou ("何/河楼") stemmed from the wrong pronunciation of "Xing Lan (行滥)" because they sounded similar. In Wu Zhou Dynasty (a period in Tang Dynasty in the reign of Empress Wu Zetian), a saying went that "gold and silver utensils are all fake with poor quality". Hu Sanxing in Song Dynasty noted: "In the market, some counterfeits and inferior goods are mixed among gold and silver utensils to be sold for profits. Thus the common people called them 'Xing Zuo Lan E' (counterfeit and shoddy goods)"[61] Hu's explanation of "Xing (行)" in "Xing Lan (行滥)" was different from that of *Law Code of Tang Dynasty*, but it is worth noticing that the common people already used "Xing Zuo Lan E" to refer to counterfeit and shoddy goods in Tang Dynasty, otherwise it would not have been recorded by Hu. Therefore, it is more likely that "Xing Lan (行滥)" and He Lou ("何/河楼") sounded close to each other, and Ruan's opinion, which was inconsistent with history, could not hold water.

At the level of civil morality, honesty and good faith is regarded as the root of being a human. The traditional Chinese culture features establishing oneself based on honesty and good faith, educating offsprings and emphasizing virtues. Honesty and

---

[57] *Criminal Code of Song Dynasty.* Volume 26. *Law of Trivia.*

[58] Zhou Mi. *Wu Lin Jiu Shi.* Volume 6. *You Shou (Idleness).*

[59] *Dongjing Menghua Lu (The Eastern Capital: A Dream of Splendor).* Volume 1. *Streets and Alleys in the Dongjiaolou.*

[60] Ruan Yue. *Shi Hua Zong Gui.*

[61] *History As A Mirror.* Volume 206. Item "August 25th in the 1st Year of the Reign of Shengli".

good faith is a kind of "virtue (德, De)" as well as "faith (义, Yi)". Self-cultivation in one's personality can be called "virtue", while interpersonal relationship stresses "faith", both of which are highly valued and respected by the people. Kou Juan in Southern and Northern Dynasties was righteous and kind as it recorded: "He never puts financial profits on heart. Once his family sold things to people and left out five Pi (a unit of measurement) of silk purposefully. He said: 'If I lose my virtues in order to get profits, I would never do that.'"[62] Meng Xin, a contemporary of Kou Juan, still lived a righteous and virtuous life after he resigned from office, "Xin lived a life of poverty, difficult to sustain his life. He only had a sick cow, which was sold by his nephew behind his back in an attempt to eke out a living. His nephew secretly completed the deed with the buyer, concealing the fact that it was a sick cow. Since the location of the owner's residence had to be stated in the deed, the buyer then went there to fetch the cow. It happened that Xin came back from the outside and saw the buyer, and then knew the cow was sold. He immediately told him: 'This cow is sick and will have a seizure after a little labor. It is of no use to you.' Then he punished his nephew with twenty floggings. The buyer was quite amazed."[63] Kou and Meng's righteous behaviors could be viewed not so much as law-abiding, but as in fear that their virtues as a "gentleman" would be harmed. Bearing virtues and integrity in mind even in face of benefits and profit was the character of intellectuals, so was that of businessmen and landlords. Tao Siweng, a person who ran a dyehouse in Song Dynasty, once spent four million Qian (a unit of money) on lithospermum (used to dye the cloths), which proved to be counterfeit. A broker offered to help him to sell those lithospermum to other small dye shops, "Weng took out all the fake lithospermum and burnt them all right in the face of the broker and said: 'I would rather be cheated myself. How can I go on and cheat others?'"[64] The Zheng family, one of the biggest and most famous families in the south of the Yangtze River that flourished from Southern Song Dynasty to Ming Dynasty, lived together with the offsprings in harmony and shared their wealth for over three hundred years. Their family rules encouraged the offsprings to do good deeds and show charity and kindness to others rather than to accumulate wealth and they viewed the ill-gotten wealth as "the door to the evil". "When expanding our industry in the case where the other party sells his or her industry by necessity, we have to bear in mind the benefits of our generations to come and put ourselves in others' shoes to estimate the actual value of the industry, so that we will pay the seller enough money. It is important not to conspire with the agents to deliberately reduce the price of land to the detriment of others' interests. Otherwise, the Heaven is very particular about retribution. Even if you temporarily get the property, there is bound to be a time of loss. Deeds and payments must be clearly delivered on the spot, and you cannot offset or delay the payment with some other goods. If there is a case of default, it has to be solved in

[62] *Book of Zhou · Biography of Kou Juan*. See more details in *Beshi (History of the North) · Biography of Kou Zan & Sun Juan*.

[63] *Beshi (History of the North): Biography of Meng Xin*.

[64] Shi Decao. *Bei Chuang Jiu Guo Lu*. Volume A.

time with compensation. Moreover, we must not secretly apportion the grain tax on others' land, doubling their taxes. This is a very serious evil deed."[65]

With regard to the principle of honesty and good faith, western neoclassical contractarians have developed a "pre-contractual obligation" for both parties to the contract, that is, to regard honesty as the prerequisite for concluding a contract. This theory was proposed by Kesler and Fine in 1964, expanding the scope of contractual responsibilities.[66] The purport of the contract theory that has risen since the middle of the 20th century is that the offeror must not deny or refuse to bear their responsibilities for the losses incurred by reasonable reliance on the offeror's related statements, guarantees and promises.[67] The "equitable estoppel", "promissory estoppel" and the theories of "reliance interest" and "expectations" are all built on the basis of the principle of "honesty and good faith" to regulate the parties' contract behaviors and seek fair and reasonable distribution of interests.[68] The "liability for negotiations" established by *The Principles of European Contract Law* is without doubt a means of limiting contract freedom, but it is based on good faith and aims to eliminate fraudulent contract behaviors. Its good intentions are the induction and summary of the 20th century legal theory, or it should be said that it is a powerful guarantee for contract freedom. *The Principles* stipulates: A party is free to negotiate and is not liable for failure to reach an agreement. However, a party who has negotiated or broken off negotiations contrary to good faith and fair dealing is liable for the losses caused to the other party. According to *The Principles*, it is contrary to good faith and fair trading, in particular, "for a party to enter into or continue negotiations with no real intention of reaching an agreement with the other party."[69]

A review of ancient Chinese contracts shows that although there was no theories or concepts such as "pre-contractual obligation" or "contractual liability", the principle of "honesty and good faith" was taken as the highest principle to judge a case where negotiations went against good faith and fair dealing in judicial practices. For example, Zhen Dexiu, a government official appointed by the imperial court in Song Dynasty, reprimanded in deep hate the evil practice of "depriving farmers of their tenancy rights selfishly", "In the remote rural areas, a brutal villain wanted to rent a field initially, which was rented by someone else at that time. He told the owner that he would pay more for the tenancy, so the owner expelled the original tenant. However, the villain breached the agreement and refused to rent the field. Thus the field was left uncultivated and deserted."[70] A case in *Law Reports of Southern Song Dynasty* also illustrated the situation of breaching the "pre-determined agreement" and the government's attitude: Li Maosen rented Jiang Bangxian's hostel and lived in it, but he remodelled and renovated the house without establishing a written contract

[65] *The Family Rules and Guidelines of Clan Zheng in Pujiang.*

[66] Wan [16].

[67] Grant [17].

[68] Yang [18].

[69] The Principles of European Contract Law. revised in July 1998 Article 2: 301 clauses 1, 2, 3. Trans. by Han Shiyuan. Cited in *Classic Journal of Foreign Law.* 1999 (1).

[70] Zhen Dexiu. *Collection of Zhen Wenzhong's Works* (Volume 8).

with Jiang. After the completion of construction, Jiang Bangxian brought a lawsuit against Li, requiring restoration of the house and claiming damages. Hu Shibi's judgement handled the dispute cleverly and tactfully:

> Li Maosen rented one's hostel and took the liberty of renovating the house without getting consent of the owner. It is true that he is guilty in this sense. However, the construction lasted such a long time from early October last year to March this year, why didn't Jiang Bangxian know it at all? If he did not allow it, he would not have waited until the day of completion to litigate. Why did he wait for so long to bring the case? Moreover, after the work was done, there was a handwritten note to inform Jiang of the cost of remodelling the house. Judging from this, there must be pre-determined agreement. Otherwise, Li Maosen would not be so foolish and ignorant as to invest money and efforts into someone else's house! The real reason why Jiang brought the case was not to restore his house, but must be that he doubted the cost of renovation and wanted to reduce the price, which he thought was too high. It is not difficult to see through his fraudulent trick! Since the two are relatives, there is no need to be penny wise and pound foolish. I would call on their neighbors and relatives to mediate between them and help settle this problem. They have to be fair and unbiased...

According to the judgement, the inference that Li and Jiang had an agreement beforehand was reasonable. However, there was controversy over the cost of renovating the house. The real purpose of Jiang Bangxian's litigation against Li Maosen using no written contract as an excuse was to reduce the price to gain his own benefits rather than restore the house and claim damages. Hu's judgment was in reasonable accordance with the law, thus it could be described as a fair judgment. The circumstance of this case was the same as that of one in the U.S. in 1950s despite different judgments[71]: Company A verbally promised to B that if B left the airline that he originally worked for, he would get a two-year offer after company A obtained the traffic rights between Alaska and Seattle. B relied on the promise, resigned from his post, and moved his family to Alaska, where company A was located. However, after obtaining traffic rights, A refused to fulfill their agreement on the grounds of no written contract. The court, based on the principle of estoppel, ruled that Statute of Frauds applied to the oral promise, which should be enforceable, thus ensuring the reasonable rights and interests of B.

Third, the principle of equality. Equality is the guarantee of justice and freedom. Without equality, it would be difficult to achieve justice and freedom. The psychological and sociological basis of equality is that people want to be respected by other social members and obtain equal social status and authority.[72] The reason why equality is protected by the law is the ideal of everyone to become their own master, without being ruled or constrained by others.

It is necessary to relate to a concept in the sociology and ethics of a traditional Chinese society here: "face (面子, Mian Zi)". A foreign expert believed that "face" was the first feature of Chinese people,[73] but "face" belonged to a conceptual category that could not be seen or touched. Lu Xun held that "face" was something that

[71] Alaska Airlines, Inc · V · Stephenson, 15 Alaska 272, 217 f · 2d 295 (9th cir · 1954), See footnote 68, p. 193.

[72] Edgar [19].

[73] Smith [20].

"would be OK without much thinking, but would definitely puzzle you when you reflect on it."[74] Lin Yutang also thought that "face" could be "illustrated by examples easily but rather hard to be defined".[75] From an external point of view, "face" seems to be only a value orientation of social behaviors, and its essence is to obtain personal social status through this social behavior orientation, of which there are four ways[76]: (1) Establishing one's authority. As stated above, China's equality is a kind of ethical equality, in which ascribed parameters such as seniority in the family and ties of blood, and the way of behaving can help establish personal authority for every social member and win respect from others. Weber held "the theory of the Chinese people fully shows the Charisma characters of the monarchical power, which are attached to one's qualifications and value".[77] In fact, in the traditional Chinese society, the "Distributive Justice" proposed by Aristotle existed in all the rankings, hierarchies and relationships apart from the supreme authority ("only one sun in the sky and one king in the world"), and this "equality" was the real means to establish personal social status and authority. (2) Morality. This is closely related to "face" in that "face" or social status could be achieved through morality. Starting from Confucianism, the distinction between "gentlemen (君子, Jun Zi, virtuous men)" and "little men (小人, Xiao Ren, ignoble men)" was no longer a purely ethical classification, but also an important criterion for balancing and exercising social power. The idea of "everyone is able to make a difference as long as he or she does good deeds" proposed by Mencius led to a common conception shared by later confucians and the whole society, that was, a gentleman could improve his own moral level through self-cultivation. One of high "morality" could bring great "reputation", and then he or she could become a "sage", which was the prerequisite for a "ruler" to master power. Self-cultivation of morality could help a person to be a "gentleman", and this theoretically provided each member of the society with equal opportunities so that one could become a person of social prestige through his or her own efforts. (3) "The courtesy of reciprocity". Courtesy on one side was in contempt of others' authority or statuses, which was a shame in traditional Confucianism. The courtesy of reciprocity showed recognition and respect for others' social statuses as well as improved one's own personal status, so that individuals could be on an equal level in terms of spirit and external etiquette. (4) Nepotism. In the intertwined social relations, traditional Chinese society formed countless connected networks due to blood, geopolitical, and industrial ties. They shared together honor and disgrace, prosperity and poverty, advance and retreat, and happiness and bitterness. These external social organizations like families, guilds and clubs maintained and balanced everyone's status and wealth, and finally evolved into a powerful lever that coordinated and stabilized social relations. B. Russell thought highly of the Chinese concept of "face", holding that "maintaining face safeguards the dignity of every Chinese person".[78] By contrast,

[74]*Selected Work of Luxun.* 1991. Vol. 6. *On Face.* People's Literature Publishing House.

[75]Lin [21].

[76]See Zhai [22].

[77]Weber [23].

[78]Russell [24].

Weber clearly saw the negative effects of the Chinese "face", proposing that it was the "face" that prevented Chinese from developing contractual social organizations.[79] To be more specific, Weber believed that maintaining face hindered the development of the ancient Chinese contracts in two aspects: first, it hindered equality; second, it blocked the psychological motivation among members of society to pursue profit maximization as a "rational person". The historical facts indicated that the latter point contributed to China's unique social characteristic of "mutual assistance", whereas the former point was the opposite of Weber's view: although maintaining face failed to stimulate the "entrepreneurship" in every member of the society, it indeed gave everyone equal opportunities and premises to "self-cultivate" regarding morality level and social statuses, thus helping the common people to climb the social ladder.

The equality in sociology is in line with the equality in law. Hegel illustrated contractual relationships as "the mutual treatment of the parties with direct and independent personalities".[80] His emphasis on the equality of subject personality was the premise of the commodity economy and meanwhile the precondition of the contract. The basic idea that ran through the contract law was that in terms of entity, the rights and obligations of the parties to the contract were equal, and in terms of procedures, the personality and procedural interests of both parties to the contract were equal.[81]

The records of the traditional Chinese contracts demonstrate that the principle of equality has always played a very important role in the development of contract, which is divided into legislation equality and exchange equality. These two categories are the product of western legal philosophy.[82] Legislation equality means the legal confirmation of the equality in the rights and obligations of both parties to the contract and in procedural guarantee; and exchange equality is to distribute the benefits of both parties at a fair and reasonable price and maintain equal personality and equal exchange of interests. As for the former one, there were laws and regulations in all dynasties of China advocating "fairness" and "harmonious purchase", the premise of which was voluntariness and equality, otherwise justice in exchange could not be achieved. As for the latter one, the nobilities, ministers of the government and the common people were all equal, and their personality and interests being exchanged were equal as well. Once this legal spirit and ethics of dealing were destroyed, the government and the people must take timely and effective measures to correct them. When the system of equal exchange ran smoothly without any problems, the government should treat the free exchange of interests among the people with a generous attitude. On the other hand, the civil society put more emphasis on the equality of rights and obligations. The ancient Chinese partnership contracts (those from Han Dynasty to the Republic of China) were cases in point, underlining equal interests of both contractual parties. In Ming Dynasty, the partnership contractsentered an era of standardization. For instance, *Chi Du Shuang Yu (尺牍双鱼)* "contracts part", *Yan Yu*

[79]Weber [25].

[80]Hegel [26].

[81]Liu and Liu [27].

[82]See footnote 72, p. 287.

Jin Jian (雁鱼锦笺) "contracts", *Yun Jin Shu Jian (云锦书笺)* "contracts", and *Xin Ke Hui Jun Bu Shi Shi Min Bian Du Tong Kao (新刻徽郡补释士民便读通考)* with records of "contracts" format, etc. A sample of partnership contracts was recorded in volume five of *Ao Tou Za Zi (鳌头杂字)* "contracts", which clarified in detail the rights and obligations of the contractual parties[83]:

> Party A and Party B reached an agreement to do business together since cooperation generates more profit. Therefore, both parties contribute a certain amount of money as the initial capital, making concerted efforts to operate the business. The profits generated are to be reviewed and divided up yearly in the presence of each other, with the capital remained to continue the business. Personal expenditure should be taken care of by oneself and must not concern the capital. The oath is sworn by the ritual of smearing the blood of a sacrifice on the mouth. Both parties should work and cooperate in harmony without willfulness and selfishness. Anyone who violates this agreement will be severely punished by the gods and people.

One point worth noting here is that the equality of rights and obligations of the parties, or the exchange equality, did not mean the equality in the identities or the social statuses of parities to the contract. Equality of identities was like a chronic disease that could not be cured in ancient Chinese society, but it was interesting that this did not prevent the equal rights of interests that unequal subjects should enjoy when they exchanged. For example, bullying the underprivileged and the weak in dealings were strictly forbidden by both laws and folk trading practices. And in Liao, Jin and Yuan Dynasties, police patrol stations were set up to specially supervise "civil matters and supply and demand",[84] or to "administer the civil matters in the capital city",[85] conducting administration of the market. During the reign of Emperor Jin Zhangzong, a servant of Madam Jin State (the younger sister of Queen Xiao Yi) refused to pay for the lacquer he bought. The seller complained to the authorities. Wan Yan Bo Jia was the judge at that time, "Bo Jia put the several servants involved in the case into jail. Madam Jin State told Zhangzong about it, and he replied: 'aunt, your servants would be released as long as you pay for the lacquer.' From then on, the privileged class did not dare to do that again".[86] Even though she was the emperor's aunt, she still had to abide by the principle of exchange equality, then we could infer that other rich or privileged class were also treated the same way. Such examples of "sympathizing the common people" presented by the supreme ruler abounded in ancient China, manifesting to some extent that both parties were equal and reciprocal in dealings.

Fourth, the principle of fairness. It is the most direct tool for regulating and balancing the interests of the parties to a contract, and also a symbol to indicate whether the official laws are in harmony with the folk customary law. Fairness is the ultimate goal of the principles of equality, voluntariness, and good faith. At the same time, it is also the ultimate embodiment of ethical justice (rationality). The rationale behind the principle of fairness is the limitation of social resources and

[83]Cited from Kong [28].

[84]*History of Yuan · Bai Guan Zhi.*

[85]*Records of the Unification of Yuan.* Edited by Zhao Wanli.

[86]*History of Jin · Biography of Wan Yan Bo Jia.*

the reasonability of the allocation of those limited resources. It aims to balance the resources enjoyed by different social subjects as a way to prevent social riots or turmoil. According to Karl Polanyi, three major exchange systems have been formed in the process of sharing resources among human beings: the first is reciprocal exchange; the second is redistributive exchange; and the third is market exchange.[87] All the forms of exchange rotate around the principle of fairness; otherwise the tilt of interests will inevitably lead to the overall "disorder" of the society. Therefore, fairness is not a product of laws and morality. It is only an objective reproduction of the economic law of interests distribution. Laws and morality serve only as an intermediary means.

The principle of fairness embodied in the ancient Chinese contract culture is no exception. The unreasonable (i.e., unfair) phenomenon in civil relations were strictly forbidden by the authorities and the civil society and related measure would be taken to remedy or correct those unfair practices, so as to create a virtuous cycle for various contractual relationships in the market, ultimately ensuring the rationality of trading results and the safety of trading orders. It can even be said that the ancient contract spirit valued safety instead of efficiency when weighing the two, and the most important one is the concept of fairness.

On the official level, there were generally three ways to regulate contractual relations: The first was to strengthen the market management mechanism, i.e., to constrain the behavior of market players from the external system. The second was to directly regulate various types of contractual relations, making clear and specific adjustments to the distribution of rights and obligations, so that the interests of both parties would be eventually balanced. The third was to adopt administrative measures to adjust the mutual interests of civil contract entities, and to redefine or eliminate related contractual rights and obligations in the form of gifts.

As mentioned above, from Western Zhou Dynasty to late Qing Dynasty, the government was always an active intervener and manager of the market. The collection of taxes to increase national profits was a major factor, but its greatest motivation was to stabilize the dealing orders and allocate social resources in a rational way. Since Tang and Song Dynasties, the government had imposed strict prohibitions on such acts as bullying, hegemony, ganging up, monopolizing prices, cheating, and profiteering in market transactions, and those prohibitions were accompanied by criminal punishments.[88] Taking Ming Dynasty as an example, fair trading and buying and selling without deception were the basic principles of the government's control and management of the market. At that time, the price was assessed by the middlemen. "Any middleman who assesses the prices of goods unfairly, either overrating or underrating the prices, will be identified as committing corruption. Any one who takes illegal possession of the goods and property will be regarded as committing larceny".[89] Such penalties had been more common in Han Dynasty. During the reign

[87]Karl Polanyi et al. 1957. Trade and Market in the Early Empires. Cited from Wang [29].

[88]Refer to *Law Code of Tang Dynasty*. Volume 26. *Law of Trivia. Criminal Code of Song Dynasty · Law of Trivia · Adjustments of Unbalanced Measurements*, etc.

[89]*Law Code of Ming Dynasty · Hu Lv · Shi Chan (Stores in a market).*

of Emperor Han Jing, it was expressly stipulated in the law: "Any official who uses his power to buy something at a low price and sell it at a high price will be punished as committing larceny and the goods shall be confiscated."[90] In the Second Year of Jia Jing Period (1523 A.D.) in Ming Dynasty, various laws of market transactions and trading were made: "Of all the agencies and shipping agents in the cities and in the countryside, only those with property that can be mortgaged are qualified to do business in the industry. The government will stamp their documents attached with the names and addresses of the merchants and ship owners, name and number of their passes and the amount of the goods. They must go to the government to go through monthly inspection. Jactitators will be punished by floggings. Any middleman who assesses the prices of goods unfairly, either overrating or underrating the prices, will be penalized according to the price gap. Businessmen who force dealings and manipulate the market price, and those who act in alliance with the agencies to disrupt the market will all be penalized severely with floggings."[91] The laws of Qing Dynasty mostly followed those of Ming Dynasty and stipulated the penalties in more detail, "Businessmen who force dealings and manipulate the market price, and those who act in alliance with the agencies, either overrating or underrating the price to disrupt the market, will all be penalized with eighty floggings. Anyone who tries to puzzle others when seeing them making a deal in order to gain benefits will be punished with forty whippings. The goods or benefits gained from this shall be considered as stolen goods, and more serious cases will be punished as committing larceny".[92]

The government's direct intervention, interference in contract terms, and the establishment of the boundaries of rights and obligations in the form of laws and cases dated back to Tang and Song Dynasties, which were implemented by the government as a peremptory norm to harmonize the interests of both parties to the contract. Taking paid (interest-bearing) loan contracts as an example, the interest-bearing debt was not protected by the law in Tang Dynasty, and bartering loans were also subject to private contracts without intervention from the government. However, if there was "illegal profit-making, that is, if the interest of the loan exceeds the range permitted by the law, people are encouraged to report it to the government, after which the principal and interest would all be given to the person who reports it". At the same time, the law strictly prohibited usury and compound interest. If these happened, the government should actively intervene and penalize those usurers. According to the historical records, the contracts of private lending and leases in early Tang Dynasty were quite developed, but the general drawbacks lay in the prevalence of usury and compound interest. People led a miserable life as the higher interest rates were up to 15–20%, and the lower ones were also 6–10%.[93]Many of the insolvent poor people were even imprisoned, unable to make a living. In view of this situation, the central

[90]*Book of Han · Biography of Emperor Liu Qi.*

[91]*Institutional History of Ming · Penalties and Punishments (6) · Shi Chan.*

[92]*Law Code of Qing Dynasty.* Volume 15. *Hu Lv · Shi Chan.*

[93]As above, the interest rate of the *Money Loan by Bu Laoshi in the Second Year in the Reign of Lin De* was 10%, and that of the *Silver Loan by Zheng Haishi in the first Year in the Reign of Qianfeng* was 15%.

government of Tang Dynasty issued a number of decrees that must be complied with by local governments at all levels. In the sixth year of the reign of Kai Yuan Period (729 A.D.), Emperor Xuan Zong of Tang Dynasty ordered: "Recently both public and private lending have made such a huge profit that the interests of the poor have been harmed, thus reform is imperative. Henceforth, the interest rate on private lending cannot exceed four percent while that on public lending cannot exceed five percent."[94] *The Law of Trivia (Za Lv) of Tang* stipulated that "the monthly interest rate must not exceed six percent. Even though the lending would last for a long time, the profit must not surpass the amount of the principal…and compound interest is forbidden",[95] this was a mandatory requirement for interest rate clauses in lending contracts. For those who were unable to repay their debts as scheduled, the imperial court also promulgated a very merciful imperial edict to forcibly extend the time limit by administrative ways. For example, in the eighth year of the reign of Xian Tong Period (867 A.D.), Emperor Tang Yizong ordered: "Defaulting on the loan is not considered as a felony. But if a person is imprisoned because of debt, he or she will be deprived of the right to earn a living. There must be provisions to guarantee people's basic living. Therefore, when a debtor with no official titles and no stable income defaults on the loan and has nothing to pledge, the local government and officials should extend his or her time limit properly. Imprisonment and penalties that would lead to one's unemployment are not allowed…Violations of this regulation would result in the impeachment and interrogation of the officials."[96]

Corresponding to the above examples, the official government's direct intervention in private contracts was reflected in frequent enactment of decrees of amnesties and merciful imperial edicts to acquit the debtors of a part of their debt, so as to balance the interests of both parties to the contract. This kind of prohibitive provisions aimed not only to protect the interests of debtors but also to protect those of creditors, preventing further exploitation at the same time. For instance, in the fourteenth year of Yuan He Period (819 A.D.), Emperor Tang Xianzong enacted the decree of amnesty: "In the situation where the debtor or the guarantor flees, if the interest of more than ten times the principal has been paid, or the interest of more than five times the principal is shared by the guarantor when the liabilities are transferred, the debt shall be cancelled."[97] Another example was the merciful imperial edict enacted by Emperor Tang Wenzong in the eighth year of the reign of Tai He (834 A.D.) in Tang Dynasty: "As for all the officials in the capital of the country who make profits from loans, if their debtors already paid the interest of more than five times the principal, then the principal and interest shall both be acquitted. In the cases where the debtor fled or died and the liabilities were transferred to the guarantor, if the guarantor pays the interest of more than twice the principal, then the principal and interest shall also be acquitted."[98]

---

[94] *Institutional History of Tang*. Volume 88.

[95] *Criminal Code of Song Dynasty*. Volume 26. *Law of Trivia*. Cited from *Za Ling* of Tang Dynasty.

[96] *The Collection of Edicts in Dang Dynasty · Government Affairs · Amnesty (6).*

[97] *Wen Yuan Ying Hua. Volume 442.*

[98] *Wen Yuan Ying Hua. Volume 441.*

On the private level, "Gong (公, the first character of '公平')" meant "unselfishness" and "Ping (平, the second character of '公平')" meant "equality". One of the peculiar phenomena in ancient Chinese contracts was that the laws and customary law maintained justice while tolerated injustice at the same time. Injustice to individuals might turn out to be fair and just to the family as a whole, and similarly, justice to the country might not necessarily be fair and just to the family. This is a universal and symbiotic phenomenon in the history of the world's legal development.[99] In other words, justice is always relative, and the principle of justice in folk customary law has been embodied in the following aspects:

1. Public property system. Accumulation of private wealth and appropriation of public property were strictly forbidden. For the family per se, it was not only a positive and effective way to protect the family's common property, but also the prerequisite for the equitable distribution of family resources. For the clan, their ancestral property, property for sacrifice, land property for supporting the big clan and the poor, and the land property for running schools were all publicly owned by the clan and were confirmed by the government to maintain the order of public affairs in the clan, the disturbance of which would be punished. Taking Qing Dynasty as an example, in the eleventh year during the reign of Emperor Qian Long (1746 A.D.), Zhuang Youmu, the governor of Jiangsu, proposed to the imperial court and was approved: "Any unworthy descendant who secretly sells one to ten Mu (a unit of area, one Mu equals 0.0667 ha) of the land property of the clan shall be beaten with one hundred floggings and wear the pillory for one month. One who sells more than ten Mu of the public land property would be directly banished to remote areas." And the buyer would be considered as "committing the same crime as the seller did, and the land property shall be returned to the clan that originally owns it. The money paid to buy the land shall be confiscated".[100] What was extremely unfair to the buyer in this case was that he or she lost both the land and the money. However, a further study into the purpose of this legislation showed that it tried to protect the public property from being stolen and sold.
2. The pre-emption right of the relatives and neighbors in the clan system. It was common knowledge that traditional Chinese families and clans, which were built on a self-sufficient system, were relatively stable constituent parts of the society. The flow of their property, especially the outflow of their real estate property, would result in a loss of shared resources, thus impacting the entire family's living environment. Since Northern and Southern Dynasties, the pre-emption right of the relatives and neighbors had been widely applied to the pawning and selling of real estate property in a clan, and gradually became established as ordinances till Song and Yuan Dynasties. Please refer to the previous chapter for more details about this.

[99] See footnote 72. More details in E. Bodenheimer's View of Equality, p. 285.

[100] *Guang Xu Da-Qing Huidian Shili (Laws, Regulations and Cases of Qing Dynasty).* Volume 755. *Hu Lv · Stealing and Selling Land and Houses. Petition for Deciding the Cases of Larcenous Sale and Purchase of the Land Property.*

3. The autonomy right of the contractual parties. That was, in the event of conflicts between the terms of the contract and the state's administrative orders, the government allowed one or both contractual parties to select the relevant terms independently and formalize them in the form of contract. Taking the amnesty as an example, various decrees for amnesty and merciful imperial edicts since Tang Dynasty required the cancellation or postponement of public and private debts, directly harming the actual rights and interests of creditors. So the creditors, in order to ensure their rights, would clarify this point and make an agreement with the debtors in the very first place on how to settle the matter when conflicts between contract provisions and government's order of amnesty arose and their typical forms of confrontation. This kind of clauses existed in most of the contracts (mainly loan contracts) of Tang Dynasty unearthed in Dunhuang and Turpan, which sufficed to show that their effectiveness or validity could surpass the state's administrative orders. Please refer to the section of "Amnesty and Gurantee" in Chap. 2 for more details.
4. The equality in the identity law. The class difference of lowliness and nobleness in the identity law was a very important pivot to maintain the patriarchal system in traditional Chinese society. Marriage, families and the related inheritance system indeed reflected the inequalities among different identities such as "men being superior to women", and "seniority being superior to juniority". However, it was a little different in terms of property distribution and inheritance. We could find that the reason why a married woman could not inherit the property of her original family was that she obtained the inheritance right of her husband's family. A typical example was this: in Han Dynasty, a rich man of 90 years old in Chenliu (the name of a place) still did not have a son and married a woman from the Family of Tian. He passed away after intercourse, and then the woman gave birth to a baby boy. The old man's daughter had a good reason to fight over the legacy with her stepmother: "My father died at a very old age, so how could he have a child just over one night?" The Prime Minister Bing Ji decided the case through a process similar to trial by ordeal, concluding that the woman's boy was indeed the son of the old man, so all the old man's property should be inherited by his son.[101] Moreover, according to the laws of Song Dynasty, the female "in her room" (the unmarried woman in the family) could obtain the full inheritance rights if there was "family heirlessness" (i.e., all the males in a family died without sons to inherit).[102] A more obvious example was that although legal wives and concubines and their respective sons had quite different family statuses and social statuses, there was no big difference among them as regards property distribution and inheritance. After examining the application of traditional Chinese laws and customs in Hong Kong, Mr. Su Yigong concluded that "the differences between Chinese wives and concubines lie mainly in their statuses rather than in their

[101] *Tai Ping Yu Lan (Taiping Imperial Encyclopaedia).* Volume 836. *Feng Su Tong (Customs and Habits).*

[102] *Law Reports of Southern Song Dynasty · Households and Marriages · Inheritance Rights.*

property”[103]; and more importantly, the will of the seniors would be much more effective than the statutory succession in the distribution of their legacies. Under such circumstances, the legacies were generally divided among the men and women of the family on an equitable basis. Furthermore, the fundamental reason for Chinese men’s priority right of inheritance was that they bore more social and family responsibilities than women did. The French historian Fustel de Coulanges examined the traditions of ancient Greek and Roman society and held that a man enjoyed the inheritance right of a family because he was also under the obligations to worship his ancestors and support his parents. From this point of view, it was the substantive equality in the civil identities.[104] As a matter of fact, after the Middle Ages in ancient China, the folk custom that the family property was equally divided among all the sons (both the sons of the legal wife and those of the concubines) was recognized by the government, which was commonly seen in all kinds of contracts of family property distribution. In the 12th year in the reign of Emperor Yongzheng, it was recorded in the property distribution contract of Family Chen in She County: “The father took an oath before the gods in the presence of the relatives, and wrote the will for distributing all the family property. Following the suggestions of the relatives, the father classified the land, hills, houses and the other property into eleven shares clearly for the descendants to draw lots to decide who gets which…Please make sure the process be fair and just regardless of the statuses or positions of the sons.”[105] The past governments’ attitude of “equal” inheritance had been evident in the legal documents. In Tang Dynasty, it was stipulated that “the land, house and other property of the family shall be divided equally among the brothers”,[106] which was followed by Song Dynasty without any change. In Ming Dynasty, it was stipulated that “The family property shall be distributed equally among the sons without regard to the statuses or positions of their mothers”.[107] It was the same case in Qing Dynasty,[108] which was cited for deciding a case in the judicial practices in Hong Kong.

A study into many ancient cases revealed the good intentions of traditional Chinese “rulers” in the process of safeguarding equality and justice. The following are a couple of cases to elaborate the point.

In Han Dynasty, there was a tycoon in Pei County whose family property was worth 30 million. His concubine gave birth to a son and his wife gave birth to a daughter who was not very virtuous. When the man was dying from severe illness, he made a will in the presence of the members of his clan in case his children would fought over wealth: All the property would be inherited by the daughter except that

---

[103] Su [30].

[104] de Coulanges [31]

[105] Cited from Zhang Youyi. *Selected Documents of Household Division and Inheritance of Landlords in Huizhou in Ming and Qing Dynasties.* As in Collected Papers of Institute of Economics, Chinese Academy of Social Sciences (Series 9), p. 98.

[106] *Law Code of Tang Dynasty.* Volume 12. *Hu Hun (Marriages).*

[107] *Law Code of Ming Dynasty.* Volume 6. *Hu Lv (Households).*

[108] *Law Code of Qing Dynasty.* Volume 10. *Hu Lv (Households).*

the son could only get a sword, which should be handed over to him at the age of fifteen by the elder sister. When the son was fifteen years old, he requested for the sword but was refused by his sister. So he lodged an accusation. At that time, the Great Minister of Public Works (an official title) He Wu accepted the case. After carefully examining the will and interrogating the daughter and the son-in-law, he told the other officials: "The daughter and the son-in-law are cruel and greedy. The rich man was worried that they would kill his son to forcibly occupy the family property. Moreover, his son was too young to keep the property even if he got it. So he pretended to give it to the daughter, intending her to keep it for the son as a matter of fact. The sword was just a tool for deciding the case and getting the property back to his son. The man knew that his daughter and son-in-law would refuse to return the sword when his son reached 15, but then his son would be intelligent and independent enough to bring the case to the county magistrate, who would be likely to investigate into it so as to protect his son and the property. How can the ordinary man be so far-sighted?" Therefore, He Wu decided that the son should recover all of his father's legacies and told the daughter and the son-in-law that they were already fortunate enough to live on her younger brother's property.[109] This case created much of a stir at that time and the people were all convinced, saying Wu's judgment was rather reasonable and justified. Looking into the case more carefully, the reason why He Wu judged it in this way was that he concluded the old man's unconventional decision of giving all his legacies to his daughter, plus leaving a sword to his son and setting the age of obtaining it at 15 must contain profound meaning, which was, the man was actually worried that his daughter and son-in-law would plot against his son for the legacies. That's why he purposefully set up this puzzle in the first place. He Wu solved it and returned the property to his son in a fair and just way, right in accordance with the rich man's original intention. A case in Song Dynasty bore much resemblance to this. The decedent stated in his will that three-tenths of his legacies should be inherited by his son and the remaining seven-tenths by his son-in-law. The local official Zhang Yong judged the case in the opposite way, distributing seven-tenths of the legacies to the son and third-tenths to his son-in-law. This judgment was also made based on the principle of equality because the son was so young that he could easily be harmed by the son-in-law if he got seven-tenths. People then were greatly convinced by Zhang Yong's "fair judgment".[110]

Another case was the dispute over entrustment contracts. In Tang Dynasty, Wang Jing, from Xinxiang County of Weizhou, entrusted his six cows to the care of his uncle Li Jin since he was going to garrison the frontiers. After five years, the cows produced 30 calves and Wang Jing finished his service. When he wanted to bring back his cows from Li Jin, Li only returned four old cows and told him the other two already died from the disease. Wang was not convinced and sued Li. The county magistrate Pei ruled: "The cows should be returned immediately. What else do you need to say? Li Jin is able to keep five cows as the reward for raising the cows over the

[109] *Tai Ping Yu Lan (Taiping Imperial Encyclopaedia)*. Volume 836. *Feng Su Tong (Customs and Habits)*.

[110] *History of the Song Dynasty · Biography of Zhang Yong*.

five years and has to return all the rest to his nephew Wang Jing."[111] Pei's judgement was also referred to as "fair judgment" in that Li Jin received reasonable reward for his efforts and labor, and meanwhile Wang Jing also claimed his rights and got his fructus as the original owner. In conclusion, the judgment was fair and just.

References

1. Jaspers, Karl Theodor. 1989. *The Origin and Goal of History*, 66, 73. Huaxia Publishing House.
2. Kluckhohn, Clyde, et al. 1986. *Culture and Personality*, trans. Gaojia et al., 5. Zhejiang People's Publishing House.
3. White, Leslie Alvin. 1988. *The Science of Culture: A Study of Man and Civilization*, trans. Cao Jinqing, et al., 323, 326. Zhejiang People's Publishing House.
4. Kardiner, Abram, and Edward Prable. 1987. *They Studied Man*, trans. Kaixiang Sun, 54–55. Joint Publishing Company.
5. Hsabine, George. 1986. *A History of Political Theory*, trans. Shan Liu et al., 523. The Commercial Press.
6. Ba, Xinsheng. 1997. On the origins and evolution of Pre-Qin "Virtues". *Journal of Chinese Historical Studies* (3).
7. Wang, Yaxing, and Zhiping Liang (ed.). 1998. *Civil Trials and Private Contracts in Ming and Qing Dynasties*, 307. Law Press China.
8. Unger, R.M. 1996. *Law in Modern Society*, trans. Yuzhang Wu, and Hanhua Zhou. China University of Political Science and Law Press.
9. Li, Jinyi. 1998. Legal thoughts of John Locke. *Journal of Renmin University of China* (4).
10. Atiyah, P.S. 1982. *An Introduction to the Law of Contract*, trans. Zhengkang Cheng, and Zhonghai Zhou, 5. Law Press China.
11. Su, Haopeng. 1999. On the historical background and value of the freedom of contracts. *Science of Law* (5).
12. Tsunoshi, Hirano. 1995. Functions of the principle of good faith and the legal principle of prohibiting the abuse of rights, trans. Jingkun Fu. *Classic Journal of Foreign Law* (2).
13. Fu, Jingkun. 1995. On the historical development of American contract theory. *Classic Journal of Foreign Law* (1).
14. Takashi, Uchida. 1997. Modernization of contract law, trans. Baohai Hu. *Civil and Commercial Law Review*, vol. 6. Law Press China.
15. Scogin, Jr. Hugh T. 1994. Between heaven and man: Contracts and the state in Han Dynasty in China. *Recent American Academic Writings on Traditional Chinese Law*, ed. Karen Turner et al., 192, 210. China University of Political Science and Law Press.
16. Wan, Qun. 1997. History and origins of American contract law. *Civil and Commercial Law Review*, vol. 6. Law Press China.
17. Grant, Gilmore. 1997. The death of contract. *Civil and Commercial Law Review*, trans. Cao Shibing et al., vol. 3. Law Press China.
18. Yang, Zhen. 1997. *Anglo-American Law of Contracts*, 333. Peking University Press.
19. Edgar, Bodenheimer. 1999. *Jurisprudence: The Philosophy and Method of the law*, trans. Deng Zhenglai, 288. China University of Political Science and Law Press.
20. Smith, Arthur Henderson. 1998. *Chinese Characteristics*, 1–4. Xue Yuan Publishing House.
21. Yutang, L. 1935. *My Country and My People*, 200. New York: John Clay Book.
22. Zhai, Xuewei. 1999. Personal status: A concept and its analytical framework. *Social Sciences in China* (4).
23. Weber, M. 1997. *Economy, Society, Religion*, 193. Shanghai Social Sciences Press.

[111] *Chao Ye Qian Zai.* Volume 5.

24. Russell, B. 1996. *The Problem of China*, 161. Academia Press.
25. Weber, M. 1995. *Confucianism and Morality.* The Commercial Press.
26. Hegel. 1961. *Law Philosophy,* trans. Yang Fan and Qitai Zhang, 82. The Commercial Press.
27. Liu, Kaixiang, and Liu Jiagang. 1997. Theory of contract procedures. *Tribune of Political Science and Law* (6).
28. Kong, Qingming, et al. 1996. *The History of Chinese Civil Law*, 561. Jilin People's Publishing House.
29. Wang, Mingming. 1997. *Social Anthropology and Chinese Studies*, 143. SDX Joint Publishing House.
30. Su, Yigong. 1999. Case studies of applying Chinese traditional legal customs in Hong Kong. *Social Sciences in China* (3).
31. de Coulanges, Fustel. 1938. *A Study of Ancient Greek and Roman Society* (Chapter 7 of Volume 2), trans. Xuanbo Li. The Commercial Press.

Chapter 6
The Flag of Desires: The Humanity Basis of Contract and the Evolution of Contractual Rights

Malinowski holds that the decisive factor of culture came from human's basic physiological needs and the derived social needs, which were sometimes regarded as certain means.[1] In the light of the comparison between Chinese and western theory of human nature, it seems that we can find a clear and strong progressive line between man's physiological needs and social needs, that is, human beings set up various social desires to satisfy their natural desires and the need for the satisfaction of both kinds of desires has generated social concepts such as education, law, morality and social groups like economic organizations. The core of this chapter explores the humanity basis and social foundation of contracts based on the comparison of Chinese and western ideas of the evil of human nature, and finds out different qualities and causes of Chinese and western contract culture. Western contract culture focuses on the satisfaction of human desires. Therefore, the contract takes individual rights, freedom and equality as the core, and the sociological and economic theories guiding contracts are the so-called "rational person" or "enterprise spirit" and the "natural obligations" of the government and state to protect the right to freedom. On the contrary, the contract spirit of traditional Chinese culture puts emphasis on restraining or even offsetting individual desires with "rite", "law" under the premise of satisfying individual desires, and thus guiding them with the ethical concept of "mutual aid" for both families and the society. In terms of contract spirit, Chinese and western cultures tend to be two extremes due to different values and institutions. Western countries advocate freedom of contract and individual rights, regarding them as the "natural obligations" of the law and government; whereas those of China are weakened or even replaced by the parental authority of "common good" (families and clans, the state). However, the traditional culture of "rite" and "law" did not completely block the path of realizing human desires, and individual desires always existed and grew under the waves of family and royalty histories. With the passage of time, contractual rights have grown constantly and become an independent form of right in the era of the Republic of China. Conversely, western freedom of contract was hindered in the

[1] Adamson Hoebel [1].

Y. Liu, *The History of the Contractual Thoughts in Ancient China*,
https://doi.org/10.1007/978-981-15-5768-2_6

early 20th century when individual rights and contract freedom evolved to socialization, aiming to safeguard social public interests and good customs. In conclusion, the spiritual changes of Chinese and western contract culture have been in continuous recurrence and development with their respective historical and cultural foundations, embodying different directions of Chinese and western cultures.

The Flag of Desires: The Humanity Basis of Contract

When it came to the formation of the concept of property, Morgan, the excellent American anthropologist, expounded that "the concept of property was shaped slowly in human's mind over a long period of time during which it had always been in a weak budding state…when the desire for property prevails over all other desires, that symbolizes the start of civilization."[2] In short, the evil of human nature not only marks the start of civilization but also drives it forward. By comparing Chinese and western theories of the evil human nature, we can find remarkable similarities between the two. A closer look into it would help us to touch upon the prototype sources from and by which the contract culture originated and developed.

In the history of western philosophy, the French philosopher Claude–Adrien Helvetius clearly elevated human beings' pursuit of physical pleasure and desires for interests to a rational level. In his *De l'homme*, he held that "the joy and suffering of the human body are always the sole principle of dominating people's action", and "the joy and suffering of the human body are the only real hinge of all rule". And in the *De l'esprit*, he believed "interests govern all our judgments".[3] Machiavelli found the connection between politics and humanity: "Human nature is essentially selfish. Thus the effective incentive that politicians must rely on should be self-interest, just as the masses desire to gain guarantees and the ruler long for power," as a result, "the government is indeed built on the weakness and incompetence of the individual."[4] He expounded that the real essence of the origins of the state and government was human beings' selfishness and the desire for their personal interests to be protected by the powerful side, which in turn served as the resources and the original driving force for the politicians. After Machiavelli, Hobbes analyzed the two principles of humanity more clearly: desires and reason. Desires propelled people to grab what others need, causing endless competition whereas reason produced a force of coordination. The society consisted of individuals motivated by selfishness who expected to get protection from the law and the government in order to rival other selfish people just like themselves, in an attempt to seek maximum personal interests in a peaceful

[2]Morgan [2].

[3]*Selected Readings of Western Philosophy* (Volume 2). 1982. Edited and trans. by the Teaching and Research Office of Foreign Philosophy of the Department of Philosophy, Peking University. The Commercial Press, pp. 179–182.

[4]Sabine [3].

condition.[5] Locke directly extended and deepened Hobbes' theory, presuming that the existence of the government and society was to safeguard personal interests, the irrevocability of which constituted the limits of the governmental and social authority. On the basis of this point, Locke categorized human beings' rights and obligations into a dialectical system where everyone was endowed with the rights to life, liberty, property and so on but at the same time he or she was also obliged to respect the same rights of others.[6] Tracing back through the history of wisdom, an ancient sage's idea about this could be highlighted here. In his work *The Republic*, Plato talked about the politicians or the ruler "the purpose of judging is to prohibit everyone from infringing upon others' property so as to protect the property of everyone", and meanwhile defined "justice" as "to enjoy your own things and do your own things".[7]

Exploring the long course of human civilization from the perspective of human desires, the "theory of mutual adaptation" in Darwin's theory of "evolution" had a more profound rational kernel. In *The Decent of Man*, Darwin explained that humans' physiological weaknesses were their best wealth in that they urged individuals to keep a highly cooperative relationship with each other. It was this history of mutual adaptation that contributed to the birth of human society. He held that all human beings bore two kinds of instincts: one was egoism and the other altruism. The coordination and compromise of these two instincts generated complicated systems that forced individuals to submit to the common interests of the collective in order to survive. Social aggregation was based on the combination of the religion and tribal government. In *Principles of Sociology*, Darwin thought that "the fear of the living became the root of political control, and the fear of the dead became the source of religious control".[8] "The fear of the living" here, which was elaborated by Sir James Frazer in his outstanding masterpiece *The Golden Bough*, was the taboos and worships arising from the shift of social power from the majority to the authoritative individuals, that was, from the formation of social supremacy and individual ownership.

He held that golden fruits of law and morality were grafted on the boughs of taboos and the primary function of Totem was to bring people into social groups as well so that they could take collective actions and develop a sense of responsibility. Then, in order to meet the needs of civilization progress, Totem and taboos bore rich fruits such as cooperation, dependence and kindness including an individual's submission to a community.[9] Bronislaw Malinowski examined the control mode of humanity instinct, and was inclined to believe in the external family system and intrinsic cultural needs. In his opinion, the family was the key to modify an individual's instinctive impulse to adjust it to social conditions of survival. And it was the loving relationship in the

[5]ibid., pp. 523, 589.

[6]ibid., pp. 590–593.

[7]*Selected Readings of Western Philosophy.* 1981. Edited and trans. by the Teaching and Research Office of Foreign Philosophy of the Department of Philosophy, Peking University, p. 117.

[8]Kardiner and Preble [4].

[9]ibid., pp. 110, 128, 136.

family that formed the original cores of clan spirit, friendship among neighbors and the loyalty and morality of tribal members; on the other hand, religions constituted the society's basic integrating power, which did not grow out of fantasies, reflection or misunderstanding, but was the reaction to the need for cultural survival.[10] The above three sages all explained the necessity and historical perspective of the emergence of law and morality from two aspects: one was to restrain the instinct of self-interest by religion, and to propel humans to choose reason over instincts. The other was to submit individuals to collective groups by the control mechanism of the external society. The combination of the both enabled humans to choose reason over instincts and maintain instinctive desires at the same time.

Returning to the philosophical track again, we could deduce the following conclusions from the Kant and Hegel's philosophical systems: The evil of human nature promoted the advancement of social history, and shaped the beautiful modern civilization as well. Kant believed that human being's anti-sociality (outliers) eventually formed the society (community). It was the evil of individuals that contributed to the overall good of the whole, developing everyone's talents through competition, confrontation and conflicts with others pushing the human history forward to the goal of moral ideal. In his discussion on instinctive desires of humanity, the philosopher Kant's ingenious arguments were reflected in the mottled light of history. He said that without the desires for honor, power, wealth and so on, human beings would live in harmony, mutual love and self-content as the shepherds in Agadia, thus burying their various talents. "If people are as good-tempered as the flock of sheep they breed, they cannot achieve a higher value than their livestock."[11] Hegel, the great master of dialectics, saw clearly into the essence of Kant's philosophy and sublimated it to the height of history with abstraction of it. He believed that between the good and evil of human nature, it was precisely the evil part that formed the driving force of history. Human activities were driven by various desires and enthusiasm to pursue their own interests. The self-interest principle or selfishness of humans impacted and offset each other's efforts, thus giving rise to the concept of reason and promoting the establishment of state institutions such as laws and political systems. As a result, mankind ended the history of primitive state at the level of the state, realized the harmonious development of the society, and welcomed the dawn of human civilization.[12] Hobbes also held that the state and its social structure per se was a necessary evil, the causes and consequences of which were to avoid greater evil. Sabine explained from another perspective: maintaining the peaceful order of the society per se was an inherent good.

The external forms of human instinctive desires were those for the legalization of property privatization and for the protection of static property ownership and dynamic transference by national laws, and at the same time the freedom of contract became the supreme principle of disposing one's property. Some scholars believed

[10]ibid., pp. 259–263.

[11]Cited from W. H. Walsh. 1960. *Philosophy of History: An introduction. Harper Torchbooks*, p. 125. See Li [5].

[12]Liu [6].

that Hugo Grotius, the founder of classical Jus Naturale, was the first to consider the freedom of personal property and contracts as human' eternal natural rights. Locke systematically demonstrated the legal value of individual freedom (including the freedom of contract).[13] In fact, as early as Ancient Rome times, many sages and jurists noticed the importance of the property itself. Domitius Ulpianus expounded that "the word 'bona' is within the scope of Jus Naturale, or it means property in Jus Civile. According to Jus Naturale, it is said to be something that makes people happy and thus it is something useful".[14] The core of Hugo Grotius' Jus Naturale system was the property rights. He held that the law originated from the individuals' desire to maintain the social order, and the basic idea of law was: "Not taking possession of the property of another, returning the things that may be possessed by us to its original owner together with the benefits that we may have derived from it, fulfilling the obligations of promises, compensating for losses caused by our faults, and being punished for our offences accordingly."[15] Two important rules were implied here: one was the formation and protection of ownership, and the other was the freedom of contract and the justice of fulfilling the contracts. It could be said that these two contributed to the emergence and development of modern capitalism. In Marx's discussion on the inheritance system of primogeniture (inheritance by the eldest son of the legal wife) in the manorial economy of western Europe, he believed that the hereditary ownership of the land formed "hardened private property", which was also "the most independent and most developed private property".[16] Engels demonstrated the importance of ownership from the negative side and indicated that any major change in the society "can only be achieved through open violation of property ownership".[17] French economist Blanqui regarded ownership as "the most powerful driving force for the promotion of human wisdom".[18] And the instinctive desires of human nature in turn constituted the essence and source of ownership. Hobbes, Spinoza and Montesquieu all explored the natural attributes of human beings from different perspectives, i.e., human emotions and desires constituted human nature; interests were the driving force of desires and emotions; and all human behaviors were to satisfy individual desires and emotions. Therefore, human beings were in nature selfish and evil. Kant's argument was more logical and empirical: the weaknesses of human nature referred to "not only the lack of moral goodness, but also the powerful factors and motives for the inclination to be evil". There exists positive evil instead of positive good in human beings, and the driving force of history cannot be anything but the evil humans or the evil of humans.

---

[13] Wang and Du [7].

[14] *Corporis Iuris Civilis Fragmenta Selecta · III · Property and Property Rights*. 1993. Edited by Sandro Scibani. Trans. by Fan Huaijun. China University of Political Science and Law Press, p. 23.

[15] See footnote 4, p. 480.

[16] Marx's Critique of Hegel's Philosophy of Right. 1962. *Karl Marx and Frederick Engels* (Volume 1). People's Publishing House, p. 369.

[17] *Marx Engels Collected Works*. Volume 4, p. 111.

[18] Proudhon. 1996. *Qu'est-ce Que la Propriété*. The Commercial Press, p. 34.

At this point, it is necessary to make a generalization of the western theories of human nature and their legal mechanisms: humans' instinctive needs and self-interest gave rise to ownership; contracts were made to improve or realize ownership, and laws and the state were created to guarantee and realize the freedom of contract and contractual rights. From the vertical point of view, classical Jus Naturale upheld the banner of freedom of contract and established the value system of individualism which centered around individuals and advocated personality liberation and freedom of will.[19] This value system constructed the "yesterday" of "modernization" in capitalist countries. At the beginning of the twentieth century, the significance of the freedom of contract ebbed in the tides of socialization with public welfare coming to the fore. The public power of the state started to get involved in the contracting process, thus ushering in a new era of "modernity".[20] The difference between "modernization" and "modernity" was that the former saw the growth of modern society as a "natural" and "desirable" process, while the latter viewed the "discourse" of the process as an ideology and power structure and reflected on it.[21]

The contract culture in traditional Chinese society was also founded on human nature. However, its basic idea was to correct the evil through the good, to regulate self-interest through morality and justice, and to improve customs through rites (customary law).

The importance of property rights had been highly valued since the most remote times of Xia, Shang, and Zhou Dynasties. The economic and legal thoughts revealed in *Book of Documents* (*Shang Shu*, a collection of the historical literature of ancient China), were worthy of intensive study. "There are eight kinds of important affairs in the society. Agricultural production ranks first, and the exchanges of commodities ranks the second". "Agricultural production" (meaning food), as the most important issue on the list, was the earliest source for value judgment in the Confucian concept of "Shi, Se, Xing Ye (食色性也, The desire for food and sex is part of human nature)". The *Chapter of Hong Fan* (laws of ruling) in *Book of Documents* listed "Fu" (富, wealth) as one of "Wu Fu" (五福, the five kinds of blessings) and "Pin" (贫, poverty) as one of Liu Ji (六极, the six kinds of misfortunes), presenting them from a different perspective. *Chapter of Lv Xing* (*Criminal Code of Western Zhou Dynasty*) explained the functions of law from the judicial perspective, which was, "the main goal of judicial adjudication is not to serve as the deterrent or to establish prestige, but to safeguard property rights". *Chapter Li Yun* of *The Book of Rites* described the wealth distribution rules between social groups and individuals: "In Western Zhou Dynasty, the emperor granted most of his land to his dukes and princes, who distributed a portion of the land to their high-ranking officials in the form of fief, who again transferred some of the fief to their own subordinates. In this way, a strict hierarchy land system was hence standardized." The most fundamental principle of Confucianism was "benevolence", which not only embodied a moral state of mind, but also a materialized state, meaning the material state by which

---

[19] See Su [8].

[20] Fu [9].

[21] Wang [10].

to survive. The most effective way of ruling a nation was to prioritize the material basis of people over the indoctrination of them. Mencius put more emphasis upon "managing the people's property" as "stable property" generated "loyalty", which served as the premise of social prosperity and stability.

The great significance of wealth lay in the fact that it was the basis for survival, a precondition for satisfying instincts as well as the authentic reflection of human nature. As regards human nature, Mencius defined it as humans' social morality, while Xuncius (Xun Zi) saw it as the natural physical desires. In the eyes of Mencius, Ren (仁, benevolence), Yi (义, righteousness), Li (礼, rite) and Zhi (智, intelligence) were the prerequisites for a human to be a human. By contrast, Xuncius was much more straight forward, holding that "the human nature is the inborn attributes that cannot be acquired or learned after birth".[22] On another occasion, Xuncius referred to "nature" as "desires": "The human desires are the desires for the eyes to see all the scenes, for the ears to hear all the sounds, for the mouth to taste all the flavors, for the nose to smell all the scents and for the heart to pursue all the comforts. These are five irresistible desires in humans."[23] Based on this point, he further inferred that "the human nature is evil, and the good is only evil in disguise". Moreover, although Mencius and Shang Yang both used "water" as a metaphor, they held quite different views on human nature. Mencius stated that "the human nature must be good just as the water must flow downwards. There is no one that is not good, and no water that would not flow downwards", whereas Shang Yang stated: "Humans pursuing interests is just like water flowing downwards, with no other choices."[24] Shang Yang publicized human nature to a great extent, and developed Xuncius' theory, "It is human nature to look for food when one is hungry, to seek for comfort when one is exhausted, to long for happiness when one is suffering from hardship, and to pursue honor when one is in disgrace".[25] Guan Zhong proposed that the basic instinct of human beings was pursuing profits while avoiding harms, "It is human nature to strive for profits and elude harms".[26] The scholar Xun Yue in Han Dynasty developed a new theory different from those of Mencius and Xuncius, proposing that the human nature was either evil or good. "The evil and good of human nature go hand in hand", "It is easy to be evil, but hard to be good".[27] It was worth noticing that Sima Qian, the historian in Han Dynasty, showed historical humanistic concerns on the instinctive desires of human beings in his discussion of the issue "Huo Zhi" (货殖, engaging in business). He stated: "pursuing for wealth is human nature which comes naturally without learning", "Therefore, in the governance of business, the first-class ruler would govern by non-interference; the second-class ruler would guide people by giving them interests; the third-class ruler would educate people with edification; the fourth-class ruler would discipline and regulate people's behaviors with intervention,

[22] *Xun Zi · Xing E (The Evil Nature).*

[23] *Xun Zi · Wang Ba.*

[24] *Shang Jun Shu · Suan Di.*

[25] *Shang Jun Shu · Suan Di.*

[26] *Guan Zi · Jin Cang.*

[27] *Shen Qian.* Volume 5. *Discussion* (b).

and the worst ruler would go against his people and compete with them." In the meantime, he also justified the existence of merchants in conformity to the historical rationality, "The common merchants who do no harm to politics or people accumulate wealth through a long time by doing business, from whom scholars can also draw a lesson", "people fulfill their duties and try their best so as to get what they want".[28] This kind of thought had been kept in silence for thousands of years under the Confucian tradition of "repressing commerce", and did not prevail again among intellectuals and squires until after Mid-Ming Dynasty. Wang Chuanshan advocated "New Theory of Four Kinds of People", "Theory of Governing People", stating that a scholar should achieve economic independence first in order to uphold his dignity and personality. The famous Confucian scholar Wang Gen had once been a cook and a merchant; and many of his disciples were also merchants, potters and peasants. Wang Gen proposed that "The daily life of common people is Tao", "It is my duty to be common and get down-to-earth. Through guiding peasants, workers and merchants, I am followed by thousands of them". Under the influence of the trend of thought, Huang Zongxi presented his idea of "industry and business being of equal importance to agriculture", a big change from the traditional thought that agriculture was the foundation of a society while business only accounted for a small part.[29] Studying domestic disciplines and family rules in Qing Dynasty, there were much concern over the careers of offsprings, and doing business also stood out. "Scholars, farmers, artisans and merchants are the four basic careers for human beings to make a living. Apart from those, the right posts can be doctors and augurs. Those doing indecent jobs such as loafing around, learning to be actors or actresses, serving others as servants or runners, and participating in heresy, shall not enter into the ancestral hall".[30] "Scholars, farmers, artisans and merchants are the basic jobs, by which one can support oneself and enjoy all necessary resources as long as one learns by heart. Though being servants or runners for others can also guarantee a well-off life, such posts will only be laughed at by friends and relatives. If a person doing such jobs exists in this clan, he shall be expelled, and deprived of the right to enter into the ancestral hall, otherwise it would be disrespecting the ancestors. This shall be obeyed by everyone."[31] "Scholars, farmers, artisans and merchants, are called four basic kinds of people in China, and four basic kinds of jobs in foreign countries. All descendants in this family shall be edified and guided to do one of these jobs in order to make a living, and not to fall into a wrong path in the future."[32] "Among scholars, farmers, artisans and merchants, scholars rank first", "The four basic kinds of jobs in one's life are scholars, farmers, artisans and merchants. Do not do more than one job

[28] *Records of the Historian · Doing Business.*

[29] Huang [11].

[30] Wang Jiyou. *Family Rules of the Zhu in the District of Changgou, Piling.*

[31] In the tenth year during Guang Xu Period of Qing Dynasty (1884 A.D.). *Family Rules of the Xiong in the District of Ningxiang.*

[32] In the twelfth year during Guang Xu Period (1886 A.D.). *Family Rules of the Fang in the District of Cidong.*

at the same time, and do not loaf around. One can distinguish himself in any trade".[33] Although those sayings reflected distinctions or rankings among different jobs, doing business indeed became a decent career rather than an inferior post, which testified that business or commerce had been attached great importance to since Ming and Qing Dynasties.

When the Confucians coordinated the relationship between human desires and the evil of human nature, they adopted a perspective which was seemingly paradoxical but in fact ingenious: On the one hand, they openly acknowledged the importance and rationality of the human desires. On the other hand, they raised the moral personality to the highest level, internalizing it as the ideal of life and externalizing it as a behavioral pattern through their demonstration and explanation. The remarkable feature of this process was that the scholars who safeguarded the ruler's power set up systems such as "rites and music" and "rites and law", attempting to control people's behaviors from the inside to the outside and coordinate the contradiction between morality and desires; In addition, they took "righteousness and interests" as the criterion of different value orientations and the standard of judgment, restraining the behaviors of "gentlemen" by subjective ethical requirements, which was, "The gentlemen know what is right and justice, but the villains only focus on getting interests". Confucian scholars had a lofty sense of historical responsibility and ethical sublimity when they explored the prosperity of rites and music culture: "The purpose of establishing rites and music culture by the former ruler is not to satisfy the desires of the mouth, stomach, ears and eyes, but to educate people to distinguish between good and bad and return to the right path of being a human. It is natural for humans to be peaceful and quiet at birth, and it is also instinctive to have different feelings, likes and dislikes generated under the influence of the outside world, thus humans start to have their good and evil part. If the good and evil in humans are not controlled and chained, the human nature would be overwhelmed by the endless temptation of the outside world. At that time, they would be completely conquered by and indulged in their desires, their human part as dead as emotionless things. Then people would begin to commit crimes with thoughts of arrogance, rebellion and cheating. The strong oppress the weak; the majority bullies the minority; the wise deceive the honest, and the brave torment the timid. The sick cannot be taken care of, and the old and the young are rendered homeless, leading to the chaos of the society."[34] The design of rites and music was to prevent people from turning into things, i.e., to prevent social people from becoming biological people who were purely controlled by desires and passions. Unbounded ("uncontrolled") desires and passions would inevitably drive everyone in the world to pursue their own interests at the cost of hurting others. An important hypothesis of Confucianism here was: humans in nature longed for nothing, whereas human desires driven by external stimuli would never end. Because of this, the wise ruler and intellectuals resorted to rites and music to control human desires, prevent conflicts and maintain the stability of the society. The whole project was called "Education by Rites and Music" (礼乐教化, Li Yue Jiao

[33] *Family Rules of the Long in the District of Shouzhou.*

[34] *The Book of Rites · The Chapter of Music.*

Hua), which thrived and was developed into a system in Han Dynasty. The classic book *Baihu General Sense*, starting from the concept of cosmic order and comparing it with the order of human society, took rites and music as the criterion and symbol to balance social interest and moral justice: "What on earth are rites and music? Rites set up regulations for words and deeds, which must be followed and practiced. Music is happiness. The gentlemen derive their happiness from self-cultivation and self-improvement, while people of vile characters obtain happiness from satisfying their own desires. Why does the ruler advocate the system of rites and music? It is used to regulate people's emotions. Music is like the boundless heaven and rites resemble the earth. Everyone is born with the Yin and Yang of the heavens and the earth. Naturally, they all have in their characters the five principles of Wu Chang (五常, the code of conduct of benevolence, morality, rites, intelligence and faith). Therefore, music can purify the soul of human beings and prevent the evil of human nature; the rites can restrain human greed and guard against extravagant living. As *The Principles of Filial Piety* says: 'There is nothing better than rites to govern the people, and there is nothing better than music to change prevailing habits and customs.' Confucius says: 'There would be no disrespect or disobedience when the monarch and his subjects listen to the music together in the ancestral temple; there would be no discord or disharmony when the elders and the younger generation listen to the music together in the patriarchal clan or the village; there would be no unkindness or unfriendliness when the father and the sons do so in a family. Thus the first thing is to keynote the whole melody in making music so as to coordinate the tones. Then a variety of instruments can be used to express harmonious rhythms, forming the smooth movement of the melody. By making music like this, the previous ruler aimed to harmonize different relationships including that between the ruler and his subjects, that between the father and sons, and that among all the people.' 'Rites are the point where Yin and Yang meet as well as the convergence of various things, which are complied with to honor the heaven and earth, to expel ghosts and spirits, to sort out orders, and to standardize human morality'. 'The monarch and fathers abide by etiquettes and rites; the subjects and sons have faith and courtesies. This leads to a harmony of the heaven, the earth, and the people, which gives birth to everything.'"[35] Rites and music were regarded as the tool and means to regulate humanity and human relations, and this idea was a great creation of Confucianism that enjoyed a long-lasting historical vitality, accounting for the result that rites was internalized as the basis for civil moral self-discipline and externalized as the customary law of human interactions. In Xuncious' exploration of the origin of rites, he provided very incisive insights with the emphasis on its effectiveness: "Where do rites originate from? The answer lies in the fact that human beings are born with desires. If they cannot get what they want, they would never give up pursuing it; if they pursue it blindly without limits, there must be conflicts. The conflicts lead to disorders, which give rise to poverty. The previous ruler hated disorders, so he established the rites to divide people into different classes in order to satisfy their desires and pursuits

[35] *Baihu General Sense.* Volume 1 (b), *Rites and Music.*

to an appropriate degree."[36] The idea was inherited by Sima Qian: "Rites stemmed from humans. Humans are born with desires. If they cannot fulfill their desires, they would feel indignation. Uncontrolled indignation causes conflicts, which result in disorders. The previous ruler hated disorders, so he established the rites to satisfy people's desires and pursuits to an appropriate degree where the desires would not exceed the limits of material supply and meanwhile the material supply would not meet their desires infinitely. These two aspects constrain each other and increase simultaneously and this is the origin of rites."[37]

Although Confucians adopted different attitudes towards human nature, just as Mencius advocated it was naturally good while Xuncius held the contrary opinion, their ideas all boiled down to controlling human desires by rites to shape people's moral personality. If rites and music could not achieve the goal of education and civilization, the "law" would be resorted to as the complement. Xun Yue from Han Dynasty advocated that human nature could be either good or evil, "If the ruler allows people to abandon themselves to their feelings and desires freely and unrestrainedly, the quality of governance of the country wouldbe reduced to a low level." "Good as human nature is, it needs to be improved by education; evil as human nature is, it could be restrained by law", "Education cultivates the good of human nature, and laws remove the evil of it". Hence, the Xun believed that "A virtuous man is driven by his kindness whereas a vile person is driven by interests", "The best way to govern people is to cultivate their human nature", "Failure of education pushes common people into the vile ranks; while success of education guides them to become virtuous men".[38] Rites and law complemented each other and laid the foundation for the sociology and psychology of Confucianism.

One question worthy of reflection was that western culture analyzed the rationality of human desires in an objective and calm way, thus developing the sacred principle of individual freedom and establishing the "government by the people" to obtain their desires. This served as the guarantee of a happy and free life, with freedom as the mainstream of the contract spirit. Traditional Chinese culture also took into account the importance of human desires, but they were always suppressed by "Tian Li" (天理, heavenly principles). Therefore, a typical culture of honoring the ruler, which took the ideal model of the social elites as the ruling tool, was promoted. It attached importance to the harmony, stability and justice of the collective whole instead of the individual freedom pursued by the western culture. In short, the essence of western culture featured the accumulation of each individual's freedom and happiness so as to form the peace and stability of the whole society, but the logical starting point of Chinese culture was just the opposite, which was, the whole society had to achieve stability and security before each individual could lead a happy life. Although both China and the West considered contract as a means of realizing rights, their emphasis were quite different. Western contract spirit placed emphasis on the realization of individual rights and balanced interests among individuals and groups.

---

[36]*Xun Zi · the Chapter of Rites.*

[37]*Records of the Historian · the Chapter of Rites.*

[38]*Shen Jian.* Volume 1, *System of the Government.*

By contrast, the Chinese contract culture underlined refraining from the desires by reason, prioritizing the group's (the country's) interests at the cost of individual interests and freedom to maintain social stability. The judicial principle of the government was mainly to resolve disputes and educate people to be moral rather than to safeguard individual rights, so contractual justice was abstract "rationality" instead of concrete rights.

Rights Under Ethical Justice: Generalization of Contract

A Webster summarized three characteristics of the "traditional society": the first was worshipping antiquities, which meant a lack of new cultural capacity to adapt to the new environment; the second was that the lineage system determined all social practices and became a major tool to implement political, economic and legal control; the third was the tendency to view the world with fatalistic eyes full of emotional colors.[39] There have been many controversies in the academic circle as to whether or not the Chinese society ever achieved or has achieved modernization. We would use these as references and solve the following questions in this section to examine whether traditional Chinese contracts transformed from traditional ones to modern ones as well as the internal and external forces in the process of transformation.

Firstly, the existing forms of contractual rights: from groups to individuals.

Mr. Zhang Jinfan believed that the most important part of the statutory civil law in Chinese history was the innumerable private contracts.[40] American scholar Bao Heng, after studying the development history of the Chinese contracts, thought that contracts played a major role in adjusting social relations, commercial affairs, laws and other relationships.[41] It should be said that his argument was based on a large number of historical records rather than groundless assumptions. However, if we study those contract documents from another perspective, we are able to capture some other ideas: first, the existence of such a huge amount of contracts has proved that the Chinese traditional society paid full attention to contractual rights, and the contract itself acted as a tool for the realization of rights; second, the appearance of contractual rights can date back to Western Zhou Dynasty. After the implementation of the taxation system (initial farm tax on land per-Mu) in the Lu State, contractual legal acts such as purchase and sale, lease, and guarantee became more developed than before with an increasing degree of land privatization. Over the course of Tang, Song, Yuan, Ming, and Qing Dynasties, China's legal system of contract took shape and was further improved. This external legal system indicated the growth of contractual rights per se. Third, although contractual rights in China lacked the foundation of the

[39]Webster [12].

[40]Zhang [13].

[41]Bao Heng. Comparative Research on Legal History of Chinese Contract Law, Roman Law, Unified Law and Jewish Law. Cited from *Tradition and Modernization of Chinese Law*. Edited by Zhang Jinfan. 1996. China Democracy and Law Publishing House.

western social contract theory, it did not mean contractual rights per se was impeded or deterred. The existence of contracts was the clear evidence of the existence of contractual rights, and the rationale of the existence of contracts, as in the western contract law theory, was the autonomy of will and the pursuit of interests by the contracting parties.

On the diachronic level, we believe that there was a clear clue in the existing forms of contractual rights in China, which was, individual rights were liberated from group rights in persistent pursuit of the interests and rights of the contracting parties under the protection of the relevant guarantee clauses and breach clauses.

As mentioned earlier, traditional contracts were derived from the system and philosophy of governmental contracts, therefore private contracts focused more on the rights and obligations agreed upon by both parties while stressing the validity of contracts per se, so as to ensure the smooth operation and functions of civil and commercial activities. It could be said that the establishment of a contract, being the materialized state and the evidence of human desires, was to pursue the realization of rights. Desires led to the birth of contracts while contracts embodied desires; these two were always supplementary and interconnected to each other. However, in terms of the system of traditional Chinese society, the interests of groups were always superior to those of individuals, which inevitably resulted in the mutual elimination and mutual recognition of the contract values between the government and the common people, and between the groups and the individuals.

The interests of groups in traditional Chinese society were mainly manifested in the following aspects: the interests of the public power, i.e., the interests of the rulers represented by the monarchy; the public interests of the families, i.e., the family interests represented by clan rights; and the public interests of certain social classes, i.e., the interests of various industries centered on their rights and the special interests centered on the rights of certain social classes such as squires. The above-mentioned three categories constituted different interest groups including monarchy, clan power, gentry power, village autonomy, and industry power, which limited individual rights. For example, the guild, as a kind of "social force created by the people", recognized the equal value of each member's interests and feelings, and treated them as common interests and feelings to be safeguarded. The Japanese sinologist Tachibana Shiraki compared the family spirit with the guild's spiritual foundation.[42] The family was built on the basis of loving kindness of the seniors and filial piety of the youth, which meant the moral ethics constituted the core of the family system; whereas the spiritual pillar of the guild was the moral consciousness of mutual aid. It should be said that the guild could promote the generation of individualism, and this was quite obvious in the development history of western European businessmen. However, it was deflected in China: All members of the guild were subjected to the absolute authority of the guild, submitting themselves to the rules and control of the guild at the expense of personal will and rights. Seriously sorting out the various systems of the guild, we could find that the basic spirit of the guild was to protect

---

[42][Japan] Tachibana [14]. Cited from Kishimoto Mio. *"Civil Society Theory" and China.* As in Wang and Liang [15].

individual interests on the premise that the group interests were not infringed upon. In other words, the individual interests of the guild members must not precede or prevail over the interests of the group, otherwise they would be punished by the guild. Taking as an example the Suzhou Handicraft Guild System in Early Qing Dynasty, all workshops must comply with the rules and regulations of the guild, and their locations and amount were strictly limited, with the price and quality of their products under regulations as well. "Cheating has to be stopped for the prosperity of the business. Conducts such as counterfeiting products with low quality, copycatting others' brand names, or cheating were all damaging others' reputation and disturbing the business. Once they are found out, they must be punished accordingly." In addition, the number of recruits and employees was also limited in many industries. For instance, the guild regulations in the wax and paper industry were that "recruiting an apprentice every six years". Once, the manager of a gold foil workshop violated the rules. He was then publicly criticized and severely penalized.[43] In general, the existence of such disciplines mostly served the justifiable purposes of preventing competition, keeping technological secrets, and safeguarding the common interests of the industry.[44] However, it was indeed a historical regret in that the regulations blocked the road of free competition at the expense of individual interests and will. Under careful consideration, it was not difficult to find out that the guild limits were followed due to the influence of the traditional family life. Characterized by obedience and sacrifice, the guild tried to maintain the relations among different classes in it by the patriarchal system to achieve the even distribution of benefits. It was the infiltration of this identity management mode based on family blood ties into the guild systems and the egalitarian principle of distributing interests that held together the authority and autocracy of the guilds, leading to the suppression of individual interests.

The same mechanism and its historical consequences were more evident in the family life. The esteemed high status brought by blood ties enabled the elders in a family to control all aspects of the juniors including their bodies and property, making it difficult for the humble juniors to independently exercise their civil rights and pursue their individual interests. The common interests of the whole family clan always prevailed over the benefits of an individual group and the individual interests of family members. The cultivation of the moral consciousness of "selflessness" and the strict family rules controlled an individual's words and deeds from inside to outside, while the even distribution of existing and available interests objectively promoted the original democratic mechanism of public ownership and the management mode of seniors controlling wealth. By comparing the different values in Chinese and western cultures, Hiroaki Terada believed that the west, with individuals as the starting point, regarded protecting the legitimate interests of each individual as the purpose of order maintenance, whereas traditional Chinese culture, on the basis of the coexistence of all individuals, advocated maintaining harmony or

---

[43] *The Selected Works of Stele Inscriptions since Ming and Qing Dynasties in Jiangsu Province*. 1959. Edited by Jiangsu Museum. SDX Joint Publishing Company, pp. 104, 160.

[44] Kong [16].

reconciling human relationships through mutual consent. Since the "Confucianism popularization" in late Ming Dynasty, local townships and villages incessantly indoctrinated such ideas through preaching and reading by the squires and governments to suppress and punish the growing selfish desires of individuals. Terada held this was the historical instinctive reaction to individual development by the national power and intellectuals,[45] which, I believe, is true.

In the traditional Chinese society where the interests of groups were prioritized, one of the major features of the rights created by contract was that they were mainly individual rights. If things like governmental and local regulations, guild regulations, and family rules were the concentrated expression of group interests, then the emergence of contracts was the tool and means to realize individual rights. More than two thousand years of civilization proved that the Chinese people were in persistent pursuit of individual rights without compromises. Human desires and passions (the desires for wealth and glory) still dominated the social structure and economic forms. To put it simply, we could examine the evolution of contractual rights from collective interests to individual interests from the following three aspects. First, the level of privatization. Privatization laid the material and economic foundation for contractual rights, whose existing forms and final realization were directly determined by the level of privatization. Taking land as an example, Mr. Fu Zhufu's study showed that the land privatization system was already established in the Warring States Period when land became a commodity to be integrated with monetary assets. Until Tang Dynasty, land privatization directly led to the purchase and sale of private land, and thanks to the policy of land equalization, land was allowed to be transferred among common people.[46] Some scholars studied Dunhuang household registration book and found that a large amount of private land existed besides the family-owned land and allocated land. The government's attitude towards the private ownership of land as well as its purchase and sale in Tang Dynasty changed from control to non-interference, and finally reaching the goal of public sale.[47] The merger of land before Mid-Tang Dynasty was mainly that of land tenure right and the right to use, which were private rights. The ownership still belonged to the state, and the taxation system was a combination of rent and levies. The land privatization system began to take shape after Mid-Tang Dynasty when the policy of land equalization disintegrated and a new contract system of land lease with complete contents and clearly-defined rights and obligations became widely prevalent. The free sale and merger of land generated a large-scale manorial economy in Tang Dynasty, which in turn promoted the development of the commodity economy and the market as well, enabling the manorial economy to mainly rely on the market instead of simple self-sufficiency.[48] Song Dynasty followed the practice of Tang Dynasty, "No restraint on mergers and

---

[45][Japan] Hiroaki [17].

[46]Zhao [18].

[47]Yang [19].

[48]Tang [20].

acquisitions",[49] "Non-interference in land affairs",[50] and the land "can be bought and sold freely by the people, and the government would help to administer their deeds and collect revenues from them".[51] In Southern Song Dynasty, Li Chunnian proposed and implemented "Jing Jie Fa (经界法)"*, registering the production of land and the number of households to base tax revenues and corvee on property rights. On the surface it aimed to suppress mergers and acquisitions, but in reality, it did unify and consolidated the property taxes, and indeed led to the improvement and perfection of the transactions of land property rights as well as the system of tax revenues in the transfer formalities.[52] Second, the free will of both parties to the contract. Ownership only dealt with the issue of static security of the property, but optimizing the accumulation of property interests still depended on the transfer of property, that was, the owner of the property could dispose it out of free will within the scope of laws or customary law. Meanwhile, the other party must also determine out of free will whether or not to enter the contractual relationship with the owner. Taking the employment contract as an example, Mr. Zhao Gang believed that there had been a labor market in China since Warring States Period, where the employers and employees simply depended on market trading relationship instead of feudal personal attachment.[53] Another example was the tenancy agreement. Prior to Tang and Song Dynasties, a tenant farmer was not able to end the tenancy unless he or she obtained the permission certificate from the land owner. The laws of Song Dynasty expressly prohibited such personal attachment conditions: "The tenant can henceforth leave the place and end the tenancy without the permission certificate as long as he or she discusses the matter with the land owner after the harvest time. The two parties can both get what they need."[54] This kind of provision not only guaranteed the same statuses of tenant farmers and landowners in the legal sense, but more importantly provided the legislative basis and judicial criteria for their exercise of free will and pursuit of legitimate interests. Some aspects should be noted in the regulation of private contractual relations in the first year of Kai Xi Period (1205 A.D.) during the reign of Emperor Zhao Kuo. To be specific, landlords must not force the tenants' family members to serve; pawnees must not force pawners to be tenant farmers; loans should be returned purely in accordance with the written contracts, and creditors must not force debtors to serve as tenant farmers (i.e. serving to repay the debt); in case of the tenant's death, the marriage of his wife and daughter could only be decided on their own independent of the land owner's interference.[55] Till

[49] *History of Song Dynasty*. Volume 17. *Shi Huo (On National Economy)* 1.

[50] *Hui Zhu Lu (Record of Discussions) · Yu Yu.*

[51] *Works of Ye Shi · Works of Shui Xin*. Volume 2. *Jin Juan · Min Shi (Civil Matters)* 1.

[52] Gong and Yao [21].

[53] Zhao [22].

[54] *The Compilation of Song Dynasty · National Economy.*

*Translator's annotation: Jing Jie Fa (经界法) refers to the official measures in Southern Song Dynasty to check and verify the land tenure and land use of every village in order to determine the tax imposed on the grains grown on each Mu of land.

[55] Zhang [23].

Qing Dynasty, the contracts of employment and tenancy paid more attention to the equality of the legal statuses of both parties, ensuring their autonomy in civil contract relations. Employers and employees then enjoyed equal employment relationships, and employees were mostly paid by time and workload in the form of money wages. "Most private textile workshops in Suzhou employ workers to weave. The workshop owner pays for the operation, and the workers get paid by their work... The wages are calculated and decided according to their workload, professional skills and the quality of the products."[56] The tenancy relationship was more clear: the tenants and landowners "eat at the same table and treat each other as equals. There is no ordering about and no masters or servants".[57] This process of transformation from serfdom to tenancy system was directly reflected in contracts such as the following example of tenancy contracts entitled *Seng Faying's Tenancy Contract of the Vegetable Garden in the Third Year of Da Li Period during the Reign of Emperor Li Yu in Tang Dynasty* (768 A.D.)[58]:

> On October 24th in the Third Year of Da Li Period during the Reign of Emperor Li Yu, Seng Faying took up a three-year lease on the above-mentioned garden. The annual rent would be two Shi ("石") and five Dou ("斗")** of wheat for per Mu (a unit of area) of land that grows wheat; and two Shi of millet for per Mu of land that grows millet. When the crops grow ripe, Ying must deliver the specified volume of wheat and millet as the rent. The land tax should be paid by the tenant. In addition, the tenant should also deliver a certain amount of vegetables to the owner of the garden within the agreed time limit. In case of delay, clothing, sundries or others would be taken to make up for the deficiency of the volume. If the garden is cultivated well and rent is paid duly, the tenant and his disciples should not end or change the three-year lease...This contract is in duplicate and each party keeps one copy. This agreement is reached in harmony, marking by the fingerprints of the two parties.
>
> (The following is omitted.)

This contract contained a very impressively detailed and comprehensive division of the rights and obligations between the landowner and the tenant farmer, from which it was difficult to find clues of personal attachment, indicating that the land owner and the tenant in a tenancy contract in Tang Dynasty put emphasis on their rights and obligations, and that the tenant's personal attachment to the land owner no longer existed. Mr. Fu Yiling believed that the tenancy relationship based on the contract system first appeared in Song and Yuan Dynasties and prevailed after Mid-Ming Dynasty,[59] which, in my humble opinion, was against the historical facts. According to the materials I have, the tenancy relationship started to evolve from serfdom to contractualization as far back as the Three Kingdoms Period. For instance, clear specifications of the rights and obligations of the two parties were seen in a tenancy agreement unearthed in Zou Ma Lou of Changsha City, Hunan province in 1996, and there was no personal bondage:

---

[56]See footnote 43, p. 6.

[57]*Law Code of Qing Dynasty*. Volume 28. *Criminal Law · Fights*.

[58]*The Unearthed Documents in Turpan*. Volume 10. Wenwu Publishing House, pp. 292–293.

[59]Fu [24].

**Translator's annotation: Shi (石) and Dou (斗) were both units of volume in ancient China. One decaliter equaled one Dou, and ten Dou equaled one Shi.

> Huang Jun from Han Qiu rented 21 Mu of land for two years, among which 15 Mu are dry farmland and six Mu are fertile land. The rent would be collected from the six Mu of fertile land. Two Chi ("尺", a unit of length) of cloth for each Mu and thus in total one Zhang ("丈", a unit of length. One Zhang equals ten Chi) and two Chi of cloth as well as seven Hu ("斛", a unit of volume) and two Dou of grains are to be paid. The grains should be delivered to the officials of the granaries Zhang Man and Zhou Dong on December 2nd of the fifth year. No money would be paid for the dry farmland whereas eighty should be paid for each Mu of the fertile land, thus totaling 480 for the six Mu, which should be delivered to the official Pan Shun on November 10th of the fifth year.[60]

Another phenomenon could also illustrate the growth of the tenant's contractual rights in the tenancy contract relationship. Permanent tenancy***, as an important part of China's private contract system, greatly promoted the development of rural economy and gradually brought real estate to the market. Some scholars believed that the permanent tenancy was a manifestation of the will of tenant farmers and also a lever for the sustained development of the farming economy in Jiangnan regions.[61] And the reason why the permanent tenancy dominated Jiangnan regions for hundreds of years and continued to thrive and prosper was that the tenants had great autonomy and were able to use their land-use rights to compete with the owners' land ownership. Two characteristics featured permanent tenancy: the land owners must not arbitrarily withdraw the lease; the tenant farmers enjoyed the rights to inherit, lease, pawn or sell their tenancy rights, and the land owners had no right to intervene.[62] In addition, the tenants had the autonomy to operate and farm the land without the owners' intervention. At the same time, in case the owners would sell the property, the tenants enjoyed the pre-emption right. The land owners' rights mainly lay in the management of the property and the collection of rent.[63]

Third, the government's approval of contractual rights. It could be seen from historical materials that from Zhou Dynasty to Qing Dynasty, the contractual rights were approved and protected according to the contracts as long as they would not violate the law and social public welfare or hinder private transaction practices. Among them, the fatal threat to contractual rights was the social clan power embodied in the pre-emption right of kinship, and the bans and rules made by various guilds, whose interests were favored by the state public power as a way to maintain social stability. Moreover, the state tended to make judgments by an abstract criterion of "rationality" or directly entrusted the judging priority to the social organizations such as families, guilds and associations. But generally speaking, contractual rights, as the private rights of a civil individual, were basically approved by the state. Moral exhortation and the mediation of clans and guilds were always aimed to balance the

[60] Hu and Song [25].

[61] Li [26].

[62] Liu [27].

[63] For relevant contract documents refer to Yang Guozhen's *Researches on Land Contracts in Ming and Qing Dynasties*. 1988. People's Publishing House.

***Translator's annotation: Permanent tenancy (永佃制) refers to the tenancy system started in Song Dynasty in which the tenant enjoyed long-term farming rights and the right to dispose of the farming rights under the condition that he or she paid the rent according to the agreement with the owner.

interests of both parties. Mr. Huang Jingjia from Taiwan held that after Shen Jiaben was appointed the Minister of Law Amendment in Qing Dynasty, he pioneered the modernization of legal system in China, completing the transformation of the Chinese legal system from the feudal identity ethics to the civil legal system based on continental legal systems. The American legal sociologist Rosco Pound claimed that the *Civil Code of the Republic of China* was one of the most perfect Codes of the contemporary era in that it respected the rights of individuals and abolished the disparities between the privileged and the underprivileged.[64]

Secondly, the realization of contractual rights: private power—public power.

The existing forms of contractual rights have been discussed as above, but how to guarantee the complete realization of them is another important question in exploring the development of contractual rights in ancient times. In general, the remedies of ancient Chinese contractual rights were presented as two kinds of forces, i.e., the overlap and the parallel coexistence of private power and public power.

Fulfillment of contractual obligations in traditional society was not only a commitment to the contract and the recognition of its validity, but also was promoted to a high level of morality. The person who followed the contract was regarded as a man of virtue and the person who breached it as one of "disloyalty and betrayal", who would live under great psychological pressure in a difficult predicament due to the condemnation by public opinions of traditional morality. A person of honest and righteous characters would receive respect from the society and have great potentials because he or she would not only be morally charismatic but also be able to obtain more social interests and even acquire some certain social powers, thus benefiting from the honest personality in the senses of morality, materials and social authority. To put it simply, compliance with contract was considered as a moral obligation and externalized as a social obligation by the traditional Chinese society, which was acknowledged and upheld by laws and customary law.

If desires were the humanity basis through which contracts were created and developed, then compliance constituted the moral foundation of contracts. Hobbes regarded the compliance with contracts as justice and breach as injustice. Ancient Chinese regarded compliance as a symbol of high morality that distinguished a man of virtues from a man of vileness. It was worth noting that the wording of men of virtues and men of vileness in China originally fell into the political and cultural categories that evaluated social elites in terms of their social statuses and cultural accomplishments, and later developed into the criterion and principle to measure and distinguish people's moral characters. At this point, the Confucian contract ethics showed a rich moral heritage that could be elaborated from both internal thinking and external rituals. As regards internal thinking, compliance as a kind of moral obligation most likely stemmed from traditional Confucian natural law. Confucianism believed that causalities inevitably existed between the Heaven and Earth, and Ying and Yang, whose internal relations were inextricably linked. It was a natural law for people to get old and sick, and it was the moral reciprocity for offsprings to be filial to their parents

[64] Huang Jingjia. *The Modernization of China's Legal System and the Development of Taiwan since the Turn of this Century.* See footnote 41.

after being brought up by them with love and care. The cosmic order of harmony between human and nature as well as the humane ethical order of seniority were all maintained by "rites", the origins of which were already explained in the previous chapter, and the internal root of which indeed depended on reciprocal relations. The underlying reason for the seniors to get respectable authority and social authority was that they had devoted both materials and spiritual labor to the education and growth of the juniors. The premise of this ideal humanity theory was that every parent loved his or her children. At the same time, each individual would inevitably become a new "respectable senior" with the growth of age and the change of social status, gaining the power to control the family or society and getting the social benefits derived from the power and prestige. In short, from the diachronic perspective, every humble junior would eventually become a respectable senior in face of equal opportunities on condition that he or she was obedient and respectful to the senior in the first place. From the synchronic perspective, every obligation of obedience was accompanied with some certain rights; and every kind of control authority was associated with some certain responsibilities and obligations. This theory of reciprocity constituted the moral and ethical foundation of ancient Chinese contracts. As for external rituals, "the courtesy of reciprocity" was not only a concept, but a kind of reciprocal ritual as well. "People should show goodwill to others, who should also return the favor kindly. Failure to do so goes against the ritual".[65] Apart from being an economic and cultural ritual, the mutual aid of giving and receiving also embodied respect for the interests and personality of others.

When it came to the realization of the contractual rights, the laws and customary law would give the other party the right to enforce specific performance and compensate for the loss if one contracting party breached the contract, so as to urge both parties to comply with the contract and punish those lacking integrity. The large number of breach clauses and guaranty clauses we read in the contracts of Tang Dynasty actually reflected a kind of private self-remedy of contractual rights, which would be considered as "perfectly justified" as long as it did not violate the basic principles of national laws and stayed within the range of customary laws. On many occasions, the government would often punish the breaching party both physically and financially as a warning to others if it was brought to court.

Taking into account the forms of realizing contractual rights in ancient China, we examined the two remedies of private power and public power on the same plane, from which several distinctive ways to resolve or mediate traditional contract disputes were revealed. First, exhortation and negotiation. This was a typical form of settling contract disputes. The exhorter should not be a family member or relative of the involved parties, who would most likely be one of the two types: (A) a respectable senior in the family clan, or one of the leaders in various industries and civil organizations; (B) a government official. As for the former, "harmony is highly valued" was the gist of the exhortation, encouraging the parties involved to make mutual concessions in order to achieve reciprocity and avoid harm, loss of money and disorders. When the townsmen associations (an association of people from the same

[65] *The Book of Rites · Song of Rites.*

hometown) were dealing with civil disputes especially contract ones, they always stressed the tenet "harmony brings wealth". Since Ming and Qing Dynasties, various townsmen associations had been established across the country, sustaining the trade exchanges in the social economy.

The Townsmen Association of Jiangsu Province in Qing Dynasty illuminated the significant link between the "currency (泉贝, quan bei)" and the "human relations (人情, ren qing)": "The circulation of currency interacts with human relations. It is the unchangeable truth that the harmony and peace of human relations brings wealth."[66] The townsmen associations of Qing Dynasty were "important factions in the cities, towns and rural areas"[67] with considerable influence. The leader in charge of an association was called "Xiang Yue (乡约)" by Sichuan people, "Ke Chang (客长)" by the people of Guangxi, Guangdong and Fujian provinces, and "Hui Dao (会道)" by people of some other places. Such leaders served as the "key connection of the government and the citizens", and "people who are not fair and honest cannot be elected".[68] The associations were mostly engaged in trade. In the event of disputes, the internal ones would be resolved through mediation in the assembly presiding by Ke Chang or an appointed person by him while the external ones would be settled in the presence of all the relevant associations, parties, and observers.[69] What was intriguing was that the mediation principles of government officials were neither about abstract unjust ideas nor interest distribution. Rather, they put more emphasis on affecting people with morality and virtues, of which humane ethics were the important connotations. The relatives' fight over wealth is cited here as an example. Han Yanshou, the chief of Dongjun Prefecture in Han Dynasty, once dealt with a dispute over farmland among brothers in a family. He held that "filing a lawsuit against blood relatives" corrupted public morals and blamed himself for not educating the people well, thus "he refused to deal with the work on the excuse of illness, entered a small room, lay down, and reflected on his faults with the door closed"; "The brothers were blamed and reprimanded by their relatives and became deeply remorseful. They shaved off their hair, took off their coats to apologize for the offence sincerely and promised never to dispute with each other again".[70] In Eastern Han Dynasty when Xu Qian served as the prefecture chief, some brothers brought lawsuits over property against each other. Xu said with guilt: "I took on the heavy responsibilities of the state but failed to educate the people well. I should take all the blame." Then he asked the emissary to submit a written statement of the case to the higher authority. "The brothers were moved and deeply repented, asking for punishments. On account of this incident, more than a thousand people in this prefecture who did not support their own parents and fought with their brothers

[66]*The Selected Works of Stele Inscriptions since Ming and Qing Dynasties in Jiangsu Province.* 1959. Edited by Jiangsu Museum. SDX Joint Publishing Company, p. 351.

[67]*The Local Records of Fushun County during the Reign of Emperor Qian Long.* Volume 4. *Temples and Altars.*

[68]*The Local Records of Qianwei County in the Republic of China · Residents.*

[69]Lan [28].

[70]*Book of Han.* Volume 76. *The Biography of Zhao Yanshou.*

came back to provide for their family members".[71] Rare as they are in the modern era, such ways of deciding a case adopted by officials were rather popular in traditional Chinese society. In Later Tang Dynasty of the Five Dynasties, someone in Jiu Men of He Dong Region "wanted to sell the land but failed to reach an agreement on the price with his elder brother who lived in the distance (the relatives had the pre-emption right to buy the land), so he intended to sell it to others. The buyer requested the elder brother to sign the contract and was refused firmly. Therefore, he filed a lawsuit to the sheriff, who brought both of the brothers to court on grounds of their immoralities and injustice". Shi Jingtang, who just took office then as the provincial governor of He Dong, delivered a very special judgment: "I feel quite ashamed that their immoral behaviors resulted from my lack and negligence of educating the local people upon my new arrival. If we assess the case with the most fundamental reason, it was the right thing to do for the elder brother to make good use of the fertile land while the younger brother sold it for a fair price; otherwise it would be wrong. Overall, the elder brother should be whipped heavily for he was rather immoral and unjust, and the disputed farmland should be sold on the market to the highest bidder."[72] The sheriff followed the practice of traditional moral education and transferred the two brothers to the governor because of the immoralities and injustice on both parties. Although Shi Jingtang talked about education and morality, he still stressed "the most fundamental reason", thus settling this contract dispute in an appropriate fashion. Second, deciding punishments in public. Contract disputes between family members must be reported to the branch head of the clan, and the patriarch of the family would hear the case in a public family gathering in the ancestral hall to distinguish right from wrong. This point was already explained in detail before. Third, reporting to the officials for judgement of the case. Under the influence of the traditional Confucian ideas of moral justice and interests, moral justice was put in a much more important place than interests in resolving private contract disputes, this being the basic principle of the Confucian natural law and the norm of settling disputes for the government. However, as the contract itself involved the rights and even the living situations of both parties, however "trivial" they were in the eyes of the government and families, balancing the parties' interests and determining right and wrong were taken very seriously. The first two cases cited in the preceding text proved to be the political achievements by the Confucian rulers who impacted people with morality, nevertheless had little influence on civil disputes. Shi Jingtang's judgment, however, was inherited and developed by the governments after Song Dynasty. As mentioned earlier, when it came to contract disputes such as family marriage, land, and debt, the government would delegate the power to the family clans, letting them settle the disputes on their own. If the cases were too difficult to be dealt with, or were resolved in an unjust way, then they could be reported to the officials for a proper judgment to ensure the legitimate interests of the contracting parties.

Two kinds of phenomena in "deciding punishments in public" and "reporting to the officials for judgement of the case" deserved further study: One was the delicate

[71] *Book of Later Han.* Volume 106. *The Biographies of Righteous Officials.*

[72] *Old History of the Five Dynasties · Book of Jin · The Biography of the Emperor Liu Bang.*

combination of family laws and national laws; the other was that both the government and the common people tended to "pacify" and "suppress" litigations as a way to maintain social stability. As for the former, the fundamental reason for the long-lasting existence of Chinese feudal society was that family-centeredness always took precedence and became the basic operating force of the society, to which the national security and order were closely tied.

Therefore, the rulers of all dynasties attached great importance to maintaining family laws so as to uphold national laws, which in turn would consolidate and better family laws. This unification of families and the state completed the integration of their interests and built a solid mechanism of social control. In the ninth year of Xian Feng Period of Qing Dynasty (1859 A.D.), *Family Rules of the Family You in Xiangyin County* was submitted to the government for approval after its formulation. The wording of these rules was very appropriate both in sense and sensibility:

> We submit this official document of Family Rules stipulating rewards and punishments to the government for approval in hope of establishing domestic disciplines and resolving disputes. We believe that it would be of assistance to the laws and regulations of our state as people abide by the teachings of their ancestors and family rules…Our family clan is not a large one with more than one thousand family members in total, who are scattered in places over one hundred Li (a unit of length, equaling approximately 1/2 kilometer) away from the county government. Fathers and elder brothers educate their sons and younger brothers by books, and the youngsters conform to the rules and regulations. For young people who live in a place where both virtuous and ignorant people and others gather, their temperament may be changed. Meanwhile, when they live far apart from each other, it is difficult to alter their personal perceptions. As the old saying goes, it is important to destroy evils before they become real menaces. That's why the document of family rules is submitted to the government for approval, and it would be placed in the ancestral temple to warn all the family members not to commit wrongdoings, so that they must keep to the family rules as well as the national laws in awe. First offenders will be punished openly in the clan hall and ones committing serious crimes will be sent to the county bureau to get severe penalties. It is hoped that gentlemen comply with laws and regulations in reverence and support the upright ruling of the government, while the ordinary people also follow the rules and lead a happy and peaceful life. Therefore, the document is submitted for consideration.

The approval document by the county magistrate delivered more profound meaning: "I have read through all the 16 clauses of your *Family Rules*. They are extremely thorough and complete. Thus they are permitted to be publicized in the county and notify the citizens of regulations. I do have great expectations that all the juniors of the clan will promote courtesies and keep away from arrogance and abuse." In the second year of Xuan Tong Period in Qing Dynasty (1910 A.D.), *The Clan Rules of the Family Gong in Shangxiang County* stated clearly at the outset that: "Our country's preparation for making constitution requires everyone's ability of self-rule as qualified citizens, and the best way to cultivate their ability of self-rule is to start in the families and clans. If a family leads a stable and peaceful life, the clan will also enjoy stability and harmony, and so will the whole country." The specific rules and regulations clarified the functional order of the clan powers: "Any complaints shall be first reported to the head of the branch for a reliable investigation and a peaceful resolution. If the dispute is not settled, it is allowed to judge the case for a second time after the parties pay four strings and eight hundred coppers in total.

Then they will be summoned to the ancestral hall for the decision of the case…If either of the parties does not accept the result, they can appeal again to the superior level for further investigation." This *Clan Rules* won much praise after its submission to the county government. The county magistrate approved it and wrote: "It is reported that these eighteen clan rules were formulated to regulate the clan members. They are quite complete and comprehensive, by which the clan members shall abide. Anyone who does not obey the clan rules will be reported immediately to the senior and the case will then be kept on file for reference." It seemed to be of little significance that these two copies of family rules got the approval of the government. However, they indicated the government's approval and encouragement of family autonomy and showed the sequence and procedures in settling civil disputes.

"Pacifying" or "suppressing" litigations were always regarded as the obvious evidence of strangling contractual rights, but if we study this kind of phenomenon carefully, we could also manage to find out the rationality in it. "Pacifying" or "suppressing" litigation was the priority strategy for family autonomy and government rule, aiming to maintain social stability and enlighten people with Confucian ethics in order to achieve mutual reciprocity and save social costs as well. "Pacifying or suppressing litigations were demonstrated in two kinds of forms. The first is the strict prohibition of litigations in a family or clan because they see litigations as serious troubles. The family precepts made by Gao Shouxiang in Yuan Dynasty included the rule of "no disputes and litigations" that went like this: "It is common that occasional rifts occur in the community, which shall be reported to the clan-chief for impartial judgment right away. Do not make things worse and initiate litigations with increasing rancor. Any person who instigates others to institute legal proceedings is the most despicable villain. The violators shall be subjected to severe punishment."[73] The Clan Zhu in late Yuan Dynasty and early Ming Dynasty strictly forbade litigations: "People mostly file legal cases to make claims and requests. Since my grandfather's generation, our family has never been involved in any lawsuits according to the records of the government. This is why my big family is treated favorably by the county government. Only those who have no other alternatives but to sue are allowed to consult with the whole clan members for doing so. If it is possible, tolerance should be the best way."[74] Xu Zichu drafted *Rules and Regulations of the Clan Xu* in Ming Dynasty, advocating a prohibition on lawsuits: "Litigations should be the last resort just like military operations. In a morally degenerate social atmosphere with increasing accusations, most people are inclined to litigate aggressively in order to wipe out their disgrace. However, what they do not know is that when they are engaged in the court debate, they have to go through insulting words or even be framed by imaginary charges; when they kneel down in court, they demonstrated the gestures of baseness and ignobility. What is worse, those litigants could even be humiliated and threatened by the petty officials who would take advantage of the positions and ask for money while they wait on tenterhooks without good sleep. What they thought as wiping out their disgrace would merely bring more disgrace. Any one

[73]*Family Precepts of the Clan Gao in Pangu County.*

[74]*Family Rules of the Clan Zhu and Clan Feng in Baizhu.*

in my clan who violates the rules, acts litigiously, or instigate others to help people of other clans to frame his own clansman as revenge will be blamed and penalized publicly in the presence of all clan members so that litigations can be prevented. Those who are forced to sue would be able to get help and counsel from the whole clan. If things do not go intolerably bad, then tolerance should be the best way. No one shall break rules and bring disgrace on the clan by virtue of power and wealth".[75] The prohibitive regulations of the clan set by Zhang Wanda in Qing Dynasty directly concerned some certain contractual rights: "In most cases, people file a lawsuit to the government on a sudden impulse of indignation for various disputes in the clan such as those over the land sale, the neighboring land property, water resources, and even over trivial matters or just rude behaviors out of insobriety. Some of them even went bankrupt for doing so. Henceforth, the cases have to be decided openly by discussion of the whole clan. Litigations are allowed only in case of dissatisfaction with the negotiated resolution." "Some ignorant villains in the clan often instigate others to litigate or testify for wrongdoings, making mischief among people. Some, being rude and unreasonable, act shamelessly on the pretext of their seniority or their parents' old age, or claim for compensation for the debt that has already been paid off or the real estate that has already been sold. These kinds of misconduct shall be punished severely by the entire clan."[76] The four cases mentioned above aimed to illustrate that litigations were strictly prohibited in folk customary law, especially in the customary law of families and clans. The government, on the other hand, suppressed civil litigations especially contractual disputes in some other ways: First, to suspend the case. The two instances cited above including the one by Han Yanshou in Han Dynasty were cases in point. Second, to influence people with morality. People were exhorted to withdraw the lawsuit for the sake of customs and education. Third, to severely punish the overly litigious people and Song Shi (讼师, law practitioners, similar to lawyers or litigators of today). However, civil "disputes over covenants of land sale are reported every day".[77] The explicit or implicit inhibition of lawsuits by the government proved the large amount of contract disputes from the negative side. Moreover, the local customs and practices of Jiang Nan Region (south of the Yangtze River) in Ming and Qing Dynasties, further confirmed the broad scope and profound influence of contractual rights disputes in the society from the positive side, showing common people's increasing attention paid to individual rights in private contracts. Consciousness of contractual rights awakened and grew in Ming and Qing Dynasties, and were finally recognized by the national statute law and received remedies and protection of the public power. In Qing Dynasty, Mi Chaqing of the Songjiang Prefecture inspected "the social environment of litigiousness" in Shanghai and said: "Both senior citizens and little children live by litigations. The peasants in the countryside have gone so far as to become eloquent, let alone those literate ones who juggle with words…They pour into the market to buy paper to write pleadings, on account of which the paper in the prefecture have become more expensive. A shop can even earn

---

[75] *Rules and Regulations of the Clan Xu in Yuyao County, Jiangnan Region.*

[76] *The Prohibitive Regulations of the Clan Zhang inYongxing.*

[77] *The Compilation of Song Dynasty· National Economy.* Volume 3–18.

up to 30 gold coins a day…Nowadays, ninety percent of the people in the downtown area and eighty percent of the peasants in the countryside have been engaged in lawsuits."[78] Mi's words were a little exaggerated, but indeed reflected the growing trend of litigation in Shanghai. People from Wu (吴, Regions including Jiangsu, Anhui and Zhejiang provinces in eastern China) were rather famous in history for their litigiousness. "People in my county are the most litigious ones. Even peasants in remote villages are capable of readily drafting complaints with their quick wit."[79] "Wu people are particularly good at litigating…The best Song Shi are called "Zhuang Yuan" (状元, the masters), while the worst ones are termed "Da Mai" (大麦, the mediocrities)…(Song Shi) are mostly children of the intellectuals or the privileged."[80] The legal profession as Song Shi emerged in Song Dynasty,[81] and flourished in Ming and Qing Dynasties. "People of Fujian province are generally litigious, especially those in Zhangzhou and Quanzhou", and "Song Shi hive in the provincial capital. They live by inciting people to lodge complaints and helping to initiate and respond to litigations. So many people from different places flood to Song Shi for help that they almost cannot take a day off".[82] "Litigations are very prevalent in the southern part of the country, so much so that there must be Song Shi wielding their pens even in the remote mountainous regions. However, there are so many complainants keeping flooding in like great roaring rivers that litigations would never end just as one can never exhaust a river by scooping out its water."[83] The historical records cited above is very thought-provoking: Why were there so many lawsuits in Jiangnan regions (regions south of the Yangtze River)? Why were there so many Song Shi? The explanations should be as follows: since Ming and Qing Dynasties, the commodity economy in Jiangnan regions had developed by leaps and bounds. The prospering economy led to more complicated contractual relationships, thus resulting in an increasing number of civil cases. On the other hand, more people dared to protect their contractual interests by litigations, indicating the awakening and upsurge of their interest awareness. Although the social status of Song Shi seemed low and humble on the surface, they enjoyed high status as a matter of fact, and that was why many people chose to be Song Shi despite the seeming lowliness. "The laws are the main criteria for sense and reason. In ancient times the preachers and scholars also added their own annotations to legal texts. Now the law practitioners engage in legal studies, learning and specializing in what the scholars and government officials generally lack. They resort to laws and settle disputes when doubts arise in government affairs. The practitioners of the legal profession are usually those who did not

[78] Mi Chaqing. *The Collection of Mi Bang*. Volume14. *For Procurator Pan.*

[79] *The Compilation of Historical Data in Shanghai · Local Records of Waigang Town during the Reign of Chongzhen by Emperor Zhu Youjian.*

[80] Xu Fuzuo. *Essays in the Huadang Pavilion.* Volume 3. item "Zhu Yingju".

[81] [Japan] Fuma Susumu. *Litigators and Litigation System in Ming and Qing Dynasties*. See footnote 42, p. 391.

[82] *The Local Records of Jiangle County during the Reign of Emperor Zhu Yijun.* Volume 1.

[83] Yuan Shouding. *Tu Min Lu.* Volume 2. Different Customs in the South and North of China.

succeed in learning Confucianism and thus gave up and turn to laws".[84] Song Shi had been widely active in the government and among common people since Ming and Qing Dynasties, who dealt with lawsuits with their professional knowledge. It could not be denied that they pursued profits in a pragmatic way as the rich sources of civil and criminal cases in the society were what they lived by. More importantly, although Song Shi, now called lawyers, could not be described as pioneers in upholding justice, they at least acted as the intermediaries or agents for the public to safeguard their own rights (mainly contractual rights), so their historical role could not be ignored. This was also the historical reason why Song Shi continued to exist despite repeated prohibitions.

Another historical source could demonstrate that the growth of contractual rights of the Chinese public had evolved to a modern level. Since Yuan, Ming, and Qing Dynasties, people who made a living as professionals writing contracts and pleadings for others existed in all walks of life. Bookstores and book clubs repeatedly reprinted various formats of contractual documents and litigation pleadings, and this footnoted the development of contractual rights at the private level.

Third, the evolution of contractual rights: from mutual aid to reciprocity.

The above exploration of the existence and realization of contractual rights aimed to find out whether or not they existed in ancient China, their existing forms as well as realization approaches. The discussion on the evolution of contractual rights, nevertheless, analyzed the internal change of contractual interests. Since the Chinese traditions were based on the patriarchal clan system and ruling by indoctrination, the form of rights embodied by Chinese contracts experienced the shift from mutual aid to reciprocity, the latter finally becoming the central principle of contractual interests. Ultimately, contracts got to break away from the constraint of humane morality and ethics and evolved into the independent legal proof and instrument to specify the rights and obligations of civil subjects.

The rationale behind mutual aid was morality and ethics, while that of reciprocity was interests and reason. In terms of mutual aid, it was reflected internally as the ethical norms of a family or a clan, and externally as the "favor" and "moral righteousness". In his book *Mutual Aid: A Factor of Evolution* published in 1919, Kropotkin argued that interpersonal relationships were not simply direct interactions between an individual and the whole, and did not manifest as a law of scientific social control. The core spirit of them was a kind of social ethics, which, in the context of China, evolved from the family institution, namely the inheritance from the family ethics of the Confucianism of Confucius and Mencius. The "place hierarchy" established by modern sociology was also a social system centering around families and family relationships. Wang Mingming believed that the crisis transition of family property and village as well as the expansion of social economic power in China relied on non-governmental organizations with "fraternity" as their core instead of on the dominant power or control of the state or the society. "Fraternity" included three types: kinship, affinity and friendship.[85] Huang Guangguo held that "favor" or "face" also

[84]Wu Guangyao. *Official Documents of Xiushan,* The Author's Preface.

[85]See footnote 21, p. 169.

contained three layers of implications: empathy, social resources, and social norms. Behind favor and face hid all the historical experiences of mutual knowledge, interactions and mutual aid among the people, which defined and shaped the life of social groups in the history.[86] In essence, mutual aid was altruistic behaviors combined with ethical approval or praise in order to build one's living environment, whereas reciprocity was divorced from the pursuit of "eudaemonism", and took interests as the goal and motivation.

The exchange of interests or reciprocity acted as the spiritual support of ancient Chinese contracts. Studying contracts as a whole, we could easily find that reciprocity was always treated as the principle of what the contracting parties knew and did, especially in the paid contracts such as those of sale, lease and interest-bearing loans, but the social forces under the patriarchal system like the family system, guilds, business communities and townsmen associations did invisibly strengthen the concept of mutual aid that prioritized moral ethics. The contract was the result of rational choices and free decision making of the contracting parties in their pursuit of "desires", while mutual aid restrained "desires" by seeking the realization of "rationality". In his analysis of the traditional concepts in Chinese society, Hiroaki Terada held that "desires" in ancient China had to stay in a reasonable range, otherwise they would inevitably be interfered in by the local authorities and the families. The entire traditional Chinese society pursued a balanced medium state between "desires" (life) and "rationality" (justice)—"humaneness". Shuzo Shiga explained it in terms of the concept of mutual aid, i.e., average people should have expectations for the actions of others and offer appropriate help and care to each other. The idea of ownership in modern China and that of struggle for the realization of rights were not only to secure their own interests, but also to establish a higher value pursuit based on social publicity and interpersonal relationships—"good-will mutual accommodation".[87] Hirano Yoshitaro compared the nature of rights in Chinese and western culture: the west emphasized individualism and rivalry, whereas the Chinese village civilization (in essence the clan culture) was about the affinity of mutual cooperation.[88]

Examination of the history showed that the reciprocal benefits in traditional contract spirit were always constrained by the practice of mutual aid. Taking as an example the pre-emption right of relatives and neighbors concerning real estate, the owner's failure to inform the relatives and neighbors of the sale of the property could lead to the damage of contractual interests or even nullification of contracts. Since Song Dynasty, if the family property was arbitrarily disposed of by the humble juniors of the family without notifying the buyer, he or she could still get the refund; but if the buyer made the purchase in the know, the money would be confiscated by the government, thus getting virtually no interests with imminent risks (confiscation of the money and return of the property). Another example was the purchase and sale of the land or property publicly owned by the family or the temple. The buyers and

[86]Huang [29].

[87]Hiroaki Terada. *Rights and Grievances: The Litigation and Civil Procedures in Qing Dynasty*. See footnote 42, pp. 248, 263 [1], 256 [2].

[88]See footnote 42, p. 357.

sellers expected to exchange interests through the deal and took the risks brought by it willingly. However, the purchase and sale of such property were strictly confined in ancient Chinese contracts by restrictions from laws to conventions. Such exchange of interests could be abolished anytime in the name of the so-called "illegal dealings", "under-the-counter transactions", and "stealing deals". The most fundamental reason for the above scenarios was that the family property and related public property were not owned by just one person. Rather, the members enjoyed equal rights to the benefits and assumed the obligation of mutual aid because the public property served as the foundation for the survival and development of the whole family or the social group. If the legitimacy of such sales was admitted by laws or conventions, the foundation of such social organizations would be undoubtedly shaken, thus greatly disturbing the social order. This kind of property ownership of "high interdependence" (If one is injured, then all are injured; if one is honored, then all are honored.) with the concept of mutual aid at the core was the basic feature of traditional Chinese society. At the end of Qing Dynasty, civil law systems from the European continent was ushered in and helped to promote the realization of individual rights. In fact, during the period from the first year of the Republic of China to the formulation of the *Civil Code* by the government, most of the civil trials relied on the case law system of the Dali Yuan (Dali Temple, equivalent to the current Supreme Court) in Qing Dynasty, namely *The Book of Dali Yuan Cases.*[89] With the enactment of the *Civil Code of the Republic of China,* the benefits of reciprocity finally replaced the ethics of mutual aid, accomplishing the completion and finalization of contractual rights. *General Principles of the Civil Law of the People's Republic of China* and the recent *Contract Law of the People's Republic of China* inherited the idea of rights and their realization from Europe, Great Britain and America, helping to complete the modern transformation of the mainland's contract legislation and judicature. But the ethics of mutual aid still played an important role as regards folk customary law, which some scholars believed would harm the ultimate individualization of contractual rights and even affect the integrity of ownership. In my view, that was reasonable concern with excessive worries. It was not impossible that the retention of mutual aid practices at the private level would impede the full realization of contractual rights, nevertheless, great harm would be caused if the convention of mutual aid was completely abandoned at the intersection of tradition and modernity. At the same time, the contract ethics and business morality inseparable from reciprocity could also be beneficially nurtured by the traditional practices of mutual aid.

References

1. Adamson Hoebel, E. 1993. *The Law of Primitive Man,* trans. Zhou Yong, 234. China Social Sciences Press.
2. Morgan, L.H. 1995. *Ancient Society* (The translated version), 6. The Commercial Press.

[89] Hu [30].

3. Sabine, George H. 1986. *A History of Political Theory*, trans. Liu Shan, et al., 397. The Commercial Press.
4. Kardiner, Abram, and Edward Preble, *They Studied Man*, trans. Kaixiang Sun, 23, 54–88. SDX Joint Publishing Company.
5. Li, Zehou. 1984. *Criticism of Critical Philosophy*, 333. People's Publishing House.
6. Liu, Chang. 1987. *The History in Mind*, 34–35. Sichuan People's Publishing House.
7. Wang, Zhe, and Yaozhong Du. 1996. *The Status of Freedom in Law. Jilin Normal University Journal* (3).
8. Su, Haopeng. 1999. On the historical background and value of the freedom of contract. *Philosophy of Law* (5).
9. Fu, Jingkun. 1997. *Contract Law in the Twentieth Century*. Law Press China, Section II of Chapter One; Grant, Gilmore. The death of contract, trans. Cao Shibing, et al. *Civil and Commercial Law Review* 4.
10. Wang, Mingming. 1997. *The Culture and Power in the View of Village*, 122. SDX Joint Publishing Company.
11. Huang, Zongxi, *Development and Evolution of Traditional Academic Thoughts in Ming Dynasty*, vol. 2.
12. Webster, A. 1987. *Introduction to the Sociology of Development* (Chinese version), 29. Huaxia Publishing House.
13. Zhang, Jinfan. 1988. *Brief Review of Legal History*, 144. Shanxi People's Publishing House.
14. Kong, Lingqi. 1994. On the guilds of handicraft industry in Suzhou in Qing Dynasty. *Social Science Front* (6).
15. [Japan] Tachibana, Shiraki. 1996. *Research on Chinese Ideologies*, 276–2788. Nippon Hyoron Sha Co. Ltd..
16. Wang, Yaxin and Zhiping Liang (ed.). 1998. *Civil Trials and Private Contracts in Ming and Qing Dynasties*, 360–362. Law Press China.
17. [Japan] Hiroaki, Terada. 1999. The civil trials in Qing Dynasty and the modern legal order of western Europe, trans. Pan Jian. *Peking University Law Journal* (2).
18. Zhao, Yunqi. 1998. On land sale and purchase under the system of land equalization in Tang Dynasty. *Social Science Front* (2).
19. Yang, Jiping. 1998. Re-discussion of the land distribution in Dunhuang household registration in Tang Dynasty. *Researches in Chinese Economic History* (3).
20. Tang, Renwu. 1996. On the land tenancy relations in Tang Dynasty. *Hebei Normal University (Social Sciences Edition)* (4).
21. Gong, Rufu, and Xiaojian Yao. 1998. The neo-confucianist Li Chunnian in Southern song dynasty and the implementation of Jing Jie Fa. *Journal of Yantai Normal University* (3).
22. Zhao, Gang. 1996. *History of China's Economic Systems*, part II, *The Labor Market*. Linking Publishing Co., Ltd.
23. Zhang, Jinfan. 1998. *A Comprehensive Review of the Civil Law in Qing Dynasty*, 18. China University of Political Science and Law Press.
24. Fu, Yiling. 1961. *Rural Social Economy in Ming and Qing Dynasties*, 71. SDX Joint Publishing Company.
25. Hu, Pingsheng, and Song Shaohua. 1997. The significance of the newly discovered bamboo slips in Zou Ma Lou of Changsha City, Hunan Province. *Guangming Daily*, Jan 14.
26. Li, Sanmou. 1995. On the particularity of the tenancy system in South China in Ming and Qing Dynasties. *Agricultural History of China* (2).
27. Liu, Kexiang. 1986. *The Formation of the Permanent Tenancy in Qing Dynasty · Regional Distribution and Development*, 161. The 8th Collection of the Institute of Economics, Chinese Academy of Social Sciences. China Social Sciences Press.
28. Lan, Yong. 1996. Study on the name and functions of the Townsmen Association of Xi'an businessmen in Qing Dynasty. *Journal of Chinese Historical Studies* (4).
29. Huang, Guangguo. 1990. *Favor and Face: Power Game of Chinese*, 19–22. Taipei Chuliu Publisher.
30. Hu, Changqing. 1934. *The Overview of Chinese Civil Law*, 36. The Commercial Press of China.

Postscript

There are two basic motives for writing this book: one is to discuss the historical background and the internal operational mechanism of ancient Chinese contracts; the other is to explore the awareness of rights of ancient Chinese people and the history of mutual recognition and restraint between the people and the government in the course of realizing the rights.

When I entered Southwest University of Political Science and Law to study civil law under the supervision of Professor Kaiguo Li in 1998, I reported the proposal to Prof. Li and got his approval. At the beginning of this year, the outline was completed. Prof. Li reviewed it and proposed suggestions. When the draft was completed, Prof. Li was also patient and kind enough to provide me with guidance. It would be impossible to finish writing and publish this book without the careful attention and encouragement of Prof. Li.

In the process of writing this book, Ms. Guangmei Long, Mr. Zonghua Pang, and Mr. Shiping Jiang gave me generous help and care. Their friendship and support were the valuable driving force for the book to be successfully completed.

My dear wife Xinglei Li, and my parents-in-law have assumed the full responsibility for the care of our child during my studies and writing, providing a reliable backup for my academic research.

My profound gratitude is expressed by the clear lamp and my sincere heart.

Liu Yunsheng
At the foot of Gele Mountain

Y. Liu, *The History of the Contractual Thoughts in Ancient China*,
https://doi.org/10.1007/978-981-15-5768-2

Appendix

Dynasties in Chinese History

Dynasty	Time period	Capital (s)
Xia Dynasty 夏	2071–1600 B.C.	Zhenxun 斟鄩
Shang Dynasty 商	1600–1046 B.C.	Bo 亳
Zhou Dynasty 周		
Western Zhou Dynasty 西周 Eastern Zhou Dynasty 东周 Spring and Autumn Period 春秋 Warring States Period 战国	1046–771 B.C. 770–771 B.C. 770–256 B.C. 475–221 B.C.	Haojing 镐京 Luoyi 洛邑 —— ——
Qin Dynasty 秦	221–206 B.C.	Xianyang 咸阳
Han Dynasty 汉		
Western Han 西汉 Eastern Han 东汉	206 B.C.–23 A.D. 25–220 A.D.	Chang'an 长安 Luoyang 洛阳
Three Kingdoms 三国		
Wei 魏 Shu 蜀 Wu 吴	220–265 A.D. 221–263 A.D. 222–280 A.D.	Luoyang 洛阳 Chengdu 成都 Jianye 建邺
Jin Dynasty 晋		
Western Jin 西晋 Eastern Jin 东晋	265–316 A.D. 317–420 A.D.	Luoyang 洛阳 Jiankang 建康
Sixteen Kingdoms 十六国	304–439 A.D.	——
Northern and Southern Dynasties 南北朝		
Southern Dynasty 南朝		
Song 宋 Qi 齐 Liang 梁 Chen 陈	420–479 A.D. 479–502 A.D. 502–557 A.D. 557–589 A.D.	Jiankang 建康 Jiankang 建康 Jiankang 建康 Jiankang 建康

(continued)

Y. Liu, *The History of the Contractual Thoughts in Ancient China*,
https://doi.org/10.1007/978-981-15-5768-2

(continued)

Dynasty	Time period	Capital (s)
Northern Dynasty 北朝		
Northern Wei 北魏	386–534 A.D.	1. Pingcheng 平城 2. Luoyang 洛阳
Eastern Wei 东魏 Northern Qi 北齐 Western Wei 西魏 Northern Zhou 北周	534–550 A.D. 550–557 A.D. 535–557 A.D. 557–581A.D.	Ye 邺 Ye 邺 Changan 长安 Changan 长安
Sui Dynasty 隋	581–618 A.D.	Chang'an 长安
Tang Dynasty 唐	618–907 A.D.	Chang'an 长安
Five Dynasties五代		
Later Liang Dynasty 后梁 Later Tang Dynasty 后唐 Later Jin Dynasty 后晋 Later Han Dynasty 后汉 Later Zhou Dynasty 后周	907–923 A.D. 923–936 A.D. 936–946 A.D. 947–950 A.D. 951–960 A.D.	Bianjing 汴京 Luoyang 洛阳 Bianjing 汴京 Bianjing 汴京 Bianjing 汴京
Ten States 十国	902–979 A.D.	——
Song 宋		
Northern Song Dynasty 北宋 Southern Song Dynast 南宋 Liao Dynasty 辽 Western Xia 西夏 Jin 金	960–1127 A.D. 1127–1279 A.D. 907–1125 A.D. 1038–1227 A.D. 1115–1234 A.D.	Kaifeng 开封 Linan 临安 Yanjing 燕京 Ningxia 宁夏 1. Zhongdu 中都 2. Beijing 北京 3. Kaifeng 开封
Yuan Dynasty 元	1279–1368 A.D.	Dadu 大都
Ming Dynasty 明	1368–1644 A.D.	Beijing 北京
Qing Dynasty 清	1644–1911 A.D.	Beijing 北京

CPSIA information can be obtained
at www.ICGtesting.com
Printed in the USA
LVHW021103250423
745104LV00027B/480

9 789811 55767